Data Structures, Data Abstraction

A Contemporary Introduction Using C++

Mitchell L Model

Prentice Hall
Englewood Cliffs, New Jersey 07632

Library of Congress Cataloging-in-Publication Data

Model, Mitchell L
    Data structures, data abstraction : a contemporary introduction
using C++ / Mitchell L Model
      p. cm.
    Includes bibliographical references and index
    ISBN 0-13-088782-X
    1. Data structures (Computer science). 2. Abstract data types
(Computer science) 3. C++ (Computer program language) I. Title.
QA76.9.D35M62 1994
005.7'3--dc20   93-33118
                  CIP

Acquisitions editor: Bill Zobrist
Production editor: Irwin Zucker
Copy editor: Brenda Melissaratos
Production coordinator: Linda Behrens
Supplements editor: Alice Dworkin
Editorial assistant: Phyllis Morgan

 © 1994 by Prentice-Hall, Inc.
A Paramount Communications Company
Englewood Cliffs, New Jersey 07632

The author and publisher of this book have used their best efforts in preparing this book. These efforts include the development, research, and testing of the theories and programs to determine their effectiveness. The author and publisher make no warranty of any kind, expressed or implied, with regard to these programs or the documentation contained in this book. The author and publisher shall not be liable in any event for incidental or consequential damages in connection with, or arising out of, the furnishing, performance, or use of these programs.

Printed in the United States of America
10 9 8 7 6 5 4 3 2 1

ISBN 0-13-088782-X

Prentice-Hall International (UK) Limited, *London*
Prentice-Hall of Australia Pty. Limited, *Sydney*
Prentice-Hall Canada Inc., *Toronto*
Prentice-Hall Hispanoamericana. S.A., *Mexico*
Prentice-Hall of India Private Limited, *New Delhi*
Prentice-Hall of Japan, Inc., *Tokyo*
Simon & Schuster Asia Pte. Ltd., *Singapore*
Editora Prentice-Hall do Brasil, Ltda., *Rio de Janeiro*

Table of Contents

Part Three: State Structures

Part Four: Linked Structures

Part Five: Association Structures

Part Six: Appendices

List of Figures

List of Tables

Preface

This book is designed for students taking introductory data structure courses and software professionals studying on their own. It has two purposes. The first is to provide a solid grounding in the theory and application of data structures, including familiarity with the fundamental data structures that every serious programmer should know. The second is to teach a modern style of data structure implementation and use known as *data abstraction*.

Motivation

What is most difficult about programming is managing complexity. Almost everything about this book's approach to data structure theory, design, implementation, and application is motivated by the importance of reducing complexity. The most powerful tool for reducing complexity is *decomposition* — breaking a complex system into weakly interacting subsystems. The primary skill needed is the ability to perceive the joints in a complex structure. With the joints identified, the system can be teased apart into smaller, less complex entities that are easier to work with.

The earliest approach to program decomposition was *sequential* — a program would be split into separate execution phases. The first part of the program would run, output interim results, and exit. Then the second part would start, read the interim results left behind by the first, perform further computations, output its results, and exit. This would continue until all the phases of a program had executed and the final result had been produced. In part this approach was motivated by the inability to fit an entire large program into the extremely limited memories of early machines, but programmers also found sequential modularization a convenient way to divide a complicated problem into several simpler ones.

The predominant decomposition paradigm for many years has been *functional* — a program is divided into groups of related subroutines: all the input/output in one module, all the mathematical computations in another, the data management in a third, etc. Structured programming techniques tend to encourage this approach. Functional decomposition is reasonable and convenient, but it turns out not to be the most powerful way to organize a large system. The primary problem is that modifying the representation of data within the program requires changing code in many different modules.

The modern approach to decomposition is *structural* — a program is divided into many relatively small modules, most of which implement a single data type. These type modules combine the representation of the type with the operations that act on it in one module. By using only these operations the code in other modules is completely shielded from changes to the type's representation. This approach is known as *data abstraction* and will be discussed thoroughly in Chapter 1.

Relation to the CS2 Curriculum

Although no longer the official recommendation, the ACM CS2 curriculum effectively described the modern practice in second-semester courses for computer science majors. Introductory data structures textbooks have had to proclaim their adherence to this standard and explain their deviations. The current ACM curriculum recommendations do not propose specific course content, presenting instead a range of topics to be covered and a variety of course sequences as examples of how they could be integrated into a particular program. However effective this might be for computer science curricula in general, this new approach is likely to leave the CS2 "standard" intact for introductory data structures courses.

This is a book for a CS2-like course, addressing the same overall subject matter as previous textbooks for such a course. However, the approach followed here is oriented more toward structures and less toward algorithms than is traditional. The importance and beauty of data structures lie in the representational and architectural lessons they teach. Algorithms have their own beauty and importance, too, and of course structures and algorithms are closely related. Nevertheless, algorithmic concerns are different from structural concerns, and I strongly believe they should not play a major role in a data structures course. (A course on the design, implementation, and analysis of algorithms would be a natural follow-up to one using this text.)

Rather than an *ad hoc* selection of topics, this book presents an organized sequence of truly fundamental data structures; other structures are just variants of the ones included. What data structures to cover, the relative importance of algorithmic issues, and the ordering of topics are dictated here by a particular conceptual framework. The resulting choices conflict somewhat with more traditional treatments. The benefits of this approach include a more coherent presentation of data structures and their fundamental operations. Heresies include the following:

- Searching is not a separate topic, but a natural part of the implementation of many data structures and the particular province of an entire class of data structures — the "association structures" studied at the end of the book.

- Sorting is considered separately, but as part of the discussion of lists, since for the most part it is only sequential and linked lists that are sorted (as opposed to the association structures that maintain their elements in order).

- The discussions of sorting and searching, and the discussions of efficiency analysis that accompany them, are less comprehensive than in many texts. The basic ideas of algorithm analysis are discussed, including "Big O" notation (see in particular Section 8.3, page 251) but not in any great depth. Enough is included here to provide a foundation for the understanding and use of sorting and searching algorithms without unduly distracting the reader from the central structure-oriented themes of the material.

- There is little explicit discussion of alternative representations. Instructors who like to emphasize this theme in their courses will have no trouble adding it to lectures and pursuing it through exercises. Although the idea of representation-invariant interfaces to implementations of data abstractions is crucial, in truth few of the fundamental structures in this text allow much room for variation. The most common variations involve things like switching between sequential and linked lists used to support a higher-level structure. In this book, stacks and queues are considered before lists are studied, and are therefore shown using arrays directly instead of some kind of list structure. Subsequent exercises explore their reimplementation using lists.

- Certain common data structures that are often assumed to belong in a book like this — in particular strings and sets — are not treated systematically. Such structures are not themselves representationally fundamental: they are basically applications of the structures discussed here. The implementation of sets and strings is a fine theme to pursue in exercises, but they don't introduce any new ideas and don't fit within the conceptual framework of this book's presentation.

- File-based data structures (such as indexed sequential files), once a major topic in data structure books, have been omitted. They are no longer central to mainstream computer science and should be relegated to advanced courses dealing specifically with file management and database implementation.

- Very little is said about coding efficiency. Qualitative efficiency is important (justifying, for instance, the use of a balanced search tree over an ordinary one), but fine-tuning of code only distracts from the central data structure topics and makes code harder to read and write.

- Recursion is not highlighted as prominently as in many traditional texts, paradoxically because it is treated as a significant application of stacks and a fundamental programming mechanism to be used routinely. The intent is that students learn to use and understand recursion by studying the code examples in this book and doing its programming exercises. My teaching experience has convinced me that students new to recursion learn best by jumping in and using it, then later coming to an understanding of its mysteries. I am not moved by the routine examples of recursive functions that could easily be programmed iteratively, such as the factorial function. For the purposes of this course, recursive programming is necessary to support recursive data structures, and can be easily learned when presented in that spirit.

Programming Language

To show how fundamental data structures are implemented we have to use a programming language. Almost any kind will do, even an abstract pseudo-language made up for the purpose. However, the whole enterprise will be vastly more successful if we can use a language that is both supportive of data abstraction and accessible to readers.

Using a mainstream language makes a book available to a wider audience than using an exotic one would. Virtually all students and professional programmers know at least one standard algorithmic language. It is much easier to move from one of these to another than it is to move from one of these to a language with a completely different computational model. The topic of the book is data structures, and while it is reasonable to ask the reader to learn a new language similar to a familiar one, it would be unreasonable to expect the reader to learn a new *kind* of language while also studying a new subject. Thus, to be accessible means that the language should already be known to the reader or be straightforward to learn given the language(s) the reader does know.

Procedural abstraction was an implicit central theme in computer programming from the earliest days of the field. Early in the 1980s, it became an explicit foundation of modern programming textbooks and courses. Data abstraction is as important for programming as procedural abstraction. Data abstraction has long been an important implicit part of computer programming, but it does not generally get the explicit attention in textbooks and courses that it deserves. This book presents traditional data structure material inside the more modern framework of data abstraction. As a result, it needs a language that supports data abstraction.

Thus, the requirements of accessibility and the technical demands of the material lead to the use of a conventional kind of language that supports data abstraction. Being accessible means not only that the language be familiar or easily learned, but also that it be available on the computers the student will use for doing programming exercises.

When this book was written C++ was unquestionably the most conventional and available language with thorough support for data abstraction. In fact, C++ goes further than data abstraction and supports a style of programming known as "object-oriented," but the object-oriented features of C++ aren't needed to study data structures. The way it is used in this book (and often in practice), C++ is just a richer C. Everything you know (or can quickly learn) about C is part of C++. Although it can be used unconventionally (for object-oriented programming), C++ is fundamentally an extension of C, a conventional language. Its support for data abstraction is excellent. Availability has been a concern until recently. However, use of C++ has grown rapidly, and since it was intentionally designed for portability, it is available on a wide variety of computers. In particular, several good implementations are available for personal computers.

What about learning C++? This book shows how to use C++ for data abstraction programming. A working knowledge of C, though not necessarily proficiency, is assumed. The first chapter will review some important features of ANSI C — the more modern C standard — for the benefit of readers whose C experience is with pre-ANSI compilers. It will also introduce some small improvements C++ makes to ANSI C. The second chapter introduces the data abstraction mechanisms of C++. In short, all that is needed to get started with this book is some experience with classic C, and only those features of C++ needed for this book are presented.

Be warned, though: becoming adept at C++ is a challenge for even the very experienced C programmer. Many powerful features are provided through subtle variations to C. Mechanisms are frequently invoked "behind the scenes," without the programmer realizing it. My experience teaching C++ in a variety of contexts has shown me the importance of insisting on a careful introduction with plenty of hands-on practice. Even though the more advanced features of the language, including those specifically added for object-oriented programming, are not used in this text, there are still plenty of new concepts and intricate details to learn. Even though students and instructors will be impatient to get to the meat of this book, a deliberate study of the preliminary chapters will be very much rewarded. The C++ concepts introduced there are not hard to understand, but many will be quite unfamiliar to most readers. I strongly recommend beginning with lots of short programming exercises, like études for a musical instrument.

Code Examples

This book contains a lot of code. One wonders how much of the vast amounts of code in-cluded in programming and data structure books is actually looked at by readers. It is with a certain amount of reluctance that all this code is included in this text, and I hope that certain features of this code will attract more than the average attention given to such examples. To improve readability, most of the code here is broken up into relatively small chunks. Indentation and white space is used to show the conceptual structure of a piece of code more clearly than the more commonly used styles tend to do.

The code shown has been tested using various C++ systems, on both PC-compati-bles and Unix workstations. The code requires a compiler that supports templates. In mid-1993, some vendors were *still* shipping compilers that didn't. Other vendors were shipping compilers that did not completely implement the template facility or had serious bugs hindering its use.

A lot of work went into simplifying the use of templates in the code so that it could be processed by the greatest number of compilers possible, even though that sometimes meant using a less elegant formulation of some particular detail. In particular, nested classes had to be avoided — for example, `list_node` is a separate class, not a class `node` nested inside the class `list`. Initialization of static members was another problem area, and a few ambitious initialization schemes had to be weakened somewhat. In general, the code uses templates in only the most straightforward ways. Compilers that provide the necessary support include the following:

- Borland C++ 3.1
- Unix cfront-based compilers from various vendors
- Digital's C++ compiler for Ultrix
- GNU g++ from the Free Software Foundation

Every choice in formulating the book's code examples has been made based on what would best serve the presentation of the conceptual material. The modules shown are de-signed for clarity and generality, not to be the ultimate implementation of their data structure. Simplicity, readability, and consistency have been favored over efficiency, sub-tlety, and conformity to professional large-scale programming practice. What is useful in a three-year twenty-person development effort will often have adverse effects in the con-text of an introductory course. There are many places where the coding of an individual function might strike the experienced professional, classically trained academic, or C++ expert as deviant. I ask you to evaluate these situations in light of the goals of this book and the importance of a delicate touch in presenting material that forms the foundation of so much programming and computer science. Students introduced to this cognitively oriented style of coding have found that it greatly facilitates their work, both academic and professional.

I claim no rights and make no restrictions to the use of any code shown here (as opposed to the text proper, for which I do assert the usual proprietary rights). I would, however, appreciate hearing about ways in which it may have proved useful beyond the scope of this book and a course using it. As the object revolution matures, may it soon be the case that the only time anyone ever has to write code for any of these data structures is for the exercises of an introductory course!

Provided Code

The diskette accompanying this book contains complete implementations of the data structures discussed. For the most part these consist of the code shown in the chapters plus programs to test the modules and, in some cases, small programs showing their use. The diskette is set up to facilitate access to the code from a PC: follow its README instructions to unpack the archive it contains and use the directory tree that results. The disk contains mechanisms to facilitate porting the code to a Unix environment, but readers with Internet access will find it easier to obtain already prepared code by anonymous ftp or by gopher.

I plan to maintain the code and periodically make updates available on the Internet. I expect to provide versions for both PC and Unix systems. The archive site is prenhall.com. The directory for ftp access is /ftp/pub/software/for_PH_texts/ model. Don't forget to use binary mode for the transfer of code archives. For further information see the README and similar files on that directory. The files can also be accessed with gopher at gopher.prenhall.com; follow instructions that appear on your screen.

The code on disk is not exactly the same as appears in the book. Comments tend to be more elaborate in the disk files than in the code shown here, since they are not supported by surrounding text. Some of the structures have been given additional functionality to support their use by other structures later in the book. Some C++ details that are finessed for pedagogical purposes in the book are handled slightly differently in the online files; in particular, the online code makes many reference arguments const that are not const in the book. Finally, errors and omissions will continue to be detected and fixed after the book goes to press — if a piece of code in the book looks suspicious, compare it to the code in the latest version of the corresponding file.

Punctuation, Grammar, and Typography

Writing about programming presents difficult challenges in the areas of punctuation, grammar, and typography. Part of the difficulty stems from the incessant intermixing of two linguistic domains: the ordinary English of what one is trying to say and the programming language constructs one is talking about. Sentences full of technical terms, function and variable names, and different kinds of quoting need whatever assistance that can be mustered. Conventional American usage has been moving in the direction of simplifica-

oriented programming, are not used in this text, there are still plenty of new concepts and intricate details to learn. Even though students and instructors will be impatient to get to the meat of this book, a deliberate study of the preliminary chapters will be very much rewarded. The C++ concepts introduced there are not hard to understand, but many will be quite unfamiliar to most readers. I strongly recommend beginning with lots of short programming exercises, like études for a musical instrument.

Code Examples

This book contains a lot of code. One wonders how much of the vast amounts of code included in programming and data structure books is actually looked at by readers. It is with a certain amount of reluctance that all this code is included in this text, and I hope that certain features of this code will attract more than the average attention given to such examples. To improve readability, most of the code here is broken up into relatively small chunks. Indentation and white space is used to show the conceptual structure of a piece of code more clearly than the more commonly used styles tend to do.

The code shown has been tested using various C++ systems, on both PC-compatibles and Unix workstations. The code requires a compiler that supports templates. In mid-1993, some vendors were *still* shipping compilers that didn't. Other vendors were shipping compilers that did not completely implement the template facility or had serious bugs hindering its use.

A lot of work went into simplifying the use of templates in the code so that it could be processed by the greatest number of compilers possible, even though that sometimes meant using a less elegant formulation of some particular detail. In particular, nested classes had to be avoided — for example, `list_node` is a separate class, not a class `node` nested inside the class `list`. Initialization of static members was another problem area, and a few ambitious initialization schemes had to be weakened somewhat. In general, the code uses templates in only the most straightforward ways. Compilers that provide the necessary support include the following. Unfortunately, at the time of this writing, GNU `gcc` does not provide sufficient template support to compile the book's code.

- Borland C++ 3.1
- Unix `cfront`-based compilers from various vendors
- Digital's C++ compiler for Ultrix

Every choice in formulating the book's code examples has been made based on what would best serve the presentation of the conceptual material. The modules shown are designed for clarity and generality, not to be the ultimate implementation of their data structure. Simplicity, readability, and consistency have been favored over efficiency, subtlety, and conformity to professional large-scale programming practice. What is useful in a three-year twenty-person development effort will often have adverse effects in the context of an introductory course. There are many places where the coding of an individual function might strike the experienced professional, classically trained academic, or C++ expert as deviant. I ask you to evaluate these situations in light of the goals of this book and the importance of a delicate touch in presenting material that forms the foundation of binding, or polymorphism. Appendix D (page 471) briefly discusses additional features of C++ that support object-oriented programming. Second, *this is not a handbook for the implementation of a robust, general-purpose collection library.* The design and implementation of data structure modules to be used for serious application development raise many issues that are outside the scope of this book.

Consequently, certain C++ details that must be carefully attended to in a professional data structure library have been purposely ignored here, to avoid over-complicating the presentation and code. (Some of these are discussed in Appendix E, page 479.) For example, most reference arguments and many functions in the modules shown here should be `const`, but substantial complexities arise in such uses of `const` that would significantly distract from the discussion here while contributing nothing. Similarly, the C++ community has widely adopted a strategy of using separate iterator structs to support traversal over the elements of a collection, but here traversal functions are built right into the data structures themselves. Although there are many important reasons why it is better to use separate iterator structs in serious development work, they offer no advantages for the topics of this book that would compensate for the complexity their use would add. Professionals from the C++ community (programmers, teachers, consultants, authors, etc.) will easily find many superficial aspects of the code shown here that offend their sensibilities. I ask that C++ professionals keep in mind the purposes and intended audiences of this book while evaluating it. This book is not designed to teach professional software development in C++, although it would be a good foundation for that.

All discussion in this book is presented within a conceptual framework of fundamental operations common to all data structures. It is not easy to work out a clear, consistent, complete framework for talking about data structures, categorizing and naming functions, determining what to include in an implementation, and so on. This book distills fifteen years of experience refining the conceptual approach and using it in my teaching and programming. Lots of small details could be handled differently. (Should the function be called `empty`? `is_empty`? `EmptyP`? something else?) The components of the scheme are highly interdependent and stabilized quite a while ago. The importance of a scheme like this is not the exact way it names or classifies functions but that it provide a structured context that facilitates discussion and guides students in their programming.

Acknowledgments and Requests

I wrote but didn't publish a book like this one more than ten years ago, while an assistant professor at Brandeis University. That project collapsed for a number of reasons, but what primarily made it impossible to complete was the lack of a widely available language supporting data abstraction. Nevertheless, I learned a great deal from that effort and thank my students from those days for their enthusiasm, challenging intellect, imagination, and encouragement. The earlier unpublished book, and therefore this one, grew out of the explorations we made together. I similarly thank Ellis Cohen, my colleague from those days, for his support and contributions of technical knowledge, insight, and perspective.

In recent years, one of my major activities has been teaching courses in object technology to professional software engineers and managers, sometimes as an employee of a technology vendor, sometimes as a subcontractor to a vendor, and sometimes as an independent consultant. This book has benefited in many ways from comments, suggestions, and war stories contributed by participants in those courses and from my interactions with people associated with the vendors with which I have worked.

I tested an earlier draft of this book on an unsuspecting class in a supposedly C-based data structures course at Boston University's Metropolitan College in the fall 1991 semester. I thank the students in that class for their patience and suggestions. More than anything else it was that experience that impressed upon me the importance of providing ready-to-compile code along with the text.

Reviewers of various drafts contributed enormously to the final result, both by their specific suggestions for changes and as experimental subjects responding to my efforts to articulate this material. Others have helped me move the code through various C++ compilers. I thank all these people for their contributions. I especially thank those people who over the years have furthered my understanding of C++ as I attempted to plumb its depths.

I thank Clive Lee, founder of Semaphore, for his support and encouragement and for the opportunity to teach and consult for Semaphore's clients, which allowed me to work on this book free from the constraints of a full-time job or the burden of finding my own consulting clients. Finally, I thank my editor, Bill Zobrist, for his enthusiasm, encouragement, and, above all, gentle patience as he endured month after month of distractions that delayed the completion of the book.

I hope this book will teach and inspire you. I welcome your comments, which may be communicated via email (mlm@acm.org) or the publisher. Please tell me about any mistakes, ambiguities, and omissions you encounter, so that such problems may be rectified in a future edition for the benefit of other readers.

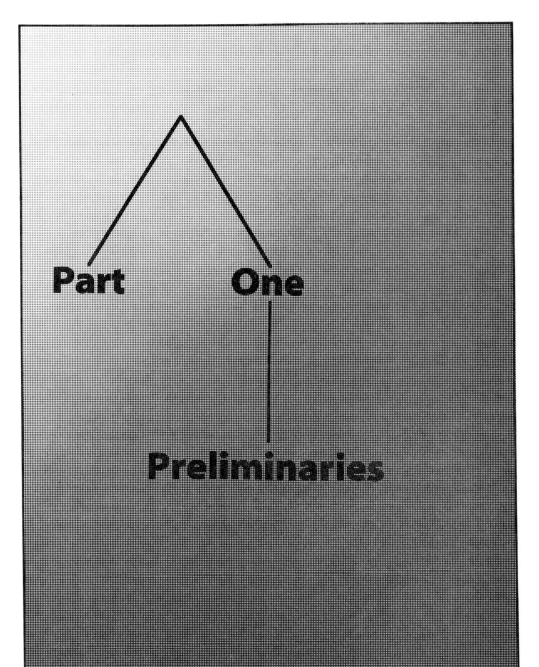

Part One

Preliminaries

Part One:

Preliminaries

This book is divided into five main parts. Each of the parts after this one is devoted to a particular class of data structure. An additional sixth part contains various appendices. This first part considers data structures in general and data abstraction programming. It also introduces the features of C++ needed for the book's examples and exercises.

Introduction

The main purpose of this book is to teach you about *data structures*. We'll look at data structures in general as well as specific structures that every programmer should know how to use. A secondary purpose of this book is to teach you good programming practices that support the use of data structures, following a powerful modern approach known as *data abstraction*.

0.1 Data Structures

What's a data structure? Computer hardware represents information in the simplest form possible: sequences of *bits*, each in one of two possible states. Bits are grouped into *bytes*, which are sequentially numbered *locations* constituting the computer's memory. Computer hardware is designed to store bits to and fetch bits from a specified location. Locations are designated by *address*es. Figure 0.1 depicts a sequence of bytes starting at location 4000200.

Data types are mechanisms for *interpreting* bit sequences to give them program-level meaning. Programming languages like Pascal and C provide a vocabulary of primitive types and a grammar of ways they may be manipulated. In using these primitive types, a programmer relies on the compiler to maintain the illusion that there are such things as numbers and characters in the computer. For instance, in Figure 0.1 the first byte could be interpreted as the character 'D' or part of a 4-byte integer (among other things), depending on the type the compiler expects to find there. Of course primitive types do correspond fairly well to the range of bit interpretations supported by hardware operations, which is why they are primitive. Computer hardware directly supports operations such as integer addition, floating-point multiplication, and character comparison.

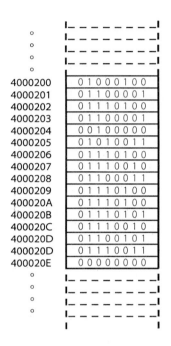

Address	Bits
4000200	0 1 0 0 0 1 0 0
4000201	0 1 1 0 0 0 0 1
4000202	0 1 1 1 0 1 0 0
4000203	0 1 1 0 0 0 0 1
4000204	0 0 1 0 0 0 0 0
4000205	0 1 0 1 0 0 1 1
4000206	0 1 1 1 0 1 0 0
4000207	0 1 1 1 0 0 1 0
4000208	0 1 1 0 0 0 1 1
4000209	0 1 1 1 0 1 0 0
400020A	0 1 1 1 0 1 0 0
400020B	0 1 1 1 0 1 0 1
400020C	0 1 1 1 0 0 1 0
400020D	0 1 1 0 0 1 0 1
400020D	0 1 1 1 0 0 1 1
400020E	0 0 0 0 0 0 0 0

Figure 0.1   Memory as a Sequence of Bytes

0.1.1 Structure

Data structures are higher-level interpretative constructs built out of primitive types and structuring mechanisms. Programming languages typically provide strings, records, arrays, and some kind of support for input and output. As a system-programming language (rather than a "high-level" language), C is a little less rich, but it still provides records (structs), simulates arrays, and supports strings and input/output through library facilities.

The built-in data structures of a language are used on their own for a wide variety of programming purposes. In addition, they are used to construct higher-level data structures, either by application programmers or by developers of software libraries used by application programmers.

The study of data structures lies at the heart of computer science. This book provides both a conceptual framework for understanding data structures in general and an introduction to the techniques used in the design and implementation of particular important ones. There are many data structures known, but most are variants of the dozen or so fundamental ones discussed in this book. To study or use a specific kind of data structure requires knowing both how to describe, or *declare*, instances of that structure as well as how to manipulate, or *process*, them. The term 'data structures' emphasizes their passive representation, but active behavior is also part of each structure's nature.

The essence of a data structure is the organization it imposes on the otherwise un-differentiated sequence of bytes in the computer's memory. A data structure is an *interpretation* — a way of seeing a sequence of bytes as the components of a compound entity with certain behavior. For instance, the sequence of bytes shown in Figure 0.1 can be interpreted as the C string "Data Structures", including the NUL character that by definition ends strings in C. There is nothing in those bytes that dictates that interpreta-tion, however — it's imposed entirely by the program that accesses the bytes.

Another example of the interpretation of memory bytes is shown in Figure 0.2, which depicts the layout of a C struct representing information about a person as it might appear in a payroll program: a pointer to a string representing the person's name, a struct representing a birth date, an int for a Social Security number, and a double for a salary. As the diagram shows, this is a two-level interpretation, since the birth date is itself a struc-ture, represented as three 2-byte shorts for the month, day, and year.

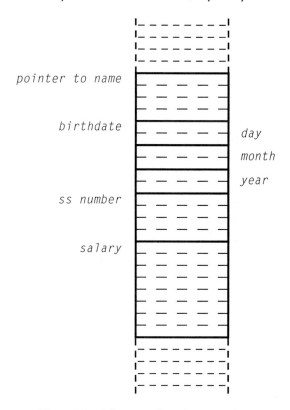

Figure 0.2   A Structure Is an Interpretation

More specifically, a structure's *representation* is the way its components are ar-ranged, including their types and the organization principle that assigns them their role in the structure's interpretation. Each component is itself another structure or else a primi-tive value, but either way it is a further interpretation of raw memory. In the case of a C string, the representation is a sequence of bytes ordered as they appear in the string termi-nated by a NUL byte. That is a natural representation, but nothing would prevent, say, storing all the odd-numbered characters before all the even-numbered characters — the important thing is that the interpretation is consistent across all uses of the bytes.

In more formal terms, a structure's representation is a *mapping* from a conceptual program-level expression to a set of bytes in memory. We store information through that mapping, which transforms the program-level expression into a set of operations on memory, and we get the information out by passing it back through the same transformation (or, more accurately, its inverse). As long as the value returned when a specified component is accessed is the same as was stored previously, it really doesn't matter how the bytes are stored. For instance, many Pascal compilers happen to allocate the bytes constituting a record structure in the reverse order of their appearance in the declaration, but few Pascal programmers ever realize that. As long as a particular field of a record means the same thing all throughout the program, it doesn't matter whether that field is stored first, last, or somewhere in between.

Another example is the storage of multidimensional arrays in languages that support them. Consider the following two-dimensional array of characters:

```
A B C D
a b c d
```

We could store the rows first, storing the bytes in the order ABCDabcd, or we could store the columns first, yielding the order AaBbCcDd. We could also store the characters in reverse order: dcbaDCBA or dDcCbBaA. All that matters is that when we request, say, the element in the second column of the first row we get back B.

For structures directly supported by a language — arrays, records, strings, etc. — the compiler implements a representation by turning a particular access expression, such as chars[0][1], into references to particular bytes in memory. Higher-level structures are implemented through declarations and operations defined by a programmer in terms of language types and other programmer-defined structures.

0.1.2 Fundamental Data Structures

Fundamental data structures can be grouped into four categories. Appendix A summarizes the categories and data structures discussed in this book. Each category is the subject of a separate section. Each kind of data structure is the subject of a separate chapter.

The basic structures provided by a programming language directly control memory layout. We'll call these *storage structures* to emphasize their direct role in storing data. Storage structures section the computer's linear sequence of raw memory bytes into individual computational entities with internal organization. The essential storage structures are the *array*, *record*, and *stream*.

State structures are those used to keep track of the tasks a process needs to perform. The main state structures are *stacks*, *queues*, and *priority queues*. Generally, these are represented as arrays or lists with special rules governing their manipulation.

The third kind of fundamental structures are the *linked structures*. The basic linked structures are *lists*, *trees*, and *graphs*. Linked structures are usually implemented using special support records called *nodes*. Since each node contains one or more pointers to other nodes, we could also call these *recursive structures*.

Finally, *association structures* implement correspondences between access keys and other data. *Tables* are association structures built on arrays or lists. *Search trees* store data in trees, ordered by their keys. *Indexed files* are also association structures, and many older data structure texts featured them prominently; however, as technology has advanced, the study of file organization techniques has become less central to computer science, so they are not covered in this book.

There's another important kind of data structure that is not included in this categorization. They are omitted because although frequently used, they aren't very, well, *structural*. The most prominent members of this group are *strings* and *sets*. These are more like primitive types, and in fact many high-level languages include them. As primitive types are little more than interpretations of the fundamental bits and bytes of the computer hardware, these simple data structures are little more than interpretations of other fundamental data structures. For example, a C string is nothing more than part of an array of chars, running from the first component of the array through the first NUL character. Operations on these structures — those provided by the C string library, for example — must adhere to their representational conventions, but they don't introduce any new structuring mechanisms. These simple structures are excellent material for examples and exercises, but there wouldn't be much to say about their structural aspects, so they aren't explicitly covered in the text.

0.2 C++ Basics

With that preliminary characterization of data structures behind us, we can turn our attention to C++, the programming language used in this book. C++ was developed to support three kinds of programming:

1. traditional programming
2. data abstraction programming
3. object-oriented programming

C++ features that support traditional programming are discussed in this section. The next chapter discusses using C++ for data abstraction programming. Object-oriented programming is not needed for an introductory discussion of data structures, so C++ features that support it are not discussed here. (However, Appendix D presents an overview of object-oriented programming and the C++ features that support it.)

To get started with C++, we'll look first at some simple ways in which the language improves on classic C. (Appendix B reviews data declaration in C, which is otherwise assumed to be familiar.) This chapter and the next will present only the features of C++ that will be needed for the examples, implementations, and exercises of this book. This is therefore not a thorough introduction to the language.

This might seem odd. Most widely used languages are reasonably concise, and to use them in any kind of serious programming requires knowing most of their features. C++ is not like that, however: it offers an unusually wide range of mechanisms and supports a variety of programming styles. C++ extends C, which is itself reasonably rich, so it shouldn't be surprising that it is more elaborate than most languages. Studying the entire language is a rather substantial enterprise that would go far beyond the needs of this text.

0.2.1 ANSI C

C++ is based on ANSI C, so we'll start by considering the ways ANSI C differs from classic C. ANSI C was the result of an effort to standardize C and various developments of that language since it was introduced. It also provided an opportunity to resolve some ambiguities that plagued the classic language as well as introduce a few new mechanisms whose absence had become a problem.

Function Prototypes

The only really significant change ANSI C introduced into C is the way arguments to functions are specified. In ANSI C the argument types are included within the parentheses of function declarations, unlike classic C, in which only the parentheses appear. In function *definitions*, the types are specified along with the arguments, rather than after the parenthesized argument list, as in classic C. The following classic C function

```
char* append();
 .   .   .

char* append(str1, str2)
    char *str1, *str2;
{
     .   .   .
}
```

would appear in ANSI C as

```
char* append(char*, char*);
 .   .   .

char* append(char *str1, char *str2)
{
     .   .   .
}
```

This fuller kind of declaration is called a *function prototype.* Note that a type is needed for each argument: you can't omit the second char in the above ANSI C example as you could in a variable declaration. In declarations, argument names are optional; some people always include them while some include only those that seem helpful as documentation. In definitions, of course, arguments names must be specified for the argument to be referenced. (Actually, argument names can be omitted from function definitions too. An unnamed argument indicates one that is never used. The compiler may issue warnings about named arguments that are never used; omitting the name is a way to suppress those warnings.)

ANSI C also permits old-style function declarations, with no arguments inside the parentheses. However, this makes it impossible for the compiler to tell whether `fn()` is meant to be an old-style declaration of a function with any number of arguments or a new-style declaration of a function with *no* arguments. ANSI C resolves this ambiguity by requiring that functions of no arguments be declared as `fn(void)`. C++ allows, but does not require, this form — in C++, `fn()` too is a function of no arguments. C++ does not allow old-style function declarations, so there is no ambiguity — function declarations must always contain the types of their arguments.

Constants

ANSI C introduces a new type specifier, `const`, which replaces many uses of `#define`. The type specifier `const` may be added to any type and designates values that may not be altered. In particular, the value of a `const` variable cannot be changed.

```
const double PI = 3.141593;
. . .
PI = 3.0;    /* illegal */
```

In more advanced programming, `const` is used in other contexts too, especially function arguments and return values. Writing professional C++ code requires careful thought to the appropriate use of `const`. However, in this book `const` will be used only for global variables of built-in types, simply as a replacement for the less accurate `#define`. Other uses involve surprising subtleties that are best avoided for the purposes at hand (see the discussion of `const` in Appendix E, page 481 ff.).[1]

The type `void`

Although not in the original language, the type `void` found its way into most implementations of C and was accepted for ANSI C. Used as a function's return type, `void` signifies that the function does not return a value. As the type of a pointer, `void` is used to escape the type system — it signifies 'any type'. Thus, the declaration

```
void* ptr;
```

indicates that `ptr` can point to anything.

A function declared as

```
void DrawShape(void* shape, enum shapetype shtyp);
```

takes a pointer to anything and an enum as its arguments and returns no value. Any pointer can be assigned to a `void*` variable or passed as a `void*` argument without explicit cast, in both ANSI C and C++. In order to use the contents of a `void*` variable, the pointer

---

[1]You may, however, notice constant arguments in the declarations of library functions. These are there to allow pointers to `const` values to be passed to functions that don't change the objects passed to them through pointers. The compiler can always promote a non-`const` to a `const`, just as it can promote a `short` to an `int`.

must be cast to a specific type. ANSI C allows that cast to be left implicit, but C++ requires an explicit cast. Thus, the following is permitted in ANSI C, but not in C++.

```
void DrawSquare(square* s);
void DrawCircle(circle* c);
void DrawLine(line* l);

void DrawShape(void* shape, enum shapetype shtyp)
{
    switch (shtyp)
    {
        square:
            DrawSquare(shape);
            break;
        circle:
            DrawCircle(shape);
            break;
        line:
            DrawLine(shape);
            break;
    }
}
```

In C++, shape would have to be explicitly cast to the appropriate type.

```
void DrawSquare(square* s);
void DrawCircle(circle* c);
void DrawLine(line* l);

void DrawShape(void* shape, enum shapetype shtyp)
{
    switch (shtyp)
    {
        square:
            DrawSquare((square*) shape);
            break;
        circle:
            DrawCircle((circle*) shape);
            break;
        line:
            DrawLine((line*) shape);
            break;
    }
}
```

In classic C, char* is used to mean both 'pointer to anything' and 'string'. Using char* to mean 'pointer to anything' worked only because char happens to be C's fundamental unit of storage, equivalent to 1 byte. Having a void type allows distinguishing a 'pointer to anything' from a 'pointer to char' (or 'string'). ANSI C interprets pointer types more rigorously than classic C, so char* arguments no longer accept arbitrary type values — that's what void* is for.

The assert Macro

ANSI C specifies an extremely useful assertion macro, defined in assert.h. It takes an integer-valued expression as its argument and expands to a test of that condition. If the condition is true the expansion does nothing, but if the condition is false a message is printed out that indicates the file name, line number, and condition of the assertion.

Assertions simplify code by performing tests that the rest of a function doesn't have to worry about. Assertions are also a way to document program assumptions explicitly. They can be considered an active form of comments such as "N should always be positive." or "Assumes the pointer is not null." They are superior to such comments because they actually test the documented assumption, as in this example.

```
void DrawShape(void* shape, enum shapetype shtyp)
{
    assert(shape != 0);
    . . .
}
```

Assertions can even be used to write test programs. Most test programs print output and expect a person to check that the output is correct. This leaves open the possibility of an error slipping by the person reading the output. It is also difficult to automate the testing process. An interesting alternative approach is to write a program consisting entirely of assertion statements. If everything is correct, the program runs to completion; if not, then it stops at the first problem and outputs an explanation. No human intervention is required to run the test.

0.2.2 Minor C++ Features

C++ offers a variety of improvements on ANSI C in the area of standard programming. Some are trivial, some are nice conveniences, and a few are quite important.

Type Checking

The most important of the improvements is that C++ enforces type consistency to a much greater extent than C does. In particular, function declarations are checked across separately compiled files as they are linked together into an executable program. You'll see some consequences of serious type checking when you start using a C++ compiler.

Single-Line Comments

C++ users have a choice between traditional C comments and a single-line comment form: // starts a comment that goes to end of line. For example:

```
        const int bufsize = 512;              // size of buffer
```

Declaration Statements

In C++, declarations are statements and can appear wherever other statements can. This encourages the use of initializers, since a variable's declaration can be deferred until its initial value has been determined. Defining a local variable without an initializer allows accidental attempts to use the variable before it has been initialized. Deferring the definition until the initial value is known avoids such errors.

Similarly, C++ interprets the syntax of `for` statements slightly differently from the way C does: the first clause may be either an expression or a declaration statement. The scope of a variable defined inside a `for` is the rest of the enclosing block, so its value is available after the loop. However, this means that it would be an error to declare the same variable in a subsequent `for` within the same block. Instead, the variable should just be used normally in subsequent statements in the same block.

```
double average(double values[], int size)
{
    fprintf(stderr, "Computing the average. . . \n");
    double total = 0. 0;
    for (int i = 0; i < size; i++) total += values[i];
    return total/size;
}
```

enum and `struct`

In C++ enum and `struct` define type *names* as well as types. If you've defined

```
        enum direction {up, down, left, right};
```

then you declare a variable or function argument as

```
        direction d;
```

instead of having to say

```
        enum direction d;
```

There is therefore no need to use `typedef` to define type names for enums and structs.

Two struct types with exactly the same field names and types are nevertheless different types. Each enumeration is a separate type; in particular, values from one enumeration cannot be assigned to a variable of another, and an enumerator can be part of just one enumeration.

Optional Arguments

C++ functions can have optional arguments. A function declaration makes an argument optional by providing a default value for it. If an optional argument is omitted in a function call, the compiler substitutes the default value. All optional arguments must follow all required ones — otherwise there would be no way for the compiler to tell that a call had omitted an optional argument between two required ones.

```
date* MakeDate(int day = CURDAY,int month = CURMONTH,int year = CURYEAR);

date* d = MakeDate(4, 7, 1776);
date* d = MakeDate(4,7);                  // July 4th of this year
date* d = MakeDate(4);                    // 4th day of this month
date* d = MakeDate();                     // current date
```

Generalized Initialization of Static Variables

Static variables can be initialized with any legal expression, not just constants as in C.

```
int CURDAY = get_currentday();
```

Undefined global variables are given a default definition that zeros the storage they occupy. Initialization expressions that cannot be completely evaluated during compilation constants are evaluated at the start of execution.

More Convenient Dynamic Allocation

C, like many other languages, maintains a *heap* for dynamic memory. C's malloc function allocates a number of bytes from the heap and returns a pointer to the first one. If no chunk of space of the specified size is available on the heap, malloc returns 0.

To dynamically allocate an instance of a type requires calling malloc with the number of bytes to allocate for that type. C provides the sizeof pseudo-function for this purpose. The compiler replaces calls to sizeof with the number of bytes taken by its argument, a detail the compiler of course knows. For example, in many implementations sizeof(int) is 4.

The pointer malloc returns is a void*. To assign that pointer to a variable whose type is a pointer to the struct being created requires a cast. (In ANSI C that can often be left implicit, but in C++ it must be made explicit.) Altogether, then, the idiom for allocating a new instance of any type T is

```
(T*) malloc(sizeof(T))
```

C++ provides an additional operator, new, to package this idiom. Instead of the above, you can just say

```
new T
```

To allocate an array of n Ts in C, you'd have to multiple T's size by n:

```
(T*) malloc(n * sizeof(T))
```

In C++, you would just write

```
new T[n]
```

For example, the following C code dynamically allocate an instance of a date struct and assigns a pointer to it to a variable.

```
date* d = (date*) malloc(sizeof(date));
```

The equivalent in C++ would be simply

```
date* d = new date;
```

We'll see later that the new operator has another important aspect, but for now we can consider it simply a convenient replacement for standard malloc idioms.

Both malloc and new return zero if they fail to allocate the requested space. Serious code should test the return and take appropriate action when zero. However, it is not necessary to do so in an educational context, and since the tests can add distracting detail they will not be included in the code shown in this book.

In C, data allocated with malloc is deallocated with free. The argument to free is a pointer to the space to be deallocated, as in this example.

```
date* d = (date*) malloc(sizeof (date));
 .   .   .
free(d);
```

The amount of space allocated by malloc is recorded on the heap so free can tell how much space to deallocate. Deallocated storage can be reused by malloc.

C++ provides another operator, delete, in place of C's free function. It shares the other feature of new that we aren't going to discuss yet, but otherwise is just like free.

```
date* d = new date;
 .   .   .
delete d;
```

To delete an array allocated with new delete must be followed by a pair of square brackets to indicate that it is an array being deleted rather than a single instance.

```
date* dates = new date[20];
 .   .   .
delete[] dates;
```

Data allocated with new should be released with delete; data allocated with malloc should be released with free. There is rarely any reason to use malloc in a C++ program. Note, however, that a few ANSI C library functions return pointers to data allocated with malloc; these must be deallocated with free, not delete.

0.2.3 Reference Types

Reference types are an important C++ feature. References are specified with ampersands the way pointer types are specified with asterisks. Although confusing at first, they soon seem natural — so much so, that it is generally better to references than pointers. The following defines d as a reference to TODAY.

```
date TODAY;
date& d = TODAY;
```

Functions can take reference arguments and return reference values just as they can take and return pointers. This section provides a first look at references. Later chapters will say more about them.

The main use for references is to pass arguments and return values "by reference" where traditional C programs pass pointers. (Other languages also make mechanisms for this available, such as var parameters in Pascal.) Arrays and functions are automatically passed as pointers (i.e., by address) in C and C++, but everything would otherwise be passed (copied) as a value. Using references prevents unwanted (inefficient) copying as well as allowing functions to change external values passed to them.

```
void enter(entry&, table&);

void increment_count(entry& e)
{
    e.count++;                      // modifies the entry passed to the function
}

main()
{
    table tbl;
    entry e;
    e.count = 0;
    increment_count(e);
    printf("%d\n", e.count);    // prints "1"
    enter(e, tbl);              // arguments passed by reference (address)
}
```

Functions can even return references as values, and a function that does can appear on the left side of an assignment statement! In a program to manage a corporate phone directory we might have the following.

```
int& lookup(table& tbl, char* str);

int get_extension(char* name)
// return the phone extension for a person
{
    return lookup(extensions, name);
}
```

```
void set_extension(char* name, int newext)
// Change the phone extension for a person to newext
{
    lookup(extensions, name) = newext;
}
```

The assignment statement in set_extension works because what lookup returns is actually the *address* of the place in some table where the integer representing the person's phone extension is stored. The compiler generates appropriate code for dereferencing that address where its value is needed, as in get_extension.

Code written using references is often clearer than equivalent code using pointers. Compare the following

```
// pointer-based definition
void int_exchange(int *a, int *b)
{
    int c = *a;
    *a = *b;
    *b = c;
}

// pointer-based call
int x, y;
.  .  .
int_exchange(&x, &y);                    // using addresses
```

to the more natural

```
// reference-based definition
void int_exchange(int &a, int &b)
{
    int c = a;
    a = b;
    b = c;
}

// reference-based
int x, y;
.  .  .
int_exchange(x, y);                      // more natural
```

In effect, specifying reference arguments to a function directs the compiler to insert pointer-dereferencing asterisks for you. Your code is relieved of all those distracting asterisks, but the end result is the same. Note, however, that you cannot distinguish an ordinary argument from a reference argument by looking at the call — you have to consult the function declaration.

0.3 Some Important Distinctions

Our study of data structures requires a better understanding of some important concepts at the foundations of C than most programmers can be expected to have, even after years of professional experience. Most readers will find these familiar to some extent, but a clear understanding of some distinctions presented here will significantly facilitate digestion and exploration of the material in the rest of the book.

0.3.1 Variable Scope and Extent

Two fundamental characteristics govern the use of variables in programming languages: *scope* and *extent*. You probably have an intuitive notion of these, but as C jumbles the two ideas somewhat you probably aren't very clear about them. Further, C++ introduces new variations on C's variable scope rules. Thus, although fundamental, these aspects of variables often cause confusion and therefore warrant review.[2]

A *variable* is an *identifier* together with its *value*. The *scope* of an identifier is the part of a program that knows about it during compilation. The *extent* of a value is the time when it exists during execution (i.e., when storage is allocated for it). Scope is a phenomenon in the *spatial* dimension of program *text*; extent is a phenomenon in the *temporal* dimension of program *execution*.

There are three possible scopes for C identifiers:

local	only code in the same block can refer to the identifier
file	only code in the same file can refer to the identifier
global	any code in any file can refer to the identifier

There are three possible extents for C values:

local	allocated on block entry; deallocated on block exit
static	exists for lifetime of program
dynamic	allocated by a call to `malloc` (or, in C++, `new`); deallocated by a call to `free` (or, in C++, `delete`)

Note that dynamically allocated memory can, and typically does, survive the exit of the block in which it was created. Strictly speaking, variable values never have dynamic extent. However, variable values can be *pointers* to dynamically allocated storage — the kind you get when you use `malloc` (in C) or `new` (in C++).

C has various kinds of variables, with a confused mixture of scopes and extents. The two basic kinds of variables and their default scope and extent are as follows.

---

[2]The description here is somewhat informal. For instance, the term *block*, common to other programming languages, is used to mean what technically would be either a *compound statement* or a *function body*. Some relatively arcane details are omitted, such as `register` variables. Also ignored is the fact that a variable is known from the point in a compilation unit where it is first declared, not from the beginning of the compilation unit.

automatic[3] variables declared in a block, including function arguments (which belong to their function's outermost block)

     scope: *local*

     extent: *local*

external[4] variables accessible outside the file in which they are defined

     scope: *global*

     extent: *static*

C allows variables to be qualified by a *storage class specifier*, two of which are commonly used: `extern` and `static`. These storage class specifiers are used to change scope or extent from the default. Declaring an identifier `extern` (without providing an initializer) means that it is not a new identifier but rather a reference to another module's global variable that will be resolved by the linker. The most confusing aspect of all this is the effect of declaring an identifier `static`: used with a file-level variable `static` changes the *scope* of the *identifier* to *file*, but used with a variable defined inside a block `static` changes the *extent* of the *value* to *static*.

0.3.2 Name Spaces in C and C++

C permits the same identifier to be used for different purposes at the same time. (Whether it is advisable to take advantage of this is a different question!) There are five separate identifier classes, or *name spaces*, in C. An identifier in one class is entirely independent of an identifier in another class that happens to have the same name. The name spaces are:

- preprocessor macro names
- statement labels
- structure, union, and enumeration names
- structure and union field names
- everything else (variables, functions, typedefs, enumeration values)

C++ originally put everything except preprocessor macro names, statement labels, and field names in the same class, but objections were raised concerning certain inconveniences and incompatibilities this caused. A compromise was developed that allows reasonable traditional uses of the same name for identifiers of different classes (e.g., having a function and a structure with the same name). It is probably best to avoid difficulties in this area by simply never using a name for more than one kind of thing (function, variable, etc.) in any scope. (Of course there's no problem with two identifiers in different scopes; in particular, an automatic variable in one block may have the same name as one in another block without any interference.) The issue of name spaces is raised here only to warn knowledgeable C programmers of an area in which C++ is subtly different from C.

---

[3]*Local* in most programming languages.

[4]*Global* in most programming languages.

0.3.3 Miscellaneous Clarifications

Our discussion of C++ basics ends by clarifying some terms that will be used a lot in this book. Probably your previous training and experience in computer science introduced you to these, but just to make sure and also to remove some potential ambiguity, they'll be reviewed briefly here.

Compile Time versus Run Time

Programs are processed in three major phases: compilation, linkage, and execution. Some languages, including C, add an additional preprocessor phase. What gets done in each of these phases depends partly on the language definition and partly on its implementation. The C preprocessor strips comments, expands #define macros, inserts the text of #include files, and removes the text of false branches of #if and related conditionals. The compiler checks syntax, builds a table of symbols and their definitions, checks for syntactic and semantic consistency, generates code, and so on. The linker combines the symbol tables and code of the separate compiled (i.e., 'object') files, extracts definitions from libraries, and checks for missing functions and variables. During execution, functions are called, local variables are allocated on the stack, space is allocated from the heap, and interaction between the program and the outside environment is managed in cooperation with the operating system.

Sometimes it is important to distinguish when a particular mechanism is active or a particular kind of event occurs (errors, in particular). The terms *compile time*, *link time*, and *run time* are used to refer to things that happen during compilation, linking, and execution, respectively.[5]

Stack versus Heap

The *program stack* is a data structure used to manage the call and return of subroutines, including passing parameters and returning results. The stack is manipulated by the run time environment; most languages give the programmer no way to reference it directly. Stacks in general are the topic of Chapter 5, so you'll learn how they work there, if you don't already know. For present purposes it's enough to understand that automatic variables are allocated on the stack (or in a closely related data structure) and managed by the run-time support system without any programmer intervention. (Global variables may be allocated in a special chunk of memory and don't participate in the block entry and exit mechanisms the stack is there to support.)

The topic of *dynamic memory allocation* was discussed briefly when the C++ new operator was introduced above. Many readers will not have had any experience using dynamic allocation, which will therefore seem quite mysterious. Dynamic memory allocation is based on another data structure of the run-time support system, called the *heap*. Storage allocated dynamically, by using malloc (in C) or new (in C++), is allocated from the heap. Allocation consists of finding the requested number of bytes in a contiguous

---

[5]Other terms include 'compilation time' and 'execution time'. 'Link time' is not a common term, presumably because in most languages little of interest to the programmer happens at link time. C++ implementations may perform several kinds of significant actions during linking, however, including cross-module type checking and template instantiation.

chunk somewhere in the heap and returning a pointer to the first one. The heap management code keeps track of the size of each allocated piece and which parts of the heap are available (as opposed to having been allocated and not yet released).

The program stack and heap are similar in that storage space is allocated from both structures. They are separate because their storage management strategies support different kinds of allocation: the stack provides space that is automatically allocated and deallocated, while the heap supplies space that is explicitly allocated and deallocated by the programmer.

Declarations versus Definitions

Informally, *declaration* and *definition* are often used interchangeably, but there are significant differences with real consequences in C. A *declaration* of a variable or function specifies its type. A *definition* also specifies the type of a variable or function, but goes further. The definition of a variable causes storage to be allocated for it. The definition of a function causes code to be generated. For the most part, header files contain declarations, and other files contain definitions.

A variable or function may be *declared* any number of times within a *compilation unit* (a file plus its #include files). All declarations of a variable or function in the same compilation unit must agree with one another. For the most part, declarations are used only by the compiler. *Definitions*, however are used in all phases of program processing — compilation, linkage, and execution.

A function may be declared without being defined as long as it is never called, but a call to an undefined function results in a link-time error. There can only be one definition of each function. If there are more, the linker complains about the multiple definitions, even if they are identical.

C was originally ambiguous about whether a declared variable had to be defined, whether it could have multiple (mutually consistent) definitions, and how to decide which declarations were definitions. ANSI C resolved much of this ambiguity, but C++ goes further. In C++, a variable declaration is a definition unless it contains the extern specifier and no initializer, and there must be exactly one definition of each variable in a program. (There can, of course, be many *declarations* as long as they are consistent with one another.) One interesting case of a definition in C++ that is not necessarily a definition in ANSI C is

```
int a;
```

This is interpreted exactly the same in C++ as

```
int a = 0;
```

Initialization versus Assignment

Variable definitions usually include initialization expressions:

```
int cur = -1;
```

Initializations look just like assignments:

```
cur = -1;
```

However, the two are different constructs. There are a few minor places where this difference matters in C — in particular, an array-valued variable may not be assigned to, but it may be initialized. However, in C++ the difference becomes quite significant, as you will see later, especially when we consider copying of structures.

Objects

Finally, the term *object* will be used loosely in this text, as it is in discussions of traditional C, to mean any kind of computational value. There wouldn't be any problem with this, except for confusion with terms from the rapidly growing popularity of *object-oriented programming* and other aspects of *object technology*, including *object-oriented analysis, object-oriented design, object-oriented user interfaces,* and *object-oriented databases.* Since C++ is one of the predominant languages used for object-oriented programming there is special opportunity for confusion in this book.[6]

The term *object* has additional ramifications in the context of object technology, but all we mean in this text by the term *object* (except for the discussion of object-oriented technology in Appendix D) is a computational value — a piece of data in memory. Unfortunately, there just isn't another commonly used generic term for the entities in memory. Often, the term *object* is used in a way that implies a structure instance, rather than a value of a primitive type such as int, but it really means *any* computational value, including primitives. (That generality is what makes the term so usefully noncommittal.) The term is often used to emphasize the integrity, or independence, of the computational entity as opposed to the sequence of bytes that comprise it.

Sometimes, *object* is used in yet another way — to distinguish structure *instances* from *pointers* to structure instances. For instance, we can note that declaring a pointer-valued automatic variable does not cause space to be allocated for the *object* to which the pointer points when its block is entered during execution. In designing and using data structures there is often an important choice to be made as to whether a particular value or component will be a *pointer* or an *object*. Generally, both are meaningful choices, but they have different consequences.

0.4 EXERCISES

1. Get an existing C program to work with C++. If it was already in ANSI C, this should require few if any changes. If it was not already in ANSI C, change all function declarations and definitions to use function prototypes. Then,
   (a) Look through the program for places where a C++ feature would have been more convenient, and change the program to use those features.
   (b) Did you discover any mistakes or problems in your old program? If so, describe and explain them and how C++ helped you find them.

2. Practice using malloc then new in a simple program.

---

[6]A different meaning of *object*, as used in the term *object file* from the early days of programming languages, shouldn't cause any confusion because 'object' would never be used with this other meaning apart from phrases such as *object file, object deck,* and *object code.*

(a) For instance, write a C program that reads text from stdin and writes it to stdout in reverse order. Read each line into a buffer. Then, dynamically allocate a long enough array
of characters to hold the line (including the final null byte) and copy the buffer to the dynamically allocated string. Store a pointer to the string in an array used to hold all the lines
of the program.

(b) Change the malloc calls to new and compile with a C++ compiler.

3. Use some of the C++ features discussed above to write a program that represents a date as a
struct with fields day, month, and year. Include at least the following. (MakeDate should allocate memory from the heap.)

(a) `date* MakeDate(int day=CURDAY, int month=CURMONTH, int year=CURYEAR);`
   `// CUR variables initialized at start of program`

(b) `int diff(date& d1, date& d2);`
   `// number of days separating d1 and d2`

(c) `void incr(date& d, int n = 1);`
   `// change d to n days later`

(d) `date* CopyDate(date& d);`
   `// allocate a new date and copy field values from d`

Data Abstraction in C++

Data abstraction is an approach to programming that insulates users of a data structure from its implementation. In particular, details of a structure's representation are known only to the functions that embody the most fundamental operations on the data structure. Those details are entirely hidden from code that uses the structure. This *information hiding* is a critical tool in the never-ending battle against program complexity. It enables a programmer to use a data structure without having to deal with all the tedious details of its implementation. Because programs are expressed in terms of abstract data structure operations, the conceptual level of application code is raised, allowing it to be expressed more naturally.

Modularization is an organizational technique that decomposes a program into pieces that interact only weakly. Ideally, changes inside one module have relatively little effect on code in other modules. Data abstraction emphasizes decomposition based on data structures. It contrasts with the more traditional approach of procedural abstraction, which bases decomposition on functionality by putting together functions that perform similar or related actions. Good modern programming requires both approaches, but structural modularization provides a more stable foundation and should be the starting point of all program development.

1.1 Modularization

C, and therefore C++, provides a very direct mechanism for dividing a program up into separate modules. Programmers write two kinds of files: *implementation* and *header*. Implementation files are compiled into *object* files, which are linked together into *executable* files — programs that can be run on the computer. Header files are incorporated into C implementation files by the #include directive.

One header file can be included by many implementation files. The primary purpose of header files is to provide shared declarations for macros, types, functions, and variables used throughout the program. There is no direct expression of the *module* con-

25

cept in C++, but informally a module usually consists of an implementation file together with a header file that publicizes declarations of some of its functions.

Data abstraction is best supported by putting each data type into a separate module. The header file specifies the *interface* to the type — the ways its instances can be manipulated by other code. The implementation file supplies the definitions of the functions declared in the header file, along with internal functions used in those definitions. In this style, each header file defines a new type and declares the functions that constitute its interface. Normally, each header file would define only one type, but sometimes it is reasonable to define a supporting type in the same header file.

1.1.1 An Example

Let's look at a simple implementation of a string type. In place of the null-terminated strings of C we'll define a struct that has a size and an array of characters (without a final NUL). We'll start with a straight ANSI C implementation, then develop it through several stages to illustrate the application of some of the C++ features discussed in the previous chapter and some new ones that support structural modularization. Along the way, we will see code that does not reflect good C++ practice — this is a pedagogical sequence that motivates the various features introduced, and until all the features have been introduced we can't show the kind of code we'd want to see in a realistic implementation.

> *In all of this book's examples, code from header files appears between double-line rules, while other code appears between single-line rules.*

A Basic C Module

```
/* stringt.h, version 1: straight C */

#ifndef STRINGT_H
#define STRINGT_H

#include <stdio.h>          /* needed by write_string */

struct _string
{
    int size;
    char* chars;
};

typedef struct _string string;
/* A standard C trick to turn a struct into a type name.
   With just    "struct string", all uses of the struct name
   would have to be preceded by 'struct'.1
*/

/*  Argument names are omitted here. */
string* make_string(int);
string* convert_to_string(char*);
void destroy_string(string*);
char string_char(string*, int);
```

```
void string_replace(string*, int, char);
int string_length(string*);
string* concatenate(string*, string*);
int string_equal(string*, string*);
int string_lessthan(string*, string*);
void write_string(string*, FILE*);

#endif /* STRINGT_H */
```

There are various ways to pass strings as arguments to functions. Here, the choice was made to always create strings dynamically and pass them around as pointers. As we consider the rest of the C++ features to be discussed we'll see better ways to create strings, pass them as arguments, and return them as values.

There are advantages and disadvantages to putting #includes in header files. The main advantage is that the header file is self-contained — to use a module users need only to include a header file; they do not need to specify the #includes the module needs. However, including a header file multiple times would cause multiple definition errors and other chaos. To prevent these problems, it is common practice to enclose the entire header file in a conditional that sets and tests a "guard" symbol indicating that the header file has already been included during a compilation. Several different conventions are widely used for naming these guard symbols; we'll use the approach that appends _H to the capitalized name of the struct the module defines.

```
#ifndef STRINGT_H
#define STRINGT_H

. . . header file contents . . .

#endif /* STRINGT_H */
```

The first time such a header file is included during a file's compilation, its guard symbol will not have been defined, so the rest of the file will get processed. For subsequent inclusions within the same compilation, the guard symbol *will* be defined, so the rest of the file will be skipped. Even with a guard symbol time is still spent opening the file and scanning for the matching #endif, which can be significant in long, complex compilations. Also, this technique requires that all system files as well as files from other users all incorporate guards. Other disadvantages arise in practice, including preprocessor limitations on deeply nested headers. As a result, it often ends up in practice that header files do not #include all headers they need, requiring the user to add those to programs using that header. Even so, header files should always be enclosed in an #ifndef guard.

---

[1] Making the typedef be for a pointer to _string is perhaps the more common approach, but it is useful to see the asterisks explicitly in this example. It is even possible in ANSI C to use the same name for both the struct and the typedef. Another approach is to combine the two in one statement:

```
typedef struct string { } string;
```

and even to omit the name of the struct in doing so.

It is often appropriate to begin designing a new module by writing its header file. After the header file is ready, writing the code that implements the declared functions will often reveal inadequacies and mistakes in the header file, which can then be corrected. Writing a test program for the module will also reveal inadequacies and errors, and the module can be extended or corrected to fix those. For instance, this string module was originally written without convert_to_string. That function was added when the test program was written, to provide a convenient way to initialize a string from a C string instead of having to store characters one at a time. (It could be argued that this string module should not provide a way to modify individual characters.)

```c
/* stringt.c, version 1: straight C */

#include "stringt.h"
#include <string.h>                      /* for strlen, memcpy, etc. */
#include <stdlib.h>                      /* for malloc */
#include <assert.h>

string* make_string(int siz)
{
    assert(siz >=0);
    string* str = (string*) malloc(sizeof(string));
    /* Technically, we should test str -- malloc returns 0 if fail.
       However, we will not bother with this nicety in this book.
    */

    str->size = siz;
    str->chars = (char*) malloc (str->size * sizeof(char));

    return str;
}

string* convert_to_string(char* cstr)
{
    assert(cstr != 0);
    string* str = (string*) malloc(sizeof(string));

    str->size = strlen(cstr);            /* not +1: don't need final null */
    str->chars = (char*) malloc (str->size * sizeof(char));
    memcpy(str->chars, cstr, str->size);
    /* memcpy is a standard C library function that we'll use instead of a
       for loop to copy bytes; not using strcpy because our strings don't
       end in a null byte.
    */

    return str;
}

void destroy_string(string* str)
{
    assert(str != 0);

    free(str->chars);
```

```c
        free(str);
}

char string_char(string* str, int n)
{
    assert(str != 0);
    assert(n >= 0 && n < str->size);
    return str->chars[n];
}

void string_replace(string* str, int n, char ch)
{
    assert(str != 0);
    assert(n >= 0 && n < str->size);
    str->chars[n] = ch;
}

int string_length(string* str)
{
    assert(str != 0);
    return str->size;
}

string* concatenate(string* str1, string* str2)
{
    assert(str1 != 0);
    assert(str2 != 0);
    string* str = make_string(str1->size + str2->size);

    memcpy(str->chars, str1->chars, str1->size);
    memcpy(str->chars+str1->size, str2->chars, str2->size);

    return str;
}

int string_equal(string* str1, string* str2)
{
    assert(str1 != 0);
    assert(str2 != 0);
    int i;

    if (str1->size != str2->size)
        return 0;
    else
        for (i=0; i<str1->size; i++)
            if (str1->chars[i] != str2->chars[i])
                return 0;

    return 1;
}

static int min(int a, int b)
{
    return (a<b ? a : b);
}
```

```
int string_lessthan(string* str1, string* str2)
{
    assert(str1 != 0);
    assert(str2 != 0);
    int i;

    for (i=0; i < min(str1->size, str2->size); i++)
        if (str1->chars[i] < str2->chars[i])
            return 1;
        else if (str1->chars[i] > str2->chars[i])
            return 0;

    return (str1->size < str2->size);
}

void write_string(string* str, FILE* fil)
{
    assert(str != 0);
    int i;

    for (i=0; i<str->size; i++) putc(str->chars[i], fil);
}
```

There are two forms to #include directives: double quotes indicate that the file is a user file, while angle brackets indicate a system file. Double quotes cause user directories — in particular, the current[2] one — to be searched before system directories.

Next is a short test program. This is far from an adequate test, but it gives enough examples for us to explore the language features we'll discuss. Note that a minimal application using a data structure module will involve at least three files: the header file for the module, the implementation file for the module, and the application program itself. The module implementation file and the application file get compiled separately then linked together into an executable program. Both include the header file.

```
// stringt tst.c, version 1

#include "stringt.h"
#include <assert.h>

main()
{
    string *str1, *str2;
```

---

[2]But what does 'current' mean? In Unix implementations double quotes mean 'first search the directory of the file with the #include', whereas in DOS implementations double quotes mean 'search starting in the directory from which the compiler was originally invoked'. A problem with the DOS interpretation is that if the path of an included file has directories in it and that file uses double quotes to include others in its directory, the preprocessor will look for them in the directory from which the compiler was invoked. Since it won't find it there, the other directory would have to be added to the list of system directories to search, even though the original #include explicitly specified a full path. In Unix implementations this wouldn't be necessary.

```
    str1 = convert_to_string("abc");
    assert('a' == string_char(str1, 0) && 'b' == string_char(str1, 1) &&
           'c' == string_char(str1, 2)
          );
    assert(string_length(str1) == 3);

    str2 = concatenate(str1, convert_to_string("def"));
    assert('a' == string_char(str2, 0) && 'b' == string_char(str2, 1) &&
           'c' == string_char(str2, 2) && 'd' == string_char(str2, 3) &&
           'e' == string_char(str2, 4) && 'f' == string_char(str2, 5)
          );
    assert(string_length(str2) == 6);

    assert(string_equal(str1,str1));
    assert(string_lessthan(str1,str2));

    printf("The concatenation of '");
    write_string(str1, stdout);
    printf("' and 'def' is '");
    write_string(str2, stdout);
    printf("', which has %d characters.\n", string_length(str2));

    destroy_string(str1);
    destroy_string(str2);
    /* Notice that a string was created from "def" that didn't get
       assigned to anything, so there's no way now to free its storage.
    */

    printf("Test completed.\n");
    return 0;
}
```

A Basic C++ Module

Next we'll rewrite the string module using some of the simple C++ features discussed earlier. Changes from the previous version are underlined. Different C++ systems have different conventions for the extension to be given to the names of header and implementation files. In this book we'll use H and C, analogous to the h and c used for C files.[3]

```
// stringt.H, version 2: using simple C++ features
// Single line comments are convenient.
// Note that the extension is now H instead of h.

#ifndef STRINGT_H
#define STRINGT_H

#include <iostream.h>              // replaces stdio.h

struct string                     // no typedef needed in C++
```

[3]This assumes an operating system that is case-sensitive. DOS, in particular, is not, so either a different convention must be used, or the environment must be set up so that all .c files are processed by a C++ compiler.

```
{
    int size;
    char* chars;
};

string* make_string(int);
string* convert_to_string(char*);
void destroy_string(string*);
char string_char(string*, int);
void string_replace(string*, int, char);
int string_length(string*);
string* concatenate(string*,string*);
int string_equal(string*, string*);
int string_lessthan(string*, string*);
void write_string(string*, ostream& = cout);
// default argument; can appear with or without name

#endif /* STRINGT_H */
```

```
// stringt.C, version 2: using simple C++ features
// The extension is now 'C' instead of 'c'.

#include "stringt.H"
#include <string.h>
// for string functions used in convert and for memcpy
#include <assert.h>

string* make_string(int siz)
{
    assert(siz >=0);
    string* str = new string;
        // replaces (string*) malloc(sizeof(string))

    str->size = siz;
    str->chars = new char[str->size];
    /*  new works with primitive types too; since we previously had:
            (char*) malloc (str->size * sizeof(char))
        which is an example of the malloc array-allocation idiom with
        T = char, we replace it as shown.
    */

    return str;
}

string* convert_to_string(char* cstr)
{
    assert(cstr != 0);
    string* str = new string;
        // see note in make_string, above

    str->size = strlen(cstr);              // not +1: don't need final null
    str->chars = new char[str->size];      // see note in make_string, above
    memcpy(str->chars, cstr, str->size);
```

```
    return str;
}

void destroy_string(string* str)
{
    assert(str != 0);

    delete [] str->chars;
    delete str;
}

char string_char(string* str, int n)
{
    assert(str != 0);
    assert(n >= 0 && n < str->size);

    return str->chars[n];
}

void string_replace(string* str, int n, char ch)
{
    assert(str != 0);
    assert(n >= 0 && n < str->size);

    str->chars[n] = ch;
}

int string_length(string* str)
{
    assert(str != 0);

    return str->size;
}

string* concatenate(string* str1, string* str2)
{
    assert(str1 != 0);
    assert(str2 != 0);
    string* str = make_string(str1->size + str2->size);

    memcpy(str->chars, str1->chars, str1->size);
    memcpy(str->chars+str1->size, str2->chars, str2->size);

    return str;
}

int string_equal(string* str1, string* str2)
{
    assert(str1 != 0);
    assert(str2 != 0);

    if (str1->size != str2->size)
        return 0;
    else
```

```
        for (int i=0; i<str1->size; i++)
        // eliminated declaration at start of block and moved here
            if (str1->chars[i] != str2->chars[i])
                return 0;

    return 1;
}

static int min(int a, int b)
{
    return (a<b ? a : b);
}

int string_lessthan(string* str1, string* str2)
{
    assert(str1 != 0);
    assert(str2 != 0);

    for (int i=0; i < min(str1->size, str2->size); i++)
        // eliminated declaration at start of block and moved here
        if (str1->chars[i] < str2->chars[i])
            return 1;
        else if (str1->chars[i] > str2->chars[i])
            return 0;

    return (str1->size < str2->size);
}

void write_string(string* str, ostream& strm)
// Note that the default argument appears only in the header file.
// The compiler inserts default arguments into the calls; the function
// itself is unaffected.
{
    assert(str != 0);

    for (int i=0; i<str->size; i++) strm << str->chars[i];
    /* Notice how much more compact this function looks without the
        initial declaration of i and with the use of the insertion operator
        for output.

        str->chars[i] could be replaced by string_char(str,i) and str->size
        by string_length(str).
    */
}
```

1.1.2 Overloading

Most of the functions in the string module are the sort that would appear in many different
kinds of modules. We'd see names like `write_date` and `write_name` analogous to
`write_string`; `date_equal` and `name_equal` analogous to `string_equal`, and so on.
These kinds of names soon get tedious. Not only are they awkward, but they may be con-

structed according to various conventions, and it is easy to get confused: is it `write_`
`string`, `string_write`, `WriteString`, `StringWrite`, `STRWrite`, or what? Wouldn't it
be nice to be able to just call these functions `write`, `equal`, and so on, and let the compiler
figure out which version to use?

C++ allows you to do just that. You can give any number of functions the same
name. The compiler chooses the appropriate one for any call by matching the types of the
arguments in the call to the types of the arguments in the declarations of each of the functions with the same name. The name of a function together with its sequence of types con-
stitutes its *signature*. The ability to use the same name with different argument patterns is
called *overloading*.

At first, this seems pretty exotic, but actually overloading is present in a limited form
in traditional languages. The machine code generated for an expression like a+b depends
on the types of a and b, since computers have different instructions for different kinds of
arithmetic (integer, floating-point, etc.). Traditional languages, however, overload only
operators, not function names, and they give the programmer no way to define new
overloadings. C++ allows you to overload function names as well as define new overloadings for built-in operators.

An Example of Function Overloading

Here's a simple example of overloading. Instead of having `int_exchange`, `char_ex-`
`change`, `double_exchange`, and `date_exchange` (assuming a `date` struct), we can just
call all of them `exchange`. Note the use of reference arguments in the example and the
lack of anything special in calls to the functions using them.

```
// exchange.H
void exchange(int& a, int& b);
void exchange(char& a, char& b);
void exchange(double& a, double& b);
void exchange(date& a, date& b);
```

```
#include "exchange.H"

void exchange(int& a, int& b)
{
    int c = a;
    a = b;
    b = c;
}

void exchange(char& a, char& b)
{
    char c = a;
    a = b;
    b = c;
}

void exchange(double& a, double& b)
```

```
{
    double c = a;
    a = b;
    b = c;
}

void exchange(date& a, date& b)
{
    date c = a;
    a = b;
    b = c;
}
```

```
#include "exchange.H"

//. . .

main()
{
    int x, y;
    date dept_mtg, dept_party;

    //  . . .
    exchange(x,y);
    exchange(dept_mtg, dept_party);
    //  . . .
}
```

Two kinds of overloadings can be distinguished: intermodule and intramodule. Having one `write` that takes a string and another that takes a date would be intermodule overloading. Intramodule overloading is also useful — it allows an operation to have different patterns of arguments without your having to use a different name for each pattern. For instance, we could have definitions of `convert_to_string` taking an `int` (to get a string with the characters representing an integer), a `double` (similar to `int`), or a `FILE*` (which might read the contents of the corresponding file into a string).

Operator Overloading

In C++, operators can be overloaded in the same way functions are. In fact, to define an operator overloading you *do* define a function. The only trick is knowing the name of the function to define.

The name of a function specifying an operator overloading is composed of the keyword `operator` and the operator's symbol. For instance, we could replace `string_equal(string&, string&)` with `operator==(string&, string&)`. Then, instead of calling `string_equal(str1, str2)` we could write the more C-like expression `str1==str2`. We could also explicitly call the operator function as `operator==(str1, str2)`, but there's rarely any reason to do that. Note also that `string_equal` was changed here to take references to strings instead of pointers to strings — operator functions normally work with objects rather than pointers. White space is permitted between the keyword operator and the operator symbol in the function name.

C++ includes a sophisticated input/output library that replaces the stdio.h facility. It is accessed by including iostream.h. You should immediately start using its basic feature — operator overloadings for simple input and output. (Other features will be discussed in a Chapter 4.)

Here's how it works. The global variables cin, cout, and cerr replace stdin, stdout, and stderr, respectively. Two operators are used: << for output (called *insertion*) and >> for input (called *extraction*). Overloadings are provided for all the built-in types, plus char* and void*. These operators return their stream argument, so they can be chained:

```
cout << "The sum of the " << n << " integers is "
    << total << '\n';
```

You will find the insertion operator quite convenient. Other features of the stream library provide enough control over I/O that you would rarely have to use printf or scanf.

The real power of the stream operators is that it is straightforward to define overloadings for the types you define. We can see by the way the insertion operation is used that its first (left) argument must be an ostream (output stream) and its second (right) argument the kind of thing being printed. Both are passed as references, the stream because the function must modify it and the thing being printed to avoid copying. Finally, to support chaining, the function must return the stream. The signature for a user-defined insertion operator for a type *T* will therefore always be

```
ostream& operator<<(ostream&, const T&).
```

In the string module, for instance, we can replace

```
void write_string(string*, FILE*)
```

with

```
ostream& operator<<(ostream&, const string&).
```

The extraction operator works similarly. Notice that operator>> does not return what it extracts — like operator<< it returns its stream argument. An already allocated value (primitive or struct instance) is passed (by reference) as the second argument to receive the input.

Here's the whole module and test program again, this time using overloading and operators wherever appropriate. That turns out to be many places — we can even overload operators like [ ] for index operations! (So much has changed here that the changes are not underlined.) A major advantage of the ability to overload operators is that it makes it possible to write expressions with your types in terms of the usual operators. Without overloading, a programmer's types could be manipulated only by functions, reducing them to a second-class role.

```
// stringt.H, version 3: using function and operator overloading

#ifndef STRINGT_H
#define STRINGT_H

#include <iostream.h>

struct string
{
    int size;
    char* chars;
};

string* make_string(int);
void destroy(string*);                 // "_string" omitted

// two overloadings of convert_to_string:
string* convert_to_string(char*);
string* convert_to_string(istream&);   // declared, but not defined

char& nth(string&, int);
// Because it returns a reference (!), this version of nth can be used
// instead of string_replace!

int length(string&);

string operator+(string&,string&);
int operator==(string&, string&);
int operator<(string&, string&);
ostream& operator<<(ostream&, string&);
// no longer has a default file argument

#endif /* STRINGT_H */
```

```
// stringt.C, version 3: using function and operator overloading

#include "stringt.H"
#include <string.h>
#include <assert.h>

string* make_string(int siz)
{
    assert(siz >=0);
    string* str = new string;

    str->size = siz;
    str->chars = new char[str->size];

    return str;
}
```

```
string* convert_to_string(char* cstr)
{
    assert(cstr != 0);
    string* str = new string;

    str->size = strlen(cstr);
    str->chars = new char[str->size];
    memcpy(str->chars, cstr, str->size);

    return str;
}

void destroy(string* str)
{
    // no need to test str -- references can't be null!
    delete [] str->chars;
    delete str;
}

char& nth(string& str, int n)
{
    // no need to test str -- references can't be null!
    assert(n >= 0 && n < str.size);

    return str.chars[n];
}

int length(string& str)
{
    // no need to test str -- references can't be null!
    return str.size;
}

string& operator+(string& str1, string& str2)
{
    // no need to test str1 and str2 -- references can't be null!
    string* str = make_string(str1->size + str2->size);

    memcpy(str->chars, str1->chars, str1->size);
    memcpy(str->chars+str1->size, str2->chars, str2->size);

    return *str;
    // returning a value now, instead of a pointer
}

int operator==(string& str1, string& str2)
{
    // no need to test str1 and str2 -- references can't be null!
    if (&str1 == &str2) return 1;        // str1 and str2 are the same!
    if (str1.size != str2.size)
        return 0;
    else
        for (int i=0; i<str1.size; i++)
            if (str1.chars[i] != str2.chars[i]) return 0;
```

```
        return 1;
}

static int min(int a, int b)
{
        return (a<b ? a : b);
}

int operator<(string& str1, string& str2)
{
        // no need to test str1 and str2 -- references can't be null!

        if (&str1 == &str2) return 0;          // str1 and str2 are the same!
        for (int i=0; i < min(str1.size, str2.size); i++)
            if (str1.chars[i] < str2.chars[i])
                return 1;
            else if (str1.chars[i] > str2.chars[i])
                return 0;

        return (str1.size < str2.size);
}

ostream& operator<<(ostream& strm, string& str)
{
        // no need to test str -- references can't be null!

        for (int i=0; i<str.size; i++) strm << str.chars[i];

        return strm;
        // All operator << and >> functions end this way, to support chaining.
}
```

```
// stringt tst.C, version 3: using overloading

#include "stringt.h"
#include <assert.h>

main()
{
        string& str1 = *convert_to_string("abc");
            // We switch to a object perspective instead of a pointer.
        assert('a' == nth(str1, 0) && 'b' == nth(str1, 1) &&
               'c' == nth(str1, 2)
               );
        assert(length(str1) == 3);
            // 'string' has been removed from many function names.

        string& temp = *convert_to_string("def");
            // Result given a name so we can delete it later
        string str2 = str1 + temp;
            // str2 is now an object, not a pointer
            // Note use of + operation on string objects.
```

```
    assert('a' == nth(str2, 0) && 'b' == nth(str2, 1) &&
           'c' == nth(str2, 2) && 'd' == nth(str2, 3) &&
           'e' == nth(str2, 4) && 'f' == nth(str2, 5)
          );
    assert(length(str2) == 6);

    assert(str1 == str1);                   // Note use of operator==.
    assert(str1 < str2);                    // Note use of operator<.

    cout << "The concatenation of '" << str1 << "' and 'def' is '" << str2
         << "', which has " << length(str2) << " characters.\n";

    destroy(&str1);
    destroy(&str2);
    destroy(&temp);

    cout << "Test completed.\n";
    return 0;
}
```

Limits on Operator Overloading

Operator overloading is a very convenient and powerful feature of C++. Nevertheless, it is not completely unrestricted. The basic rule is that while operators can be *defined* for various overloadings, an operator's basic characteristics cannot be changed:

- number of arguments
- precedence
- associativity

There are other restrictions, but in practice these rarely prevent you from using operator functions where appropriate. Only operators already in the language can be overloaded — there is no way to define new ones. Every operator function must have at least one struct argument — operators that act entirely on built-in types may not be overloaded. Operator functions may not have optional arguments.

It is up to the programmer to enforce any standard meanings of, or equivalences between, operators. For instance, if the result of += should be just like the combination of + and =, then operator+= must be defined accordingly. The compiler will not generate operator+= from the definitions of operator+ and operator=.

1.1.3 Encapsulation

The functions of the string module versions above are only loosely connected to the type definition. For full support of data abstraction we want to bind its operations more tightly with the data structure. We really want the operations to be *part of* the string type. C++ provides an effective mechanism for doing this: structs can include *functions* as well as data. Functions included in a struct are called *member functions* (not 'function member'). We thereofore say that a C++ struct declaration can include both *data members* and *member functions*.

Grouping the functions that operate on a data structure with its representation is called *encapsulation*. Member function definitions are entitled to use any of the structural details of the type they manipulate — the names of its fields in particular. Outside the implementation module, code *using* the module has access only to a restricted interface defined by the member functions the type makes available.

Look back at version 3 of the header for the string module (page 38). Notice that most of the functions take a `string*` as their first argument. These functions should be moved into the struct definition. This first argument becomes implicit — it is omitted from the argument list of both declarations and definitions. The compiler automatically adds it to declarations inside the struct, giving it the name `this`. This is a pivotal change: the structure begins to play a more prominent role and become more self-sufficient, rather than being just another argument to some function.

Here's the header file with some of the functions made members of the string structure. The ones not made members don't have an initial `string*` argument. We've also changed `nth` to `operator[]`, extending our use of operator functions.

```
// stringt.H, version 4: functions encapsulated with data

#ifndef STRINGT_H
#define STRINGT_H

#include <iostream.h>

struct string
{
    // data members
    int size;
    char* chars;

    // member functions
    void destroy();
    char& operator[](int n);
    int length();
    string operator+(string&);
    int operator==(string&);
    int operator<(string&);
};

string* make_string(int);
string* convert_to_string(char*);
ostream& operator<<(ostream&, string&);

#endif /* STRINGT_H */
```

Making a function a member affects calls to it in addition to its declaration. Member functions are invoked with a slightly different syntax than ordinary (nonmember) functions. Calls to member functions use the same sort of member access syntax as is used for data members, for example:

```
str.length()
```

The function's argument list follows the access of the member. In the case of length, the argument list is empty. Here is an example of a member function call with arguments:

```
str1.operator+(str2)
```

which of course could also be expressed simply as

```
str1 + str2
```

Here's our test program again. The only changes are to the calls to nth and destroy.

```
// stringt tst.C, version 4: using member functions

#include "stringt.h"
#include <assert.h>

main()
{
    string& str1 = *convert_to_string("abc");
    assert('a' == str1[0] && 'b' == str1[1] && 'c' == str1[2]);
    // Note use of operator[]
    assert(str1.length() == 3);              // member function notation now

    string& temp = *convert_to_string("def");
    string str2 = str1 + temp;

    assert('a' == str2[0] && 'b' == str2[1] && 'c' == str2[2] &&
           'd' == str2[3] && 'e' == str2[4] && 'f' == str2[5]);
    assert(str2.length() == 6);

    assert(str1 == str1);                    // Note use of operator.
    assert(str1 < str2);

    cout << "The concatenation of '" << str1 << "' and 'def' is '" << str2
         << "', which has " << str2.length() << " characters.\n";

    str1.destroy();                          // member function notation
    str2.destroy();                          // member function notation
    temp.destroy();                          // member function notation

    cout << "Test completed.\n";
    return 0;
}
```

Calls to a member function within the implementation file will also use the new form. For instance, if a function with str as an argument had called length(str), that call would be replaced by str->length(). If str had been the first argument of the function and therefore omitted in the new format, it would be omitted from the call to length too — we'd just write length(). This is just shorthand the language allows in place of this->length(). In effect, the compiler adds this-> before every member (data or function) used on its own (i.e., not following a dot or arrow).

Thus, a member function definition involves a new kind of identifier scope in which all references to members implicitly apply to the `this` argument, unless they explicitly specify a different value and a dot or arrow. One problem remains. How does the compiler know the type with which a member function definition is associated? The *declaration* is inside the struct itself, so there the type is clear. However, in the implementation file there is no indication other than the inclusion of a particular header file, which is too subtle a clue for the compiler to use. Besides, nothing says you can't put definitions of member functions of more than one data type in the same file, although structural modularization discourages that. You could also spread the definitions of a type's member functions over more than one file.

In short, although the implementation file is *conventionally* associated with the type by name as well as by use of include directives, there's no *formal* connection between a file and a type. Therefore, each function must indicate the type with which it is associated. This is accomplished by using a new compile-time operator introduced by C++, the *scope operator*, written as two colons. The full name of the `length` function in the string module would be `string::length`. Normally, such full names are used only at the beginning of a function definition, not in its body, since the full name at the beginning establishes that type as the scope for the statements in the body.

Each struct introduces a new scope in C++. This adds a fourth scope — structure — to the three listed in Section 0.3.1, page 19. Structure members are accessible only in the following contexts:

- in a member function of the structure
- after the `.` operator applied to an instance of the structure
- after the `->` operator applied to a pointer to an instance of the structure
- after the `::` scope resolution operator applied to the name of the structure

Notice that only the names of member functions include the name of the type that declares them. Nonmember functions do not have an implicit `this` argument, so the problem doesn't arise for them. Strictly speaking, nonmember functions defined in a type's module aren't part of the type's definition — they are just loosely associated with it. Their names are not qualified with the scope resolution operator since they have global, not structure, scope.

In certain specialized situations, you may have to call a globally scoped function when there is another function of the same name in the scope from which the function is to be called. You do this by using the scope resolution operator without a preceding name, for example `::make_string`.

Here's the implementation file for the string module, with some of the functions modified to be members, corresponding to the new version of the header file.

```
// stringt.C, version 4: functions encapsulated with data

#include "stringt.H"
#include <string.h>
#include <assert.h>

string* make_string(int siz)
```

```
// not string::make_string because it is a global, not a member, function.
{
    assert(siz >=0);
    string* str = new string;

    str->size = siz;
    str->chars = new char[str->size];

    return str;
}

string* convert_to_string(char* cstr)
// not string:: because it is a global, not a member, function
{
    assert(cstr != 0);
    string* str = new string;

    str->size = strlen(cstr);
    str->chars = new char[str->size];
    memcpy(str->chars, cstr, str->size);

    return str;
}

void string::destroy()                  // Note absence of argument
{
    delete [] chars;                    // equivalent to this->chars
    delete this;                        // explicit use of this
}

char& string::operator[](int n)
{
    assert(n >= 0 && n < size);
        // size is a data member, implicitly this->size
    return chars[n];
}

int string::length()
{
    return size;
        // size is a data member, implicitly this->size
}

string string::operator+(string& str2)
{
    string* str = make_string(size + str2.size);

    memcpy(str->chars, chars, size);
    memcpy(str->chars+size, str2.chars, str2.size);

    return *str;
}

int string::operator==(string& str)
{
```

```
    if (this == &str) return 1;              // same strings!

    if (size != str.size)
        return 0;
    else
        for (int i=0; i<size; i++)
            if (chars[i] != str.chars[i]) return 0;

    return 1;
}

static int min(int a, int b)
{
    return (a<b ? a : b);
}

int string::operator<(string& str)
{
    for (int i=0; i < min(size, str.size); i++)
        if (chars[i] < str.chars[i])
            return 1;
        else if (chars[i] > str.chars[i])
            return 0;

    return (size < str.size);
}

ostream& operator<<(ostream& strm, string& str)
// not string::operator<< because it is a global, not member, function
{
    for (int i=0; i<str.size; i++) strm << str.chars[i];

    return strm;
}
```

1.1.4 Information Hiding

As developed so far, the string module binds together a representation and a set of operations. However, its representation details are actually still available to user modules. We could add comments indicating which of the members are meant for users and which are only part of the implementation, but the compiler would not be able to detect violation of the encapsulation. User code could still refer to the internal details of the representation even though the documentation says not to.

What we really want is a way to *enforce* the distinction between information available to users and information available only to the type itself. This kind of protection is called *information hiding* — we want details of the representation, especially the names and types of data members, to be enforceably hidden from users of the module. C++ does provide such a mechanism, allowing each member (data or function) to be declared either *public* or *private*. The compiler enforces the privacy of private members, allowing only member functions of the type to access them. Public members, however, can be accessed from anywhere.

Public and Private Members

The struct definition is divided into public and private sections by the *access specifiers* public and private, each followed by a colon. An access specifier designates the accessibility of all of the members that follow it, until a different one appears. Thus, you can have any number of public and private sections. In the beginning of the struct declaration the members are *public*, until a private appears. There is no way to make a nonmember function private.

With this feature, we are at last in a position to define a truly modularized data type, including:

- the name of the type
- the type's representation — a sequence of fields, each with a name and a type
- a set of operations that act on instances of the type
- a specification of which operations and fields are available to users of the type

Furthermore, in most approaches to data abstraction, *data members are never publicized* — the public interface is entirely procedural.

All of the string module's operations should be available to users. Therefore, we want all its data members to be private and all its function members to be public. (Its nonmember functions are necessarily public.) This kind of extreme division into all private data members and all public member functions is fairly common, especially with relatively simple structures. More complex structures might have private member functions. These would support the implementation of other member functions but would not be part of the public interface.

Here's the header file for this version. The implementation file and test program are unaffected. In this particular version, we do not take advantage of the default being public — we explicitly indicate public or private right from the beginning. Remember also that you can organize your struct into any number of private and public sections.

```
// stringt.H, version 5: information hiding added (public vs. private)

#ifndef STRINGT_H
#define STRINGT_H

struct string
{
  private:
    // data members
    int size;
    char* chars;

  public:
    // member functions
    void destroy();
    char& operator[](int n);
```

```
    int length() const;
    string operator+(string&);
    int operator==(string&);
    int operator<(string&);

};

// necessarily public because global:
string* make_string(int);
string* convert_to_string(char*);
ostream& operator<<(ostream&, string&);

#endif /* STRINGT_H */
```

Thus, the (public) member functions of a struct constitute its *public interface*. Users of the struct need only consult the public parts of its declaration to find out what they can do with it. There is nothing a user can do with a private member, so it would really be better if there were two header files for each struct — a public one for people and compilers to read and a private one that only the compiler sees. No such distinction is available, however, so users just have to learn to ignore the private parts. In a commercially delivered header file, it is customary to put the public parts first, to facilitate human reading. Since this book is about the implementation of data structures, however, the basic representation is shown at the beginning of its struct declarations.

Friendship

Version 5 still isn't quite right. Look at the definitions (from version 4, page 44) of the module's global (i.e. nonmember) functions. They use field names of the struct. However, all the field names are private, and only member functions of a struct can use its private members. Here's an example of an invalid attempt to access a private member.

```
ostream& operator<<(ostream& strm, string& str)
{
    for (int i=0; i<str.size; i++) strm << str.chars[i];
        // error: no access to private members size and chars!

    return strm;
}
```

One option is to rewrite these to use the public interface, as follows.

```
ostream& operator<<(ostream& strm, string& str)
{
    for (int i=0; i<str.length(); i++) strm << str[i];
        // replacing size (private) with length() (public) and
        // using public operator[] instead of .chars

    return strm;
}
```

There is an alternative, however, that is sometimes more attractive or even necessary. C++ allows a struct declaration to declare a nonmember function (either a global function or a member of a different struct) to be a *friend*. Friends of a type have all the access privileges of the type's own member functions — they can access any of the type's members.

Friendship is granted by the struct in its declaration. The friend function is declared inside the struct, preceded by the keyword `friend`. (It doesn't matter whether this goes in a private or public section of the struct declaration.) That's all. The definition of the friend function doesn't change, but its access privileges do. The friend declaration inside the struct is a declaration of the function — the function need not be declared outside the struct too. The function's scope remains global — it's a friend, not a member function.

Some functions, in particular `operator<<`, must be made friends if their definitions make use of private members. They couldn't be made members of the struct because their first argument is of another already defined type. Similarly, functions that are associated with a type even though they don't operate on one of its instances, such as `convert_to_string`, must be made friends if they require access to internal implementation details.

One struct can make *all* the member functions of another its friend by declaring the other struct a friend. For example, if there was a class `character` that `string` functions used, the class `character` could declare `string` a friend by including in its definition the declaration.

```
friend struct string;
```

Sometimes it is better to make a function global even when it *could* be a member. In particular, binary operators should usually be global rather than members. First of all, since they are symmetric they seem more natural expressed as a function of two arguments, rather than as a member function of one. Second, they are rarely called using the member access notation, since the infix operator syntax is so convenient and familiar. (Expressions using the operator functions would look the same whether they were members or friends.) Finally, there is a subtle loss of flexibility when member functions are used: in the case of a function of two arguments, the compiler can attempt to coerce given arguments to the types of the required ones, but types through which member functions are called using access notation are not coerced. It would be strange to have a binary operator for which the first argument couldn't be coerced but the second could (especially when the operator is commutative), so it is generally better to declare these friends rather than members.

Global functions can be made friends if they need access to internal details, but often they don't. In fact, one style of defining operator functions has them turn around and call a regular member function, giving user's a choice of either operator or function call notation. A side effect of declaring global functions friends is that the declarations move inside the struct with the rest of the type's interface. This makes the functions look like they are truly encapsulated inside the type, even though they are still global. Presenting this impression may be reason enough to make the global functions friends even if they don't need access to private members.

Here's the header file for the string module with the global functions and binary operators as friends.

```
// stringt.H, version 6: information hiding + friendship

#ifndef STRINGT_H
#define STRINGT_H

#include <iostream.h>

struct string
{
  private:
    // data members
    int size;
    char* chars;

  public:
    // member functions
    void destroy();
    char& operator[](int n);
    int length();

    // friend operator functions
    friend string operator+(string&, string&);
    friend int operator==(string&, string&);
    friend int operator<(string&, string&);

    // friend functions
    friend string* make_string(int);
    friend string* convert_to_string(char*);
    friend ostream& operator<<(ostream&, string&);
};

#endif /* STRINGT_H */
```

Since they are no longer member functions, the operator function definitions return to the form they had in version 3, before we made the data members private. Actually, we could use operator[] in place of ->chars, and length() instead of ->size. Then, operator== and operator< could be ordinary, nonfriend, global functions placed outside the struct definition. There's no compelling reason for doing this, however, and functions inside the struct definition seem more clearly part of the interface than those placed outside, so we'll leave them as is. In fact, it seems odd to take advantage of an access function for one field, but not the other; since we're leaving these as friends we'll use the internal field names directly.

```
// operator functions from stringt.C, version 6: information hiding
// Note that friendship is declared in the header, but not here

char& string::operator[](int n)
{
    return chars[n];
}

int string::length()
{
    return size;
}

string operator+(string& str1, string& str2)
{
    string* str = make_string(str1.size + str2.size);

    memcpy(str->chars, str1.chars, str1.size);
    memcpy(str->chars+str1.size, str2.chars, str2.size);

    return *str;
}

int operator==(string& str1, string& str2)
{
    if (&str1 == &str2) return 1;        // same strings!
    if (str1.size != str2.size)
        return 0;
    else
        for (int i=0; i<str1.size; i++)
            if (str1.chars[i] != str2.chars[i]) return 0;

    return 1;
}

static int min(int a, int b)
{
    return (a<b ? a : b);
}

int operator<(string& str1, string& str2)
{
    for (int i=0; i < min(str1.size, str2.size); i++)
        if (str1.chars[i] < str2.chars[i])
            return 1;
```

```
        else if (str1.chars[i] > str2.chars[i])
            return 0;

    return (str1.size < str2.size);
}
```

Static Members

Consider the function make_string, now a friend.

```
string* make_string(int siz)
{
    assert(siz >=0);
    string* str = new string;

    str->size = siz;
    str->chars = new char[str->size];

    return str;
}
```

Unlike some of the other friend functions we've seen, there is simply no way to write this one using only the public interface. It could be made a friend, but there's a better mechanism available. You can declare them *static*, which makes them part of the encapsulated type but independent of any instances of the struct. Both data members and member functions may be made static.

Static data members are essentially global variables of struct scope. Inside member function definitions, they are accessed normally, since member functions are within the struct's scope. To access a static data member outside a member function of its struct, you must prefix its name with the struct name and the scope resolution operator (::). For example, string might declare a member null. Since there's no need for each string to have its own personal null string, null would be declared static. Inside string member functions null would be accessed normally. Outside, it would be referred to as string::null.

There are many uses for static data members. Global variables should be avoided wherever possible in data abstraction programming. Most variables you'd be tempted to make global should really be static data members. In particular, global variables of file scope (i.e., static global variables) act as module-level global variables by virtue of the fact that they are accessible from within the function definitions in their file but not from outside the file. Where the file is the implementation of a data type, such file-scoped global variables should be made static data members of the type.

Static member functions are just global functions with struct scope. Like static data members, they are accessed normally from within member functions and by names qualified with the struct name and scope operator outside. Static member functions are used for actions that are clearly part of the type, but not associated with any particular instance. Since they do not act on an instance, they don't have an implicit this argument.

You won't see many static members in this book. They are usually found in application-level structs, not implementations of fundamental data structures. In this section they are used to create new instances of string. Functions that create new instances *must* be static (or global) because before the instance is created it doesn't exist, so the instance can't be used to call an ordinary member function. However, C++ features discussed a bit later make explicit creation functions unnecessary, so this use of static member functions here is mostly for pedagogical purposes.

Static members follow the usual rules of access according to whether they are public or private, with one exception. As global variables, static data members must be initialized at the file level. File level is outside of any function scope, so they must be qualified with the name of the struct. Normally, there would be no way to access a private member at file scope (we can make *functions* friends, but not *files*). Because there would otherwise be no way to initialize a private static data member, an exception is made to allow private static members to be defined at file scope.

Making make_string and convert_to_string static instead of friends gives us the next version of the string module. Code calling these functions must use the scope resolution operator to explicitly identify the struct from which they come — string::make_ string, for example. Thus, the syllable string in the names of these functions is really redundant and can be omitted. Note that there are no longer any functions declared outside the struct — those that used to be outside are now either friends or static declared inside the struct.

```
// stringt.H, version 7: using static members

#ifndef STRINGT_H
#define STRINGT_H

#include <iostream.h>

struct string
{
  private:
    // data members
    int size;
    char* chars;

  public:
    // member functions
    static string* make(int);
    static string* convert(char*);
    void destroy();
    char& operator[](int n);
    int length();

    // friend operator functions
    friend string operator+(string&, string&);
```

```
    friend int operator==(string&, string&);
    friend int operator<(string&, string&);
    friend ostream& operator<<(ostream&, string&);
};
#endif /* STRINGT_H */
```

Here are the definitions of the two static member functions. The definition of operator+ is also affected: its call to make_string becomes a call to string::make.

```
// static functions from stringt.C, version 7
// Note that members are declared static in the header, but not here.

string* string::make(int siz)
{
    assert(siz >=0);
    string* str = new string;

    str->size = siz;
    str->chars = new char[str->size];

    return str;
}

string* string::convert(char* cstr)
{
    assert(cstr != 0);
    string* str = new string;

    str->size = strlen(cstr);
    str->chars = new char[str->size];
    memcpy(str->chars, cstr, str->size);

    return str;
}

string operator+(string& str1, string& str2)
{
    string* str = string::make(str1.size + str2.size);

    memcpy(str->chars, str1.chars, str1.size);
    memcpy(str->chars+str1.size, str2.chars, str2.size);

    return *str;
}
```

The test program is similarly affected: calls to convert_string become calls to string::convert.

```
// stringt tst.C, version 7: using static member functions

#include "stringt.h"
#include <assert.h>

main()
{
    string& str1 = *string::convert("abc");
        // convert is now a static member function of string
    assert('a' == str1[0] && 'b' == str1[1] && 'c' == str1[2]);
    assert(str1.length() == 3);

    string& temp = *string::convert("def");
    string str2 = str1 + temp;

    assert('a' == str2[0] && 'b' == str2[1] && 'c' == str2[2] &&
           'd' == str2[3] && 'e' == str2[4] && 'f' == str2[5]);
    assert(str2.length() == 6);

    assert(str1 == str1);
    assert(str1 < str2);

    cout << "The concatenation of '" << str1 << "' and 'def' is '" << str2
         << "', which has " << str2.length() << " characters.\n";

    str1.destroy();
    str2.destroy();
    temp.destroy();

    cout << "Test completed.\n";
    return 0;
}
```

This is as much as needs to be said about data abstraction for now. This section has introduced some important new features that C++ adds to C. Most of these will be used extensively throughout the rest of this book. This first glance is only an introduction — the implementations of various data structures that begin in the next chapter will further clarify their use.

1.2 Fundamental Operations

Once you've implemented a few data structure modules, you begin to notice that certain operations show up over and over again. These operations are fundamental in several senses:

- They are common basic operations that should be understood by anyone using and implementing data structures.
- They are intimately tied up with the representation of a data structure.

- They define the essential behavior of instances of the data structure.

There are some things we can say about fundamental operations abstractly, independent of any particular data type. The schematic overview presented in this section will be used to organize the implementations of the data structures shown in the rest of the book. You should use them to help you think about and organize the data structures that you use and implement, too. Appendix A includes a summary of the fundamental operations.

There are four broad classes of fundamental operations:

Lifetime   the core of a structure's implementation

Traversal   mechanisms for performing actions on each of a collection's components

Content   manipulations based on the meaning of the type and the states of its instances

Support   auxiliary operations less intimately tied to the implementation, but still common to most structures

Each of these groups contains various generic fundamental operations. In this book these will be distinguished typographically by capitalization and a different typeface — **Modify**, for example. Some generic operations have several manifestations in a particular data type, so really we have four groups of *kinds* of operations. For instance, **Modify** includes **Add**, **Remove**, **Replace**, and **Exchange**. Even something as specific as **Add** might be implemented by several different functions: for example, `add_at_front` and `add_at_back`.

1.2.1 Lifetime Operations

Lifetime operations provide the core of a structure's implementation. The operations could also be called *existential operations* because they deal with an instance's existence. Figure 1.1 illustrates the lifetime of a computational object.

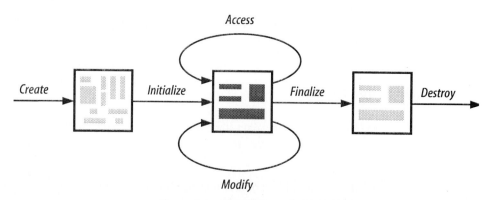

Figure 1.1   The Lifetime of a Data Object

An object's life begins when it is created and ends when it is destroyed. Our string module has make and destroy, as well as convert, a variation on make. The definitions of make and convert really perform two separate actions: allocate space for the object and establish a meaningful initial state. We'll call the first of these **Create**, since once space is allocated the object exists, and the second **Initialize**.

Traditional programming style often combines **Create** and **Initialize** into one operation, as in make and convert. That makes sense since we don't want to allow an object to be used before it is initialized. However, **Create** and **Initialize** are conceptually distinct operations and should be recognized as such. A language may support these two fundamental operations with different mechanisms, as, in fact, C++ does. Also, we may want the ability to reinitialize a used object, requiring operations that initialize without creating.

Just as we don't want to use an object before it is initialized, we don't want it to be destroyed before any necessary cleanup actions are performed. As the diagram shows, a **Finalize** action should precede any **Destroy**. (The term 'finalize' is chosen as the opposite of 'initialize', in that 'final' is the opposite of 'initial'; other terms could be used, including 'terminate' and 'cleanup'.)

In between **Create-Initialize** and **Finalize-Destroy** is the object's useful lifetime. At the lowest level of interpretation, the only things we really can do to a computational object is **Access** and **Modify** its components. Several kinds of **Modify** operations are common, including **Add**, **Remove**, **Replace**, and **Exchange**. Collection structures often provide **Clear** (**Remove** all). Our string module provides operator[], which, since it returns a reference, can be used for both **Access** and **Replace**. **Remove** and **Exchange** are not provided, though they could be. (Cf. Exercise 1.)

1.2.2 Traversal Operations

Some data structures represent individual entities, and some represent *collections* of entities. The representation and implementation of individual entities are usually very simple and straightforward, so for the most part studying data structures means studying collections. Given a collection of objects, it is frequently necessary to *traverse*, or go through, the entire collection performing some operation. There are two ways to traverse a collection: an *iterator* performs some action for every element of a collection, while a *generator* supplies one element each time it is invoked.

Several of the string module functions contain for loops. These loops are examples of "open-coded" iterations — traversals expressed directly in the programming language. It would be wonderful if the language provided a generalized foreach statement, so we could just write something like.

```
foreach ch in str do fn(ch);
```

Some avant garde languages provide such constructs, but C++ doesn't.

Open-coded traversals are a source of a large percentage of programming errors: expressing initialization, stepping calculations, accesses, and termination tests just right can be tricky and may require a detailed understanding of the implementation of the collection structure. It is better to encapsulate traversal operations in functions than to open-code them. Traversals involve four basic actions: initializing the process, stepping to the next component, accessing the current component, and testing for termination. Ideally, each data structure should provide traversal operations as part of its implementation, so that users never have to worry about these details.

One approach to encapsulating traversal is to provide iterator functions. A traversal using an iterator function would be expressed in C++ as follows:

```
str.foreach(fn);
```

Another kind of iterator function not only performs some operation on each component of a collection, but *collects* the result into a new instance of the type. Unfortunately, iterator functions get awkward in C-based languages for technical reasons having to do with parameter typing. (Cf. Appendix C, page 465.) Because there is no way to conveniently generalize iterators in C++, the more common approach is to use generators.

Iterator operations would support the most common kinds of collection traversals. They would handle initialization, stepping actions, component access, and termination tests all in one construct. Generators are similar, but they provide these aspects of traversal separately. To traverse an entire collection using a generator requires code in a form something like

```
initialize-generation();
while (! termination-test())
    { generate-next(); use-current(); }
```

Because generators are a lower-level mechanism, they can be used to construct specialized loops that would not be handled by routine iterators. Generators can be used wherever iterators would be, though less conveniently. It turns out to be fairly straightforward to express generators in C++.[4] Generator operations are therefore used throughout this book, including situations which would call for iterators in a language that facilitated their implementation and use. Section 1.3.5 below shows a simple approach to the implementation of basic generator operations in C++.

A difficult problem to deal with is the consequences of modifying a structure while in the midst of traversing it. Will newly added elements be seen by the traversal? Will removing an element cause another to be missed by the traversal? The implementation approach taken by a commercial data structure library would have to confront these issues, but they are beyond the scope of our discussions here. The assumption in this book is therefore that traversals are "read-only" regarding the contents of the structure which they traverse. The individual elements may be modified, but there are no guarantees on what will happen if elements are added or removed between steps of a traversal.

1.2.3 Content Operations

Operations that reflect the meaning of a type will be called *content operations*. There are several different kinds:

---

[4]C++ makes generators so straightforward to implement and use and makes iterator functions so difficult that iterator functions are almost never used, and the term 'iterator' is used in the C++ community to describe what is more accurately termed a 'generator'. In any case, the rest of this book will simply refer to 'traversal'.

Attribute	special states or properties, either predicative (e.g., `empty`) or quantitative (e.g., `length`)
Compare	comparison of two objects for equality, order, etc.
Combine	combination of two objects in type-dependent ways, broadly subdivided into **Add** (e.g., set `union`), **Subtract** (e.g., set `difference`), and **Multiply** (e.g., set `intersection`)

Our string module contains several typical content operators.

Attribute:	`length`
Combine:	`+`
Compare:	`==`, `<`

All collection structures inherently have an attribute that indicates the number of elements they contain. However, different spatial metaphors are used in talking about different kinds of collections, and 'length' only applies to structures pictured as linear, such as arrays and lists. Other similar terms include 'depth' for stacks and 'cardinality' for sets.

It will be convenient to use a single term for this attribute for all kinds of structures. Candidates for a generic term meaning 'number of elements' include 'size', 'count', and 'cardinality'. All of these have problems: 'size' is easily confused with the number of bytes the structure occupies in storage, 'count' sounds more like something to do than an attribute, and 'cardinality' technically applies only to sets. Some theorists also use 'cardinality' to denote the number of values a type can have: the cardinality of Boolean is two, and the cardinality of C's `char` is 256. One possible solution would be to use 'number_of_ elements', which clearly indicates its meaning; however, that name is inconveniently long for a function that will be used frequently.

This issue will be resolved by using 'size' in the rest of the book to mean the number of elements in a collection. To talk about the amount of storage a structure occupies, the term 'space' will be used. Implementations of structures that maintain an internal count of elements will store that count in a data member called 'length'. This works well because typically it is only linear collections that store such a count, and 'length' is entirely applicable to them. Other kinds of structures must compute their size somehow. The use of the terms 'length' and 'string' in the string example will be left as is, however — 'length' the **Attribute** function and 'size' the internal count. In part this is because C's `strlen` function conditions programmers to think about string 'length' and in part because strings really aren't full-fledged collections like the other structures studied in this book.

1.2.4 Support Operations

The last group of fundamental operations is to some extent a catch-all for the ones that don't fit neatly into any of the other three groups. For the most part these operations are so commonly used that data structure implementations should provide them as a convenience. Many don't need access to internal details and can be implemented in terms of more fundamental operations. For some, however, implementation is simpler or more efficient when the internal representation is accessed directly. Occasionally such access is necessary. Categories of *support operations* include the following:

Copy	various kinds: partial or full, same order or reverse, etc.
Process	Sort, Search
Input/Output	text and graphics: **Read**, **Write**, **Display**, etc.

The only example (so far) from the string module is `operator<<` (**Write**). Others we could add include `operator>>`, `reverse`, and `copy`. It is a lot easier to specify a general output operator for a structure than a general input operator. Input gets very messy in that all sorts of validation tests have to be performed on the characters being parsed, and different formats may have to be accommodated. To simplify things, the structures in this book don't define **Read** operators.

1.2.5 Summary

The summary of fundamental operations in Table 1 shows *categories* of fundamental operations. For a given structure, a particular category may have several manifestations. For instance, **Access** operations on a set type might include **Add**, **Remove**, and **Replace**. Those manifestations can be given generic names, but often specific names are used for a particular kind of structure. In a set module, for example, **Combine** would be **Union** (**Add**), **Difference** (**Subtract**), and **Intersection** (**Multiply**).

Lifetime	Traversal	Content	Support
Create/Destroy	Foreach	Attributes	Copy
Initialize/Finalize	Collect	Compare	Process
Access/Modify	Generate	Combine	Input/Output

Table 1   Summary of Fundamental Operation Categories

Convert

There's one more category of operation that might theoretically be included in this scheme: **Convert**. Conversion plays a major role in C programming: various kinds of scalar values are converted to each other, pointers of one type are converted to pointers of another, etc. Some conversions are performed automatically by the compiler and some because the programmer has written an explicit cast. C++ extends the concept of casting to cover one-argument constructors that can be used by the compiler or programmer to convert the argument type to the constructor's type, as will be seen in the next section.

Conversion has wider meaning that just casts. C library functions that parse strings into numbers are often called *text conversions*. Input and output can even be considered conversion between text strings and a program's values. A function that returns the number of characters in a string or elements in a set could be considered a conversion from a collection structure to an integer.

Not only does conversion have wide applicability, but it plays the kind of central role that other fundamental operations do. Many conversion operations, in particular one-argument constructors, are unavoidably linked to internal implementation details. Clearly **Convert** qualifies as a fundamental operation.

Why isn't **Convert** included here then? Partly because of the introductory level of this text and partly because C++ implements conversion operations with too varied a range of mechanisms, considering **Convert** as a separate fundamental operation would detract from the discussions here more than it would add to them. One-argument constructors can be considered special kinds of **Initialize** operations, rather than **ConvertFrom**. Treating input and output as conversion between structures and text streams is an interesting approach but doesn't really contribute anything to the way data structures are designed or implemented. Sophisticated uses of **ConvertTo** operations usually appear only within a carefully integrated library of related data structures, not in the simple stand-alone types described here. Simple uses of **ConvertTo**, like converting a collection to an int indicating whether or not it is empty, can easily be treated as ordinary predicate operations.

1.3 C++ Support for Fundamental Operations

C++ provides various kinds of mechanisms that help make the principled implementation and use of fundamental operations quite natural. The simplest is the availability of operator overloading, since so many fundamental operations can be naturally expressed as operators. More substantial support is provided for **Create/Destroy**, **Initialize/Finalize**, and **Copy**. C++ also supplies mechanisms for defining operations that convert an object of one type to an object of another type, which will be described even though not used in the rest of the book.

1.3.1 Create and Destroy

Create and **Destroy** in C++ are implemented through the operators `new` and `delete`. Variable declarations also lead to objects being created and destroyed. Global definitions are supplied for `new` and `delete`.

Structs can define their own version of these operators. Furthermore, both global and struct-specific versions can be defined for various signatures. The details of overloading `new` and `delete` are beyond the scope of this text, but it is worth mentioning this here to show that C++ does give programmers control over the behavior of **Create** and **Destroy** for their types. The default global definitions of `new` and `delete` are entirely sufficient for of the purposes in this book.

1.3.2 Initialize and Finalize

Looking at the code for `string::make` we can see that the **Create** operation is performed by the C++ `new` operator. The rest of the function performs the **Initialize** actions. Similarly, `string::destroy` performs **Finalize** actions and then invokes `delete` to actually deallocate the space (i.e., **Destroy** the instance). Functions that combine **Create** and **Initialize**, and **Finalize** and **Destroy**, are common in traditional data structure implementations. As pointed out earlier, however, there are advantages to splitting these dual-purpose operations into separate functions.

In any case, C++ has special mechanisms for initialization and finalization, which lead to entirely separate implementations of **Create, Initialize, Finalize,** and **Destroy.** Keeping **Initialize** and **Finalize** operations independent has another very important advantage beyond the ones mentioned earlier: the combined functions (**Create-Initialize** and **Finalize-Destroy**) manage only dynamically allocated objects, whereas the C++ mechanisms apply also to global and local object-valued variables.

In C++, a special initialization function, called a *constructor*, is automatically invoked whenever an instance of a struct is allocated (created), whether it be the value of a local or global variable or dynamically created with new. Similarly, before any struct instance is destroyed — either by a variable going out of scope or by a delete of a dynamically allocated instance — a special finalization function, called a *destructor*, is automatically invoked. Constructors are member functions with the same name as their struct and no return type (not even void). Destructors are member functions whose name is the name of their struct preceded by a tilde and no return type.

A constructor (but not a destructor) may take arguments. In fact, a struct may define several constructors, each with its own signature (pattern of argument types). A constructor that can be called with no arguments (either it has no arguments or all its arguments are optional) is called a *default constructor*. Arguments are passed to a constructor by putting them in an argument list that follows the variable name (for global and local variables) or the struct name (in a new expression). (There are further syntactic forms for specifying initialization arguments that won't be discussed just yet.)

```
struct date
{
    // . . .       (Ellipsis comments represent omitted details.)

  public:

    date();                                 // default constructor
    date(int day, int month, int year);     // other constructor

    ~date();                                // destructor
    // . . .
}

// . . .

main()
{
    date d1;                                // default constructor called
    date d2(4, 7, 1776);                    // other constructor called
    // . . .
    // destructor for d1 and d2 called on exit
}
```

Most default constructors take no arguments, as shown in the above declaration. However, it is often convenient to specify a default constructor with all optional arguments. Thus, the two date constructors above could be combined as

```
date(int day = CURDAY,
     int month = CURMONTH,
     int year = CURYEAR);
```

Because in C++ constructors are called whenever an instance of a struct is created, we don't really need functions like `string::make`. We *do* need a constructor (initializer) called `string::string`, but **Create** in C++ is handled by the new operator and the mechanisms that allocate space for global and local variables. Similarly, **Destroy** is handled by the `delete` operator and the mechanisms that deallocate global and local variables when their scope is exited. In short, basic language mechanisms take care of **Create** and **Destroy** for us, including always invoking the appropriate **Initialize** and **Finalize** operations. Our data structure implementations just need to supply constructors (for **Initialize**) and a destructor (for **Finalize**).

Constructors and Destructors in the String Module

Here is the header file for the string module modified to use constructors and destructors in place of `make`, `convert`, and `destroy`. The constructors and destructors implement **Initialize** and **Finalize**, whereas the old functions also performed **Create** and **Destroy** operations. In C++, we don't need functions that both create and initialize or both finalize and destroy. **Create** and **Destroy** are invoked through the mechanisms of variable allocation and operators `new` and `delete`. **Initialize** and **Finalize** are automatically invoked whenever **Create** and **Destroy** operations are performed. All the programmer needs to do is define the appropriate constructors and destructors.

```
// stringt.H, version 8: constructors and destructors added

#ifndef STRINGT_H
#define STRINGT_H

#include <iostream.h>

struct string
{
  private:
    // data members
    int size;
    char* chars;

  public:
    // member functions

    // make, convert, and destroy replaced by constructors and destructors:
    string(int);                        // constructor (initializer)
    string(char*);                      // constructor (initializer)
    ~string();                          // destructor (finalizer)

    char& operator[](int n);
    int length();

    // friend operator functions
```

```
    friend string& operator+(string&, string&);
    friend int operator==(string&, string&);
    friend int operator<(string&, string&);
    friend ostream& operator<<(ostream&, string&);
};
```

The constructors and destructor are defined as follows. They replace the static functions make, convert, and destroy, though they only initialize and finalize strings, not create and destroy them. **Create** and **Destroy** are handled by C++ variable definitions, new, and delete.

```
// Constructors and Destructors, version 8

// Note the absence of a return type.
string::string(int siz)                         // In place of make-string
{
    assert(siz >=0);
        // Note that there's no new here: the string has
        // already been created by the time this is called.

    size = siz;
        // Note that there's no str-> here or anywhere else in these defs
    chars = new char[siz];

        // Note the absence of a return.
}

// Note the absence of a return type.
string::string(char* cstr)
{
    assert(cstr != 0);

        // Note that there's no new here.
    size = strlen(cstr);
    chars = new char[size];
    memcpy(chars, cstr, size);

        // Note the absence of a return.
}

// Note the absence of a return type.
string::~string()                               // In place of destroy
{
    cout << "Deleting string at address " << this << '\n';
    delete [] chars;
    // Note that there's no delete this - the string gets destroyed later
}
```

Next is the test program modified to use constructors and destructors. Note that the strings are now created as objects instead of pointers — the variable definitions cause space to be allocated, so dynamic allocation using new is not needed here.

```
// stringt tst.C, version 8: using constructors and destructors

#include "stringt.h"
#include <assert.h>

main()
{
    string str1("abc");
    // Note absence of function call: the initializer is called
    // automatically and passed the argument "abc".
    assert('a' == str1[0] && 'b' == str1[1] && 'c' == str1[2] );
    assert(str1.length() == 3);

    string temp("def");
    // Note absence of function call:
    // The initializer is called automatically.

    string str2 = str1 + temp;

    assert('a' == str2[0] && 'b' == str2[1] && 'c' == str2[2] &&
           'd' == str2[3] && 'e' == str2[4] && 'f' == str2[5]);
    assert(str2.length() == 6);

    assert(str1 == str1);
    assert(str1 < str2);

    cout << "The concatenation of '" << str1 << "' and 'def' is '" << str2
         << "', which has " << str2.length() << " characters.\n";

    // Finalizers are called automatically when the strings go out of
    // scope (when the function returns). Their calls don't appear in code.

    cout << "Test completed.\n";
    return 0;
}
```

One-argument constructors can be interpreted as conversions from the argument type to the constructor's type. In fact, that's what was done in this last implementation of the string module: `string::convert(char*)` became an initializer. The compiler is free to use one-argument constructors for type casting whenever it wants to cast something of a constructor's argument type to the constructor's type. Not all one-argument constructors are meant as conversion constructors: `string::make(int)` initializes the string to hold a certain number of characters, but it would not be reasonable to interpret this as a conversion from int to string. Unfortunately, there's no way for the compiler to know which one-argument constructors do make sense as conversion operations and which don't, and problems sometimes arise when the compiler unexpectedly uses a one-argument constructor in a way the programmer didn't intend.

Note that the string module does not have a default constructor. In this implementation it would be pretty meaningless to create a string without specifying either its size or its characters. If a default constructor is needed for a struct that doesn't provide *any* constructors, the compiler will normally generate one that does nothing. However, as long as the struct defines at least one constructor, the compiler will not generate a default one.

Member Initialization Lists

One final detail of constructors remains to be discussed. What happens if a data member is a reference or a const (e.g., a person's Social Security number)? How could it ever be initialized, since an assignment would be flagged as an error? To get around this problem, constructors can have a *member initialization list*, which specifies initial values for members. This distinction is just like that between initialization of local variables and assignment to already declared local variables. The (comma-separated) list specifies members and their initial values in the format

```
member1(value), member2(value), ... , membern(value)
```

The member initialization list is placed after a colon following the argument list in the constructor's definition.

There are reasons to use member initializers even for members that could be assigned to. If a member with built-in type is not mentioned in a member-initialization list, it won't be initialized, and assignment in the body will be fine. However, if a struct-valued member is not mentioned, it will first be initialized via the default constructor for its type. That will in general be wasted effort if there's an assignment to that member in the constructor's body, since the work that assignment will do is usually very similar to the work done in the structure's default constructor. Furthermore, if no default constructor is defined or generated for the struct, the compiler will complain if the struct-valued member is not included in the member initialization list.

In sum, you *must* use the member initialization list to initialize things that cannot be assigned to, such as const and reference members, and you *should* use the member initialization list (instead of assignment) for struct-valued members. (If you want the default initialization for a struct-valued member, leave it out of the member initialization list.) Members with nonconst, nonreference built-in types are the only thing left for which assignment is acceptable. For consistency it makes sense to use the member initialization list for these too. About the only time assignment in a constructor is appropriate is inside a loop used to initialize the individual elements of an array allocated by an expression in the member initialization list.

```
// Constructors from string.C, version 9: using member initialization lists

string::string(int siz) : size(siz), new char[siz])
{
    // nothing else to do!
}

string::string(char* cstr)
    : size(strlen(cstr)), chars(mempcy(new char[size], cstr,size))
{
```

```
    // Members are initialized in the order in which they appear in the
    // struct declaration, so the memcpy call can use size.

    // nothing else to do!
}
```

_____

1.3.3 Compare

C provides six comparison operators: ==, !=, <, <=, >, and >=. Not all kinds of data structure have natural notions of ordering, but nearly all have natural notions of equality. Note
that equality of structures is a weaker condition than identity. Identity would be tested by
comparing the addresses of two structures to see if they are actually the *same*. Equality is
tested by comparing the components of the two structures and, for some kinds, their
shape. Similarly, there are two kinds of equality tests for structures: one based on whether
the components are *identical* and another based on whether the components are *equal*.
Unless otherwise stated, equality of structures will in this book be the kind based on equality, not identity, of components.

The convention adopted for this book is that all structure modules will provide implementations of equal and compare operations. Templates (see Section 1.4.1, page 73
ff. below) in standard.H provide operator functions that call equal and compare, so that
users can program with the more convenient operator notation. Equal functions return
bools. An enum order is defined in standard.H, containing BEFORE, EQUAL, AFTER, and
NO_ORDER. Compare functions return orders. The value NO_ORDER is used when order
comparison is inappropriate or impossible.

Equal should normally be implemented in all structure modules. A function testing
the equality of two structures must be able to test the equality of their components, so all
structure implementations in this book assume that their component type also provides
an equal operation. Similarly, structures for which order comparison makes sense require component types to implement compare. Because the structures described in the
text can themselves be used as components of each other, they too must always implement
equal and compare. If the operation doesn't makes sense for that kind of structure, then
its implementation can signal an error indicating that the corresponding function
shouldn't be called.

1.3.4 Copy

Copy has two manifestations in C++, one for initialization and one for assignment. In the
initialization of one struct instance from another of the same type, the constructor that
takes an argument of that type is invoked. In other words, copy initialization is like a conversion to a struct instance from another of the same type. For assignment from an instance of the struct to another instance of that struct, operator= is used. In both cases,
the argument is passed as a reference. The signatures of the two operations are always, for
a given type *T*, as follows.

```
        T::T(T&);                              // copy constructor
        T& T::operator=(T&);                   // copy assignment
```

In both cases, if the struct doesn't define the appropriate member function the compiler will (in most circumstances) generate one automatically if it is needed, but the definitions generated are usually inappropriate for collection structures. They copy structures by copying each member. Pointers are copied to the other structure, rather than what the pointers point to, leading to two collections having members pointing to the same auxiliary storage — almost always an error.

For a variety of reasons, it is good practice to always define both copy initialization and copy assignment (presumably with essentially the same external behavior). In particular, wherever a structure instance is passed or returned by value (perhaps accidentally) the compiler invokes a copy constructor, defining one if necessary. It is better to keep control over the definition of **Copy** operations by defining them yourself, even if you don't expect users of your module to invoke them. For this reason, all the modules shown in this book will include copy constructors and assignment operators. It is especially important to define **Copy** operations when a struct allocates storage in its initializers because **Copy** almost always means allocating new storage and copying values from the old. You'll find that the definition of the two forms of **Copy** are quite similar, so a good practice is to abstract that common code to a private member copy that both call.

It turns out that the code shown to this point has been implicitly using compiler-generated copy constructors! String's operator+ returned a string — not a string& or string*. Returning an object by value is one of the standard situations in which copying occurs — the operator+ function creates a string, then returns a copy of it. Then, another copy operation occurs, as the returned value is used to initialize str2. (A smart compiler might optimize away the second copy by making the first one in str2 directly.) The compiler-generated copy constructors are incorrect, since they copy the chars pointer rather than the characters to which chars points. Note also that the string dynamically created inside the operator+ function is never explicitly deleted, a serious design error that we can finally rectify.

Copy Operations in the String Module

Following are declarations and code for the **Copy** operations in the string module. **Reverse** is a fairly common operation that can be understood as a variation of **Copy**, and we'll include that here too. Similarly, **Copy** operations sometimes include only some of the old structure's components in the new one; in the case of strings, substring would be an example of a partial **Copy**.

```
// stringt.H, version 10: Copy operations added

struct string
{
    // . . .

  private:
    void copy(string&);
```

```
  public:
    string(string& string);              // copy initialization
    string& operator=(string&);          // copy assignment
    string reverse();                    // reverse copy
    string substring(int start, int end = -1);  // partial copy

    // . . .
};
```

```
// stringt.C, version 10: Copy operations and corrected operator+

// private function supporting copy operations
void string::copy(string& str)
{
    size = str.size;
    chars = new char[size];
    memcpy(chars, str.chars, size);
}

string::string(string& str)
{
    copy(str);
}

string& string::operator=(string& str)
{
    if (this != &str)                    // assign string to itself?!
        {
            delete [] chars;             // must first delete old array
            copy(str);
        }
    return *this;
}

ostream& operator<<(ostream& strm, string& str)
{
    str.reset();
    while (str.next()) strm << str.current();

    return strm;
}

string& string::reverse()
{
    string* str = new string(*this);

    int mid = size/2;
    for (int i = 0; i < mid; i++)
        exchange(str->chars[i], str->chars[size-i-1]);
        // exchanges two values (from standard.H, discussed below)

    return *str;
}
```

```
}

string& string::substring(int start, int end)
{
    assert(abs(end) <= size && start > 0);
    if (end < 0) end += size;          // -1 is last, -2 next to last, etc.
                                       // Note that size = lastindex+1
    string* str = new string(end - start + 1);
    for (int i = start; i <= end; i++)
    str->chars[i - start] = chars[i];

    return *str;
}

string operator+(string& str1, string& str2)
{
    string str(str1.size + str2.size);

    memcpy(str->chars, str1.chars, str1.size);
    memcpy(str->chars+str1.size, str2.chars, str2.size);

    return str;
        // OK to return local variable since it will get copied.
}
```

1.3.5 Traversal

C++ offers no special support for traversal operations. However, it is straightforward to add member functions to data structures to support them. There are a number of different approaches. The one used in this book is the simplest possible: traversals are accomplished via an idiom supported by member functions that together provide a generalized generator facility. Functions are provided that

- initialize the process
- step to the next component
- tell whether or not there are any more components to process
- supply the current component

For convenience, there will also be a function to supply an index or counter as the traversal proceeds. Here are the member functions for string. Other structs will have the same functions, differing primarily in the component type (here a char).

```
// stringt.H, version 11: Traversal operations added

typedef int bool;

struct string
{
    // . . .
```

```
    // Traversal
    void reset();                     // initialize the traversal
    bool finished();                  // any components left to process?
    bool next();                      // step and return finished()
    char& current();                  // current component
    int index();                      // number of current component
};
```

There are many ways to organize traversal operations. The approach used here is that reset positions the process *before* the first component, so a next must be performed before attempting to access the first component. This facilitates using the traversal operations. Note also that for convenience, since next doesn't have any other value to return, it will return the result of finished. Here are the implementations.

```
// stringt.C, version 11: Traversal operations

/* Traversal */

void string::reset()
{
    cur = -1;
}

bool string::finished()
{
    return cur >= size;
}

bool string::next()
{
    cur++;
    return !finished();
}

char& string::current()
{
    return chars[cur];
}
```

The basic traversal idiom is as follows:

```
string str;
// . . .

str.reset();
while (str.next())
    // do something to str.current()
```

Here's how `string::operator<<` would be coded using these traversal operations.

```
ostream& operator<<(ostream& strm, string& str)
{
    str.reset();
    while (str.next())
        strm << string.current();

    return strm;
}
```

The advantage of using traversal operations in place of the original formulation of `operator<<` is that it leaves the function independent of the implementation of `string`. If we change to a different representation for strings, this function is unaffected. This is important not only for arbitrary external code but also for the less central operations of a structure's module. To the extent that dependence on a structure's implementation details can be minimized, maintenance is facilitated, and many errors are avoided.

There are two major problems with the simplistic approach used here:

- Every instance of the struct incorporates space for the traversal state even when no traversal is in process.

- Worse, only one traversal at a time can be in progress on any instance.

More sophisticated approaches use separate "iterator" structs that maintain traversal state independently of the struct instance. That would resolve these two problems, but for the purposes of this book the increased complexity of the resulting implementations would not be worth the trouble.

1.3.6 Input/Output

The basic features of the C++ `iostream` library were introduced earlier (page 37). Chapter 4, on streams, discusses its facilities further. Although strictly speaking not yet part of the language (just as `printf` and related functions were not strictly speaking part of the classic C language), the `iostream` facility is supplied as part of virtually all C++ implementations. It provides a rich, convenient set of mechanisms for defining input and output operators tailored for each data structure. It's good practice to define an output (insertion) operator for every struct, if only to support debugging.

Input (extraction) operators are also useful, but it's much harder to discuss their implementation in general and they are ignored in the rest of this book. The main difficulty is the range of possible formats (and the code needed to parse and validate input). There's more flexibility on output, where any reasonable format can be understood by the human reader. For input, data would have to conform to a specifically defined arrangement, perhaps one of several. Also, various verification issues arise on input to make sure that the values read are valid.

1.4 Other C++ Programming Issues and Features

This section covers a few remaining technical issues of various degrees of significance. This material will complete the introduction to data abstraction programming in C++. After this, the central part of the book begins.

1.4.1 Templates

Templates are a major new feature that began appearing in C++ implementations by the end of 1991. This feature will be used heavily in the code shown in this book, as it required for the implementation of data structures in a type-safe language. It is also useful for defining a class of simple type-independent utility functions, such as `min`, `max`, and `exchange` that would otherwise be defined less safely with macros.

Motivation

Suppose you wanted to implement a set of integers, using an array to hold its elements. The elements would be stored contiguously in the array, and the struct would need a member to keep track of the number of elements. The technical term for the number of elements in a set is *cardinality*, but 'size' is used for the **Attribute** function here, to be consistent with the way it is used in the rest of the book, as discussed in Section 1.2.3, page 58. We'll use 'cardinality' for the internal count since sets don't really have a 'length' as do linear structures. The header file would look something like the following.

```
// Sketch of set.H

typedef int bool;
const int set_limit = 100;              // assuming fixed size limit

struct set
{
  private:

    int cardinality;
    int elements[set_limit];

  public:

    set();

    int size();

    set& operator+=(int);                 // add to the set
    set& operator-=(int);                 // remove from the set

    bool contains(int);

    friend ostream& operator<<(ostream&, set&);
    friend bool operator==(set& s1, set& s2);
    friend bool operator!=(set& s1, set& s2);
```

```
    friend set operator+(set& s1, set& s2);     // Union
    friend set operator-(set& s1, set& s2);     // Difference
    friend set operator*(set& s1, set& s2);     // Intersection

    // Traversal
    void reset();                               // initialize the traversal
    bool finished();                            // any components left to process?
    bool next();                                // step and return finished()
    int& current();                             // current component
    int index();                                // number of current component
};
```

Suppose that later, after writing and debugging this module, you are working on another program and you realize that you need a set module again. However, in this program sets must contain strings (char*) instead of integers. What do you do? The time-honored maneuver in this situation is to make a copy of both the header and implementation files and use an editor to replace every occurrence of int with char*. Careful, though! Not every int was there because it is the type of the set's components. For instance, the type of the cardinality member is an int and should stay that way, not be changed to a char*.

After a few experiences like this, you might hit upon the clever idea of using typedef to simplify the whole process. You could take your original header and implementation files and replace all component-type ints with something neutral sounding like element and add to the beginning of the header file:

```
        typedef int element;
```

With the typedef inserted, every place the compiler encounters element it will be as if the file had int instead. The header file would then look something like the following.

```
// generalized set header file

typedef int bool;
typedef int element;

const int set_limit = 100;              // assuming fixed size limit

struct set
{
  private:

    int cardinality;
    element elements[set_limit];

  public:

    set();

    int size();
```

```
    set& operator+=(element&);
    set& operator-=(element&);

    bool contains(element&);

    friend ostream& operator<<(ostream&, set&);


    friend bool operator==(set& s1, set& s2);
    friend bool operator!=(set& s1, set& s2);

    friend set operator+(set& s1, set& s2);
    friend set operator-(set& s1, set& s2);
    friend set operator*(set& s1, set& s2);

    // Traversal
    void reset();                       // initialize the traversal
    bool finished();                    // any components left to process?
    bool next();                        // step and return finished()
    element& current();                 // current component
    int index();                        // number of current component
};
```

Now, to make a module for sets of strings, you would copy the header and implementation files (giving the copies new names), change the typedef to say char* instead of int, and compile the new implementation file. You end up with three files — header, implementation, and compiled — for each copy of the module that you make. Programs select which to use by #includeing the appropriate header file in their program text and including the appropriate compiled file in their list of files to link. You can do this over and over again, creating a whole library of set-of-whatever types. To make a new set module, all you actually change is the typedef in the header and implementation files.

The basis for this trick is the observation that *none of the text in the module files depends in any way on the type of the collection's components.* The characters in the different files are identical except for the single typedef. This trick in effect creates a *generic* set module — one that can be *instantiated* for any particular component type. *The component type becomes a parameter of the set type.* Parameterization is an important aspect of all collection types: collections must contain elements of some specific type, and nothing about the component type affects the collection's implementation.

There are several problems with this approach, however. One is that with the simplistic approach outline so far, any given program can include only one instantiation of a generic module. Although *you* might think of each set module as being a set-of-something module, the *compiler* would just see definitions of set and its member functions. Each copy of the module defines a struct named set, so using two of them in the same program would lead to many compilation and linkage errors due to multiple definitions. To solve this problem, you'd have to find some trick to parameterize the *name* of the type in addition to the type of the component, to get structures with names like intset and stringset.

The main problems with this approach arise from the proliferation of module copies. Each version of the module needs its own name for the struct it defines and the files comprising it and takes up space in the file system. Worse, if a bug is fixed in, or a new feature is added to, the original module, the changes have to be propagated to all the copies. That is tedious enough, but it may not even be possible to find out where all the copies are — someone might have made a copy without telling the original author. Copying modules inevitably leads to all sorts of maintenance headaches.

C++ Support

Historically, various macro-based approaches have been developed that support more sophisticated versions of the above copy-and-edit scenario. Ultimately, however, effective type parameterization requires language support, and C++ now supplies it. The mechanism used is the *template*, which is essentially a way to specify parameters of a type in both generic modules and in program declarations. Only one copy of the module text is maintained, with the compiler automatically generating the instantiated copies. This eliminates all the maintenance problems associated with multiple copies of modules, the space necessary to store them, and even the work necessary to produce them. The template facility also provides syntax for parameterized type names, so that there's no problem using several different parameterizations of the same type in one program and no work to do to generate type-specific collection names. Sophisticated implementations can even avoid generating functions of a particular instantiation that aren't used, so the size of the generated code would be less than if a complete copy had been manually made for each instantiation.

    Only the basics of the parameterized type mechanism will be considered here — advanced features and other ways to use them are beyond the scope of this text. Superficially, just about the only thing added to C++ syntax for this is a new keyword `template` and one new bit of notation: a list of template parameters enclosed in angle brackets. The `template` keyword and the type parameter list precede the `struct` that begins the definition of a parameterized type. For instance, a `vector` type could be parameterized on the number of dimensions by defining the template

```
template<int ndimensions> struct vector
{
    // . . .
};
```

    Then, throughout that definition, the template parameter can be used just as if it had been defined with a #define or a `typedef`. The name of the parameterized type is used in the definition just as if it were not parameterized. In short, the only thing different about the definition of a parameterized struct is a few extra things that appear before it; the body of the definition is unchanged.

    Usually, but not always, the parameter is a *type* name rather than a value such as appears in the vector example above. C has no mechanism for passing a type as an argument, so something new is needed: the keyword `class` in a template parameter list designates a type argument.[5] No doubt you have never seen a type passed as a *function* argument (as opposed to a value), but you may have seen type names used as *macro* arguments, and the idea here is similar. Here's the header file for a type-parameterized set module.

```
// parameterized set header file

const int set_limit = 100;              // assuming fixed size limit

typedef int bool;
template <class element> struct set      // replaces typedef
{
  private:

    int cardinality;
    element elements[set_limit];

  public:

    set();

    int size();

    set& operator+=(element&);
    set& operator-=(element&);

    bool contains(element&);

    friend ostream& operator<<(ostream&, set&);

    friend bool operator==(set& s1, set& s2);
    friend bool operator!=(set& s1, set& s2);

    friend set operator+(set& s1, set& s2);
    friend set operator-(set& s1, set& s2);
    friend set operator*(set& s1, set& s2);

    // Traversal
    void reset();                        // initialize the traversal
    bool finished();                     // any components left to process?
    bool next();                         // step and return finished()
    element& current();                  // current component
    int index();                         // number of current component
};
```

The only change from the ad hoc typedef-based solution shown earlier is to replace the typedef with template<class element>. This says that element is a type that will be specified in declarations that use set. The header and implementation file just use el-

---

[5]'Class' is used instead of 'type' because 'class' pretty much means 'type' in the object-oriented aspects of C++ that we are not considering, and 'type' is too common a word in existing C programs for C++ to appropriate it as a reserved word.

ement as if it were really a type — as if it had been defined with #define or typedef. Declarations of instances of parameterized types also use the angle brackets.

```
#include "student.H"

set<char*> course_names;          // a set of C strings
set<student*> CS1, CS2, CS40;     // three sets of student*s
```

Parameterization is not limited to just one argument. We could make the maximum size of the set a parameter of the type.

```
template<class element, int limit> struct set
{
  private:

    int cardinality;
    element elements[limit];
    // . . .
};
```

This would mean that set<int,50> and set<int,100> are different types. Each parameter of a template is either of the form class *T*, where *T* is the type argument that will be used in the template, or type *X*, where type is an already-defined type and *X* is the expression argument that is used in the template. Then, when using the template, type names are supplied for type parameters, and expressions are supplied for other kinds of parameters.

Template Functions

Member functions of parameterized types must be parameterized in the same way. Each template function begins with the same template preface as the declaration of the struct to which it belongs (either as a member or a friend).

```
template <class element> bool operator==(set& s1, set& s2)

{
    if (s1.cardinality ! = s2.cardinality) return FALSE;

    for (int i = 0; i < cardinality; i++)
        if (! s2.contains(s1.elements[i]))
            return FALSE;
    // could use traversal operations, but that would disturb
    // any traversal in progress, so for convenience this is
    // implemented directly in terms of the set's representation.

    return TRUE;
}
```

A member function has the template preface and a parameterized name.

```
template <class element> int set<element>::size()
{
    return cardinality;
}
```

Independent Template Functions

Template functions are also useful independently of parameterized types. Consider a small function like min.

```
int min(int i, int j)
{
    return (i < j) ? i : j;
}
```

What about min for other numeric types? It seems pretty tedious to define a simple function like min for every kind of numeric type with which it might be called. Templates make it possible to write just one generic definition that the compiler will instantiate as needed.

```
template <type T> T min(T& i, T& j)
{
    return (i < j) ? i : j;
}
```

That template function can be invoked with any type that defines operator<, built-in or user-defined. Using reference arguments avoids the overhead of copying when T is a struct type.

Functions like min are typically defined as macros in C. One aspect of the flexibility macros provide is that the types of their arguments are ignored when they are expanded. Of course that flexibility is also a danger, and in C++ type safety becomes much more important a consideration than it is in C. Templates are much better than macros since they generate real, type-checked functions.

Final Details

Template functions are more like macros than actual functions, since they are used by the compiler to generate actual function definitions. In many implementations, templates get included by source files that use them, just as macros are, in which case the *implementation* file gets included in addition to the header file. In more sophisticated implementations, only the header file is included and the compiler places the definitions it generates into separate files that are later compiled and linked in to the executable. In either approach, a separate function definition is generated for each type with which the template

function is called. Simple implementations generate definitions for every template function in a module whenever any are needed. More sophisticated implementations generate definitions only for those functions actually called with a particular type.

If a regular function is defined with the same signature as some template function,
then the compiler will not generate a definition for that function from the template. The
regular definition preempts the template. This allows tailoring a module for a specific
type by explicitly defining a few of its functions.

The straightforward approach of generating definitions for every function in the
module whether or not it is called makes certain demands of component types. If a structure's template function invokes some function on one of its components, then the component type must provide that operation. Given the design of the modules in this book,
there are three functions like this: `equal`, `compare`, and `operator<<`, each of which must
call the corresponding function on the components of the structure. Suppose, however,
you want to use one of these structures with a component type that doesn't have any reasonable definition of, say, `equal`. If you try to construct an application, you'll get linker
errors indicating that `equal` wasn't found for the component type. Presumably, your
program would not call the structure's `equal` operation, since you know that the component type you are using doesn't support `equal`.

However, in the straightforward approach, a definition of `equal` would still be generated, and it would contain an invocation of the component type's `equal`, causing the
linker to look for it. For this reason, you would have to define these three functions even
if all they do is complain that they shouldn't be called. Similarly, for this reason, all the
structure modules shown in this book are given definitions of these three functions in case
they are themselves used as the components of other structures. Of course, a more sophisticated template implementation would avoid generating definitions for template
functions that don't get called, in which case modules would not have to provide functions
that were never going to be invoked.

1.4.2 Exception Handling

As you get comfortable with the process of writing modular data abstractions, you will notice that their fundamental operations should check for certain common aberrant
situations. For instance, set **Add** should check to see if the underlying array that holds the
components is full before trying to add a new component. The term *exception* is used to
refer to the identification of such aberrant situations. *Exception handling* refers to a
mechanism for *signalling*, or *raising*, exceptions and responding to them. The term *exception* is more general than *error*, which implies something incorrect has happened. Exceptions include errors as well as other unusual but expectable situations such as the end
of a file. Consequently, exception handling may be applied to a wider range of situations
than just detecting errors.

We've already seen one primitive exception handling mechanism: the `assert` macro (cf. page 13). This is a convenient way to state an expectation and halt the program if
it is violated. It is meant to be used during program development and testing, then turned
off when the program is prepared for delivery. It is too crude a mechanism for applica-

tions that are actually being used. A better mechanism is needed that allows the program to detect and handle the exception yet retain control.

Motivation

What should a fundamental operation do when it detects an aberrant situation? Although a structure's operations may *detect* aberrant situations, it can't really know how to handle it — the appropriate action really depends on the application and the context. Exception handling mechanisms are like conditional statements in that they divert the flow of control if a certain condition occurs. They are unlike conditional statements in that the action to perform gets specified somewhere else — typically, in an entirely different part of the program. A common way of visualizing exception handling is to use a *catch-and-throw* metaphor: the code detecting the unusual situation *throws* an exception and other code *catches* it.

A catch-and-throw mechanism must be supported by the language, giving the programmer a way to express raising and catching exceptions. It also be supported by the run-time system, which must be able to find a catcher for any exception thrown and divert control to it. Rudimentary exception handling mechanisms have appeared in some commercial languages for many years — for instance, PL/1 had some in the 1960s. Exception handling has also been the theme of many experiments in languages and systems, but it has yet to become a part of the mainstream language paradigm. An exception handling mechanism has been planned for C++ that, though somewhat limited, is straightforward and takes care of the most common uses. Unfortunately, commercially available compilers have yet to support it. For this book's purposes, the `assert` macro and various error functions defined in `standard.H` will be entirely adequate. However, it is worth considering briefly what the exception handling mechanism proposed for C++ looks like.

The Proposed C++ Exception Handling Mechanism

Handlers will be established with a new kind of statement called a *try block*. The try block has two parts, an ordinary compound statement (block) and a sequence of handlers. Each handler has the form

```
catch (argument-declaration) compound-statement;
```

The declaration is like the declaration of a function argument. Exceptions are (created and) thrown by a *throw expression*:

```
throw expression;
```

When an exception is thrown, control is immediately transferred to the "nearest" handler that matches the type of the expression thrown. 'Nearest' means the handler whose try-block was most recently entered and not yet exited — i.e., is still on the program stack. Once control is transferred, all intervening stack function calls are abandoned; thus, control never returns to where the throw was executed.[6] When control is trans-

---

[6]The alternative of allowing control to continue at the throw was considered and rejected. C++ exception handling is intended primarily for error handling and will not support some of the more sophisticated control regimes that require *continuation semantics*.

ferred, the value thrown is passed as the argument to the handler, and the handler's statement is executed.

One of the difficulties in implementing such a mechanism for C++ is that the intervening functions may contain local variables whose values are objects. Normally, entering a block will cause the constructors of such objects to be invoked, and exiting the block
will cause their destructors to be invoked. If an exception causes a function to be abandoned, the exit code that invokes the destructors for its object-valued variables will never
be reached. Therefore, the throw mechanism must somehow explicitly invoke their destructors.

Exception Handling Examples

Here's an example of general-purpose handler that might be part of a try block wrapped
around the body of a program.

```
main()
{
    try
        {
            doit();
        }
    catch(char* msg)
        {
            cout << "Sorry, " << msg << ".\n";
            exit(1);
        }
}
```

Code anywhere in the program can signal an exception that will print a message and terminate the program by throwing a char*, as in the following example:

```
set& set::operator+=(element* elt)
{
    if (contains(elt)) return;              // no duplicates

    if (cardinality >= set_limit)
        throw "an attempt was made to add to a full set"

    elements[cardinality++] = elt;
}
```

Note that the throw and corresponding catch are in two different files and have no
knowledge whatsoever of each other.

The type of the handler argument is not restricted. You can throw an integer, enumerator, or any other kind of value that seems useful. You can throw an instance of a
struct that capture details of the error situation, after creating and filling its fields with appropriate values. Since there can be more than one handler associated with a try block,
try statements can catch exceptions of more than one type.

The declaration of a handler can be an ellipsis (. . .), in which case that handler will catch anything that reaches it. Inside the block of a handler, a `throw` can be performed without an argument. That passes the exception the handler caught on to the next handler on the stack whose argument matches it, as if the exception hadn't been caught. There is also syntax for declaring what exceptions a function might throw.

1.4.3 Objects, References, or Pointers

When deciding on the type of any variable, data member, or function argument, one is always faced with a decision whether to use an object (value), a reference, or a pointer. For the purposes of the code in this book it would be useful to adopt a consistence convention about what collections will hold and how their components will be passed to and from functions. There are many issues here, and the requirements of commercial software are different from those of pedagogical examples. Basically, we want simple, flexible conventions that will support work with the structures that will be discussed.

Consider the set module above as a concrete example. Should the array of elements hold objects, references, or pointers? A key consideration is the assignment of a component to a location within the structure, as when adding a new element to a set. For an array-based structure, references are not an option because there's no way to store references in an array! (References are synonyms for something else and don't exist on their own, so they can't be stored.) More flexible kinds of collections, however, use newly created auxiliary storage for each component they contain and therefore could store references. However, there would still be no way to replace a reference without replacing the auxiliary storage.

Storing objects in the array would work, but doesn't necessarily produce the desired result with user-defined types, since assigning one value to another copies the first to the second. One problem with copying is its inefficiency, especially with large objects. More importantly, copy semantics are not usually what's wanted. Suppose a program creates an instance of a `student` struct, stores it in a set, makes some modifications to it, and later gets it out of the set. Should the `student` instance reflect changes made to the original after it was added to the set? If objects are copied into the set, subsequent changes won't affect the instance in the set, just the original instance outside the set. There will be two different objects ostensibly representing the same student while potentially having different states (values for their data members). (This issue doesn't arrive with primitives like integers, because two different integers with the same value are in effect the same integer.)

The simplest, most flexible, and generally most efficient approach is for collection structures to contain pointers. Using pointers avoids the inefficiency and questionable semantics of copying, and pointers, unlike references, can be replaced. A further advantage of pointers is the availability of a special null value to indicate 'nothing here' or 'not found'. It turns out that objects stored in collection structures are usually allocated dynamically (via `new`, which returns a pointer), so it ends up being just as natural to use pointers as anything else. For commercial libraries of collection types, other considerations apply, and pointers throughout might not be the most appropriate solution, but the approach is fine for the purposes of an introductory text.

There is one significant problem with pointer-based implementations, however. In general, collection structures need to know nothing about the types they contain. That is the fundamental fact making parameterization on the type of the component possible. Normally collections do nothing with their components except take them in, hold them, and hand them out. However, there are two kinds of operations on components that operations on collections need to invoke: **Output** and **Compare**. A collection's **Output** operation, implemented as `operator<<` in C++, typically traverses the collection outputting each component. Similarly, two collections are compared by traversing them in parallel and comparing their components pair by pair.

Since the collections will be holding pointers, these operations will have to dereference the pointers to invoke the **Output** or **Compare** operations on the objects pointed to. This may require the component type to supply **Output** and **Compare** operations even if they don't make sense, since those operations in the collection structure will attempt to invoke them. (If the template implementation generates definitions only for those functions called, then these functions would not have to be provided by the component type, as long as the corresponding function was never called with the collection type.)

The template mechanism offers further flexibility. The modules shown in this book could be used with primitive types, except for two problems: the **Output** and **Compare** operations expect to dereference pointers, and in some places, null pointers are interpreted specially. However, because template functions won't be used to generate definitions for functions that are explicitly declared, special-purpose variations on these modules can be created simply by explicitly defining the few functions that depend on pointers. For example, a set module could be used with integers as long as its **Output** and **Compare** operations were replaced by versions that didn't dereference component pointers.

1.4.4 Missing Types and Operations

C is missing two important types provided by many other languages: *string* and *Boolean*. Strings are represented as arrays of characters conventionally ending in a NUL (0 byte) and manipulated via the library functions declared in `string.h`. Although there is no type `string`, manipulating character arrays through the library function achieves almost the same effect as having a built-in type.

Integers are used for Boolean values, with zero meaning *false* and nonzero *true*. However, just as it is better to use `void*` to mean 'pointer to anything' instead of the technically equivalent `char*`, it would be better to have a separate type for Booleans to avoid confusion with other uses of `int`. It is common practice to define such a type, along with values for *true* and *false*. There are several of ways of doing so, each with its own advantages and disadvantages. For the work in this book, `bool` will be defined as a synonym for `int` and `TRUE` and `FALSE` defined as `bool` constants. That allows using the result of a logical expression (e.g., `a==b`) as if it were a `bool`. The more obvious approach of making `bool` an enum wouldn't allow using the result of an expression as a Boolean value, too great an inconvenience to accept, in particular for function returns.

Also missing from C, but frequently needed, are `min` and `max`, which, as shown above, are easily implemented as templates. We'll package `bool`, `TRUE` and `FALSE`, `min` and `max`, and other useful tidbits into a header file called `standard.H`. For convenience that file will also include iostream.h, string.h, and assert.h, since they are almost always needed. All implementation files shown in the rest of the book are presumed to include standard.H.

Section 1.3.3 (page 67) showed that an enum for order comparisons is convenient to have and will be used frequently here, so that goes in the standard header file, too. That section showed how functions for the six comparison operators can be defined using a central comparison function. Because this will be so common, and the operator definitions take up so much space without adding any information, standard.H will have template functions for the six operators. Incidentally, if a definition for a template instantiation is explicitly provided, the compiler won't generate one, so it is always possible to define one of these operators specially for some structure even though a template for it is defined.

Bits and pieces of other conveniences are also found in standard.H. Two of the functions found there are spaces to print a number of spaces and timestamp to output the current date and time. Some useful error-reporting macros include error, error2, warning, and notimp. Similarly, there are macros for issuing a warning and aborting out of a function — abortv, abort0, abort1 — that differ by what they return from the function (void, 0, and 1, respectively). Another convenience is a template for exchange.

```
template <class T> void exchange(T& a, T& b)
{
    T c = a;
    a = b;
    b = c;
}
```

The library functions for manipulating C strings include functions that copy the characters from one string into another, but they require that the other string already be allocated. Some versions of string.h include a strdup function, but ANSI C's doesn't. Since strdup encapsulates such a convenient idiom, standard.H will include a macro for it. Like many of the other functions and macros in standard.H, this could have been coded as a macro, a function, or an inline function, and there are various considerations for and against each approach. One of the reasons it is coded as a macro here is to avoid conflicts where strdup happens to be present in string.h. Conditional compilation would be another option, but there isn't any way to test whether a particular function has been declared!

```
#define strdup(str) (!str ? 0 : strcpy(new char[strlen(str)+1], str))
```

The functions in the file really should go in a .C file, but there are only a few, so to simplify things they are left here. The only disadvantage is that each compilation unit will contain its own copy of the functions. As you'll see, the use of templates for the implementation of all the data structures ends up meaning there will only be one or two compilation units in the programs that use them, so this turns out not to be a significant issue.

There are a lot of subtle choices involved in formulating utilities like these in C++. The exact mechanisms used here in each case were the result of pragmatic considerations involving interactions with various compilers and the way these utilities are used in the book's data structure modules. The definitions in standard.H are not meant to be recommendations for how such things should be handled in actual software development work; they are a compromise designed to make it easier to use the code files accompanying the book.

1.5 EXERCISES

1. The string module discussed in the chapter does not have any **Remove** or **Exchange** operations.
   (a) Define some.
   (b) Show how they are used.
   (c) Discuss advantages and disadvantages to including them from the point of view of the module's users.

2. In the first version of the string module (page 26), strings are always dynamically created and passed to string functions as pointers. What changes could you make to hide the details of the structure's definition from module users *in straight C*?

3. If module users are prohibited from referring to the fields of a struct, why does the struct declaration go in the header file?

4. Why can't the string in the names make_string and convert_to_string be eliminated in version 3 of the string module (page 38)?

5. At the end of the implementation for version 2 of the string module (page 32) the comment is made that str.chars[i] could be replaced by string_char(str,i) and str.size by string_length(str). What are the advantages and disadvantages of doing this for version 2?

6. In version 3 (page 38), str.chars[i] is replaced by str[i] in operator== and operator<. What are the advantages and disadvantages of doing this? Are any of these affected by the changes made for version 4? (page 42)

7. Write operator> and operator>= for the string module.

8. What would operator- for the string module mean? Code it.

9. Write operator>> for the string module.

10. Write a complete module for a date type and test it.

11. Write a complete module for large, an integer with as many as 100 digits.
    (a) Design a representation for the type.
    (b) Define and test appropriate **Initialize** operations.
    (c) Define and test input and output operators.
    (d) Define and test arithmetic operators.
    (e) What other operations would be useful for this module? Define and test them too.

12. Can you think of an advantage if the language were changed to allow you to omit parentheses in a member function call when the function takes no arguments (other than the implicit this)?

13. Implement a module for set of unsigned char, analogous to the string structure shown in the examples throughout this chapter. Start with a straightforward representation, such as an array indexed by char with each element a flag indicating whether or not the corresponding character is in the set.

(a) Make sure you define an appropriate range of **Combine** operations, including at least `union` and `intersection`, and perhaps `difference`.

(b) Once everything's working, try changing the representation to be more compact. Since there are only a small, fixed number of possible members, you can use a bit-level representation: have an array of `unsigned int`, with each bit set to 1 if the corresponding character is in the set, 0 if it's not. If, for example, your machine has 32-bit integers, then the indicators for characters 0 through 31 would be in the first integer, 32 through 63 in the second integer, etc.

(c) How many elements do you need in your array?

(d) Does it matter whether your bit indicators go from left to right or right to left within their bytes? Why?

14. Define `struct word` (simply), as for a text-processing application.

(a) Declare simple versions of its fundamental operations.

(b) Define in particular `operator<<` and `operator>>`. (Let a word be any contiguous sequence of nonwhite characters. Note that all `operator>>` functions stop at white space, so this should be trivial.)

(c) Write a short program that reads all the words in a file and prints each one on a separate line, in the order in which they appear in the file. The program should also count the number of words found and print that out after the last one.

(d) Organize things so that the main program innocently asks for words without ever checking for end of file, and have `word::operator>>` check end of file. Only the main program should know the number of words read. The main program should catch an exception thrown by `set::operator>>`. If your C++ doesn't have an exception-handling mechanism, use `setjmp` and `longjmp`, from the ANSI C library.

15. Parameterize the set module from Exercise 13.

16. Use the parameterized set module to store a set of characters, as in the nonparameterized version defined in Exercise 13. You'll have to explicitly declare and define replacements for any of its functions that treat components as pointers, but otherwise you can use the module as defined for Exercise 15.

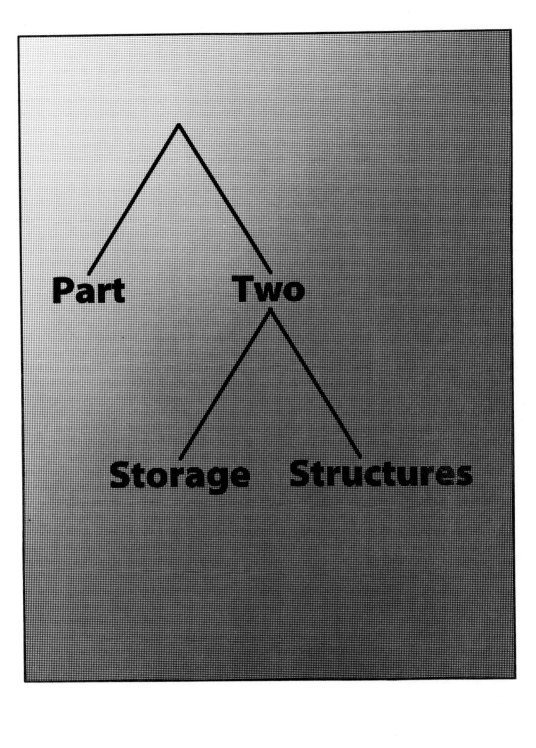

Part Two:

Storage Structures

Storage structures are the fundamental structuring mechanisms of computer languages. All other data structures are built on top of them. Storage structures directly manage raw memory, either internal (RAM) or external (disks, tapes, etc.). There are three fundamental kinds: the *array*, the *record*, and the *stream*. Modern programming languages provide these either directly in the language itself or as part of a standard run-time library.

Storage structures are little more than containers that hold computational objects. *Arrays* provide a fixed sequence of numbered locations into which objects can be stored. *Records* provide a fixed set of *named* locations. *Streams* do not have a fixed size; their elements are accessed one at a time. Thus, while components of arrays and records are accessed directly, stream components are accessed *sequentially*. All components of an array or stream are of the same type, so these are *homogeneous* structures. Record components can be of any type, so records are *heterogeneous*. In sum:

array	fixed-size sequence of directly accessible homogeneous components
record	fixed-size sequence of directly accessible heterogeneous components
stream	indefinite-size sequence of sequentially accessible homogeneous components

In sum, all three fundamental storage structures are sequences of components. The differences between them stem from whether or not they have a fixed size and whether or not their components are all of the same type. From the former follows whether or not their components are directly or sequentially accessible, since sequentially accessible structures can grow indefinitely. Table 2 summarizes the kinds of storage structures and their distinguishing properties.

	Homogeneous?	Access
Array	yes	direct
Record	no	direct
Stream	yes	sequential

Table 2   Kinds of Storage Structures

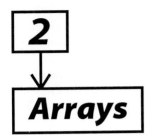

Arrays

An array is a *fixed-size sequence of directly accessible components of the same type*. Individual elements are accessed by an integer *index* into the array. In C

```
int month_days[12];
```

declares an array called `month_days` that holds 12 integers, as illustrated in Figure 2.1. C

```
month_days
        0    31
        1    28
        2    31
        3    30
        4    31
        5    30
        6    31
        7    31
        8    30
        9    31
       10    30
       11    31
```

Figure 2.1 An Array

array slots are always numbered starting with 0. (In some languages, indexing starts from 1; in others, indexing starts from an initial index specified in the array declaration.) Individual array elements are accessed by expressions such as

```
month_days[month]
```

Pascal's declaration syntax is more revealing of the array's nature:

```
VAR MONTH_DAYS ARRAY[0..11] OF INTEGER;
```

(In Pascal, any range of integers can be specified for the index range.) The underlying generic form of declarations for any kind of collection structure in any language is

```
STRUCTURE OF TYPE
```

(The variable name is not part of the type declaration for the structure.) In the present example, the structure is `ARRAY[0..11]`. Note that in this case the structure specifies both an organizing *mechanism* (the array) and a specific set of component *names* (in a form unique to the array mechanism).

Each variable in a program gets assigned to a particular memory location by the compiler or run-time environment. The amount of space reserved for the variable's value is determined by its type. In the case of an array-valued variable, the number of bytes (ignoring alignment considerations) would be

$$\text{number-of-elements} * \text{element-size}$$

The essence of the array mechanism is that the element designated by `a[n]` is located at address

$$\text{address-of}(a[n_0]) + ((n-n_0) * \text{element-size})$$

where the ampersand is the C "address-of" operator and n_0 is the value of the first value of the index range. In C, where the first index is always 0, the computation reduces to

$$\text{address-of}(a[n_0]) + (n * \text{element-size})$$

The quantity added to the initial address is called the *offset*. An array access expression is translated by the compiler into code that computes the offset and adds it to the address of the array.

2.1 An Array Type

C's implementation of the array concept is quite weak. In fact, C doesn't really have arrays, just an array-like notation that gets translated into equivalent pointer manipulations. An array-typed variable is equivalent to a pointer to the array's first element. There's no real distinction between a type `array-of-component` such as `int[12]` and the type `pointer-to-component` (`int*`). Wherever an array is expected as a function argument, a pointer to the first argument is accepted equivalently.

The C bracket notation in expressions such as `months[n]` is equivalent to access via pointer arithmetic:

```
*(months + n)
```

That in turn has a special interpretation: the offset is implicitly considered to be in units of the size of the array's components. Thus, if `months` is an array of 4-byte integers at address A, then `months[5]` is the integer at location A+(5*4). Neither the C compiler nor the C run-time environment checks that the index is within the bounds of the array — if the program attempts to access a component beyond the limit of the array, random havoc ensues.

At the price of only a little extra storage and a few extra instructions per operation, we can have a robust array type. Let's look at a possible definition. The array type will be implemented as a struct that contains a C array of components along with the specified bounds. While we are at it, let's loosen C's requirement of zero-origin indexing. We'll record the value of the first and last indices. The number of components can be derived from the two index values. (Equivalently we could store the number of components and just one of the indices, deriving the other index from those two values.)

2.1.1 Representation

The `array` structure will be represented as follows. (Ellipses appearing in class declarations indicate the omission of other aspects of the declaration.)

```
template <class elt> struct array
{
  private:

    // Representation
    elt *elts;                  // C-array of elts
    int first;                  // first index value
    int last;                   // last index value
    // . . .
};
```

The `elts` member is a C-array of `elts`. The array of `elts` will be dynamically allocated during the initialization of an `array` instance.

2.1.2 Lifetime Operations

The lifetime operations have the following declarations. To make this array type behave like one built in to the language, `operator[]` is provided instead of an ordinary function to obtain the nth element.

```
template <class elt> struct array
{
    // . . .
  public:

    // Initialize/Finalize
    array(int size, int origin = 0);
    ~array();

    // Access/Modify
    elt& operator[](int n);
};
```

Users will specify the size of the array as a constructor argument. A second argument will allow the user to specify a first index. The constructor will store the lower bound as well as a computed upper bound in the struct instance. (The code is more conveniently expressed in terms of the first and last indices, while users will find it more convenient to specify an array size. This is a simple example of how the interface to a structure might be different from its representation.)

Having the user specify the size instead of the last index makes it possible to take advantage of C++'s optional parameter feature. If we had made the first argument the last index value, we could have defaulted the origin, but an initialization of just one integer seems more readily understood as the array size rather than a bounds. Putting the lower bound first, of course, would mean having to always provide two arguments to the constructor, since there wouldn't be a sensible default value for the size or upper bound. Another alternative would be to have two different constructors: a one-argument constructor that takes a size and requires the offset to be zero and a two-argument constructor that takes a lower and upper bound, in that order. There are significant interface design choices for even the simplest of structures!

The constructor will store the values of `first` and `last` and allocate the `elts` array. We'll have the constructor zero all the pointers. That way, if someone gets an element out of a location of an array before anything has been stored into it they'll get a null pointer rather than whatever bits happen to be there.

```
/* Initialize/Finalize */

template <class elt> array<elt>::array(int size, int origin) :
    first(origin), last(origin+size-1), elts(new elt[size]), cur(no_pos)
    // cur and no_pos are discussed under 'Traversal', below
{
    // initialize all elts to zero:
    for (int i = 0; i < size; i++) elts[i] = 0;
}

template <class elt> array<elt>::~array()
{
    delete [] elts;
}
```

We can get by with a single all-purpose **Access/Modify** operation, as programming languages do with the array facilities they provide. The `operator[]` member will return a reference to the corresponding component of the array. The compiler will handle the reference appropriately, according to whether it occurs in an **Access** context (in which case the value will be fetched) or a **Modify** context (in which case the corresponding component will be replaced). For example, we could write a statement like the following.

```
a[n] = a[n+1];
```

This means assign to the nth component the value of the $n+1$th component, just as with ordinary built-in arrays.

To more fully support the array concept, `operator[]` will check that the index is within the array's bounds, using the `assert` macro. Implementation is straightforward.

```
/* Access/Modify */

template <class elt> elt& array<elt>::operator[](int n)
{
    assert(n >= first || n <= last);
    return elts[n-first];
}
```

2.1.3 Traversal Operations

The traversal operations for arrays are very much like the ones shown for strings in Section 1.3.5, page 70. Here are their declarations.

```
template <class elt> struct array
{
    // . . .
    // Traversal
  private:
    int cur;                // position of traversal's current element
  public:
    void reset();
    bool finished();
    bool next();
    elt& current();
    int index();
};
```

Definitions for the **Traversal** operations are next. Note that current verifies that the current position is valid — that the traversal has been initialized, at least one next has been performed, and that the traversal hasn't yet been completed. A simple assert really isn't adequate in this situation, because traversal mistakes are easy to make and assert error messages would refer to entirely internal details.

```
/* Traversal */

static const int no_pos = -1;    // value of cur for uninitialized traversal

template <class elt> void array<elt>::reset()
{
    cur = first-1;
}

template <class elt> bool array<elt>::finished()
{
    return cur > last;
}
```

```
template <class elt> bool array<elt>::next()
{
    cur++;
    return !finished();
}

template <class elt> elt& array<elt>::current()
{
    if (no_pos == cur)
        error("[array::current] traversal not yet initialized");
    if ((first-1) == cur)
        error("traversal initialized but not yet stepped");
    if (finished())
        error("traversal already finished");
    return elts[cur-first];
}

template <class elt> int array<elt>::index()
{
    return cur;
}
```

2.1.4 Content Operations

Arrays have three **Attributes:** size, first_index, and last_index. Any one of these can be computed from the other two, so the module only has to provide two, but the idea is to make things convenient for the programmer using the module. Besides, how would you decide which of these are primary and which should be the derived one?

Combine does not have a natural interpretation for arrays, so it is not supported in this implementation. Of course, many structures that are implemented on top of arrays would implement meaningful **Combine** operations. Nor would it make much sense to **Compare** two arrays for order — order would be a property of a structure implemented on top of an array, not of the array itself.

Equality tests would be useful, however: two arrays are equal if they are the same size and the components at corresponding indices are themselves equal. (This definition allows the arrays to have different index ranges as long as they have the same size.)

```
template <class elt> struct array
{
    // . . .
  public:

    // Attributes
    int size();
    int first_index();
    int last_index();

    // Combine not supported
```

```
    // Compare
    friend order equal(array<elt>&, array<elt>&);
    friend order compare(array<elt>&, array<elt>&); // not implemented
};
```

The definitions of the **Attribute** operations are simple.

```
/* Attributes */

template <class elt> int array<elt>::size()
{
    return (last - first) + 1;
}

template <class elt> int array<elt>::first_index()
{
    return first;
}

template <class elt> int array<elt>::last_index()
{
    return last;
}
```

The simplicity of definitions such as these for array attributes is one of the hallmarks of the data abstraction style of programming. It would be easier to write a.first rather than a.first_index() in code using array. In older programming styles, functions are used primarily to package together a significant amount of code that is used in more than one place. In data abstraction programming functions are used also as an *abstraction mechanism* that hides the details of an operation's implementation from its users. It doesn't matter that the implementation happens to be trivial — the user shouldn't have to know about it at all. We want to be able to change the internal representation without affecting code that uses the structure. Here, if we decided to store the size instead of the index upper bound, code calling the attribute functions would be unaffected, whereas code directly accessing fields of the struct would have to be edited extensively.

Comparing two structures typically involves traversing them both in parallel and comparing the pairs of elements encountered at each step. The traversal can end as soon as nonequal elements are found.

```
/* Compare */

/*  tests equality of elements, not just ==, so two pointers could
    point to elements that test equal even though they are different.

    equal(elt&, elt&) is presumed defined.
*/
template <class elt> bool equal(array<elt>& a1, array<elt>& a2)
```

```
{
    if (&a1 == &a2) return TRUE;              // same arrays!
    if (a1.size() != a2.size()) return FALSE;  // different sizes

    a1.reset();
    a2.reset();

    while (a1.next(), a2.next())
        if (!equal(*a1.current(), *a2.current()))
            return FALSE;

    return TRUE;
}
```

The code for `equal` uses traversal operations. Given the primitive traversal mechanisms used in is book, it would generally be better to code a structure's operations without using it's traversal operations so as not to disrupt user traversals of the same structure. Here, it probably doesn't matter, since `equal` would not normally be called in the midst of a traversal and it's worth showing a few uses of traversal operations. In principle, of course, one never knows the uses to which one's structure will be put, so assumptions like this are dangerous.

Note also that `equal` is one of those functions that invokes operations on the objects pointed to by its elements. For the purposes of this book's code, as discussed in Section 1.4.3 (page 83), it is assumed that every struct (both collection and component types) supplies `equal` and `compare`. Types for which `compare` doesn't make sense will provide a definition that says that.

2.1.5 Support Operations

No **Process** operations are supported. The array is simply too low-level a structure to have a generally useful interpretation of these operations. However, all our modules will have **Copy** and **Write** operations.

```
template <class elt> struct array
{
    // . . .
    // Copy

    array(array<elt>&);                      // copy constructor
    array& operator=(array<elt>&);           // copy assignment operator

    // Output

    friend ostream& operator<<(ostream&, array<elt>&);
};
```

The copy constructor is similar to the regular constructor seen earlier. However, the initial values of the data members are based on those in an already existing instance instead of being provided explicitly. Also, instead of zeroing the elts array, the pointers in the array are copied from the old array. Some of them may be zero, of course.

```
/* Copy */

template <class elt> array<elt>::array(array<elt>& a) :
    first(a.first), last(a.last), elts(new elt[a.size()]), cur(no_pos)
{
    memcpy(elts, a.elts, sizeof(elt) * (1 + last - first));
}

template <class elt> array<elt>& array<elt>::operator=(array<elt>& a)
{
    if (this == &a) return a;                    // assignment to self!

    if (size() != a.size())
        {   // free old elts and reallocate
            delete [] elts;
            elts = new elt[a.size()];
        }

    first = a.first;
    last = a.last;
    cur = no_pos;   // abandon any traversal in process

    memcpy(elts, a.elts, sizeof(elt) * (1 + last - first));

    return *this;
}
```

For the output operator, we'll be a little fancy and print out the elements one to a line, along with their index enclosed in square brackets. Note the dereference of the pointer returned from current.

```
/* Output */

template <class elt> ostream& operator<<(ostream& strm, array<elt>& a)
{
    a.reset();

    while(a.next())
        strm << "\t[" << a.index() << "]\t" << *a.current() << '\n';

    return strm;
}
```

The definition of the output operator is a good example of why low-level traversal operations are sometimes needed even if iterators that traverse the entire structure in one operation were available. The oddities of comma-separated sequences requires that either the first or last element be handled specially, since there is one fewer comma than there are elements in the sequences. Note how compact the traversal code is, even though it is handling a special case of iteration.

2.2 Multidimensional Arrays

In some programming languages, including C, arrays are fundamentally one-dimensional structures. Other languages support *multidimensional arrays*. Even languages that have only one-dimensional arrays often provide syntax that simulates multidimensionality. For instance, a calendar could be declared in C as:

```
entry* calendar[12][31];
```

and accessed similarly:

```
calendar[0][0] = new entry("New Year's Day");
```

Here, entry is simply an array of 12 arrays, each holding 31 entry*s, as illustrated by Figure 2.2.

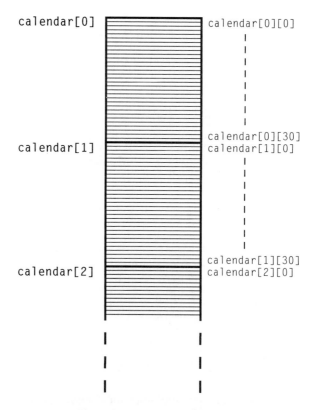

Figure 2.2 An Array of Arrays

Languages that have true multidimensional arrays interpret them similarly. The differences are mostly syntactic: elements of true multidimensional arrays are referenced by a single index expression: `calendar[0,0]` as opposed to a sequence of indices such as `calendar[0][0]` in C. One interesting variation from language to language is the order the elements of multidimensional arrays are stored. In Figure 2.2 the components of the two-dimensional array are arranged so that all the components of `a[0]` are first, followed by all the components of `a[1]`, and so on. Technically, we describe this by saying that the elements are stored with the last subscript varying most rapidly. Some languages that support multidimensional arrays arrange components the other way, storing arrays with the first subscript varying most rapidly.

Consider the abstract `array` type of the previous section. Declaring an array of arrays using C++ parameterized type notation is straightforward.

```
array< array<entry*> > calendar;
```

(When nesting parameterized type names like this, be sure to separate `>>` pairs with a space; otherwise, the compiler will treat the pair of angle brackets as a right-shift operator!) However, as defined above the array module does not provide a default constructor, so this declaration would not be accepted by the compiler! (How large should the outer array be? The inner arrays?)

We could add a constructor argument for the outer array:

```
array< array<entry*> > calendar(12);
```

but there's still no way to provide constructor arguments for the inner arrays. An alternative would be for the outer array to contain *pointers* to arrays:

```
array< array<entry*>*> calendar(12);
for (int i = 0; i < 12; i++)
    calendar[i] = new array<entry*>(31);
```

The use of `operator[]` and reference returns from functions would allow accessing an element of an array of arrays just like ordinary C array-of-array indexing:

```
calendar[month][day]
```

That expression would first invoke `operator[](month)` on `calendar`, then `operator[](day)` on the array returned. An array of pointers to arrays, however, would require slightly more awkward syntax:

```
(*calendar[month])[day]
```

Another drawback of using the array module for multidimensional arrays is that although the smaller arrays all have the same shape, each contains its own `first`, `last`, and `elts` fields. This wastes space and may result in unnecessary bounds checking.

Let's consider what it would take to have a separate multidimensional array type. We'll call it a *multarray*. We'll use as an example a decade-long hourly appointment calendar. For simplicity, let's assume that every day of every month needs to be represented, but only the hours from 8 AM to 5 PM need entries. This calendar could be represented as a four-dimensional array, with index ranges $1991:1999$, $1:12$, $1:31$, and $8:17$. (We won't worry about the pointers allocated for days that months don't have, such as April 31.) Figure 2.3 illustrates the layout of the components of the multarray representing the calendar. (The indices are shown there in basic C form, not in the application-level indices reflecting years, months, days, and hours.)

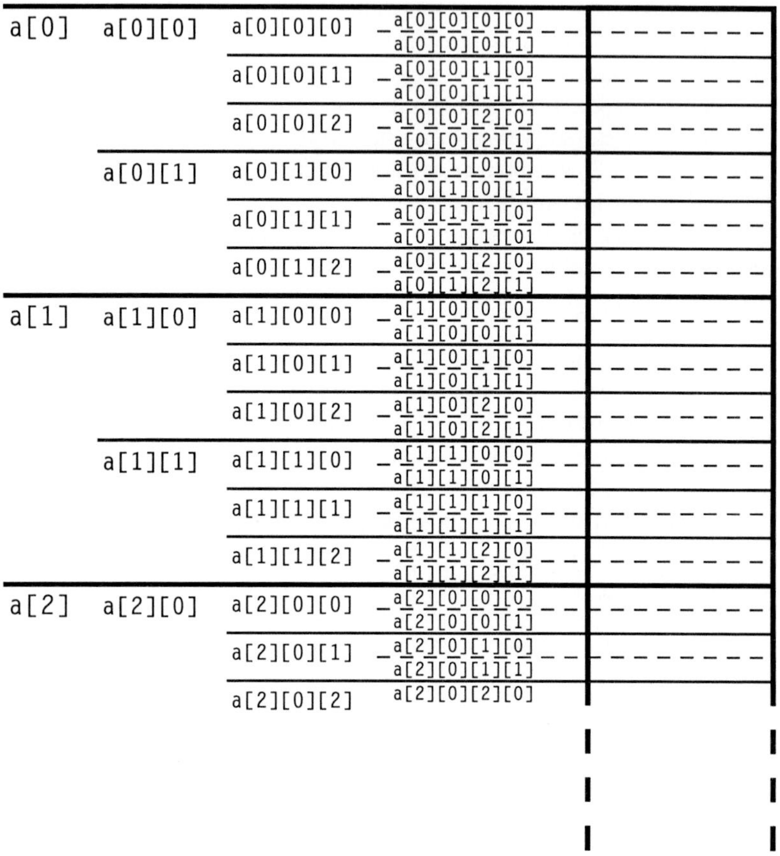

a[0]	a[0][0]	a[0][0][0]	a[0][0][0][0] / a[0][0][0][1]	— — — — — — —
		a[0][0][1]	a[0][0][1][0] / a[0][0][1][1]	— — — — — — —
		a[0][0][2]	a[0][0][2][0] / a[0][0][2][1]	— — — — — — —
	a[0][1]	a[0][1][0]	a[0][1][0][0] / a[0][1][0][1]	— — — — — — —
		a[0][1][1]	a[0][1][1][0] / a[0][1][1][01]	— — — — — — —
		a[0][1][2]	a[0][1][2][0] / a[0][1][2][1]	— — — — — — —
a[1]	a[1][0]	a[1][0][0]	a[1][0][0][0] / a[1][0][0][1]	— — — — — — —
		a[1][0][1]	a[1][0][1][0] / a[1][0][1][1]	— — — — — — —
		a[1][0][2]	a[1][0][2][0] / a[1][0][2][1]	— — — — — — —
	a[1][1]	a[1][1][0]	a[1][1][0][0] / a[1][1][0][1]	— — — — — — —
		a[1][1][1]	a[1][1][1][0] / a[1][1][1][1]	— — — — — — —
		a[1][1][2]	a[1][1][2][0] / a[1][1][2][1]	— — — — — — —
a[2]	a[2][0]	a[2][0][0]	a[2][0][0][0] / a[2][0][0][1]	— — — — — — —
		a[2][0][1]	a[2][0][1][0] / a[2][0][1][1]	— — — — — — —
		a[2][0][2]	a[2][0][2][0]	

Figure 2.3   Layout of Components in a Four-Dimensional Array

2.2.1 Representation

The representation of multarray will be as follows. Changes from array are underlined — the basic idea is similar, but a more complex representation is needed to support multiple dimensions.

```
template <class elt> struct multarray
{
  private:
    int ndimensions;
    elt *elts;                    // C-array of elt*
```

```
    int * first;                    // array of first index values
    int * last;                     // array of last index values
    long * sizes;                   // [see text]
    // . . .
};
```

What have we changed from `array`? Instead of a single `first` and `last`, we need a `first` and `last` for each dimension of the array. To allow full generality, the dimensionality of the array will be specified in initialization. (We could also use a parameterized type to create a different type for each number of dimensions we need. Cf. Exercise 1.) The array of elements is basically unaffected — all the elements of the multidimensional array will be stored in one long sequence. Only the access operator will interpret this sequence as a nesting of arrays of progressively lower dimensionality. (This parallels the way that built-in arrays interpret sequences of bytes as arrays of indexable components.)

2.2.2 Lifetime Operations

Initialize/Finalize

The arguments to **Initialize** change in the transition from `array` to `multarray`. Also, **Initialize** and **Finalize** now have two other dynamically allocated arrays to manage. To allow an arbitrary number of dimensions, the constructor takes a sequence of integers alternately indicating lower and upper bounds. To avoid the intricacies of variable argument lists, which are handled by macros defined in `stdarg.h`, we'll take the crude approach of specifying five pairs of arguments, with all but the first pair defaulting to zero. That will allow users to specify an array with as many as five dimensions and arbitrary integers for the lower and upper bound of each dimension. (We'll require that the lower bound is not greater than the upper for each dimension.)

```
template <class elt> struct multarray
{
    // . . .
  public:
    // Initialize/Finalize
    multarray(int l1, int u1, int l2, int u2, int l3, int u3,
              int l4, int u4, int l5, int u5);
    ~multarray();
};
```

We would declare our calendar as

```
        multarray<entry*> calendar(1991,1999,1,12,1,31,8,17);
```

This isn't pretty, but it's good enough for present purposes.

Access/Modify

The **Access** operation must be similarly flexible. There is some awkwardness in formulating this, however. Ideally, we'd like to define operator[] like the constructor — with a sequence of up to five index values (or more generally, using variable argument lists). However, there's no way to change the number of arguments an operator function expects, and operator[] takes only one argument. Moreover, operator functions may not have optional arguments, which we need here to allow for different number of dimensions. Therefore, we'll have to use an ordinary function, which we'll call sub. The function will return a reference, so we can use it for both **Access** and **Modify**.

```
template <class elt> struct multarray
{
    // . . .
  private:
    void validate_index(int, int);

  public:
    // Access/Modify
    elt& sub(int i1, int i2 = 0, int i3 = 0, int i4 = 0, int i5 = 0);
};
```

The calendar entry for noon on July 4, 1996, would be accessed with the following expression:

```
            calendar.sub(1996, 7, 4, 12)
```

Assignment to that entry would use exactly the same expression. Since sub returns a reference, it can be used on the left side of an assignment operation:

```
            calendar.sub(1996, 7, 4, 12) = new entry("Holiday");
```

Offset Computation

The central feature of multidimensional arrays is the generalization of the offset calculation. The formula can be derived by inspecting Figure 2.3 on page 104, as follows. Indices into an n-dimensional array are sequences of n integers. It will be simpler to number each index value according to the dimension to which it corresponds. In other words, the first index will be i_n, and the last i_1. We can write an index sequence just as it would appear in a language that supported multidimensional arrays:

$$(i_n, i_n-1, i_n-2, \ldots , i_1)$$

Let $card_k$ be the number of components in arrays corresponding to index value i_k in an index sequence for the array ('card' for 'cardinality'). For $k \neq 1$, the components of the arrays corresponding to i_k are themselves arrays of dimension $k-1$. (The components of arrays corresponding to i_1 are arrays of dimension $1-1$, i.e., 0, i.e., *scalars* — individual values.)

The number of components in the arrays corresponding to index i_k is simply

$$card_k = upper_k - lower_k + 1$$

since there's one component for each value in the index range for the corresponding dimension. Let $size_k$ denote the total number of elements in the arrays corresponding to index i_k. The one-dimensional arrays corresponding to index i_1 have $card_1$ components, each an individual component, so

$$size_1 = card_1$$

The two-dimensional arrays corresponding to index i_2 have $card_2$ components, each an array of $card_1$ components, so the total number of components in each two-dimensional array is

$$size_2 = card_2 * card_1$$

Generalizing, the number of components in the entire n-dimensional array is

$$size_n = card_n * card_{n-1} * \ldots * card_2 * card_1$$

or more succinctly

$$size_n = \prod_{k=1}^{n} card_k$$

The components of arrays corresponding to index i_k have $size_{k-1}$ components. (Components of index i_1 therefore have $size_0$ components; since we know that these are scalars, we see that we can treat $size_0$ as 1.) The first component of any array is at offset 0 from its start, regardless of its dimensionality. The second component is at offset equal to the size of the components. The third component is at offset equal to twice the size of the components, and so on. For a moment, assume that the lower bounds of all dimensions is 0. The offset within the full n-dimensional array of the i_n^{th} array (which has dimension $n-1$) is $i_n * size_{n-1}$. Then, within that array of dimension $n-1$, the offset of the i_{n-1}^{th} array (which has dimension $n-2$) is $i_{n-1} * size_{n-2}$. Thus, offset of the i_{n-1}^{th} array (with dimension $n-2$) relative to the start of the entire n-dimensional array is

$$i_n * size_{n-1} + i_{n-1} * size_{n-2}$$

Continuing to the last dimension, we arrive at a formula for the offset of the i_1^{th} component (which is an elt — a single pointer) relative to the entire n-dimensional array:

$$i_n * size_{n-1} + i_{n-1} * size_{n-2} + \ldots + i_2 * size_1 + i_1 * 1$$

Finally, revising the formula to use the actual lower bounds of each dimension instead of 0 and expressing it more succinctly gives us

$$offset = \sum_{k=1}^{n} ((i_n - lower_n) \times size_{k-1})$$

Table 3 shows the values of the various quantities involved in the four-dimensional calendar.

unit	dimension	lower	upper	card$_k$	card$_k$ * elt. size	total cardinality
hour	1	8	17	10	10*1	10
day	2	1	31	31	31*10	310
month	3	1	12	12	12*310	3720
year	4	1991	1999	10	10*3720	37200

Table 3   Structure of a Four-Dimensional Appointment Calendar

Intricate calculations like these must be performed for every **Access/Modify** operation. Note, however, that the various $size_k$s never change after an array is created with a particular shape (number of dimensions and cardinality of each). It certainly seems reasonable, then, to store the $size_k$s in the multarray to facilitate both the expression of the offset value in code and its actual calculation. The declaration of `multarray` included a `size` member, an array of integers, for this purpose.

To simplify the initialization and offset calculation code, the arrays representing the lower bound, upper bound, and size of each dimension will have $n+1$ elements for an n-dimensional array. That way, `first[i]` will represent the lower bound of the i-dimensional arrays. This wastes `first[0]` and `first[1]`, but allows assigning 1 to `size[0]` to represent the size of scalars — the components the multarray holds. If we didn't do that, we'd have to handle the 1-dimensional arrays specially in the size and offset computations.

```
/* Initialize/Finalize */

static int check_dimensions(int l1, int u1, int l2, int u2, int l3, int u3,
                            int l4, int u4, int l5, int u5)
{
    int n = 1;
    assert(l1 <= u1);

    if (l2 == 0 && u2 == 0) return n;
    assert(l2 <= u2);
    n++;

    if (l3 == 0 && u3 == 0) return n;
    assert(l3 <= u3);
    n++;

    if (l4 == 0 && u4 == 0) return n;
    assert(l4 <= u4);
    n++;

    if (l5 == 0 && u5 == 0) return n;
    assert(l5 <= u5);
    n++;

    return n;
```

```
}

template <class elt>
multarray<elt>::multarray(int l1, int u1, int l2, int u2, int l3, int u3,
                          int l4, int u4, int l5, int u5) :
    ndimensions(check_dimensions(l1, u1, l2, u2, l3, u3, l4, u4, l5, u5)),
    sizes(new long[ndimensions+1]),
    first(new int[ndimensions+1]), last(new int[ndimensions+1])
/* Note: data members are initialized in the order in which they appear in
   the class declaration, not the order in which they appear in the member
   initialization list. Since ndimensions is first in the declaration, once
   it has been set the others can use its value.
*/
{
    // store bounds
    first[ndimensions] = l1;
    last[ndimensions]  = u1;
    if (ndimensions > 1)
        {
            first[ndimensions-1] = l2;
            last[ndimensions-1]  = u2;
        }
    if (ndimensions > 2)
        {
            first[ndimensions-2] = l3;
            last[ndimensions-2]  = u3;
        }
    if (ndimensions > 3)
        {
            first[ndimensions-3] = l4;
            last[ndimensions-3]  = u4;
        }
    if (ndimensions > 4)
        {
            first[ndimensions-4] = l5;
            last[ndimensions-4]  = u5;
        }

    //  compute size of multarray:
    sizes[0] = 1;                          // size of 0-dimensional multarray
    for (int i = 1; i <= ndimensions; i++)
        sizes[i] = (last[i] - first[i] + 1) * sizes[i-1];

    // allocate and zero storage for elts:
    elts = new elt[sizes[ndimensions]];
    for (i = 0; i < sizes[ndimensions]; i++) elts[i] = 0;
}

template <class elt> multarray<elt>::~multarray()
{
    delete [] elts;
    delete [] first;
    delete [] last;
}
```

```
/* Access/Modify */

template <class elt> void multarray<elt>::validate_index(int indx, int i)
{
    assert(indx >= first[i] && indx <= last[i]);
}

// Very crude code. Could be cleaned up by using varargs.
template <class elt>
elt& multarray<elt>::sub(int i1, int i2, int i3, int i4, int i5)
{
    int& n = ndimensions;                    // for convenience

    validate_index(i1, n);
    int offset = (i1 - first[n]) * sizes[n-1];

    if (n > 1)
        {
            validate_index(i2, n-1);
            offset += (i2 - first[n-1]) * sizes[n-2];
        }
    if (n > 2)
        {
            validate_index(i3, n-2);
            offset += (i3 - first[n-2]) * sizes[n-3];
        }
    if (n > 3)
        {
            validate_index(i4, n-3);
            offset += (i4 - first[n-3]) * sizes[n-4];
        }
    if (n > 4)
        {
            validate_index(i5, n-4);
            offset += (i5 - first[n-4]) * sizes[n-5];
        }

    return elts[offset];
}
```

2.2.3 Traversal Operations

The traversal operations for multarrays aren't much different from the ones for arrays. They still step through the components one at a time. The way the offset calculations are phrased leads to storing the elements with the last subscript varying most rapidly, which for most purposes is the natural ordering. For instance, in the calendar example, a straightforward traversal of elts would generate the array's elements in the following order.

```
1991   January     1   8am
1991   January     1   9am
         . . .
1991   January     1   5pm
1991   January     2   8am
1991   January     2   9am
         . . .
1991   January     2   5pm
         . . .
1991   January    31   5pm
1991   February    1   8am
         . . .
1991   December   31   5pm
1992   January     1   8am
         . . .
```

```
template <class elt> struct multarray
{
    // . . .
    // Traversal
  private:
    int cur;
  public:
    void reset();
    bool finished();
    bool next();
    elt& current();
    void index(int*);          // pointer to array of ndimensions ints
                               // to be filled with current index

};
```

```
/* Traversal */

template <class elt> void multarray<elt>::reset()
{
    cur = -1;
}

template <class elt> bool multarray<elt>::finished()
{
    return cur >= sizes[ndimensions];
}

template <class elt> bool multarray<elt>::next()
{
    ++cur;
    return !finished();
}

template <class elt> elt& multarray<elt>::current()
{
    if (no_pos == cur)
```

```
            error("[array::current] traversal not yet initialized");
        if ((first-1) == cur)
            error("traversal initialized but not yet stepped");
        if (finished())
            error("traversal already finished");

        return elts[cur];
}

template <class elt> void multarray<elt>::index(int* indx)
{
        for (int i = 0; i < ndimensions; i++)
            indx[i] = first[ndimensions-i] +
                        ((cur % sizes[ndimensions-i]) / sizes[ndimensions-i-1]);
}
```

A minimal example of traversal is counting the number of entries in the whole calendar. (Since we are assuming that our structs all hold only pointers, we can use the null pointer to indicate 'nothing here'. In the calendar example, a null pointer would indicate that there's no entry stored for the corresponding time.)

```
int number_of_appointments(multarray& cal)
{
        cal.reset();
        int count = 0;

        while (cal.next()) if (cal.current()) count++;

        return count;
}
```

2.2.4 Content Operations

A multarray module would provide all the operations an array module would. The array **Content** operations were the **Attributes** size, lower_bound, and upper_bound and the **Compare** operation equal. The definitions of these functions change only slightly for multarray: size returns the total number of components, and the two bounds functions take an additional argument to select a dimension. Multarrays have some additional operations, too: dimensions (an **Attribute**) and isomorphic ('same shape'), which is another form of **Compare**. **Equal** is defined to be same shape with corresponding components equal.

```
template <class elt> struct multarray
{
    // . . .
  public:
    // Attributes
```

```
    int size();
    int first_index(int dimension);
    int last_index(int dimension);
    int dimensions();

    // Combine not supported

    // Compare
    friend bool isomorphic(multarray<elt>&, multarray<elt>&);
    friend order compare(multarray<elt>&, multarray<elt>&);
    friend bool equal(multarray<elt>&, multarray<elt>&);
};
```

```
/* Attributes */

template <class elt> int multarray<elt>::size()
{
    return sizes[ndimensions];
}

template <class elt> int multarray<elt>::first_index(int dim)
{
    return first[dim];
}

template <class elt> int multarray<elt>::last_index(int dim)
{
    return last[dim];
}

template <class elt> int multarray<elt>::dimensions()
{
    return ndimensions;
}
```

```
/* Compare */

template <class elt>
bool isomorphic(multarray<elt>& a1, multarray<elt>& a2)
{
    if (&a1 == &a2) return TRUE;          // same!

    if (a1.ndimensions != a2.ndimensions) return FALSE;

    for (int i = 1; i <= a1.ndimensions; i++)
```

```
        if (a1.first[i] != a2.first[i] ||
            a1.last[i] != a2.last[i]) return FALSE;

    return TRUE;
}
```

```
template <class elt> order compare(multarray<elt>&, multarray<elt>&)
{
    warning("compare not implemented");
    return NO_ORDER;
}

template <class elt> bool equal(multarray<elt>& a1, multarray<elt>& a2)
{
    if (&a1 == &a2) return TRUE;                    // same arrays!

    assert(isomorphic(a1, a2));

    a1.reset();
    a2.reset();
    while (a1.next(), a2.next())
        if (!equal(*a1.current(), *a2.current()))
            return FALSE;

    return TRUE;
}
```

2.2.5 Support Operations

The **Copy** operations are more involved here than they are for regular arrays, but they have the same general shape. A reasonable **Output** operation would be to print all nonzero elements, one to a line, showing their indices. It would also be reasonable for the **Output** operator to just print a description of the array. (Cf. Exercise 5.) No **Combine** or **Process** operations other than **Output** are defined.

```
template <class elt> struct multarray
{
    // . . .
    // Copy
  private:
    void copy_elements(multarray<elt>&);
    void copy_dimensions(multarray<elt>&);
  public:
    multarray(multarray<elt>&);
    multarray<elt>& operator=(multarray<elt>&);
```

```
    // Output
    friend ostream& operator<<(ostream&, multarray<elt>&);
            // show all non-empty entries
};
```

```
/* Copy */

// private support function
template <class elt>
void multarray<elt>::copy_dimensions(multarray<elt>& old)
{
    ndimensions = old.ndimensions;
    memcpy(first, old.first, (ndimensions+1)*sizeof(first[0]));
    memcpy(last, old.last, (ndimensions+1)*sizeof(last[0]));
    memcpy(sizes, old.sizes, (ndimensions+1)*sizeof(sizes[0]));
}

// private support function
template <class elt>
void multarray<elt>::copy_elements(multarray<elt>& old)
{
    elts = new elt[sizes[old.ndimensions]];
    memcpy(elts, old.elts, old.size()*sizeof(elts[0]));
}

// Copy constructor
template <class elt> multarray<elt>::multarray(multarray<elt>& old) :
    sizes(new long[old.ndimensions+1]),
    first(new int[old.ndimensions+1]), last(new int[old.ndimensions+1])
{
    copy_dimensions(old);
    copy_elements(old);
}

// Copy assignment operator
template <class elt>
multarray<elt>& multarray<elt::operator=(multarray<elt>& old)
{
    if (this == &old) return *this;    // assignment to self!

    // free old elts and reallocate
    delete [] first;
    delete [] last;
    delete [] sizes;
    delete [] elts;
```

```
    copy_dimensions(old);
    copy_elements(old);

    return *this;
}
```

```
/* Output */

template <class elt> ostream& operator<<(ostream& strm, multarray<elt>& a)
{
    int indx[10];
    a.reset();

    while (a.next())
        if (a.current())
            {
                a.index(indx);
                strm << '\[' << indx[0];
                for (int i = 1; i < a.ndimensions; i++)
                                          strm << ',' << indx[i];
                strm << "] = " << *a.current() << '\n';
            }
    strm << "\n\n";

    return strm;
}
```

2.3 EXERCISES

1. Define a vector-of-double type parameterized on the number of dimensions.
   (a) Attributes should include length, the distance from the origin.
   (b) Include some useful **Combine** operations, such as **Add** and **Multiply**.
   (c) Define compare.

2. Section 2.2 mentions using a four-dimensional array for a decade-long appointment calendar, in which the component type is entry*.
   (a) Discuss some disadvantages of this approach, at various conceptual levels — for instance, efficiency of implementation (e.g., how many bytes are wasted by leaving 31 positions for every month), supported functionality (what might you want to store in a calendar for which there is no appropriate place in this implementation), and suitability of design for re-use in different contexts.
   (b) Is there a moral about modularization here?
   (c) How might you redesign this four-level calendar?
   (d) What are some advantages and disadvantages of your design compared to the way the example was done?

3. Write an appropriate output operator for multarrays. It should show the shape of the array as well as its contents.

4. In Section 2.2.3 the example was given of a function to count the number of nonempty entries in a a multarray. Isn't this an attribute operation? Why wasn't it described as such? Could it be? If so, what is it an attribute of?

5. Replace the **Output** operator of the multarray module with one that simply describes the array (number of dimensions and their ranges, etc.) without printing any of the elements.

SNET Yellow Pages
Connecticut's Book.

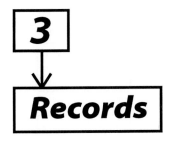

Records

Records, like arrays, are computational containers with slots for components. However, record slots are *named* rather than *numbered*. Slots of records are usually called *fields*. In C records are called *structs* and fields *members*.

Unlike arrays, records may (and normally do) contain mixed kinds of components. Each field is separately typed. Thus, a record is a *fixed-size sequence of directly accessible components of possibly mixed type*. One of the earliest descriptions of records provides a clear picture:

> Like the array, a record is intended to occupy a given number of locations in the store of a computer. It differs from the array in that the types of the fields are not required to be identical, so that in general each field of a record may occupy a different amount of storage. This, of course, makes it unattractive to select an element by means of a computed ordinal number; instead, each field position is given a unique invented name (identifier), which is written in the program whenever that field is referred to.
>
> A record may be used to represent inside the computer some discrete physical or conceptual object to be examined or manipulated by the program, for example, a person, a town, a geometric figure, a node of a a graph, etc. The fields of the record then represent properties of that object, for example, the name of a person, the distance of a town from some starting point, the length of a line, the time of joining a queue, etc. Normally, the name of the field suggests the property represented by the field.[1]

The seemingly slight difference between the homogeneity of arrays and the heterogeneity of records has substantial implications. Because all of an array's components are the same size, the location of a particular component can be computed at run time from its index. This allows code to include computed array references (i.e., indices that are variables or expressions). In contrast, record fields are accessed by fixed names specified in program code, which the compiler converts to *constant*, not computed, offsets. Figure 3.1 illustrates the storage layout of a record and the offsets of its fields. Note that the value of the birthdate field is itself a record.

---

[1] N. Wirth & C. A. R. Hoare, "A Contribution to the Development of ALGOL," *Communications of the ACM*, **9**:6 (June 1966), p. 416.

Field Name   Offset

```
struct date
{
   short day;
   short month;
   short year;
};

struct person
{
   char* name;
   date birthdate;
   int ss_number;
   double salary;
};
```

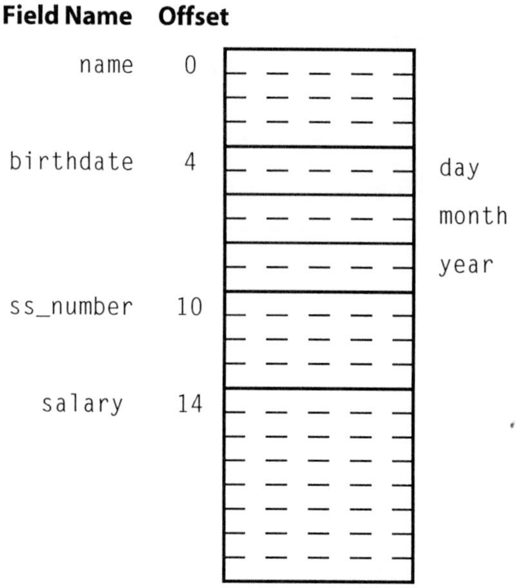

name   0

birthdate   4   day

                                           month

                                           year

ss_number   10

salary   14

Figure 3.1   A Record

3.1 Implementation

The amount of space allocated to a record is simply the sum of the space required by each field. The compiler keeps track of the location of each field in terms of an offset — a number of bytes — from the start of the record. An access expression of the form variable.-field is transformed by the compiler into an address computed as

> address-of(variable) + offset-of(field)

The offset is a constant value inserted into the generated machine instructions at compile time. There is no way in traditional algorithmic languages to designate a field with a variable or expression that changes value during execution.

There isn't really much to say about the implementation of traditional records, since they are entirely passive at run time. Because indices are not computed at run time, bugs like invalid array indices do not occur with records. The compiler handles all the details, and the record structures fade into the background. All the data structures shown in this book are implemented as records — this book is in some respects a study in the use of records — but the discussions are about the data structures, not the records. Records are profoundly important, yet entirely uninteresting!

There are no fundamental operations on records as such. Records are always interpreted as representing some other type. Any operations defined for a particular struct are for the type the struct represents, not the struct itself. With arrays, knowing only the size of the array you can **Access** and **Modify** an element or use **Traversal** operations to do something to every element. Nothing like that is possible with records. **Access** and **Modify** address the fields of a struct, but in terms of their meaning for the type they represent. There is no way to generically compute what the address of the next field is, and different fields may have different types, so there is no reasonable way to traverse the fields of a record. A function may indeed do something to each field, but that would have to be hard-wired as a series of statements each addressing one of the fields directly.

3.2 Variations

C allows two variations on the fundamental idea of records. These are used only in specialized situations. They are included not because they are important in actual programming, but because they can help to further illuminate the nature of records.

3.2.1 Bit Fields

Occasionally a struct may need to have many fields that hold only an amount of information smaller than a char, C's smallest data type. Common examples include a Boolean (1 bit), an octal digit (3 bits), or a hexadecimal digit (4 bits). Other situations include values of "flags," such as the mode of an open file or protection code of a file on disk. Such sub-char fields could easily be represented as chars, but if there are many such fields in a record and many instances of the record, a great deal of space may end up being wasted.

C solves this problem by allowing a field to designate the number of bits it should occupy. Fields that include the number of bits they require are called *bit fields* in C. What actually happens depends on the compiler. For instance, a compiler may "pack" eight consecutive 1-bit fields (Booleans, e.g.) into a single byte, but may also need a whole byte for a single 1-bit field sandwiched between two ints.

The syntax for designating the number of bits a field needs is to follow the name of the field with a colon and that number. For instance, a simplified version of information about a Unix file might be represented as

```
struct file_protection
{
    char* name;
    unsigned int is_directory : 1;
    unsigned int owner_protection : 3;
    unsigned int group_protection : 3;
    unsigned int other_protection : 3;
    unsigned long size;
};
```

The four bit fields together take up 10 bits and so can be packed into one short instead of taking up four separate shorts.

3.2.2 Unions

Called *record variants* in other languages, *unions* are a way to use one record type to store several different kinds of values. The traditional example here is a record representing an identifier in the parser of a compiler. A *token* in a program is what you think of as a single thing: a number (of various types), identifier, string, or operator. Suppose the compiler represents identifiers and strings as char*s, integers as ints, real numbers as doubles, and operators as values of an enum operator. To store tokens in an array you might define a record that had a field for each kind of token, as follows.

```
enum opsymbol { plus, minus, assign, equal, // ... and many others };

struct token
{
    char* str;
    char* id;
    int i;
    double r;
    opsymbol op;
};
```

Then, for each token, all fields except one would be ignored. For example, if the next token read were an integer, your program would store the integer in the integer field of a token. The contents of the other fields would be irrelevant. The program would still need a way to know which field to access for a particular instance of token. Therefore, another enum and field must be added to "tag" each token with the type it represents.

```
enum opsymbol { plus, minus, assign, equal, // ... and many others };
enum type {string, identifier, integer, real, operator};

struct token
{
    type typ;

    char* string;
    char* id;
    int integer;
    double real;
    operator op;
};
```

Now your program could have an array of tokens, yet store different kinds of tokens in it. Each would be identified by the value of its typ field, and one of its other fields would have a meaningful value. The rest would be ignored. Code manipulating tokens would test the typ field to know how to interpret them.

There's nothing wrong with this solution. However, it wastes space: each instance of token takes up enough space to store one of each kind, but it only represents one of them. A union is a struct in which only one of the fields is used at any time. The space a union takes up is the space required to store the largest field. The program must still determine which field to use for a given union instance, so almost always unions are fields of structs that also include a type field. The above example would be reformulated as follows.

```
enum opsymbol { plus, minus, assign, equal, // ... and many others };
enum type {string, identifier, integer, real, operator};

union token_value
{
    char* string;
    char* id;
    int integer;
    double real;
    operator op;
};

struct token
{
    type typ;

    token_value val;
};
```

Now a `token` occupies only enough space to store a `type` and the largest of `token_value`'s fields. In C++ (but not C), if the union is used in only one struct, there's no need to even give it a name. Instead, the struct can contain an *anonymous union* — simply a union without a name nested inside a struct.

```
enum opsymbol { plus, minus, assign, equal, // ... and many others };
enum type {string, identifier, integer, real, operator};

struct token
{
    type typ;

    union token_value
    {
        char* string;
        char* id;
        int integer;
        double real;
        operator op;
    } val;
};
```

The fields of an anonymous union are fields of the struct itself. With the named version, to get the integer stored in an instance of `token` called `curtoken` a programmer would write `curtoken.val.integer`. With the anonymous union, a programmer just writes `curtoken.integer`. Of course, only the module in which `token` was defined would have expressions like that. Other code would use functions such as `getInteger`, `setInteger`, `getIdentifier`, and so on, which that module would provide.

3.3 EXERCISES

1. Write a program that explores the way your C++ compiler lays out record fields.
    (a) The iostream facility includes the ability to print a `void*` pointer as a hexadecimal address. By taking the address of a struct instance's field and casting it to a (void*), you can print the location of that field of that instance.
    (b) Address of struct instances and their fields can also be cast to `longs` and subtracted to determine field offsets.
    (c) Define a set of several structs, including at least one that includes another. An example would be `Name`, `Address`, and `Person`, where `Person` includes a `Name` and an `Address` along with other information.
    (d) Define an output operation for each struct that prints out an instance's details. For example, `ostream& operator<<(ostream&, Name&)` would print the first name, middle initial, and last name stored in an instance of `Name`, separate by spaces.
    (e) Declare some instances of your structs and print their values using your output operations.
    (f) For each struct, define a function `describe` that takes an instance of that struct and prints out the type of struct it is, how many bytes it takes up, and the offset, hexadecimal address, and values of each of its fields.
    (g) Use your `describe` function to explore the way your compiler lays out storage structures.
    (h) If working on a PC, experiment with a storage model that uses 16-bit pointers and one that uses 32-bit pointers. If working on a Unix platform, notice whether there seem to be any alignment constraints (i.e., rules about what bytes records can start on — typically, multiples of 2 or 4).
    (i) (Optional.) Experiment further to determine how your compiler handles bit fields.
    (j) (Optional.) Experiment further to see how your compiler allocates fields of a union.
    (k) Summarize what you've learned about the way your compiler lays out records.
2. Write a program that uses a union to determine all the *symbols* in a file.
    (a) Use a very simple notion of *symbol*, as follows. A *number* begins with a digit or dash and ends at the first nondigit character. A *word* begins with a letter or an underscore and ends at the first character that is not a letter or an underscore. *Punctuation* is an individual non-white space character that cannot be part of a word or number.
    (b) In a union store numbers as `ints`, words as `char*s`, and a punctuation as an individual `char`.
    (c) Define an `enum symbol_type` and a struct `symbol` that stores a `symbol_type` and an instance of the union.
    (d) Store symbols in a single array, keeping track of the current number of symbols. Each time a symbol is extracted from the file, see if the symbol is already in the array and if not, add it. (You can just code this informally, but you might find it convenient to use the `Array` module of the previous chapter.) You'll need an **Equal** operation to compare two `symbols`.
    (e) (Optional.) Sort the array using any sorting method you know, or `qsort` from the C library. You'll need a **Compare** operation to compare two `symbols`.
    (f) Have the program print out all the symbols found.

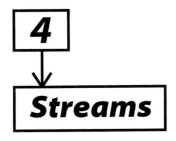

Streams

Streams are related to conventional files. For instance, the `FILE` structure of C implements a stream of characters, and C programs using the `stdio.h` facilities start with three instances of streams already initialized: `stdin`, `stdout`, and `stderr`. Pascal's `FILE` is a structuring mechanism like `ARRAY`, requiring the specification of a component type:

    VAR PERSONNEL FILE OF EMPLOYEE

Pascal's declaration for files reflects the generic `STRUCTURE OF TYPE` form, which, as pointed out on page 93, is inherent in any structure declaration. A C or Pascal `FILE` instance is a stream, but streams are not necessarily tied to files.

Arrays are sequences in space (memory), whereas streams are sequences in time. Only one element of a stream is available at a time: the current one. The basic form of **Access** is sequential: access the current component and get ready to access the next one. Stream access expressions do not specify an index or a field —since there is only one available component, it isn't explicitly named. Sequential access is a direct consequence of the temporal nature of streams — we can navigate in space, but in time there is only now.

The elements of a stream are produced as needed from a substrate that is either explicit or implicit. Ordinary files are explicit substrates from which streams can be generated — they are just arrays stored on disk instead of in RAM. Figure 4.1 illustrates the generation of a stream of characters from an underlying disk file, an array stored in external memory. The **Traversal** operations discussed throughout this book generate streams from collection structures. A traversal converts a spatially organized representation into a linear temporal one, with a collection structure the explicit substrate of the resulting stream.

Streams with implicit substrates are produced by a process that computes the next element when requested. An example is a stream derived from a function that generates a new random number each time it is called. Another example is the stream of characters typed on a keyboard — a keyboard with its supporting hardware and software is a transducer that converts a person's finger movements into a stream of characters!

A random number generator can produce numbers indefinitely. Similarly, there is no way to know in advance how many characters someone will type in response to a program's request — that is why we need special control characters to indicate the comple-

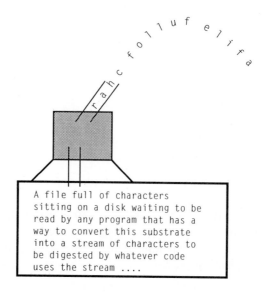

Figure 4.1 A Stream of Characters

tion of typed input. Although a file has a fixed size, that size is in general not the amount of space occupied by the number of components it contains, since for efficiency file space is allocated in units of blocks, each containing hundreds or even thousands of characters. Clearly, streams do not have a fixed size, though they do terminate. A stream, in sum, is an *indefinite-size sequence of sequentially accessible components of the same type*.

Streams are inherently directional: the components of a stream are *produced* by one process and *consumed* by another. A stream object either generates components or absorbs them; it cannot do both. (Files opened for both input and output are either a pair of streams or act more like a disk-based array with direct indexed access via repositioning operations.)

Programs perform operations on computational objects (values). How can a stream be represented in a program if it exists in time rather than space? The answer is subtle: objects represent the *ends* of the stream (producer or consumer), not the stream itself. This is illustrated in Figure 4.2.

Figure 4.2 A Stream Flows between Portals

The variables you use for input and output operations are such ends, not streams in themselves. For example, a C FILE is not itself a stream! Rather, it represents the state of a stream — the state of a traversal over an underlying file substrate. Such end objects are portals that anchor the temporal stream in computational space. (An appropriate mental picture might be a magic doorway in an adventure game or fantasy story: the doorway is real enough, but walking through it magically brings you to another time or place.)

4.1 The C++ Stream Library

C++ implementations provide an input/output stream facility in a library accessed through iostream.h. In-depth discussion of its capabilities and implementation is beyond the scope of this book, but a look at some of the highlights should help illuminate the nature of streams as well as show you some useful things you can do with the facility in C++.

We've already seen the basic use of operator<< with cout. The type of cout's value is ostream, for 'output stream'. Really, though, this value is a portal for a stream. The expression cout<<x produces the characters representing x, thereby generating more of the output stream.

Instances of ostream can be portals to either unbuffered or buffered streams. The iostream library includes implementations of buffering mechanisms. It also defines the global variables cin, cout, and cerr (unbuffered), analogous to the stdio variables stdin, stdout, and stderr. It also arranges for the creation of the corresponding buffers, which are instances of streambuf. One ostream constructor, for example, takes a streambuf* as its argument.

The value of cin is an instance of istream. The characters a user types to a program go into the streambuf associated with cin. An istream is a stream portal too. An expression like cin>>x consumes characters as the value of x is obtained.

4.1.1 Input/Output with Files and Arrays

In addition to streams for terminal interaction, the iostream library provides types to support file and memory-based (string) input and output: ifstream ('input file stream') and ofstream, istrstream ('input string stream') and ostrstream. You can easily define instances of these in your programs. The constructors for the file stream types take the name of a file, and the string stream constructors take a char array and a length. Input from or output to one of these streams is performed on the corresponding file or string, mediated by a buffer instance of an appropriate type.

In addition to constructors and the operators << or >>, stream types provide a range of other member functions. Just about all the facilities available through the traditional stdio of C are available, though often in a different form, from iostream. For instance, cin.eof() tests whether an end of file has been encountered during an input operation. As an example of file processing using C++ streams, here's code for a filter to read a file and output its words one to a line, with 'word' defined as a contiguous sequence of non-white space characters. (This code is inadequate as shown — it needs more tests to cover other problematic conditions, using features about to be described.)

```
ifstream ifil("words.txt");
ofstream ofil("words.lst");
char word[50];

while (!ifil.eof())
    {
        ifil >> word;                    // >> stops at white space
        ofil << word << '\n';
    }
```

String streams are used similarly. After outputting to an output file stream, the file substrate remains as a by-product. Likewise, after outputting to a string stream, a string remains as a by-product. That string may be accessed by invoking the `str` member function, after which no further output may be done to the stream. (Deletion of the `char*` returned by `str` is the responsibility of the programmer, even destroying the stream itself — when, for instance, it is the value of a local variable whose scope is exited — doesn't destroy that C string.)

4.1.2 Some Useful Features

In addition to operators `>>` and `<<`, input and output can be performed through a variety of member functions of the stream types. For single-character input/output, the following are available.

`put(char ch)` output `ch`

`get(char& ch)` input a single character to `ch`

`get()`   input a single character, returning integer; like `getc`, returns `-1` if end of file

`putback(char ch)` with `ch` the last character read, return it to the stream so it will be read next

`peek()`   return next character without reading

Then there are some useful functions for handling groups of characters.

`ignore(int limit=1, int delim=EOF)`
                 read and throw away at most `limit` characters, stopping when a `delim` is encountered

`getline(char* buf, int limit, char delim='\n')`
                 read at most `limit-1` characters into `buf` and add a terminating `NUL`, stopping when either end of file or a `delim` is encountered

The extraction operator (`>>`) for strings, like all extraction operators, stops at the first white space character. The only way to read past white space — in particular to read a line of words —is to use `getline`. Even extracting a char (e.g., `cin>>ch`) skips white space, so extraction cannot be used to skip one character if that character could be white space (as is typical when "gobbling" a character). Use `get` to read a single character, testing with `peek()` first if the skip depends on what's next.

The use of get becomes especially important when input is performed using a mixture of operator>> and getline, because operator>> stops before reading a newline character, but getline reads newline characters. If the last action performed before calling getline is an operator>> that reaches the end of a line, the getline will return an empty string, since it reads from the current stream position through the next newline! A get must be inserted between an operator>> that stops at a newline and the getline that follows it to have the getline read the next line.

Finally, there is a pair of functions for writing and reading the byte-level representation of any value:

```
write(char* addr, int size)      write size bytes from str to the stream
read(char* addr, int size)       read size bytes from the stream into str
```

Since any C value can be thought of as a sequence of bytes, and bytes are just chars, casting any pointer to a char* and outputting it with write will output the bytes that make up the value. Here's a small example.

```
// output an integer's bytes:
int n;
. . .
ostrm.write((char*)&n, sizeof(int));
```

This is only a taste of the range of facilities provided through iostream.h. As you find yourself needing more advanced features, you should consult the appropriate manual pages for the C++ system you are using.

4.2 General Streams

The C++ stream library is a rich facility, but it is limited to characters! Actually, it's rather more elaborate than a pure stream mechanism. A stream is a temporal sequence of components of the same type. Certainly C++ streams are ultimately sequences of characters; however, they provide rich facilities that convert between other types and their character representation. When it looks like we are adding an integer to cout, we are really asking the system to do two things for us: convert the integer to characters; then add the characters to the stream.

The fact that the conversion process is not necessarily an intimate part of the stream mechanism, but rather a secondary appendage, is demonstrated by the fact that we can add output operators to any structure we devise. These operators convert instances of our structures to characters, in part by using output operators for more primitive types as intermediaries. It happens that the implementation of C++ streams includes output operators for basic C++ types, but that is only a convenience. As character streams, all the stream structures really need are mechanisms for adding characters to an output stream and removing characters from an input stream.

The larger significance of streams is that they naturally capture fundamental patterns of processing. A wide variety of processes can be expressed in terms of streams. Especially important are processes that manipulate underlying substrates, which some pragmatic consideration limits to sequential, rather than direct, access. In traditional data processing, the largest class of such processes involves manipulations of large files on sequentially accessed files. In the old days, these files were typically stored on magnetic tape, which was inherently a sequentially accessed medium. However, even where the storage medium does not dictate a stream-based process, other considerations might. In particular, wherever separate processes cooperate to perform some task, from the viewpoint of any one process the external behavior of the others can be characterized in terms of stream-like input and output.

4.2.1 Simple Array-Based Streams

To explore further the fundamental nature of streams, we consider the implementation of a parameterized stream type that is unencumbered by extra facilities like character conversions. Like C++ string streams, this will use an array of elements as its underlying substrate. We'll actually need two types: one for producers and one for consumers. These both have fundamental operations like other data structures, but relatively few of them. After all, with access restricted to getting the next element, their basic behavior isn't going to be all that rich.

A Producer Stream

A stream is created on an array, which is provided as a constructor argument. **Access, Modify, Traversal**, and **Attribute** operations collapse into one integrated set of functions. This illuminates the close connection between streams and traversals. Most producer stream implementations provide a peek operation in addition to get; the latter removes the element from the stream while the former doesn't.

```
template <class elt> struct producer_stream
{
  private:

    // Representation
    elt *elts;                          // array of elements
    long asize;

  public:

    // Initialize/Finalize
    producer_stream(elt*, int);         // arg is C-array substrate
    ~producer_stream();

    // Access/Modify/Traversal/Attributes combined
  private:
    int cur;                            // traversal index
  public:
    void reset();
    elt &get();                         // current+next
    elt &peek();                        // current
    int index();
    bool empty();                       // empty-finished
```

```
    // Compare (from current positions)
    // Note: uses up stream elements during comparison
    friend order compare(producer_stream<elt>&, producer_stream<elt>&);
    friend bool equal(producer_stream<elt>&, producer_stream<elt>&);
};
```

In general, the traversal operations in this book's modules require a reset before they can be used. Here, reset plays the role clear does in other structures, and the constructor calls reset, so the stream can be used without calling it explicitly. The only time reset would be called by application code is to restart the stream from the beginning. Since using the stream doesn't affect the underlying array of elements, resetting involves just moving the current position back to the beginning.

Definitions of these functions are quite simple. **Initialize** stores the array and its size and sets the current position to 0. The functions for using the stream are basically traversal operations based on the current position. To allow for a stream that is shorter than the underlying array, a null pointer will be used to mark the end. A stream is empty either when the array runs out or a null pointer is encountered.

```
/* Initialize/Finalize */

template <class elt>
producer_stream<elt>::producer_stream(elt* substrate, int siz) :
        elts(substrate), asize(siz)
{
    reset();
}

template <class elt> producer_stream<elt>::~producer_stream()
{
}
```

```
/* Access/Traversal/Attributes combined */

template <class elt> void producer_stream<elt>::reset()
{
    cur = 0;
}

template <class elt> elt &producer_stream<elt>::get()
{
    return elts[cur++];
}

template <class elt> elt &producer_stream<elt>::peek()
{
    return elts[cur];
}
```

```
template <class elt> bool producer_stream<elt>::empty()
{
    return cur==asize || elts[cur] == 0;
}

template <class elt> int producer_stream<elt>::index()
{
    return cur;
}
```

The only intricate operations are those for **Compare**. What we mean by comparing two streams is that their elements are compared pairwise starting from their current positions. As the comparisons proceed, elements are removed from the stream. These are therefore invasive procedures, unlike most **Compare** operations.

```
/* Compare */

template <class elt>
order compare(producer_stream<elt>& strm1, producer_stream<elt>& strm2)
{
    order ord;

    while (!strm1.empty() && !strm2.empty())
        if (EQUAL != (ord = compare(*strm1.get(), *strm2.get())))
            return ord;

    if (strm1.empty())
        return BEFORE;
    else
        return AFTER;
}

// tests equality of elts, not just identity, so two different pointers
// could point to elts that test equal even though they are different.
template <class elt>
bool equal(producer_stream<elt>& strm1, producer_stream<elt>& strm2)
{
    while (!strm1.empty() && !strm2.empty())
        if (!equal(*strm1.get(), *strm2.get()))
            return FALSE;

    return TRUE;
}
```

A Consumer Stream

Consumer streams take elements and put them into their underlying array. Their basic operations mimic those of producer streams. As a result of the unidirectional nature of streams, any functions with a directional flavor are reversed, though: get becomes put, and empty becomes full. Since consumer streams modify their underlying array, they support **Combine** and **Copy** operations, though with a different flavor than in more typical structures. Streams are one-way, so the argument to consumer **Combine** and **Copy** operations are producer streams!

```
template <class elt> struct consumer_stream
{
  private:

    // Representation
    elt *elts;                        // array of elements
    long asize;

  public:

    // Initialize/Finalize
    consumer_stream(elt*, int);       // arg is C-array substrate
    ~consumer_stream();

    // Access/Modify/Traversal/Attributes combined
  private:
    int cur;                          // traversal index
  public:
    void reset();
    void put(elt&);                   // current+next
    int index();
    bool full();                      // full-finished

    // Combine (from current positions)
    // Args include an explicit destination to combine to.
    void concatenate(producer_stream<elt>&, producer_stream<elt>&);
    void merge(producer_stream<elt>&, producer_stream<elt>&);

    // Copy (from current position)
    // Note: uses up stream elements during comparison
    void copy(producer_stream<elt>&);
};
```

The basic operations have simple definitions like those for producer streams. The function terminate marks the end of the stream by storing a null pointer in the array.

```
/* Initialize/Finalize */

template <class elt>
consumer_stream<elt>::consumer_stream(elt* substrate, int siz)
        : cur(0), elts(substrate), asize(siz)
{
```

```
}

template <class elt> consumer_stream<elt>::~consumer_stream()
{
}
```

```
/* Access/Traversal/Attributes combined */

template <class elt> void consumer_stream<elt>::reset()
{
    cur = 0;
}

template <class elt> void consumer_stream<elt>::put(elt &e)
{
    elts[cur++] = e;
}

template <class elt> bool consumer_stream<elt>::full()
{
    return cur==asize;
}

template <class elt> void consumer_stream<elt>::terminate()
{
    elts[cur] = 0;
    asize=cur;
}

template <class elt> int consumer_stream<elt>::index()
{
    return cur;
}
```

The **Combine** and **Copy** operations have straightforward definitions, except for the twist that there are two kinds of streams involved. Two streams are concatenated simply by copying all the (remaining) elements from one to the consumer, then copying all the (remaining) elements from the other. Merging works similarly, but the elements are taken alternately from the two streams. Copying is performed by taking one element at a time from the producer stream and adding it to the consumer, checking at each step that the consumer isn't full.

```
/* Combine */

template <class elt>
void consumer_stream<elt>::concatenate(producer_stream<elt>& strm1,
                                       producer_stream<elt>& strm2)
{
    copy(strm1);
```

```
    copy(strm2);
}

template <class elt>
void consumer_stream<elt>::merge(producer_stream<elt>& strm1,
                                 producer_stream<elt>& strm2)
{
    while (!strm1.empty() && !strm2.empty())
        if (full())
            error("[consumer_stream::concatenate] consumer full");
        else
            {
                put(strm1.get());
                put(strm2.get());
            }

    // one of the streams is empty, possibly both;
    // copy the remaining elements of the other to the consumer.
    if (!strm1.empty())
        copy(strm1);
    if (!strm2.empty())
        copy(strm2);
}
```

```
/* Copy */

template <class elt>
void consumer_stream<elt>::copy(producer_stream<elt>& strm)
{
    while (!strm.empty())
        if (full())
            error("[consumer_stream::concatenate] consumer full");
        else
            put(strm.get());
}
```

4.2.2 Stream-Based Sorting

Sorting is an important part of many traditional business applications that manipulate large amounts of data stored on magnetic tape and other stream-based processes. Most sorting methods require the ability to access arbitrary elements from within a collection structure. Streams don't support that, so special sorting methods are required. The standard approach to sorting streams is based on successive passes of merging and splitting.

The basic process works as follows. For convenience, we'll use the previously described array-based streams, even though arrays certainly support direct access and so can be sorted by many other methods. A very short sequence of integers will be used to illustrate the process. First, a producer stream is split into two consumer streams by taking elements from producer stream and adding them alternately to the two consumer streams.

```
original:                            5 8 3 6 7 2 4 1

split:                               5 3 7 4
                                     8 6 2 1
```

Next, the direction of the process is reversed. A new consumer stream is created on the original array, which can be reused, since its elements are safely stored in the split arrays. Two producer streams are created for the arrays underlying the two consumer streams that received the elements distributed in the first step.

The new producer streams are merged in a special way, as follows. Their first elements are compared (accessed by peek). The lesser of the two is added to the consumer stream followed by the other. This pairwise comparison and moving from the producer streams to the consumer stream continues until the producers are exhausted. (In all processes like this, if one stream is exhausted before the other, the rest of the other is simply copied to the consumer.) The way the elements were added to the consumer stream guarantees that every two elements in the original array are now in order relative to each other:

```
merge:                               5 3 7 4
                                     8 6 2 1

    original:                            5 8

merge:                               3 7 4
                                     6 2 1

    original:                            5 8    3 6

merge:                               7 4
                                     2 1

    original:                            5 8    3 6    2 7

merge:                               4
                                     1

    original:                            5 8    3 6    2 7    1 4
```

The array is split again, but this time two elements at a time are moved over to a consumer stream. Because elements are known to be ordered pairwise, the first two elements of each stream will end up in proper order relative to each other in the consumer stream whether they are moved together or end up separated by elements from the other producer:

```
original:                            5 8    3 6    2 7    1 4

split:                               5 8    2 7
                                     3 6    1 4
```

Then, as before, the two split arrays are merged. However, this time, after the first elements are compared and one is moved to the consumer, the other is not immediately moved. Instead, it is compared to the next element in the stream from which an element was removed. However, once both elements of a pair are removed from one producer stream, any remaining elements of the pair in the other producer stream must be moved over to the consumer stream:

```
split:                              5 8   2 7
                                    3 6   1 4

    original:                             3

split:                              5 8   2 7
                                    6     1 4

    original:                             3 5

split:                              8     2 7
                                          1 4

    original:                             3 5 6

// Nothing left in the second stream's pair, so
// the rest of the first stream's pair is copied over.

split:                              2 7
                                    1 4

    original:                             3 5 6 8

// The first pairs have now been merged

split:                              2 7
                                    4

    original:                             3 5 6 8   1

split:                              7
                                    4

    original:                             3 5 6 8   1 2

split:                              7

    original:                             3 5 6 8   1 2 4

split:

    original:                             3 5 6 8   1 2 4 7
```

As you can see, the result of merging the two streams two elements at a time is that we now have runs of four elements that are correctly ordered relative to one another. The array is split again, this time by moving four elements at a time from the producer stream to one of the consumer streams. Then the two split arrays are merged again, this time comparing runs of four elements to one another. At this point, the size of the run of elements guaranteed to be in order has reached the size of the sequence of elements being sorted, so the process stops.

Here is code implementing stream-based merge sorting. To simplify things, the maximum number of elements to be sorted is defined as a constant.

```
const int asize = 8;

template <class elt>
void split(producer_stream<elt>& src, consumer_stream<elt>& dest1,
           consumer_stream<elt>& dest2, int runsize)
{
    src.reset();
    dest1.reset();
    dest2.reset();

    while (!src.empty())
        {
            // move one run of elements from src to dest1
            int i = runsize;
            while (--i >= 0 && !src.empty())
                dest1.put(src.get());

            // repeat for dest2
            i = runsize;
            while (--i >= 0 && !src.empty())
                dest2.put(src.get());
        }

    dest1.terminate();
    dest2.terminate();
}

template <class elt>
void merge(consumer_stream<elt>& dest, producer_stream<elt>& src1,
           producer_stream<elt>& src2, int runsize)
{
    int run1, run2;

    while(!src1.empty() && !src2.empty())
        {
            run1 = run2 = 0;
            while(!src1.empty() && !src2.empty() &&
                 (run1 < runsize || run2 < runsize))
                {
                    if (run1 < runsize &&
                        (run2 >= runsize ||
                         BEFORE == compare(*src1.peek(), *src2.peek())))
                        {
                            dest.put(src1.get());
                            run1++;
                        }
                    else
                        {
```

```
                                    dest.put(src2.get());
                                    run2++;
                                }
                        }
                }

        if (!src1.empty()) dest.copy(src1);
        if (!src2.empty()) dest.copy(src2);
}

template <class elt> void merge_sort1(elt a[], int runsize)
{
        elt tmp1[asize], tmp2[asize];

        // prepare streams for split phase
        producer_stream<elt> orig(a, asize);
        consumer_stream<elt> splt1(tmp1, asize);
        consumer_stream<elt> splt2(tmp2, asize);

        split(orig, splt1, splt2, runsize);

        // reverse direction; prepare streams for merge phase
        consumer_stream<elt> mrg(a, asize);
        producer_stream<elt> mrg1(tmp1, asize);
        producer_stream<elt> mrg2(tmp2, asize);

        // merge two split halves back
        merge(mrg, mrg1, mrg2, runsize);
        show(a);
}

template <class elt> void merge_sort(elt a[])
{
        int runsize = 1;
        while (runsize < asize)
            {
                merge_sort1(a, runsize);
                runsize *= 2;
            }
}
```

4.3 Pipes and Filters

An important way of organizing computational activity is as a chain of producer-consumer processes. Each process consumes the output of its predecessor and produces the input of its successor. A compiler might be organized as shown in Figure 4.3. In that diagram, the arrows represent the streams, the rectangles processes, and the ellipses files (source and sink of the process as a whole).

The lexical analyzer consumes characters generated from the text file and groups them into symbols (words). As each symbol is extracted from the stream of characters, it

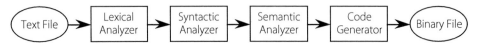

Figure 4.3   A Compiler Organized as a Producer-Consumer Chain

is generated to be consumed by the syntactic analyzer. The syntactic analyzer groups symbols into grammatical structures. This continues down the chain, each process accumulating objects generated by the previous one, analyzing the sequence of objects, and generating a new stream of objects.

A process that consumes one stream and produces another is often called a *filter*. The data pathway connecting the two processes is often called a *pipe*. Typically, the type of component produced by a filter is the same as consumed. The filter may just select a subset of components it allows to pass through (e.g., a program that removes nonprinting characters), or it may generate a different set of components based on the input (e.g., a program that replaces tabs with an appropriate number of spaces). More generally, though, a filter may consume one kind of component and generate another, as illustrated by the processes in the compiler example.

A *buffered stream* temporarily stores components in memory. Buffers are a common and important device for isolating the producer from the consumer and smoothing out uneven rates of stream traversal among interconnected processes. Within the limits of a buffer's size, the producer can go on producing stream components regardless of the rate at which the consumer consumes them. In contrast, an unbuffered stream — a random number generator, for example — generates each component immediately upon demand.

An important use of buffers is to improve the efficiency of transferring information from one computational device to another. Common examples are input/output to a peripheral device (disk, screen, etc.) and packet-based network transmission. In such situations, there is fixed overhead for each transmission — time to position the disk read head, time to handle a network packet (construct, route, receive, decipher, etc.), and so on. Individual components are accumulated in a buffer. When the buffer is full, its contents are sent in a single transmission. By transmitting components together (characters, in particular), the fixed overhead is amortized over all the components, reducing the cost for each one.

In essence, a pipe is a buffer shared by a producer stream and a consumer stream. The producer stream fills the buffer, and the consumer stream empties it. The buffering mechanism must control these two processes so that the producer doesn't try to add to a full stream and the consumer doesn't try to take from an empty one. Furthermore, the activity of the two processes must be coordinated. When the consumer stops because the buffer is empty, the producer must be reactivated so it can refill it. Note that the type of component produced into the buffer is necessarily the same as that consumed from it.

A variety of sophisticated strategies may be used to coordinate processes connected to a pipe. Here, though, we are concerned with the nature of streams and pipes, not issues in multiprocess coordination. Therefore, we'll look at an implementation that is about as simple as possible. A buffer will hold a fixed number of elements. A producer attached to it generates elements until the buffer is full or the producer terminates. When the buffer is full, control is passed to the consumer, which consumes elements until the buffer is empty. Control is then passed back to the producer, unless the producer has terminated, in which case the consumer stream terminates too.

4.4 EXERCISES

1. Why isn't their some kind of storage structure for which the values in the summary table on page 91 would both be "no" (i.e., an indefinite-size sequence of sequentially accessible components, not necessarily of the same type)?

2. Show the split and merge stages for sorting the names of the months according to their lexical order.

3. The basic merge sort process is inefficient because runs of elements are stopped at predetermined points. Suppose the first element of the next run is greater than the last element of the current run. Then there's no reason to stop the run — it can continue on as long as the next element is greater than the one that was just removed. This variation is known as *natural merging*.
   (a) Modify the code shown for merge sorting so that it keeps track of the number of comparisons performed and the number of passes needed to sort the array.
   (b) Gather some statistics for merge sort's performance on arrays of various sizes.
   (c) Modify the code to implement natural merging.
   (d) Gather statistics for the new implementation's performance on the same arrays you used for the original and compare the relative performance of the two versions.

4. Write a program to shuffle a deck of cards.
   (a) Define enumerations for suits and face values. A *deck* will be just an 52-element array of pointers to cards, not a separate type. That will allow it to be the substrate for producer and consumer streams as shown in this chapter.
   (b) Write a function cut that splits a deck into two equal halves. This will be essentially the inverse of consumer_stream::concatenate, as follows. A source deck and two empty destination decks are provided as arguments. Cards get removed from the source deck and added alternately to each of the destination decks, until the source is empty.
   (c) Write a shuffle function that cuts a deck into two, then distributes cards from the two decks (selecting a Deck at random) into another, initially empty, deck. This is basically just consumer_stream::concatenate with the elements taken randomly rather than alternately from each of the two source decks.
   (d) The shuffle function is meant to be an approximation of what people do rather than an efficient algorithm. The suggested implementation of cut is not really a good approximation of how people cut decks. Why couldn't we have it just split the deck (approximately) in half, as people do?

5. Design, implement (without using iostream facilities), and test input and output stream types that read from and write to character arrays, as do istrstream and ostrstream from the iostream library. The types should be parameterized.
   (a) In any program you've written using the C++ iostream facility, replace that file-based stream structure with your array-based one.
   (b) What aspects of your program design supported or obstructed this change to your program?

6. Using write and read implement a facility that writes and reads the memory-level representation of some simple struct to and from a disk file.

(a) Discuss adding this pair to the set of fundamental operations to be implemented by all types, like operator<< and operator>>.
(b) What major problems does this simple approach run into?
(c) Discuss a scheme to solve the problems.

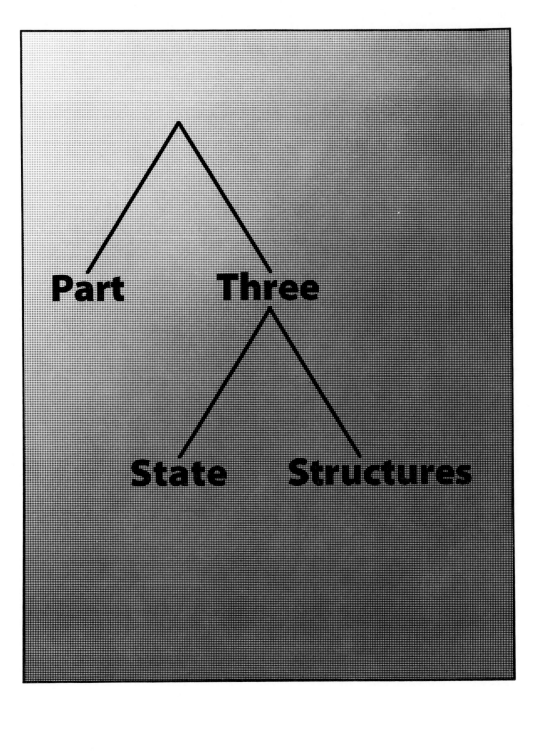

Part Three

State Structures

Part Three:

State Structures

The next group of structures we consider are those that support processes by keeping track of their *state*. There are three kinds of *state structures*: *stacks*, *queues*, and *priority queues*. Each maintains a set of *tasks*, accepting new ones and supplying the "next" one on request. The different state structures differ primarily in the meaning they give to 'next', as shown in Table 4. The different meanings of next give rise to different processing patterns.

	Next Task
Stack	newest
Queue	oldest
Priority Queue	best

Table 4   Kinds of State Structures

Simple implementations of state structures use C arrays. More sophisticated implementations could be built on top of an array type such as was shown in Chapter 2. Still more sophisticated implementations would use one of the list structures discussed later, in Chapter 8. This chapter will show only the simplest array-based representations. Variations using other structures are straightforward — what's interesting about state structures is mostly their operations and the way they are used, not their representation. (Exercises in Chapter 8 explore more sophisticated implementations.)

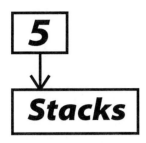

5
Stacks

The most widely used state structure is the *stack*, which supports *last-in first-out* (LIFO) processing. Under a LIFO "discipline" the next task to be invoked is the one most recently added. Stacks are used for tasks that must be suspended then later resumed. Since subroutine call and return follows a suspend-and-resume regime, the run-time environments of programming language implementations use stacks to control program execution.

5.1 LIFO Processing

Suppose you were writing a paper on supernatural beings. You are reading page 437 of a book entitled *Goblins, Ghosts, and Gremlins*. A paragraph on that page discusses the fact that ghosts frequently appear as characters in older fiction and refers you to a book called *Ghosts in Fiction*. Interested, you put down the first book and begin skimming the second. While reading a chapter on ghosts in plays, you come across a mention on page 233 that Shakespeare happens to have included supernatural beings in several of his plays. A footnote on that page refers you to *The Supernatural in Shakespeare's Plays*. You get a copy of that book and read some of its material. On page 389 the author refers to a scene in *Hamlet*, so you pick up a copy of that play to read the scene.

Having finished that scene, you return to *The Supernatural in Shakespeare's Plays* and finish the chapter. Now you can put that away and go back to *Ghosts in Fiction*. Once you are done with that book, you can return to your work on the book you first picked up — *Goblins, Ghosts, and Gremlins*.

While reading one book, you don't want to be distracted by having to remember where you were in each of the other books. Besides, interruptions may force you to put your work aside temporarily. You would therefore need a way to recall your place in each book when you later returned to your work. Your memory might suffice for one or two books, over a period of a few hours, but it would be difficult to remember much more than that.

What might you do to keep track of where you are in each book? One simple scheme would be to reserve part of your desktop for a pile of books. Every time you put aside a book that you want to return to you insert a marker (such as an index card) at the page you were reading and put the book on top of the pile.

When you finish a book you can put it back on the shelf. What would you do next? You would simply pick up the top book of the pile, open to the page where the marker was, and resume reading. (We are omitting the detail of remembering and returning to the correct line of the page, but you could write that on the index card.) That book will be the one that had most recently been interrupted, because each time you add a book to the pile you place it on top of the books added earlier.

Figure 5.1 illustrates a sequence of states of your reading process, with somewhat extended from the example above. Each state is recorded as a set of tasks. Each task records a book and a page number. Stacks are computational structures that manage LIFO processes like the one illustrated.

5.2 Implementation

The basic work of a stack is to *push* (**Add**) new components and *pop* (**Remove**) existing ones. A stack module could have just about the most minimal public interface possible: a constructor, a destructor, push, and pop. The implementation shown here will also include definitions for other operations that are sometimes convenient to have, but push and pop are the essence of a stack's behavior.

5.2.1 Representation

Stacks are commonly represented as an array of elements plus a *stack pointer* — the index within the array of the top of the stack. Real-world stacks grow upward — in the reading example above, the stack of books grows higher with every diversion. However, arrays are always pictured with higher array indices below than lower ones, and it's most natural to start the stack pointer at the first index and increment it as new elements are added. This means that stack structures typically grow downward, rather than upward.

We could define a stack with a fixed limit to the number of components it can hold. We could also define a template that has the limit as a parameter. The stack shown here uses a third approach: the limit will be a constructor argument. In this approach the same stack type can be used for stacks of different sizes. Client code specifies the limit (or accepts the default) when it creates a stack. The stack structure records the limit as well as the current position, and (pointers to) components are stored in an array dynamically allocated by the stack constructor.

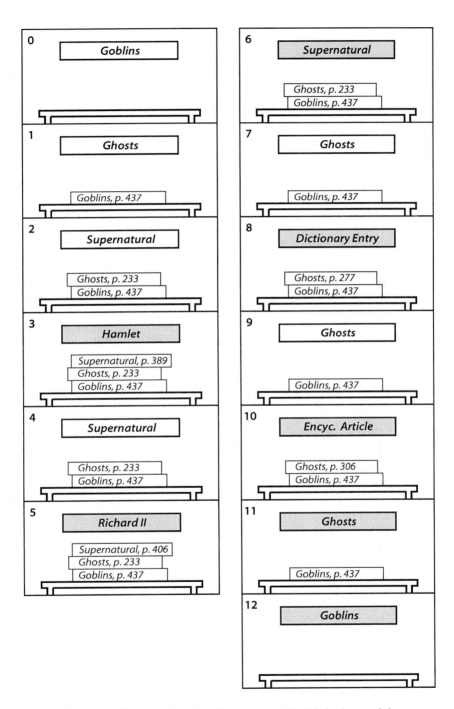

The title in the large box above the table contains the title of the book currently being read. Shaded boxes show books read to completion.

Figure 5.1   Suspending and Resuming Tasks

```
template <class elt> struct stack
{
  private:
    // Representation
    elt *elts;                          // array of pointers
    int top;                            // index of top itm
    int maxelts;                        // limit on number of elts
    // . . .
};
```

5.2.2 Lifetime Operations

Add and **Remove** are implemented as push and pop. Also, for convenience, operator+=
is defined as a synonym for push. It's sometimes convenient to be able to access the top
element without popping it, so we include topelt. Finally, so that an application can reuse a stack without having to explicitly pop remaining items, we add a clear function.

```
template <class elt> struct stack
{
  public:

    // Initialize/Finalize
    stack(int size = 100);
    ~stack();

    // Access/Modify
    void push(elt);
    stack<elt>& operator+=(elt);
    elt pop();

    elt topelt();
    void clear();
    // . . .
};
```

The constructor sets top to -1 and creates an array of elements (pointers). (It is
more common to initialize top to 0, but then 'top' would really mean 'one past the top element'; the more natural interpretation is adopted here.) Since the user specifies the stack
size limit, that must be recorded in the structure too. The destructor frees the array of
elements. Push adds an item to the stack, incrementing top; pop returns the top item,
decrementing top. The definitions of the other operations follow from these. Figure 5.2
illustrates the behavior of a stack.

Implementation details of the lifetime operations follow directly from the illustration in Figure 5.2. (The **Attributes** full and empty used in some of these definition are
discussed a little later.)

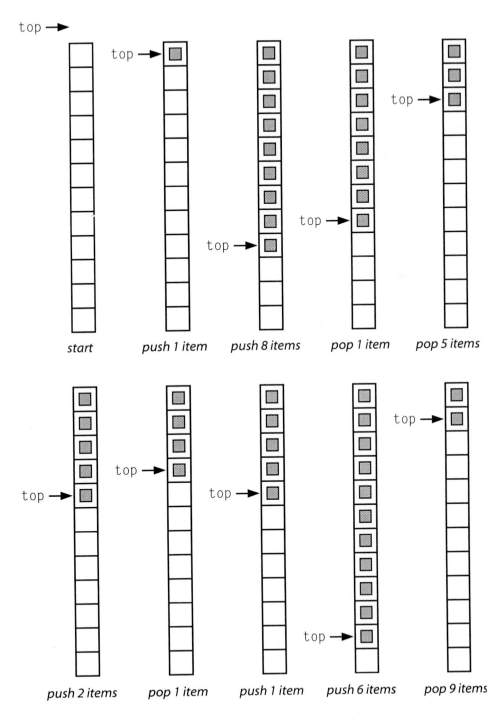

Figure 5.2   Stack Pushing and Popping

```
/* Initialize/Finalize */

template <class elt> stack<elt>::stack(int size) :
    top(-1), elts(new elt[size]), maxelts(size-1)
{
}

template <class elt> stack<elt>::~stack()
{
    delete [] elts;
}
```

```
/* Access/Modify */

template <class elt> void stack<elt>::push(elt itm)
{
    if (full())
        error("stack overflow");
    else
        elts[++top] = itm;
}

// synonynm for push
template <class elt> stack<elt>& stack<elt>::operator+=(elt itm)
{
    push(itm);
    return *this;
}

template <class elt> elt stack<elt>::pop()
{
    if (empty())
        error("stack underflow");

    return elts[top--];
}

template <class elt> elt stack<elt>::topelt()
{
    if (empty())
        error("stack empty");

    return elts[top];
}

template <class elt> void stack<elt>::clear()
{
    top = -1;                               // no need to modify elts
}
```

5.2.3 Traversal Operations

Strictly speaking, stacks allow access only to their top element. Client code would not normally traverse a stack directly. We still need traversal functions to support other operations, such as **Output**, so they are included in the module. If we wanted to absolutely prohibit client code from using them, we could make them private.

The natural traversal order for a stack is top-down. That happens to be the opposite of the natural traversal order for the underlying array. Differences like this are why it is so important to define operations for each structure even though it would seem to be just as easy to manipulate the underlying representation directly.

```
template <class elt> struct stack
{
    // . . .
    // Traversal
  private:
    int cur;                            // traversal index
  public:
    void reset();                       // Traversal order is top to bottom
    bool finished();
    bool next();
    elt& current();
    int index();
};
```

```
/* Traversal */

template <class elt> void stack<elt>::reset()
{
    cur = top+1;
}

template <class elt> bool stack<elt>::finished()
{
    return cur < 0;
}

template <class elt> bool stack<elt>::next()
{
    --cur;
    return !finished();
}

template <class elt> elt& stack<elt>::current()
{
    return elts[cur];
}
```

```
template <class elt> int stack<elt>::index()
{
    return (top - cur) + 1;
}
```

5.2.4 Content Operations

Stacks are not normally compared or combined. The only content operations we'll have are **Attributes**. Stacks grow and shrink as they are used. When a program goes to pop the next task description from a stack, the stack may be empty, in which case there are no more tasks to perform. In this implementation, there's a limit to how big each stack can get, so an attempt to push a new task description may fail. Both `push` and `pop` check for these conditions, but module users may also want to avoid provoking exceptions. The attributes `empty` and `full` are therefore provided as part of the public interface. Occasionally it's useful to know how many elements a stack contains, so we provide the attribute `size`, as usual.

```
template <class elt> struct stack
{
    // . . .
public:
    // Attributes
    bool empty();
    bool full();
    int size();

    // Compare
    friend order compare(stack<elt>&, stack<elt>&); // not implemented
    friend bool equal(stack<elt>&, stack<elt>&);
        // same elts in same order? (elt identity, not equality)
};
```

```
/* Attributes */

template <class elt> bool stack<elt>::empty()
{
    return top < 0;
}

template <class elt> bool stack<elt>::full()
{
    return top == maxelts;
}
```

```
template <class elt> int stack<elt>::size()
{
    return top + 1;
}
```

```
/* Compare */

template <class elt> order compare(stack<elt>&, stack<elt>&)
{
    notimp("compare(stack<elt>& stk1, stack<elt>& stk2)");
    return NO_ORDER;
}


template <class elt> bool equal(stack<elt>& stk1, stack<elt>& stk2)
{
    if (stk1.size() != stk2.size()) return FALSE;    // preliminary check
    stk1.reset();
    stk2.reset();

    while(stk1.next() && stk2.next())
        if (stk1.current() != stk2.current()) return FALSE;
    // NOTE: if stk1 runs out, stk2 has not yet been incremented

    if (!stk1.finished()) return FALSE;
    if (stk2.next()) return FALSE;        // stk1 is finished; step stk2
    return TRUE;
}
```

5.2.5 Support Operations

Copy operations take their usual form. It might be necessary to test whether a particular item is on a stack, so we'll provide contains (in two versions, one for identity and one for equality). **Output** is useful for debugging and sometimes to show an application's user the state of the stack, so the module will define the output operator.

```
template <class elt> struct stack
{
    // . . .
    // Copy
  private:
    void copy_elts(stack<elt>&);
  public:
    stack::stack(stack<elt>&);
    stack& operator=(stack<elt>&);

    // Process
```

```
    bool contains(elt);
    bool contains_equal(elt);

    // Output
    friend ostream& operator<<(ostream&, stack<elt>&);
};
```

/* Copy */

```
//private:
template <class elt> void stack<elt>::copy_elts(stack<elt>& stk)
{
    memcpy(elts, stk.elts, maxelts*sizeof(elt));
}

template <class elt> stack<elt>::stack(stack<elt>& stk) :
    top(stk.top), elts(new elt[stk.maxelts+1]), maxelts(stk.maxelts)
{
    copy_elts(stk);
}

template <class elt> stack<elt>& stack<elt>::operator=(stack<elt>& stk)
{
    if (this == &stk) return *this;        // copy to self!
    delete elts;

    top = stk.top;
    maxelts = stk.maxelts;
    elts = new elt[stk.maxelts+1];

    copy_elts(stk);
    return *this;
}
```

/* Process */

```
template <class elt> bool stack<elt>::contains(elt itm)
{
    reset();
    while (next()) if (itm == current()) return TRUE;        // identity

    return FALSE;
}

template <class elt> bool stack<elt>::contains_equal(elt itm)
{
```

```
        reset();
        while (next()) if (equal(*itm, *current())) return TRUE;      // equality

        return FALSE;
}
```

```
/* Output */

template <class elt> ostream& operator<<(ostream& strm, stack<elt>& stk)
{
    stk.reset();
    while (stk.next()) strm << '\t' << *stk.current() << '\n';

    return strm;
}
```

5.3 An Example

Here's a simple example showing how the stack module can be used. It reproduces the sequence of readings shown in Figure 5.1 on page 149. This program defines a type place that describes a suspended task— a book title and page number. The type chunk is used just to manage the simulation.

```
// stkdemo.C, corresponding to reading sequence of Figure 5.1 on page 149

#include <stringt.H>
#include <fstream.h>
ofstream ofil("stacktst.out");            // file output

struct place
{
    char* book;
    int page;
    friend bool equal(const place&, const place&);
    friend ostream& operator<<(ostream&, const place&);
};

ostream& operator<<(ostream& strm, const place& itm)
{
    return strm << '"' << itm.book << '"' << ", page " << itm.page;
}

bool equal(const place& itm1, const place& itm2)
{
    return ((itm1.page == itm2.page) && (!strcmp(itm1.book, itm2.book)));
}

struct chunk
```

```
{
    int page;
    place next;
};

chunk chunks[] =
    {
        {437, {"Ghosts in Fiction", 1}},
        {233, {"The Supernatural in Shakespeare's Plays", 320}},
        {389, {"Hamlet", 1}},
        {-1},
        {406, {"Richard II", 1}},
        {-1},
        {-1},
        {277, {"Dictionary Entry", 522}},
        {-1},
        {306, {"Encyclopedia Article", 979}},
        {-1},
        {-1},
        {-1}
    };

int chunkptr = 0;

/*  start reading r->bk at r->pg and keep reading until a reference that
    will be followed is encountered.  Replace r->pg with current page.
    Return 0 if book has been finished, otherwise pointer to a new
    reference.  The array chunks is used to simulate the sequence of
    references encountered.
*/
place* read(place* r)
{
    static int depth = 0;    // keep track of nesting for indentation
    chunk &chnk = chunks[chunkptr++];
    // make chnk an alias for current chunk for convenience

    spaces(2*depth, ofil);
    ofil << "Reading '" << r->book << "' at page " << r->page << "....\n";
    if (chnk.page == -1)
        {
            spaces(2*depth--, ofil);
            ofil << "Finished reading '" << r->book << "'.\n";
            return 0;
        }
    else
        {
            r->page = chnk.page;
            spaces(2*depth++, ofil);
            ofil << "Putting aside '" << r->book
                 << "' at page " << r->page << ".\n";
        return &chnk.next;
        }
}

place first = {"Goblins, Ghosts, and Gremlins", 1};
```

```
main()
{
    place *cur = &first;
    place *next;
    stack<place*> stk(10);

    while (cur)
    {
        next = read(cur);
        if (!next)
            if (!stk.empty())
                cur = stk.pop();
            else
                cur = 0;
        else
            {
                stk.push(cur);
                cur = next;
            }
    }
    return 0;
}
```

This example program produces the following output.

```
Reading 'Goblins, Ghosts, and Gremlins' at page 1....
Putting aside 'Goblins, Ghosts, and Gremlins' at page 437.
  Reading 'Ghosts in Fiction' at page 1....
  putting aside 'Ghosts in Fiction' at page 233.
    Reading 'The Supernatural in Shakespeare's Plays' at page 320....
    Putting aside 'The Supernatural in Shakespeare's Plays' at page 389.
      Reading 'Hamlet' at page 1....
      Finished reading 'Hamlet'.
    Reading 'The Supernatural in Shakespeare's Plays' at page 389....
    Putting aside 'The Supernatural in Shakespeare's Plays' at page 406.
      Reading 'Richard II' at page 1....
      Finished reading 'Richard II'.
    Reading 'The Supernatural in Shakespeare's Plays' at page 406....
    Finished reading 'The Supernatural in Shakespeare's Plays'.
  Reading 'Ghosts in Fiction' at page 233....
  putting aside 'Ghosts in Fiction' at page 277.
    Reading 'Dictionary Entry' at page 522....
    Finished reading 'Dictionary Entry'.
  Reading 'Ghosts in Fiction' at page 277....
  putting aside 'Ghosts in Fiction' at page 306.
    Reading 'Encyclopedia Article' at page 979....
    Finished reading 'Encyclopedia Article'.
  Reading 'Ghosts in Fiction' at page 306....
  Finished reading 'Ghosts in Fiction'.
Reading 'Goblins, Ghosts, and Gremlins' at page 437....
Finished reading 'Goblins, Ghosts, and Gremlins'.
```

5.4 The Program Stack

One of the most significant mechanisms of programming languages is *subroutine* (or "procedure" or "function") *invocation*. Subroutine definitions assign names to pieces of code. The code associated with a name can be invoked by using the name. When the code finishes executing, control is returned to the point where it had been invoked. From the point of view of the invoking code the subroutine is a single action. This is the fundamental mechanism of procedural abstraction.

5.4.1 Call-and-Return

We can see from this brief description that 'invocation' means 'call and return': the subroutine is *called* from somewhere and it *returns* to that point when it's done. Subroutines implicitly return when their last statement has executed. Explicit return statements allow the subroutine to terminate before its last statement has been executed. The call-and-return discipline in most languages allows the call to pass *arguments* to code that has been expressed in terms of *parameters*. This allows one procedure to express a computation generalized for different input values. Similarly, most languages allow subroutines to return a result that becomes the value of the invoking expression.

Call-and-return is implemented using a stack. The programming environment's run-time environment creates and manages a *program stack* for each program executed. Call-and-return is based on addresses of the machine-level instructions that the compiler generated from the program text. When a subroutine is called, the address of the call instruction is pushed onto the stack and control is transferred to the first instruction of the subroutine. When the subroutine returns, the stack is popped and control is transferred to the popped address. (Because subroutine invocation is so fundamental, it is generally supported directly by the CPU's instruction set.)

Consider the following primitive C code.

```c
#include "screen.h"
#include "windows.h"

void RefreshDisplay()
{
    ClearScreen();
    for (int i = 0; i < NUMWINDOWS; i++)
        {
            W = WINDOWS[i];
            DisplayWindow();
        }
}

void DisplayWindow()
{
    DisplayFrame();
    DisplayContent();
}
```

```
void DisplayFrame()
{
    DisplayBorders();
    DisplayTitle();
    DisplayBackground();
}

// . . .
```

Let's look at how the program stack is used to control execution of this program. The stack starts off empty:

Suppose RefreshDisplay is called from main, executing the instruction at location 50662. That address gets pushed on the stack, and control is transferred to the first instruction of RefreshDisplay, say, 77640. The stack now contains one address.

```
| 50662 |
```

The first thing RefreshDisplay does is call ClearScreen, so 77640 gets pushed on the stack, and control goes to that routine. The stack is now

```
| 77640 |
| 50662 |
```

When ClearScreen finishes executing, the stack is popped and control returns to the popped location — 77640, an instruction in RefreshDisplay. The stack has shrunk to:

```
| 50662 |
```

RefreshDisplay now continues with its loop. Each time around the loop, DisplayWindow is called, say from instruction 77652, so each time around the loop 77652 gets pushed onto the stack.

```
| 77652 |
| 50662 |
```

The first thing `DisplayWindow` does is call `DisplayFrame`, say from instruction 77404. The stack grows to:

```
77404
77652
50662
```

Next, `DisplayFrame` calls `DisplayBorders` from instruction 77266, say, growing the stack to

```
77266
77404
77652
50662
```

When `DisplayBorders` returns, 77266 is popped from the stack and execution continues there, shrinking the stack to:

```
77404
77652
50662
```

`DisplayFrame` continues, calling `DisplayTitle` and `DisplayBackground`. Finally, `DisplayFrame` returns: 77404 is popped from the stack and execution resumes after that instruction inside `DisplayWindow`. The stack now holds

```
77652
50662
```

Eventually, `DisplayWindow` returns. The stack is popped, and execution continues at location 77652, in `RefreshDisplay`. The stack contains only the original address in `main` from which `RefreshDisplay` was invoked:

```
50662
```

Finally, `RefreshDisplay` completes and returns to `main`. The stack is empty once again:

```
```

5.4.2 Arguments, Return Values, Etc.

The above picture is considerably simplified. The program stack also supports argument passing as part of calls and return values as part of returns. In fact, storage for all local values — arguments, local variables, and compiler-generated temporaries — is stacked. Different languages, and even different implementations of the same language, may have different ways of handling the specific details of local variables, temporaries, etc. The description here is a simplified one sufficient for the discussion of stack use.

Why can't a subroutine's local values be put in a fixed location known to that subroutine? That's how subroutine calls were implemented in older languages — FOR-TRAN for example. The compiler would allocate space for a subroutine's local values along with its machine-level instructions. This approach is too restrictive, though: it doesn't allow subroutines to call themselves or to call other routines that (ultimately) call them. The first invocation would store some values in the local variables. Then, when the subroutine was invoked a second time, it would modify the same machine locations the first invocation did. When the first invocation regains control, it would find its local variables mysteriously modified.

The second invocation may invoke the same routine a third time, and so on. Once we allow subroutines to call themselves, there's no way to know beforehand how deep it will go — the sequence is ended according to a test in the subroutine that detects a terminating condition. Therefore, there's no way in advance to know how many copies of the subroutine's local values to allocate.

The only alternative is to use a stack. A separate copy of each subroutine's local values is pushed onto the stack each time it is invoked. The return mechanism pops these along with the return address. In some implementations, the return address and local variables are stored together as one item, called a *stack frame*, on the program stack, while in others there is a separate stack holding local variables.

5.4.3 Recursion

The technical name for a subroutine's calling itself is *recursion*. Recursion may be indirect: a subroutine calls others that eventually call it. Recursion is needed when a process must perform several different actions at the same time. Since a (traditional) processor can execute only one instruction at a time, only one task can be active at any time. Descriptions of the other tasks must be saved on a stack for later execution. Even in many cases where recursion is not required, a computation can be expressed more succinctly in a recursive form. Learning to write and think recursively is a valuable programming skill.

Quicksort

As an example, we'll consider a famous clever sorting method called *Quicksort*. Suppose we have an array of n elements, and we want to rearrange the elements so that they are ordered according to their definition of compare. The heart of a Quicksort implementation is a function that rearranges the array elements in a certain way. The function, which we'll call split, takes as its arguments the array and two indices indicating a subrange, which we'll call bottom and top. It determines a special index value, called the *pivot*, and returns that index as the value of the function.

In determining a pivot, split also rearranges the elements of the array so that (assuming the array contains pointers, as usual) the following conditions are true.

$$\text{bottom} \le i < \text{pivot} \implies *a[i] <= *a[\text{pivot}]$$
$$\text{pivot} < i \le \text{top} \implies *a[i] > *a[\text{pivot}]$$

After such a split, we can sort the two sections separately. The way that split rearranges the array guarantees that the elements of each part will remain in that part regardless of any further sorting activity.

Since the pivot is not included in either section, the sections are both guaranteed to be smaller than the subrange of the array being split. (One section could be empty, if pivot equals bottom or pivot equals top, but the other section is still one smaller than the subrange since it excludes the pivot.) If we split the array, then split each section, and continue to split sections, eventually all sections are reduced to having only one or two elements. A section with only one element is necessarily sorted! A section with only two elements can be sorted by testing whether the two elements are in their proper order and exchanging them if they are not.

Each split produces one or two sections to process. However, the program can only work on one of them at a time, so a simple iterative loop won't work. If we keep splitting the section and processing, say, the lower subsection, eventually we'll get to a subsection with only one or two elements, but what happened to all the upper subsections from the various splits? They've been left out.

Using a Stack for Quicksort

What's needed is more than simple iteration — we must use a stack. Stacks record tasks to be performed. A Quicksort split generates two tasks to be performed: sort the lower subsection and sort the upper subsection. We can use a stack to record these tasks. The task descriptions are simple, consisting of just the two indices that bound the subsection to be sorted. Quicksort can be coded as a template parameterized on the type its array argument contains, as follows.

```
struct pair
{
    int bottom, top;
    pair(int, int);
};

template <class elt> void quicksort(elt arr[], int from, int to)
{
    stack<pair*> stk(to-from);              // definitely more than necessary!
    stk += new pair(from, to);

    while (!stk.empty())
        {
            pair* pr = stk.pop();
            if (pr->bottom == pr->top)      // only 1 elt
```

```
                ;
        else if (pr->bottom == pr->top - 1)      // only 2 elts
            if (AFTER != compare(*arr[pr->bottom], *arr[pr->top]))
                ;
            else
                exchange(arr[pr->bottom], arr[pr->top]);
        else                                      // > 2 elts
            {
                int pivot = split(arr, pr->bottom, pr->top);
                // after calling split, all elements before pivot
                // are <= pivot, all elements after pivot are >= pivot.

                if (pivot < pr->top)
                    stk += new pair(pivot+1, pr->top);
                if (pivot > pr->bottom)
                    stk += new pair(pr->bottom, pivot-1);
            }
        delete pr;
    }
}
```

This is pretty magical — there's not much here that looks like it's sorting anything! In fact, the bulk of the sorting work is done by the split function. That function isn't hard to write, though, and there are many interesting variations possible. (A simple one follows.) Nevertheless, this is still pretty mysterious and requires working through some examples to really see what's happening.

The Split Function

The splitting process starts by picking an element of the array with which other elements will be compared. Ultimately, the selected element will end up at the pivot location. It turns out that different strategies for selecting the value affect the performance of the algorithm in subtle ways, but that actually *any* element will work. For simplicity, we'll just pick the first element. At the end of the entire splitting process, all the elements in the array from bottom to pivot-1 will be less than or equal to the selected element and all the elements from pivot+1 through top will be greater than the selected element.

One index variable is started at bottom, and another is started at top — we'll call them lower and upper, respectively. As long as the element at lower does not belong after the selected element, lower is incremented. Similarly, as long as the element at upper does not belong before the selected element, upper is decremented. When both indices have reached an out of place element, the two elements are exchanged. The indices are moved again until another pair of out-of-place elements is found, and another exchange occurs. This continues until the two indices cross. Finally, the selected element is exchanged with the element at upper, which at this point is the desired pivot value.

```
template <class elt> int split(elt* s[], int bottom, int top)
// will be called only if lower is at least 2 less than upper
{
    elt& val = *s[bottom];   // actually doesn't matter which is picked!
    int lower = bottom, upper = top;   // start at extremes

    while (lower < upper)                    // until they cross ...
    {
        while (lower < top && (AFTER != compare(*s[lower], val))) lower++;
        // Move lower upwards skipping elts that are in their
        // correct half until a elt that is > val is encountered.

        while (AFTER == (*s[upper], val)) upper--;
        // Move upper downwards skipping elts that are in their
        // correct half until a elt that is <= val is encountered.

        if (lower < upper) exchange(s[lower], s[upper]);
    }

    /* When lower >= upper, do a final exchange, switching s[bottom] and
       s[upper] — all the comparisons were made against s[bottom], but
       s[bottom] was never moved.  Now we know where it belongs: at upper;
       also, the elt at upper is <= val or else upper would have been
       decremented further.
    */
    exchange(s[bottom], s[upper]);

    return upper;
}
```

Recursive Quicksort

Quicksort is shown here to demonstrate how stacks are used to support recursive processing. Quicksort is recursive because after splitting a section, each of as many as two subsections is separately sorted using the same process. However, the above code is not expressed recursively. It uses an ordinary iterative loop plus its own stack to manage the recursive processing. Modern languages support direct recursive expression, however. A recursive expression of Quicksort would look something like the following. In essence, the program stack takes the place of the explicit stack of the iterative formulation.

```
template <class elt> quicksort(elt* arr[], int bottom, int top)
{
    if (bottom == top)                       // only 1 elt
        ;
    else if (bottom == top-1)                // 2 elts
        if (*arr[bottom] <= *arr[top])
            ;
        else
            exchange(strings[bottom], strings[top]);
    else                                     // > 2 elts
```

```
        {
            int pivot = split(arr, bottom, top);

            if (pivot<top) quicksort(arr, pivot+1, top);
            if (pivot>bottom) quicksort(arr, bottom, pivot-1);
        }
}
```

This is more concise! There are no stacks, stack elements, while loops, or many of the other details needed in the iterative formulation. Actually, the special cases of one or two items distract from the real power of this formulation. In the next section of the book, which considers data structures that are themselves recursive, we'll see some very terse code that will better show recursion's real power.

5.4.4 Backtracking

Backtracking is a special form of recursion that attempts to attain a goal starting from an initial state. Each step applies one of a set of rules to transform the current state into a new one. A predicate is supplied that determines whether a state meets the goal criteria. To find the goal from any state, each applicable rule is tried in turn. Success is achieved when a state is generated that meets the goal criteria. Failure is encountered when a nongoal state is achieved to which no further transformations apply, either because none are applicable, or because all the applicable ones have already been tried. When failure is encountered, the process is "backed up" to an earlier state and continued from there with the application of the next transformation. The term 'backtracking' is derived from the fact that when failure is encountered the process goes back over its tracks state by state, until one is reached where further options remained.

Because there may be more than one transformation applicable to a given state, recursion is required to remember the others while one is tried. The next state may have several transformations, each of those states may have several applicable transformations, and so on. Therefore, a great many states may have to be explored before the process ever returns to the original state and the next transformation of it is tried. A stack is used to maintain the history of states that led to the current one. Whenever there are no more transformations applicable to a state, it is abandoned: the stack is popped and further transformations are tried for the previous state. As with Quicksort above, backtracking may be expressed using an explicit stack or as a recursive function that uses the program execution stack.

A simple example is a classic problem called the "Knight's Tour." A Knight is a chess piece that moves two squares either horizontally or vertically then one square in the other dimension. A Knight is placed on a chessboard, and the challenge is to find a sequence of moves by which the Knight visits every square on the board exactly once.

The transformation rules for this puzzle would describe the legitimate moves from any position. There are as many as eight moves possible from a given square: first move two in any of four directions, then move one either way in the other dimension (e.g., two to the left and one up or one down). Squares near or on the edge of the board produce fewer possibilities. Moves that land the Knight on a square already visited are discarded.

A program to solve this simply needs an appropriate structure to define a board's state, a way to generate moves from a given position, and a stack. The program would begin by pushing the initial position on the stack. On each iteration a board description would be popped off the stack and tested to see if all squares have been visited. If not, a new board description would be pushed onto the stack for every applicable move from the position currently being considered. Due to the large number of squares and possible moves, a great many positions may end up being examined on the way to a solution, but in principle the process is simple, using an explicit stack.

5.5 EXERCISES

Stacks

1. A classic example of the use of stacks is to verify for some text that every left parenthesis, left bracket, or left brace is matched by the corresponding right character. For instance, if the most recent left character is a parenthesis, then the next right character seen should also be a parenthesis, not a bracket or brace. Whenever a right character is encountered, the only question to ask, and therefore the only state information the verification process needs, is "What is the most recently unmatched left character?" Once a left character is matched, it can be thrown away. Because parenthesized, bracketed, and braced text can appear within each other, nesting can occur to any level. Therefore, a stack is needed to record the state of the scan. Write the program described, using the stack module from the course library.

2. Perhaps the simplest possible use of a stack is to evaluate algebraic expressions expressed in postfix form (where the two operands precede the operator, as in 5 9 / 98.6 32 - * to compute the Celsius equivalent of "normal body temperature" in Fahrenheit). Assume that each expression occupies a single line of input and that spaces surround every operator and operand. Note that postfix notation is unambiguous — there is no need for parentheses.

    (a) Write a simple program that reads and prints back out series of algebraic expressions consisting entirely of integers and the binary operators +, -, *, and /.

    (b) Modify the program to use a stack to evaluate and print out the value of each of the input expressions. The process is simple: integers get stacked, and operators work by popping the top two stack elements, applying the designated operation to them, and pushing the result back on the stack. Be careful to arrange the two operands in the correct order.

    (c) Extend the program so that it stores expressions instead of evaluating them, and allows expressions to contain one-letter variables and real numbers in addition to integers. Expressions will be numbered for reference. Accept input such as the following:

```
F = 98.6                        // assign 98.6 to the
variable F
(1) 5 9 / F 32 - *              // store expression #1
(2) X X * Y Y * 2               // store expression #2
? 1                             // evaluate expression
(1)
X = 3                           // assign 3.0 to X
Y = 4                           // assign 4.0 to Y
? 2                             // evaluate expression #2
F = 68                          // reassign F
? 1                             // reevaluate #2
```

Recursion

3. In the Quicksort program in Section 5.4.2, the stack was created large enough to hold as many bounds pairs as there are array elements. Intuitively this seems large enough; in fact, it is much larger than necessary. Determine the maximum depth reached by the stack Quicksort uses for sorting an array of n elements.

4. Write a program to print out the reverse of each line of text input to it.
   (a) Use a stack of characters to read the line and print its reverse. Do not use any variables to store characters except for the stack and the character just read.
   (b) Rewrite using recursion, where each call reads a character. Do not use any variables to store characters except for the character just read.
   (c) Compare the two approaches.

5. Write and test a recursive function to calculate the *greatest common divisor* of two positive numbers based on Euclid's algorithm: if $p\%q$ is 0, then q divides p and, since it divides itself, it is the largest number that divides both; if $p\%q$ is not 0, then their *gcd* is the *gcd* of q and $p\%q$. (p must be less than q.)

6. Suppose C++ had no `while`, `for`, or any other looping construct — not even a `goto`. Loop constructs are of course very useful, and you wouldn't want to program without them. All is not lost! Loops can be expressed recursively.
   (a) Write a function `dowhile` that takes two functions — a predicate and an action — and repeats the action as long as the predicate evaluates to false.
   (b) Write a function `dofor` that takes an initial value and three functions: one function to step the value, one to test for termination, and one that performs the repetition action. The function should repeatedly perform the action, stepping the value and testing for termination on each repetition.

Backtracking

7. Backtracking can be used to solve mazes. Let an N x M maze be defined as a two-dimensional array of squares, each one containing a block, the maze runner, or nothing, along with designated start and goal squares. The runner begins at the start square; the object of the program is to get the runner to the goal square. At each move, the maze runner may move to any empty adjacent square (horizontal or vertical, not diagonal).
   (a) Write a simple module implementing a maze. It should be able to read a maze specification from a file, output the current state of a maze, report the legal moves available from the current state, and perform legal moves.
   (b) Write a program that solves the maze using a stack. A state structure is necessary because there may be as many as three moves possible from a given position. (The fourth possibility is excluded — there's no need to consider the move that undoes the move that got the runner to its current square.) Only one at a time can be pursued; others have to be added to a state structure for later consideration.
   (c) One inefficiency in this program is that a given square might be reached by more than one path. If a square has already been explored once, there is no need to explore it again. Change your program so it keeps track of what squares have been reached and doesn't add them to the stack when they are encountered again.
   (d) Change the program to use recursion instead of an explicit stack.

8. Consider string pattern matching, where a `'?'` in the pattern matches any character in the string and a `'*'` in the pattern matches any sequence of characters (including none) in the string.

(a) Write a recursive function that tells whether its first argument, the pattern string, matches the second argument, the target string.

(b) Test it in a program that reads pattern-target strings, with each pattern and target on a separate line and pattern-target pairs separated by a blank line.

(c) Why does this have to be recursive?

9. Write the Knight's Tour program described in Section 5.4.4, page 167.

(a) Begin by using an explicit stack.

(b) The number of positions considered can be greatly reduced by ordering the current position's possible moves before pushing them onto the stack, so that moves with the fewest possible successor moves are considered before moves with more. Note that you must push them in the reverse of the order in which you want the moves considered, since elements are popped from stacks in the reverse of the order in which they were pushed. One way to order the moves is according to how many moves there are from each of them to an unvisited square. Another is to order them according to how close they are to a horizontal edge and a vertical edge, since edge squares and, to a lesser extent, squares one away from an edge reduce the number of moves available.

(c) Modify your program so that it uses recursive calls instead of an explicit stack. Compare the two implementations: which do you think is easier to write (assuming a stack module is already available)? Which is easier to read?

10. Another classic backtracking problem is called "Eight Queens." A Queen in chess can move any number of squares in a single direction, including diagonally. A piece is considered under attack by another piece if the second piece can reach the square of the first piece on one move. The challenge is to place eight queens on a chessboard so that none attacks any of the others. Obviously, there can only be one Queen on any row or column, so the process can be organized by placing Queens in successive rows, trying each of the still unoccupied columns. The tricky part is that the diagonals have to be checked, too: if the newly placed Queen can reach the square of any of the Queens placed earlier, the position is abandoned. Write a program that solves this puzzle, trying it out first on a 4x4 board before running it for an 8x8 one.

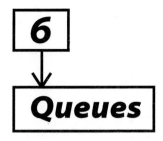

Queues

Queues are quite similar to stacks. The essential difference is that queued tasks are processed in the order in which they entered the queue rather than most recent first. The processing pattern queues generate is *first-in first-out* (FIFO). This difference is conceptually simple, but it makes the implementation and applications of queues substantially different from the implementation and applications of stacks.

6.1 Queue-Based Processing

We'll illustrate FIFO processing with a reading example similar to the one used to illustrate LIFO processing with stacks. The example is based on a student's need to keep track of reading assignments in a number of courses she is taking.

An unusually well-organized student might proceed as follows. Every time a reading assignment is given in a course the student writes information about the assignment on an index card. She places each entry on a separate index card and stores the cards in a file box, adding new cards at the back. When it is time to do some studying, the student removes the first card from the front of the box and does the reading assignment it represents.

When an assignment is completed, its index card can be thrown away. If there is time to do more studying, another card can be taken from the front of the box. In this way, readings get done in the order in which they were assigned. Figure 6.1 illustrates this approach. In contrast to the suspend-and-resume approach supported by stacks, a queue-based process completes each task before beginning the next.

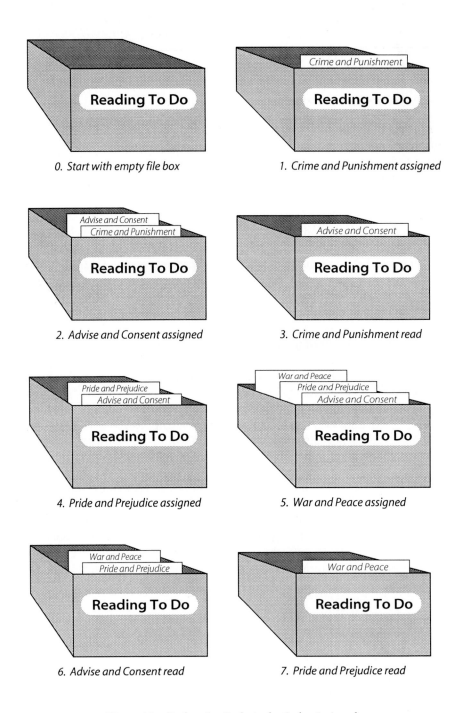

Figure 6.1   Performing Tasks in the Order Assigned

6.2 Implementation

Like stacks, queues are based on arrays. If implementation were to follow the file box metaphor exactly, when a task description is removed from the queue all the others would
have to be moved up in the array. That overhead can be avoided by treating the array as
a circular structure, as if you had grabbed it by its end, curved it around, and attached its
end to its beginning.

This can be accomplished by maintaining separate pointers to the current front and
back of the queue, as illustrated in Figure 6.2. When an item is added, back is incremented; when an item is removed, front is incremented. When back hits the end of the array,
it is reset to the beginning. Similarly, when front hits the end of the array, it is reset to the
beginning. In this way, front continues to chase back around the circular array. (If it
ever catches up, the queue is full.)

6.2.1 Representation

The data members of queue are just like those of stack. The only change is to replace
stack's single top pointer with front and back pointers.

```
template <class elt> struct queue
{
  private:
    // Representation
    elt *elts;                        // array of pointers
    int front, back;                  // indices
    int maxindex;                     // size of array - 1
    // . . .
};
```

6.2.2 Lifetime Operations

Initialize and Finalize are routine for queues. As with stacks, Add and Remove are the fundamental Modify operations. We'll include a clear to empty the queue and first and
last to access those special elements.

```
template <class elt> struct queue
{
    // . . .
  public:

    // Initialize/Finalize
    queue(int siz = 100);
    ~queue();

    // Access/Modify
    void add(elt);
```

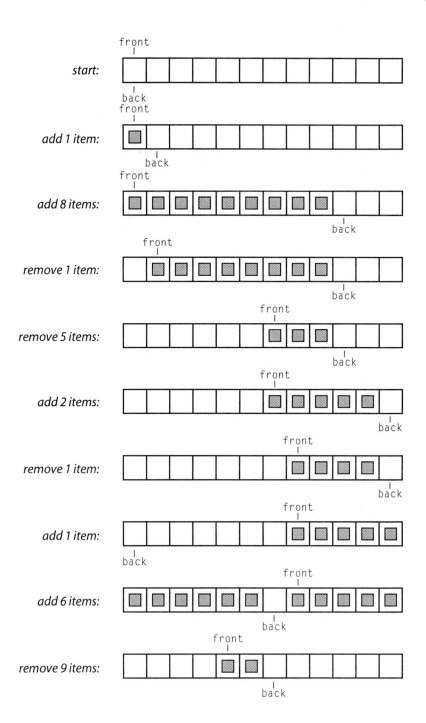

Figure 6.2 Queue Add and Remove

```
    queue& operator+=(elt itm);        // synonym for add

    elt remove();
    void clear();
    elt first();                        // first elt
    elt last();                         // last elt
};
```

It is convenient to have front==back indicate an empty queue. Since front and back will move through the array, it actually doesn't matter what array index they are initialized to as long as they start out equal. The constructor calls clear to establish the initial state; clear sets both to 0. The constructor also allocates an array to hold the elements. As in the stack implementation, the size of the array is recorded in the queue struct. (Actually, for convenience, we record the maximum index of the array — one less than its size.)

```
/* Initialize/Finalize */

template <class elt> queue<elt>::queue(int siz) :
    elts(new elt[siz]), maxindex(siz-1)
{
    assert(siz > 1);
    clear();
    // a little tricky, so abstract out as a separate
    // function that can be called on its own too.
}

template <class elt> queue<elt>::~queue()
{
    delete [] elts;
}
```

Add stores the new entry at back then increments back (or resets it to 0 if it is already at maxindex). Remove increments front and returns the entry at the old value of front. Thus, unless the queue is empty, front always points to the first item in the queue, and back points one past the last item in the queue (the place where the next item will be added).

```
/* Access/Modify */

template <class elt> void queue<elt>::add(elt itm)
{
    assert (!full());

    elts[back++] = itm;
    if (back > maxindex) back = 0;        // wrap around
}

template <class elt> queue<elt>& queue<elt>::operator+=(elt itm)
```

```
{
    add(itm);
    return *this;
}

template <class elt> elt queue<elt>::remove()
{
    assert(!empty());

    elt itm = elts[front++];
    if (front > maxindex) front = 0;        // wrap around
    return itm;
}

template <class elt> void queue<elt>::clear()
 {
    front = back = 0;
}

template <class elt> elt queue<elt>::first()
{
    assert(!empty());

    return elts[front];
}

template <class elt> elt queue<elt>::last()
{
    assert(!empty());

    if (back == 0)
        return elts[maxindex-1];
    else
        return elts[back-1];
}
```

6.2.3 Traversal Operations

Queue traversal operations are quite similar to those for stacks.

```
template <class elt> struct queue
{
    // . . .
    // Traversal
  private:
    int cur;                                // traversal index
  public:
    void reset();                           // Traversal is front to back
```

```
    bool finished();
    bool next();
    elt& current();
    int index();                              // offset 1
};
```

/* Traversal */

```
template <class elt> void queue<elt>::reset()
{
    cur = front-1;
}

template <class elt> bool queue<elt>::next()
{
    if (++cur > maxindex) cur=0;
        return !finished();
}

template <class elt> elt& queue<elt>::current()
{
    return elts[cur];
}

template <class elt> bool queue<elt>::finished()
{
    return cur == back;
}

template <class elt> int queue<elt>::index()
{
    if (front <= cur)
        return ((cur - front) + 1);
    else            // traversal wrapped around to front of array
        return ((maxindex - front) + cur + 1);
}
```

6.2.4 Content Operations

Queues have content operations similar to stacks. There are similar **Attributes** and minimal **Compare** operations. **Combine** operations would rarely be needed, but could easily be implemented (cf. Exercise 1).

```
template <class elt> struct queue
{
    // . . .
  public:
    // Attributes
    bool empty();
```

```
bool full();
int size();

// Compare
friend order compare(queue<elt>&, queue<elt>&);
friend bool equal(queue<elt>&, queue<elt>&);
    // same elts in same order? (elt identity, not equality)
};
```

A queue is full when back catches up to front. We have to be careful, though. If every element of the array contained a queue component, we'd have front==back, which is the definition of empty! There's no way to avoid this: we've arranged the queue to act as if it were a circular ring of entries, and the empty and full states must be distinguished. One of the two states can be defined as front==back, but the other must be distinguished some other way. In this implementation, full is represented by back being one behind front, rather than actually catching up to it. This means that there is always at least one unused slot in the array. In Figure 6.2 on page 174, for instance, the next to last queue state shown is a full one even though there is one empty box.

Given this interpretation of front and back, computing the number of elements currently in a queue is straightforward, though slightly tricky to express correctly. Both size and full must deal with the inconvenient details of front and back wrapping around when they get to the end of the array.

```
/* Attributes */

template <class elt> int queue<elt>::size()
{
    if (empty()) return 0;

    if (front < back)
        return back - front;
    else
        return (maxindex - front) + back + 1;
}

template <class elt> bool queue<elt>::empty()
{
    return front == back;
}

template <class elt> bool queue<elt>::full()
{
    return (front == back+1) || ((front == 0) && (back == maxindex));
}
```

Queues, like other state structures, would hardly ever be compared. We won't implement compare, but in general it's always a good idea to have equal defined, if only to facilitate testing. In any case, because of the considerations discussed in Section 1.3.3 (page 67) and at the end of Section 1.4.1 (page 79), we have to provide *some* version of equal and compare. For convenience, and to illustrate their use, equal uses traversal operators, even though this would interfere with any traversal client code might be in the midst of when it calls equal.

```
/* Compare */

template <class elt> order compare(queue<elt>&, queue<elt>&)
{
    notimp("compare(queue<elt>&, queue<elt>&)");
    return NO_ORDER;
}

// same elts in same order? (elt identity, not equality)
template <class elt> bool equal(queue<elt>& q1, queue<elt>& q2)
{
    if (&q1 == &q2) return TRUE;                     // same!
    if (q1.size() != q2.size()) return FALSE;   // preliminary check

    q1.reset();
    q2.reset();
    while(q1.next() && q2.next())
    if (q1.current() != q2.current()) return FALSE;
    // NOTE: if q1 runs out, q2 has not yet been incremented

    if (!q1.finished()) return FALSE;
    if (q2.next()) return FALSE;                     // q1 is finished; step q2
    return TRUE;
}
```

6.2.5 Support Operations

As always, we provide an operator<< function for the structure — the same considerations apply for that as for compare and equal. Again, as for stacks, we might want to see if a particular item was in the queue or not. In fact, the definition of all three support operations are essentially the same as the corresponding definitions for stack.

```
struct queue
{
    // . . .
  public:
    // Process
    bool contains(elt);
    bool contains_equal(elt);

    // Input/Output
    friend ostream& operator<<(ostream&, queue<elt>&);
};
```

```
/* Process */

template <class elt> bool queue<elt>::contains(elt itm)
{
    reset();
    while (next()) if (itm == current()) return TRUE;          // identity

    return FALSE;
}

template <class elt> bool queue<elt>::contains_equal(elt itm)
{
    reset();
    while (next()) if (equal(*itm, *current())) return TRUE;   // equality

    return FALSE;
}
```

```
/* Output */

template <class elt> ostream& operator<<(ostream& strm, queue<elt>& q)
{
    q.reset();
    while (q.next()) strm << '\t' << *q.current() << '\n';

    return strm;
}
```

6.3 An Example

```
// qdemo.C, corresponding to reading sequence of Figure 6.1 on page 172

#include <fstream.h>
ofstream ofil("qtst.out");

struct item
{
    char* title;
    item(char* t) : title(t) { }
};

ostream& operator<<(ostream& strm, const item& itm)
{
    strm << '"' << itm.title << '"';
    return strm;
}
```

```
bool equal(const item& itm1, const item& itm2)
{
    return !strcmp(itm1.title, itm2.title);
}

queue<item*> q(4);

void report(char* prefix)
{
    ofil << prefix << "queue contains " << q.size()
        << " items:\n" << q << '\n';
}

void report_contains(char* title)
{
    item itm(title);

    ofil << "The queue does ";
    if (!q.contains_equal(&itm))
        ofil << "not ";
    ofil << "contain " << title << ".\n\n";
}

void read(item* itm)
{
    ofil << "Read " << *itm << ".\n";
    delete itm;
}

void assign(char* title)
{
    ofil << '\"' << title << "\" assigned.\n";
    q += new item(title);
    report("");
}

main()
{
    report("At first, ");
    assign("Crime and Punishment");
    assign("Advise and Consent");
    read(q.remove());
    assign("Pride and Prejudice");
    assign("War and Peace");
    read(q.remove());
    read(q.remove());
    // W&P still in queue
    report("At end, ");
    report_contains("War and Peace");
    report_contains("Crime and Punishment");
        .
    return 0;
}
```

The output from this demonstration is as follows.

```
At first, queue contains 0 items:

"Crime and Punishment" assigned.
    queue contains 1 items:
    "Crime and Punishment"

"Advise and Consent" assigned.
    queue contains 2 items:
    "Crime and Punishment"
    "Advise and Consent"

Read "Crime and Punishment".
"Pride and Prejudice" assigned.
    queue contains 2 items:
    "Advise and Consent"
    "Pride and Prejudice"

"War and Peace" assigned.
    queue contains 3 items:
    "Advise and Consent"
    "Pride and Prejudice"
    "War and Peace"

Read "Advise and Consent".
Read "Pride and Prejudice".
    At end, queue contains 1 items:
    "War and Peace"

    The queue does contain War and Peace.

    The queue does not contain Crime and Punishment.
```

6.4 EXERCISES

1. Add combine(queue&, queue&) to the queue module shown in the text. The result should be a new queue, rather than modifying one of the arguments.

2. Write a program that simulates a printer queue. The program should loop accepting commands from standard input, as follows, and simulate printing at a fixed rate of characters per minute. Queue entries should record only file names and lengths (in characters) — don't bother with different user names, priorities, or other details you might find in a real printer queue.
   (a) print filename   verify that a file of that name exists and add it to the queue
   (b) status   list the entries on a queue (name plus number of characters)
   (c) time   print the total amount of time it will take to print all the queued files

3. Strictly speaking, the only **Modify** operations required for a queue are add and remove, to add elements at the back and remove them from the front. However, it might also be useful to be able to remove a particular element of the queue.
   (a) Give some examples of queue applications that might use such an operation.

(b) What signature should the operation have?

(c) Implement and test it.

(d) Add a remove filename command to the printer queue of Exercise 2.

4. Substitute a queue for the stack in the maze running program of the previous chapter's Exercise 7, page 169. Describe the difference this makes in the way the maze is searched. Which one corresponds to the way a person would normally search a maze?

5. Write a program that simulates a highway toll plaza. Assume tolls are collected in one direction only, there are three lanes of traffic, automatic toll machines take 10 seconds per car, peopled tollbooths take 20 seconds, and cars arrive at random intervals from each lane. Drivers decide which tollbooth to get on based on some combination of how far over the booth is from the driver's current lane, the length of the various lines, and awareness that peopled lanes move twice as slowly as automatic lanes. (Make up some reasonable formula.) Run simulations for various numbers of tollbooths and traffic volume and gather statistics regarding the throughput of the toll plaza, average and maximum wait of cars, etc.

Priority Queues

The essence of state structures is that they store descriptions of tasks awaiting processing. Stacks and queues embody two commonly used scheduling disciplines: LIFO and FIFO, respectively. Many kinds of processing are directly supported by either LIFO or FIFO scheduling. LIFO is used for nested suspend-and-resume processing, as in subroutine calls. FIFO is used to manage first-come first-serve ordering, such as printer queues. FIFO can also be used for suspend-and-resume scheduling: the current process is suspended and put back *at the end* of the queue. This supports processor sharing, in which each task is allowed to use a certain amount of resources before being suspended in favor of the next one waiting.

Sometimes a more sophisticated scheduling discipline is required than FIFO or LIFO. *Priority queues* are a generalization of stacks and queues that support arbitrary schedule regimes, or what might be called *best-next* processing.

7.1 Selective Processing

Stacks and queues store their task descriptions in an order reflecting the order in which they'll be processed. Priority queues can do that too by inserting each new task in its proper place relative to the others currently stored. Alternatively, they can store the tasks in arbitrary order, and **Remove** can search for the best one each time it is invoked. The latter approach is necessary if the evaluation is dependent on time or changing conditions. The former is appropriate when evaluations of queued tasks don't change, in which case the evaluations can be included in the task description. Either way, a priority queue orders its tasks according to some kind of evaluation.

For example, priority queues play an important part in allocating shared resources of a large computer system to its users. Batch (non-time-shared) systems might use a priority queue to manage job requests. Time-shared systems usually have printer queues to manage output requests. For either example, a request's priority might be calculated as a function of the size of the task to be performed, the privileges of the requester, and the amount of time the request has been waiting in the queue.

The implementation of a priority queue is similar to that of a stack or a queue. The main difference is in either **Add** or **Remove**, according to whether or not tasks are stored in order. If stored in order, then **Remove** is unaffected, but **Add** must evaluate the new item and successive old items until the new item's place in the ordering is determined, then insert the new task at that location. With an array-based representation insertion requires moving subsequent tasks down in the array.

If the tasks are not stored in order, then **Add** is unaffected, but **Remove** must evaluate all the tasks to select the one with the highest evaluation. With an array-based representation deletion of items can be managed either by marking the entry free (assuming entries are pointers, by setting the value to 0) or by moving subsequent entries up. The latter wastes a little time shuffling items in a **Remove**, whereas the former wastes a little time in each **Add** looking for an empty spot. If this inefficiency becomes significant, a more appropriate implementation would be to use a linked list, discussed in the next chapter.

One variation on the idea of priority queues combines the idea of a queue with that of a priority queue, useful when there are a small number of possible priority values. An array of queues can be maintained, each corresponding to a particular priority value. When a task is added, it is simply added to the end of the queue corresponding to the task's priority value. To find (and remove) the next task to be processed, the queue with the highest priority is examined: if nonempty, its first task is selected. If that queue is empty, the one with the next highest priority is considered, and so on.

Priority queues are often used in game-playing and puzzle-solving programs. Given a particular position in a puzzle or game, legal moves from that position are generated, evaluated, and added to a priority queue. The evaluation can be stored as part of the task description, since it does not depend on external factors such as time waiting. Since **Remove** will not reevaluate each item, the items can be stored in order of their evaluation, and **Remove** can just delete and return the first item, as in a queue.

7.1.1 Representation

Here's the declaration of a priority queue that stores elements according to their priority, rather than determining the next element each time one is to be removed. The implementation offers two choices, specified as constructor arguments: should the highest or lowest priority be the first element removed, and what function should be used to compare elements? If the optional function argument is provided, it is the name of an *evaluation function* that takes an element and returns an integer indicating its priority. If no function is provided, operator< or operator> is used, with the (necessarily pointer-valued) elements being dereferenced first.

```
template <class elt> struct pqueue
{
  private:
    // Representation
    elt *elts;
    int front, back;
```

```
    int maxelts;
    bool highfront; // do elements with highest evaluation go at front?
    int (*evaluator)(elt);              // evaluation function for elts
    // . . .
};
```

7.1.2 Operations

The implementation of the priority queue will take the implementation of a regular queue shown in Chapter 6 as a starting point. Only a small number of functions change: the constructor, add, the copy constructor, and the copy assignment operation. Except for add, and a private function insert, which it calls, the changes simply involve the initialization and copying of the new data members highest_first and evaluator. The declaration and definition of the module's other functions are the same as for regular queues and won't be shown here.

```
template <class elt> struct pqueue
{

    // . . .
    // Initialize/Finalize
    pqueue(bool highest_first = TRUE,    // else lowest first
           int (*evalfn)(elt) = 0,
           int siz = 100);

    // Access/Modify
  private:
    bool before(elt itm, int pos);
    void insert(elt itm, int pos);       // insert itm at pos
  public:
    void add(elt);
};
```

```
/* Lifetime Operations */

template <class elt>
pqueue<elt>::pqueue(bool high, int (*fn)(elt), int siz)
      : highfront(high), evaluator(fn), maxelts(siz-1), elts(new elt[siz])
{
    assert(siz > 1);
    clear();
}

// private:
// insert e at position pos; back starts off just after last elt
template <class elt> void pqueue<elt>::insert(elt e, int pos)
{
    int i = back;
```

```
    if (++back > maxelts)                       // increment back
        back = 0;                               // wrap?

    while (i != pos)
        {
            elts[i] = elts[i ? i-1 : maxelts];
            if (--i < 0) i = maxelts;           // wrap backwards
        }

    elts[pos] = e;
}

template <class elt> void pqueue<elt>::add(elt e)
{
    if (full())
        error("pqueue overflow");
    else
        {
            int val = evaluator ? evaluator(*e) : 0;
            int cur = front;

            while (cur != back &&
                    (evaluator ? (highfront ? val < evaluator(elts[cur])
                                            : val > evaluator(elts[cur]))
                              : (highfront ? operator<(*e, *elts[cur])
                                           : operator>(*e, *elts[cur])))
                  )
                if (++cur > maxelts) cur = 0;        // wrap

            insert(e, cur);
        }
}
```

```
/* Copy */

//private:
template <class elt> void pqueue<elt>::copy_elts(pqueue<elt>& q)
{
    front = q.front;
    back= q.back;
    memcpy(elts, q.elts, maxelts*sizeof(elt));
}

template <class elt> pqueue<elt>::pqueue(pqueue<elt>& q) :
    highfront(q.highfront), evaluator(q.evaluator),
    maxelts(q.maxelts), elts(new elt[q.maxelts])
{
    copy_elts(q);
}

template <class elt> pqueue<elt>& pqueue<elt>::operator=(pqueue<elt>& q)
{
    if (this == &q) return *this;                   // copy to self!
```

```
    delete [] elts;
    highfront = q.highfront;
    maxelts = q.maxelts;
    elts = new elt[q.maxelts];
    evaluator = q.evaluator;
    copy_elts(q);

    return *this;
}
```

7.2 An Example

As an example of the use of priority queues in game-playing programs, we'll consider the classic "Fifteen Puzzle." This is a 4 x 4 array of tiles, numbered 1 through 15, with one missing. Initially the tiles are scrambled. The objective is to rearrange the tiles so that they are in order: 1 through 4 across the top, 5 through 8 across the next row, etc. The only allowable maneuver is to slide a tile adjacent to the empty space into the empty space, thereby exchanging the position of the tile and the empty space.

7.2.1 Representation and Manipulation of Positions

The first thing a program to solve the puzzle needs is a representation of the puzzle. The most obvious representation would be a 4 x 4 array of integers, each representing the number of the tile in the corresponding position. It will be convenient to track the location of the blank square, rather than searching for it each time a move is made, so we include that in the representation.

```
struct position
{
  private:
    short tiles[4][4];
    short blank_row, blank_col;
    // . . .
};
```

Next, we consider what operations we want to perform on a position. Although it serves a very specific purpose, this is still a full-fledged data structure and will benefit from the same kind of organization we apply to the more generally useful ones that are the subject of this book. We need a constructor, **Access/Modify**, some **Attributes**, and the usual **Compare**, **Copy**, and **Output** operations. The **Modify** operations we need are make_move, which modifies a board by moving the blank square in the direction specified by its argument, and make_moves, a scrambling function that makes a number of random moves. The constructor will set up a board in the solution position, then call make_moves with the number of moves specified as its argument.

The main **Attribute** needed is a test to determine if a position is a solution. To support evaluating positions, we'll need **Attributes** that report other characteristics. Here, a simple approach to evaluating a position is embodied in the **Attribute** number_correct, which returns the number of tiles that are in position they'll occupy in the solution. **Compare** will evaluate boards by calling number_correct, but number_correct can also be used by a priority queue's evaluation function.

```
struct position
{
  public:
    enum direction { NONE, LEFT, RIGHT, UP, DOWN };
    // This is a struct-specific enum.

  private:
    short tiles[4][4];
    short blank_row, blank_col;

  public:
    // Initialize/Finalize
    position(int n = 5);
    // a position with n random moves

    // Access/Modify
  private:
    void make_move(direction d);
    void make_moves(int n);

    // Attributes
    bool is_solution();
    int number_correct();

    // Compare
    friend order compare(state&, state&);
    friend bool equal(state&, state&);

    // Copy
  private:
    void copy(position& p);
  public:
    position(position&);                     // copy constructor
    position& operator=(position&);          // copy assignment

    position* move(direction d);
    // exchange the blank with the square in direction d
    // We return a pointer instead of a reference so we
    // can use 0 to mean the move was not possible

    // Output
    friend ostream& operator<<(ostream&, position&);
};
```

A new puzzle is obtained by creating a `position`, giving the constructor the number of random moves to make to scramble the solution position. We can code the scrambling function so that a move never undoes the immediately preceding move (e.g., after a left, a right would not be considered). Still, random moves may eventually return the puzzle to a previously encountered order, so although the solution is guaranteed to be no longer than the requested number of moves, it might be shorter.

Given a `position`, new positions are generated from it by the `move` operation — a kind of **Copy**. That function returns either 0 if the requested move is impossible (the blank is at the edge corresponding to the direction of the move). Otherwise, it makes a copy of the position, makes the requested move in the copy, and returns a pointer to the new position. Both `move` and `make_moves` utilize a private member function `make_move` that exchanges the blank with the adjacent square.

Making the **Modify** operations private and providing no access to individual tiles mean that individual applications can create (and destroy) positions, but not modify them once created. Initialization involves making a number of random moves, and `move` produces a copy with a desired move made, but existing positions are never changed. This is necessary because the way position will be used means that they must be independent of their successors — considering a move from a position doesn't mean the position is no longer needed. By initializing moves with a scrambling function, we guarantee that only positions that can be solved are created. (It turns out that transposing any pair of non-blank adjacent tiles in a position that does have a solution produces a position that does not.)

7.2.2 Solving the Puzzle with a Queue

The following process is guaranteed to find the shortest solution to any puzzle:

- Create a `position` and add it to the queue.
- As long as the queue is not empty, remove a position and test whether it is a solution, then:
  - if yes, stop;
  - if no, spawn and queue a new position for each possible move from the current one and continue.

Once the solution is found, however, we presumably want to know how the program got there. We therefore need some way to record move sequences. There are various approaches, but probably the easiest way to do this is to define a `state` struct that holds a pointer to a `position`, an indication of the move that generated the position, and a pointer to the `state` holding the position from which this one was generated. Knowing the last move makes it possible to avoid generating a position that just undoes the move that created the current one.

Utility structures like this can be used informally with respect to modularization and data abstraction. Data members can be made public for convenience, and they don't need a full complement of fundamental operations. In addition to the members each `state` will need, the struct also defines a static member `count` to keep track of the number of states (and therefore positions) generated while solving a puzzle. (The definitions of the position and state member functions aren't shown here, but they are included in the code files accompanying the book.)

```
struct state
{
  public:
    position* pos;
    state* parent;
    position::direction move;
    static count;

    state(position* p, state* par, position::direction d);

    char move_name();
    static bool moves_are_inverses(position::direction,
                                   position::direction);

    friend order compare(state&, state&);
    friend bool equal(state&, state&);
    friend ostream& operator<<(ostream&, state&);
};
```

The first thing the program must do is initial state::count. Then a few utility functions are defined to simplify the code.

```
int state::count = 0;

void queue_move(state* s, position::direction d, queue<state*>& q)
{
    position* succ = s->pos->move(d);
    // 0 if move is invalid from s's position
    if (succ) q += new state(succ, s, d);
}

void print_solution(state* s, queue<state*>& q)
{
    cout << "Solution found after queueing "
         << state::count << " positions,\nout of which "
         << state::count - q.size() << " were considered.\n";
    cout << "\nThe path from the solution to the start was: ";
    while (s->parent)
    {
        cout << s->move_name() << ' ';
        s = s->parent;
    }
    cout << "\n";
}
```

With all that support out of the way, main can be defined.

```
// program argument is number of shuffles for
// generating an initial position, default = 3
main (int argc, char** argv)
{
    int depth = argc>1 ? atoi(argv[1]) : 3;
    queue<state*> q(int(pow(4, depth+1)));        // max needed

    position* pos = new position(depth);
    cout << "The initial position, obtained from "
         << depth << " random moves is:\n" << *pos << '\n';
    q += new state(pos, NULL, position::NONE);
    state* s;

    while (!q.empty())
    {
        s = q.remove();

        if (s->pos->is_solution())
        {
            print_solution(s, q);
            exit(0);
        };

        // otherwise, add to the queue a new state for each move
        // that can be made from the current state's position
        queue_move(s, position::LEFT, q);
        queue_move(s, position::RIGHT, q);
        queue_move(s, position::UP, q);
        queue_move(s, position::DOWN, q);
    }

    return 0;
}
```

7.2.3 Solving the Puzzle with a Priority Queue

Solving the Fifteen Puzzle with a queue obtains the shortest possible solution, but it may take a very long time. Replacing the queue with a priority queue allows pursuing the more promising positions first. There's no guarantee that the solution is the shortest possible, but the number of positions considered may be dramatically reduced. It isn't even necessary to evaluate positions accurately — any reasonable estimate will work. The **Attribute** number_correct discussed above suffices. A more accurate estimate could be obtained by summing how far away each square is from where it belongs, but all that extra computation wouldn't necessarily reduce the number of positions considered enough to make it worthwhile.

Very few changes are required to use a priority queue in place of a queue. Obviously, the declaration of the queue changes to declare a priority queue. An evaluation function that calls number_correct must be supplied to the priority queue. That's about it.

The priority queue produces its more efficient processing pattern by ordering its elements. Exercise 2 gives you the chance to experiment with this modification.

7.3 Another Example

Priority queues are often used to support simulations. In this sort of application, priority queues store *event* descriptions. Events are often ordered simply by the time at which they should occur. An ordinary queue wouldn't be sufficient, in general, because an event added later might have an earlier time than one added earlier.

The example we'll use here is a classic one: a highly simplified simulation of the flow of customers in and out of a bank. The simulation must embody the following conditions. The result produced by a simulation is the average number of time spent by customers in the bank.

1. The bank has a fixed number of tellers, each with their own line of customers waiting to do business with them.
2. The only relevant property customers have is the length of time it will take to conduct their business with a teller.
3. A customer entering the bank goes to a free teller if one is available or to the back of the shortest teller line if all tellers are busy.
4. After one customer is finished with a teller, the next customer on that teller's line leaves the line and walks up to the teller window.
5. After customers finish with a teller, they leave the bank.

From these statements we can determine that the total time spent by a customer in the bank is the time spent on line plus the time spent with a teller plus any related delays. Delays could include the time it takes the customer to select and join a line, the time it takes a customer to leave a line and walk up to the teller's window in front of that line, and the time it takes to walk from the teller's window to the bank exit.

7.3.1 Modules

A thoroughly modularized approach to programming this simulation dictates a separate module for each kind of thing involved in the situation. We therefore will need modules for bank, teller, and customer. We also, of course, need data structures to manage the simulation: the bank will include an array of tellers, lines of customers will be represented as queues, and the simulation itself will be driven by a priority queue of events. Another module is needed to define an event structure.

A program like this presents many opportunities for making design choices. For instance, should customer lines (queues) be attached to tellers or to the bank? Which events do we really need? For example, we might think we need both events to represent a customer entering the bank and events to represent a customer getting on line, but as there is a fixed delay between the two, there isn't any real advantage to having both kinds. The situation actually reduces to only two kinds of events: a customer entering the bank and a customer completing his or her business. Everything else follows from those two.

One approach to the various types needed and the information they'll include can be summarized as follows. Various other approaches are also reasonable.

bank	array of tellers
	number of customers served
	total time spent in bank by customers served
teller	queue of customers
	current customer
customer	time entering bank
	amount of time business will take
	total time spent in bank
event	scheduled time
	customer involved
	action: enter or exit

7.3.2 Declarations

```
struct teller
{
  private:
    queue<customer*> line;
    customer* current_customer;

  public:
    teller();

    queue<customer*>& get_line();

    customer* take_next_customer(int time);
    void remove_customer();

    int line_length();
    bool is_free();
};
```

```
struct customer
{
  private:
    int enter_time;              // time entering bank
    int wait_time;               // time spent on line
    int exit_time;               // time exiting bank
    int time_needed;             // time needed with teller
    int id;                      // for output and debugging
    teller* teller_used;         // teller used by customer

  public:
    customer(int t_enter, int t_needed);
```

```
    int time_in_line();
    int time_in_bank();

    friend bool equal(customer&, customer&);
    friend order compare(customer&, customer&);
    friend ostream& operator<<(ostream&, customer&);
};
```

```
const int numtellers;

struct bank
{
  public:
    static int number_of_customers;
    static int total_customer_time;

  private:
    teller tellers[numtellers];

  public:
    bank();

    queue<customer*>& shortest_line();
    void add_to_shortest_line(customer* c);
};
```

```
struct event
{
  public:
    enum type { ENTER, LEAVE };

    customer* c;
    type typ;
    int time;

    event(customer*, type, int tim);

    friend bool equal(event&, event&);
    friend order compare(event&, event&);
    friend ostream& operator<<(ostream&, event&);
};
```

7.3.3 Managing Events

The program would use a single priority queue ordering its elements according to oper-
ator<(event&, event&). Input to the program might consists of a sequence of lines
specifying customer information: time entering bank and amount of time needed with a

teller. The program can begin by reading all the input, creating a customer, and adding an enter event to the priority queue for each line. It would then loop, each time taking an event off the queue and acting on it. At the end, the total number of customers using the bank and the average amount of time each spent in the bank would be printed.

The action taken would be different for each event type. For an enter event, the customer must be added to the shortest line or sent directly to the teller if a free one is available. On an exit event, the next customer is removed from the line in front of the teller the leaving customer used. Enter events are created from input, but exit events are created as the program executes. When a customer reaches a teller, the time the customer will leave the bank is known — it's just the time leaving the line plus the amount of time to be spent with the teller (plus any fixed delays assumed). So, when a customer goes directly to a free teller as part of an enter event or leaves a line as part of an exit event for the customer who previously left that line, a new exit event is added to the priority queue.

7.4 EXERCISES

1. A priority queue would work well with the maze runner program described in Exercise 7 of Chapter 5 (page 169). A reasonable evaluation function would be the "taxicab metric":

   ```
   distance from (x1,y1) to (x2,y2) = |x1-x2| + |y1-y2|
   ```

2. Modify the Fifteen Puzzle program shown in Section 7.2.2 (page 191) to use a priority queue, as discussed in Section 7.2.3 (page 193). Generate some statistics for puzzles of various depths (number of scrambling moves made) and comment on the relative efficiency of the queue and priority queue versions of the program.

3. Implement the bank simulation using the declarations shown in Section 7.3.3 (page 196), adding additional members to the structs shown if needed.

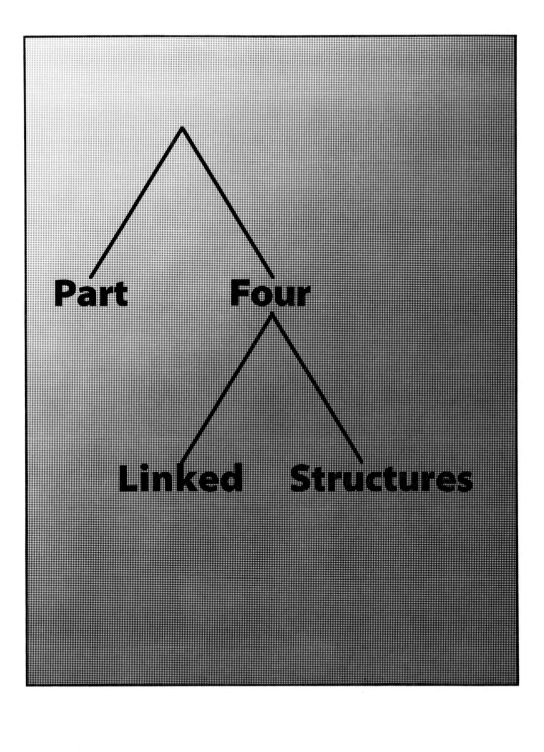

Part Four

Linked Structures

Part Four:

Linked Structures

This part of the book discusses *linked structures*. These structures are characterized by their flexibility in that they grow and shrink in size and can take on a variety of shapes. Consequently, they are often called *dynamic data structures*. The name 'linked' is used because they are composed of *nodes*, each of which holds pointers (links) to one or more other nodes in addition to an element. Because these structures have naturally recursive definitions, they may also be called *recursive structures*.

Linked structures are widely used in programming. The use of nodes to construct linked structures is probably the single most important topic in this text that would not ordinarily not be encountered in a programming or introductory computer science course. Each node of a linked structure has one or more successors and one or more predecessors. There are three fundamental kinds of linked structures, distinguished by the number of predecessors and successors allowed: *lists*, *trees*, and *graphs*. Table 5 summarizes this.

	Predecessors	Successors
List	1	1
Tree	1	1 or more
Graph	1 or more	1 or more

Table 5   Kinds of Linked Structures

From a given node only the immediate predecessor(s) and successor(s) of that node can be directly accessed (in addition to the node's data element). Therefore, most operations on linked structures require traversing them one node at a time — linked structures are sequentially accessed, like streams, rather than directly accessed, like arrays and storage structures.

Lists

Lists are the simplest kind of linked structure. In fact, they are so simple that they can even be represented in an unlinked form. We'll look at *sequential lists* first (the unlinked kind), then at various kinds of *linked lists*.

Lists are *ordered* structures. That is, the order in which a list's elements appear is typically significant to the application that uses it. **Add** and **Remove** operations must therefore preserve that order when modifying a list.

8.1 Sequential Lists

Sequential lists are collections of elements stored in an array, along with some kind of mechanism for delimiting the list within the array. Although the length of the array places an upper limit on the number of elements stored in it, the size of the list can grow and shrink within that limit as elements are added and removed. Moreover, by using a dynamically allocated array and reallocating a larger one when it gets filled up, sequential lists can be allowed to grow indefinitely large.

8.1.1 Representation

The obvious way to represent a sequential list in C++ is as a struct that contains an array of list elements and an integer that keeps track of the size of the list. A fixed array size could be coded into the list implementation, but specifying the size as a constructor argument would provide greater flexibility. The implementations of several fundamental operations use the array size, so that value must be included in the struct representing the list. Figure 8.1 illustrates this arrangement.

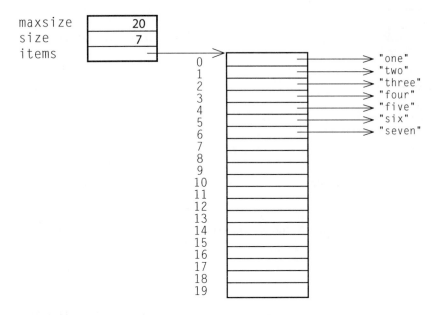

Figure 8.1   A Sequential List

```
template <class elt> struct seq_list
{
  private:
    // Representation
    elt *elts;                      // array of elt's
    int length;                     // current length
    int allocation;                 // length of allocated array
    // . . .
};
```

8.1.2 Lifetime Operations

Initialize/Finalize

Constructors initialize each of a new instance's data members appropriately: length to 0, allocation to the limit indicated by the constructor argument, and elts to a newly allocated array. The traversal state — cur — is set to a special value indicating an uninitialized traversal. The function clear is called to do the work necessary to make the list empty, in this case just setting length to 0 and making the traversal state, defined later, uninitialized. Clear is also used in the **Copy** operations, to start a copy off empty. For these purposes, clear could be made private. However, it also provides a convenient way to empty a list without having to remove each element individually, so it is made publicly available.

The destructor deallocates the dynamic array. In the approach to collections adopted for this book, elements of a collection are always independent of it. Consequently, the destructor deletes only the space allocated to store the pointers, not the data to which the pointers point.

```
template <class elt> struct seq_list
{
    // . . .
  private:
    // Initialize/Finalize
  public:
    void clear();
    seq_list(int maxlen = 100);
    ~seq_list();
};
```

```
/* Initialize/Finalize */

template <class elt> void seq_list<elt>::clear()
{
    length = 0;
    cur = no_pos;
}

template <class elt> seq_list<elt>:: seq_list(int maxlen) :
    allocation(maxlen), elts(new elt[maxlen]), cur(no_pos)
    // no_pos is discussed with traversal operations, below
{
    clear();
}

template <class elt> seq_list<elt>::~seq_list()
{
    delete [] elts;
}
```

The basic **Access** operation is nth, which, given n, returns the nth element of the list. Sequences can be indexed starting either at 0 or at 1. Here, 1 is chosen, since it is more natural — even though C array indexing starts at 0. The subscript operator is made a synonym of nth. For convenience and naturalness of expression, first and last are also provided.

A wide range of **Modify** operations makes sense for lists. We'll consider each subcategory separately — **Add**, **Remove**, **Replace**, and **Exchange**. References are returned by all **Access** operations, so these operations can be used on the left side of an assignment statement. This provides an alternative to calling a **Replace** function to replace a specific element of a list. Following is an example.

```
seq_list<char*> lst;
lst += "one";
lst += "two";
lst[1] = "three";
lst.last() = "four";
// lst now contains "three" and "four"
```

Access

```
template <class elt> struct seq_list
{
    // . . .
    // Access
  public:
    elt& nth(int n);
    elt& operator[](int n);
    elt& first();
    elt& last();
};
```

```
/* Access */

template <class elt> elt& seq_list<elt>::nth(int n)
{
    if ((n <= 0) && (n > length))
        error("[seq_list::nth] index out of bounds");
    return elts[n-1];
}

template <class elt> elt& seq_list<elt>::operator[](int n)
{
    return nth(n);
}

template <class elt> elt& seq_list<elt>::first()
{
    return nth(1);
}

template <class elt> elt& seq_list<elt>::last()
{
    return nth(length);
}
```

Add

The basic add function adds a new element at the back of the list. By default, insert adds a new element at the front; if n is provided, it adds the new element before the nth element. Another way of inserting within the list is provided: insert_before and insert_after. These take the element to be inserted and the element before or after which the new one is to be inserted. Operator+= is made a synonym for add.

```
template <class elt> struct seq_list
{
    // . . .
    // Modify: Add
    void add(elt);                      // add at back
    seq_list<elt>& operator+=(elt);

    void insert(elt, int pos = 1);
    // add at pos, moving subsequent elts down; pos can be 1 past end
    void insert_before(elt new_elt, elt old_elt);
    void insert_after(elt new_elt, elt old_elt);
};
```

Adding a new element at the end of the list is simple. First the function verifies that the list is not full. Then it stores the new element at the position indicated by size. Finally size is incremented.

```
/* Modify: basic Add */

template <class elt> void seq_list<elt>::add(elt e)
{
    if (length == allocation)
        error("[seq_list<elt>::add] list is full");
    else
        elts[length++] = e;
}

template <class elt> seq_list<elt>& seq_list<elt>::operator+=(elt e)
{
    add(e);
    return *this;
}
```

Since the order of components within a list is often significant we want to be able to add a new element anywhere in the list, not just at the end. Insertion in the midst of existing elements is more work than just adding an element to the end, because subsequent elements have to be moved down to make room for the new one. To insert at the front of the list, we can just move all the list's elements down one position and store the new one in the first array location. The C library function memmove is used to shift the array elements. (Like memcpy, this is a convenient way to copy a sequence of bytes, but unlike memcpy, memmove works even if the source and destination overlap.) For insert_before and insert_after, the position of the target element must be determined first. That will be done using position_of, a **Process** operation shown later.

```
/* Modify: Insert */

//   Insert element at position pos (offset-1), shifting subsequent ones.
//   Inserting at 1 past current end is permitted, to support insert_after.
template <class elt> void seq_list<elt>::insert(elt e, int pos)
{
    if (length == allocation)
        error("[seq_list<elt>::insert] list full");
    if (pos > length+1)
        error("[seq_list<elt>::insert] position past end of list");
    if (pos <= 0)
        error("[seq_list<elt>::insert] position before beginning of list");

    ++length;
    memmove(elts+pos, elts+pos-1, (length-pos)*sizeof(elt));
    // -1 to convert offset-1 positions to offset-0 indices
    elts[pos-1] = e;
}

template <class elt>
void seq_list<elt>::insert_before(elt new_elt, elt old_elt)
{
    int pos = position_of(old_elt);

    if (pos <= 0)
        error("[seq_list<elt>::insert_before] elt not in list");
    else
        insert(new_elt, pos);
}

template <class elt>
void seq_list<elt>::insert_after(elt new_elt, elt old_elt)
{
    int pos = position_of(old_elt);

    if (pos <= 0)
        error("[insert_after] elt not in list");
    else
        insert(new_elt, pos+1);
}
```

Remove

Unlike a set, a list may contain duplicate elements, so a user might want to remove all occurrences of an element or just remove the first. What element to remove may be indicated by providing an element or by specifying a position. The module includes several kinds of **Remove** operations to accommodate the various usages: remove to remove all occurrences of an element or the element at a particular position and remove1 to remove the first occurrence of a specific element. It is useful for remove(int) to return the element removed, but when the element is supplied in the call there's no need for any return. Operator-= is provided as a synonym of remove (elt). Some of these functions make use of a private function remove_at that does the work of removing the element at a specific position of the element array.

```
template <class elt> struct seq_list
{
    // . . .
    // Modify: Remove
  private:
    elt remove_at(int pos);          // offset-0
  public:
    void remove(elt);                // remove all occurrences
    void remove1(elt);               // remove first occurrence
    elt remove(int);                 // remove nth elt&  return
    seq_list<elt>& operator-=(elt);  // synonym for remove
};
```

```
/* Modify: Remove */

// private, doesn't test validity of argument
template <class elt> elt seq_list<elt>::remove_at(int pos)
{
    elt e = elts[pos];               // save to return

    memmove (elts+pos-1, elts+pos, (length-pos)*sizeof(elt));
    // -1 to convert offset-1 positions to offset-0 indices
    length--;

    return e;
}

// remove first occurrence of elt
template <class elt> void seq_list<elt>::remove1(elt e)
{
    int pos = position_of(e);

    if (pos <= 0)
        error("[position_of] elt not in list");
    else
        remove_at(pos);
}

// remove all occurrences of elt
template <class elt> void seq_list<elt>::remove(elt e)
{
    for (int pos = length; pos > 0; pos--)
    // backward so iteration isn't confused
    // by the removal and consequent shifting
```

```
        if (e == elts[pos-1]) remove_at(pos);
}

template <class elt> seq_list<elt>& seq_list<elt>::operator-=(elt e)
{
    remove(e);
    return *this;
}

template <class elt> elt seq_list<elt>::remove(int n)
{
    if (n <= 0 || n > length)
        error("[seq_list::remove] index out of range");
    return remove_at(n);
}
```

Replace

As with **Remove**, **Replace** may mean replace all occurrences of an element or just the first.
As we saw above, since the **Access** operations return references, they can be used to replace
the corresponding element of the list.   We won't bother including a function to replace the
n^{th} element, since the **Access** operations are so natural to use.

```
template <class elt> struct seq_list
{
    // . . .
    // Modify: Replace
    void replace(elt old_elt, elt new_elt);
    void replace1(elt old_elt, elt new_elt);
};
```

```
/* Modify: Replace */

// replace first occurrence of old_elt
template <class elt> void seq_list<elt>::replace1(elt old_elt, elt new_elt)
{
    int pos = position_of(old_elt);

    if (pos <= 0)
        error("[seq_list<elt>::replace1] elt not in list");
    else
        elts[pos-1] = new_elt;
}

// replace all occurrences of elt
template <class elt> void seq_list<elt>::replace(elt old_elt, elt new_elt)
{
```

```
    reset();
    while (next())
        if (old_elt == current())
            current() = new_elt;           // note lval function call
}
```

Exchange

In principle, all collection structures could support **Exchange** operations. **Exchange** operations are not shown for most of the structures in the book, but they are included here. They are particularly useful with lists, especially in support of sorting operations, as will be seen in Section 8.3, page 251.

```
template <class elt> struct seq_list
{
    // . . .
    // Modify: Exchange
    void exchange(int, int);
    void exchange(elt, elt);              // exchange first occurrences
};
```

```
/* Modify: Exchange */

// Exchange elts at p1 and p2 (offset-1)
template <class elt> void seq_list<elt>::exchange(int p1, int p2)
{
    if (p1 <= 0 || p1 > length || p2 <= 0 || p2 >= length)
        error("[seq_list::exchange] index out of range");
    ::exchange(elts[p1-1], elts[p2-1]);
        // The :: is needed to call the global function from standard.H.
}

template <class elt> void seq_list<elt>::exchange(elt elt1, elt elt2)
{
    int p1 = position_of(elt1);
    if (p1 <= 0) error("[seq_list<elt>::exchange] elt1 not in list");

    int p2 = position_of(elt2);
    if (p2 <= 0) error("[seq_list<elt>::exchange] elt2 not in list");

    ::exchange(elts[p1-1], elts[p2-1]);
        // The :: is needed to call the global function from standard.H.
}
```

8.1.3 Traversal

Traversal of a sequential list is simple — so simple that there seems little need for any mechanism. Suppose you wanted to count the number of occurrences of an element e in the list lst. You could write code such as this:

```
int count = 0;
for (int i = 0; i < lst.length(); i++)
    if (lst[i] == itml) count++;
```

There's an error here, however, and this kind of error is one of the strongest reasons to prohibit low-level loops like this: operator[] uses an offset-1 scheme, not the offset-0 scheme of C arrays, so, the 0 should be 1, and the < should be <=. **Traversal** operations encapsulate the tricky details of loop limits and stepping to free programmers using the structure from having to know about them and to avoid errors due to mishandling them. Traversing a structure should always be done using traversal operations, even when lower-level mechanisms are available. The above should therefore be coded as

```
int count = 0;
lst.reset();
while (lst.next())
    if (lst.current() == itml) count++;
```

Here are **Traversal** operations for sequential lists. The declarations are the usual ones. The definitions are straightforward. A special value (no_pos) is used to distinguish an uninitialized traversal from one that has been reset but not yet stepped with next.

```
struct seq_lst
{
    // . . .
    // Traversal
  private:
    static const int no_pos;        // shows uninitialized traversal
    int cur;                        // traversal index
  public:
    void reset();
    bool finished();
    bool next();
    elt& current();
    int index();
};
```

```
/* Traversal */

template <class elt> const int seq_list<elt>::no_pos = -99;
            // value of cur for uninitialized traversal

template <class elt> void seq_list<elt>::reset()
{
    cur = -1;
```

```
}

template <class elt> bool seq_list<elt>::finished()
{
    return cur >= length;
}

template <class elt> bool seq_list<elt>::next()
{
    if (no_pos == cur)
        error("[seq_list<elt>::next] traversal not yet initialized");
    if (finished())
        error("[seq_list<elt>::next] traversal already finished");

    ++cur;
    return !finished();
}

template <class elt> elt& seq_list<elt>::current()
{
    if (no_pos == cur)
        error("[seq_list<elt>::current] traversal not yet initialized");
    if (-1 == cur)
        error("[seq_list<elt>::current] traversal initialized"
                "but not yet stepped");
    if (finished())
        error("[seq_list<elt>::current] traversal already finished");
    return elts[cur];
}

template <class elt> int seq_list<elt>::index()
{
    return cur + 1;
}
```

8.1.4 Content Operations

Lists have typical **Attributes** and can be compared and combined in various ways. The standard way to combine linear structures (such as lists) is to create a new one with all the elements of the first followed by all the elements of the second. This is typically called *append* or *concatenate*. An interesting variation of **Combine** available for linear structures is merge, which creates a new list consisting of elements taken alternately from each of two existing ones. Implementation of merge is left as an exercise here (Exercise 6).

```
template <class elt> struct seq_list
{
    // . . .
    // Attributes
    int size();
    bool empty();
```

```
    bool full();

    // Compare
    friend order compare(seq_list<elt>&, seq_list<elt>&);
    friend bool equal(seq_list<elt>&, seq_list<elt>&);

    // Combine
    friend seq_list append(seq_list&,seq_list&);
    friend seq_list<elt> operator+(seq_list<elt>&,seq_list<elt>&);
                                        // synonym for append
    friend seq_list<elt> merge(seq_list&,seq_list&);  // alternate elts
};
```

```
/* Attributes */

template <class elt> int seq_list<elt>::size()
{
    return length;
}

template <class elt> bool seq_list<elt>::empty()
{
    return length == 0;
}

template <class elt> bool seq_list<elt>::full()
{
    return length == allocation;
}
```

Two linear structures are generally compared by traversing them in parallel, comparing elements pairwise. If the lists have the same number of elements, and all the elements are equal pairwise, the lists are considered equal. Lists are compared for order similarly. The two lists are traversed, and their elements are compared pairwise. When the first unequal pair is encountered, the list with the lesser element is considered "before" the other. If both lists are the same length, and no unequal pairs are encountered, the lists are considered equal.

Note that equal could just be defined as testing whether compare returns EQUAL. There are two reasons not to do that. One is that the element type might define equal but not compare. If seq_list::equal calls seq_list::compare, then when seq_list::- compare tries to call the element type's compare, an error will occur; however, if seq_ list::equal calls the element type's equal directly, there won't be any problem. Therefore, coding equal separately provides greater flexibility for users of the list module. The other reason is efficiency: comparing two elements for order may require a lot more work than just telling whether or not they are equal. Moreover, seq_list::equal can use some preliminary tests to determine inexpensively that the two lists are not equal, such as comparing their stored lengths.

```
/* Compare */

template <class elt>
order compare(seq_list<elt>& lst1, seq_list<elt>& lst2)
{
    order ord;
    int i = 0;
    int minlength = min(lst1.length, lst2.length);

    while ((i < minlength) &&
            (EQUAL == (ord = compare(*lst1.elts[i], *lst2.elts[i]))))
        i++;

    if ((i == minlength) && (lst1.length == lst2.length))
        return EQUAL;
    else if (i == lst1.length)
        return BEFORE;
    else if (i == lst2.length)
        return AFTER;
    else return ord;
}

// tests equality of elts, not just identity, so two different pointers
// could point to elts that test equal even though they are different.
template <class elt> bool equal(seq_list<elt>& lst1, seq_list<elt>& lst2)
{
    if (lst1.length != lst2.length)
        return FALSE;

    for (int i = 0; i < lst1.length; i++)
        if (!equal(*lst1.elts[i], *lst2.elts[i]))
            return FALSE;

    return TRUE;
}
```

The implementation of append is straightforward. It begins with a new empty list then traverses its two argument lists adding each element to the end of the new list. Finally, it returns a copy of the new list. (Because the list is returned by value, not by reference, the compiler invokes the copy constructor to make a copy before deallocating the locally allocated new list.) Of course, making that copy requires traversing the new list and adding each of its elements to the copy.

There is no simple way to avoid this inefficiency, and we will have to live with it for the implementations in this book. Returning a reference to a local variable is not allowed: since the variable is deallocated when the function returns, there's nothing left for the reference to refer to! It would work to allocate the new list on the heap instead of the stack, then return a reference to it. However, that would require programmers to keep track of and eventually delete lists returned from append. This is an unacceptable burden to impose.

The only straightforward workable solution is to incur the extra costs of copying a local list on return from the function. This problem arises for any function that makes a new list out of one or more existing ones — in general, **Combine** and certain **Process** operations (such as reverse, shown below). It might seem that the problem would arise for **Copy** operations too, but in C++ these do not allocate the destination lists. The copy constructor is invoked on a newly allocated list, and the copy assignment operator copies to an already existing list. Neither allocates a new list.

```
/* Combine */

template <class elt>
seq_list<elt> append(seq_list<elt>& lst1, seq_list<elt>& lst2)
{
    seq_list<elt> lst(lst1.allocation +lst2.allocation);
    // might as well make the new list big enough to hold full versions
    // of each of the lists whether or not they are currently full.

    for (int i = 0; i < lst1.length; i++)
        lst.elts[i] = lst1.elts[i];
    for (i = 0; i < lst2.length; i++)
        lst.elts[lst1.length + i] = lst2.elts[i];
    lst.length = lst1.length + lst2.length;

    return lst;
}

template <class elt>
seq_list<elt> operator+(seq_list<elt>& lst1, seq_list<elt>& lst2)
{
    return append(lst1, lst2);
}
```

8.1.5 Support Operations

In addition to the standard **Copy** and **Output** operations, lists support some interesting **Process** operations. **Search** operations include position_of, contains, and contains_ equal. **Sort** is declared, but not implemented. List sorting is discussed as a separate topic later in this chapter (cf. Section 8.3, page 251). Another **Process** operation applicable to linear structures is reverse.

```
template <class elt> struct seq_list
{
    // . . .
    // Copy
  private:
    void copy(seq_list& lst);
  public:
    seq_list(seq_list&);
```

```
        seq_list& operator=(seq_list&);

        // Process
        int position_of(elt);
        bool contains(elt);
        bool contains_equal(elt);
        seq_list reverse();
        void sort();

        // Output
        friend ostream& operator<<(ostream&, seq_list&);
};
```

Copy starts with an empty list. (The copy constructor is called when a new list is allocated, while the copy assignment operator resets the length of the list being copied to.) Then the list being copied is traversed, and each of its elements is added to the end of the destination list. In the copy constructor, the maximum size of the destination list is made the same as the maximum size of the old one, and a new array of elements is allocated. In the copy assignment operator, allocation and elts are left alone if allocation is at least as big as the allocation of the source list. Otherwise, the old array of elements is deleted and a new, larger one is allocated, with allocation set accordingly. (This is a design choice: another approach would be to always delete the old array and allocate a new one.) Also, the traversal state of the destination list is set to uninitialized.

```
/* Copy */

//private:
template <class elt> void seq_list<elt>::copy(seq_list<elt>& lst)
{
    lst.reset();
    while (lst.next()) add(lst.current());
}

template <class elt> seq_list<elt>:: seq_list(seq_list<elt>& lst) :
    allocation(lst.allocation), elts(new elt[lst.allocation])
{
    clear();
    copy(lst);
}

template <class elt>
seq_list<elt>& seq_list<elt>::operator=(seq_list<elt>& lst)
{
    if (this == &lst) return *this;           // assignment to self!

    if (allocation < lst.length)
        {
            delete elts;
            allocation = lst.allocation;
            elts = new elt[allocation];
        }
```

```
    clear();
    copy(lst);

    return *this;
}
```

The **Search** operation `position_of` was used in the implementation of various **Mod-ify** operations in the sequential list module. It is sometimes useful externally, too. Really, it's just another form of `contains` that returns the position found instead of a Boolean. (If the target is not found, then 0 is returned.) In fact, `contains` could be defined to just call `position_of`. Similarly, although `position_of` is defined here directly in terms of the list's representation, it could have been defined using traversal operations. Compare the definitions of `position_of` and `contains` — they really say the same thing in two different ways.

Both `position_of` and `contains` are based on element *identity* not *equality*. Sometimes searches based on equality are needed, so `contains_equal` is also provided. As with `compare` and `equal`, the definition of `contains_equal` makes the assumption that the element type of the list template is a pointer type. It tests for equality by dereferencing the pointer provided as an argument and each successive pointer found in the list, until `equal` of the two values is true or the list is exhausted.

Similar considerations apply to `reverse` as to the **Combine** operations discussed above. It allocates a local list, operates on it, then returns it by value, causing a **Copy** to occur. Here, the local list starts out as a straight copy. Then pairs of elements are exchanged starting at the extremes and working inward. This slightly subtle process effectively reverses the list, including handling both odd- and even-length lists.

```
/* Process */

// Positions are offset-1 for simplicity of interface.
template <class elt> int seq_list<elt>::position_of(elt e)
{
    for (int i = 0; i < length; i++)
        if (e == elts[i]) return i+1;
    return 0;                               // not found
}

// tests identity
template <class elt> bool seq_list<elt>::contains(elt target)
{
    reset();
    while (next()) if (target == current()) return TRUE;

    return FALSE;
}

// tests equality
template <class elt> bool seq_list<elt>::contains_equal(elt target)
{
```

```
        reset();
        while (next()) if (equal(*target, *current())) return TRUE;

        return FALSE;

}

// returns a reversed copy
template <class elt> seq_list<elt> seq_list<elt>::reverse()
{
        seq_list<elt>* lst(*this);                   // start with a copy

        int mid = length/2;
        for (int i = 0; i < mid; i++)
            ::exchange(lst.elts[i], lst.elts[length-i-1]);

        return lst;
}
```

There isn't really any standard way to print a list. Certainly printing a list will involve printing each of its elements, which means dereferencing each pointer and invoking the element's output operator. But how should the elements be separated? By spaces? commas? newline characters? And what about the beginning and end of the list — should the list be enclosed in parentheses? braces? brackets? extra blank lines? nothing? Here, the decision is made to enclose the list in parentheses and separate the elements by a space.

In any case, the definition of operator<< is typical of output operators for linear structures. The heart of the process is a traversal over the elements that prints each one, perhaps separated by additional characters. There may be special actions before and after the traversal. Finally, since the number of separators output will be one less than the number of list elements, the first element is printed outside the traversal loop, without a separator.

```
/* Output */

template <class elt> ostream& operator<<(ostream& strm, seq_list<elt>& lst)
{
        lst.reset();
        strm << '(';
        if (lst.next()) strm << *lst.current();
        // handle first element specially: no delimiter before

        while (lst.next()) strm << ' ' << *lst.current();

        strm << ')';
        return strm;
}
```

8.2 Linked Lists

Although sequential lists are easy to implement, their inflexibility limits their utility. Sequential lists are inefficient in several ways:

- Each list takes up a fixed amount of space regardless of its size, wasting unoccupied space.
- A list cannot contain more elements than its fixed-size array can hold.
- Insertion and deletion shift many elements in the array.

Some simple memory management techniques can be used to automatically expand and shrink a sequential list, as explored in Exercise 4. However, there isn't much that can be done to improve the performance of sequential lists for insertion and deletion, and those operations occur frequently. Achieving greater flexibility requires a different kind of list implementation: the *linked list*.

Sequential lists share some of the characteristics of linked lists, but they also share some of the characteristics of arrays. In particular, they support direct access, which linked structures do not. This means they support many important sorting and searching algorithms that depend on being able to easily obtain an arbitrary element rather than having to traverse the structure to reach it. Linked lists trade the efficiencies of direct access for the efficiencies of trivial insertion and deletion operations.

8.2.1 Links

In a sequential list, the successor and predecessor of each element are implicit in the ordering of the elements an array. In a linked data structure the successors (and possibly predecessors) of each element are explicitly represented. The order in which the elements are stored is irrelevant — the links determine the ordering of the elements at the conceptual level of the list.

A linked structure is composed of *nodes*. Each node contains two kinds of information:

- a pointer to an element
- pointers to the element's predecessors and successors

Whether an element may have more than one successor and whether it may have more than one predecessor depends on the kind of linked structure being represented. Links to an element's successors are always represented explicitly in the element's node, but whether the node also contains links to the element's predecessors is an implementation option. (Explicit representation of predecessor links, or *back pointers*, improves the efficiency of certain operations at the cost of the space taken by the extra pointers.)

Elements in a list have one successor and one predecessor. A linked list node contains just two or three pointers: one to an element, one to the next node, and, optionally, one to the previous node. Figure 8.2 illustrates a linked list and its nodes. (We'll consider only *singly linked lists* from now on; *doubly linked lists* — those with back pointers — are explored in Exercise 23.) In such figures, pointers are traditionally represented by

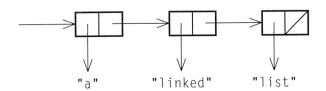

Figure 8.2   A Linked List

arrows. The absence of a pointer — a special end-of-list value — is indicated by a diagonal line across the pointer field.

The implementation of a linked data structure always involves two types: one representing instances of the structure and one representing the nodes comprising instances of the structure. The node type is "private" to the structure type — clients of the structure see only the structure's interface. Therefore, the two types may be implemented together in a single module.

Inserting a new element into the middle of a list involves the following steps, as shown in Figure 8.3.:

- Allocate a new node with a pointer to the new element.
- Store a pointer to the new node's successor in the new node.
- Change the pointer from the former predecessor of the new node's successor to point to the new node.

Insertion at the front of the list is special — here, what changes is not a node's link, since there is no previous node, but rather the pointer to the first node that is recorded in the list structure. (More will be said about this when we look at some implementations.)

The important thing to notice about linked list insertion is that *nothing gets moved!* All that changes in the list are a few pointers. Insertion into a linked list is therefore a very inexpensive operation, compared with insertion into a sequential list, which must shift elements within an array.

Deleting an element is also efficiently accomplished simply by changing links, as illustrated in Figure 8.4. Again, nothing is moved. As with insertion at the front, deletion of the first node changes a pointer in the list struct rather than a link of a node.

Many operations on lists involve traversal. The implementation of traversal is simple: start at the first node and follow the links until the end of the list is encountered. In effect, you do something like this when you read linked list diagrams.

8.2.2 Array-Based Linked Lists

We'll look first at a simple implementation of linked lists, based on arrays of nodes. The purpose of discussing this approach is to introduce the essential details of nodes and links. An array-based approach does nothing to correct the problems of fixed-size structures — it's just a pedagogical tool. Afterward, we'll look at the way linked structures are really implemented and how size limitations are avoided.

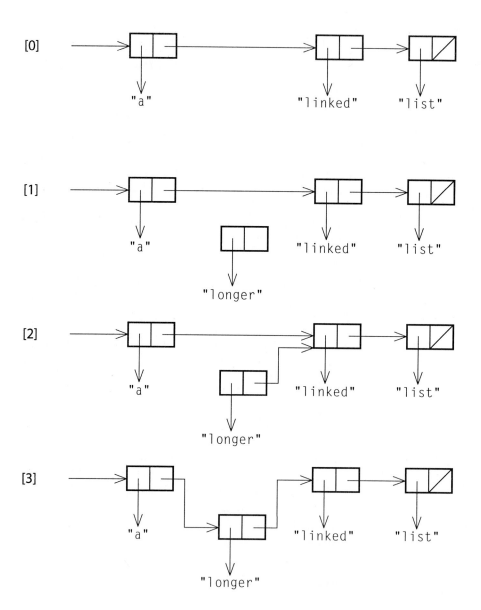

Figure 8.3   Linked List Insertion

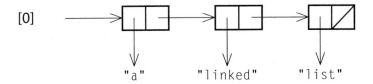

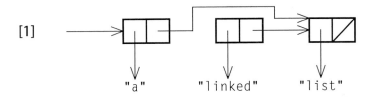

*Once the pointer from the first node to the second is re-
moved, nothing points to the second node — it's still
there, but it is no longer part of the data structure.*

Figure 8.4   Linked List Deletion

Representation

The list structure keeps track of several pieces of information, as shown in Figure 8.5:

- an array of nodes to be used to represent the list
- the size of the array
- the index of the node to be used next when a new one is needed
- the index of the first node of the list

```
typedef int link;                           // type for node addresses

template <class elt> struct linked_list
{
  private:
    // Representation
    static link endmark;                    // special end-of-list value

    list_node<elt>* nodes;                  // array of nodes
    int allocation;                         // size of nodes array
    link firstnode;                         // location of first node
    link nextfree;                          // location of next unused node
    // . . .
};
```

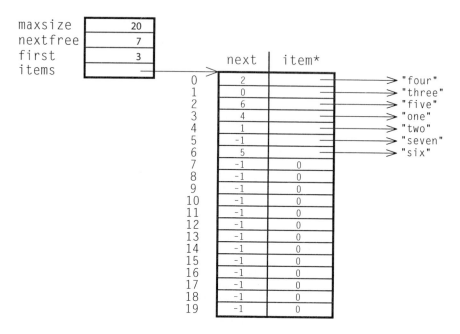

Figure 8.5   An Array-Based Linked List

The linked list module also defines a second type — a supporting structure called list_node. Users of the module will never interact with nodes directly. To enforce that, all node members are made private, and linked_list made a friend of list_node.

A list node simply contains an element and a link to another node. Its job is to hold on to the element on behalf of the list and know where the next node is to be found.[1] As a typical low-level data structure, the only operations it needs are **Initialize** and an **Access** and **Modify** for each of its fields. The node structure doesn't know anything about how it is being used — it is entirely a slave of the linked list structure that uses it.

---

[1]It is common in introductory treatments of linked lists to simply add a link field to whatever data type is used for the list elements. This leads to conceptual absurdities like a person struct that stores information about a person such as age, name, address, occupation, Social Security number, and ... a pointer to another person! A disciplined approach to data abstraction dictates that the concerns of linking nodes be isolated from the application-level information, rather than mixing the two together haphazardly. A person has a name and a node has a link; the two kinds of information are entirely unrelated.

Another problem with adding link fields to application types is that it restricts each instance to being on just one list, since there's only one link field. Suppose linked lists are used to represent students enrolled in courses. We would need to be able to store the same student instance in several linked lists. Only a disciplined approach that separates nodes and students makes this possible: a new node is created for each list the student instance belongs to. The fact that several nodes point to the same instance is largely irrelevant.

```
/* private structure */
template <class elt> struct list_node
{
    friend struct linked_list<elt>;
  private:
    elt elem;
    link next;

    list_node();
    ~list_node();

    elt& getElt();
    void setElt(elt);
    link getNext();
    void setNext(link);
};
```

```
/* list_node functions */

// a friend of linked_list<elt> so it can access endmark
template <class elt> list_node<elt>::list_node()
        : elem(0), next(linked_list<elt>::endmark)
{
}

template <class elt> list_node<elt>::~list_node()
{
}

template <class elt> elt& list_node<elt>::getElt()
{
    return elem;
}

template <class elt> void list_node<elt>::setElt(elt e)
{
    elem = e;
}

template <class elt> link list_node<elt>::getNext()
{
    return next;
}

template <class elt> void list_node<elt>::setNext(link n)
{
    next = n;
}
```

8.2.3 Lifetime Operations

Here are the lifetime operations for an array-based linked list module. Remember, this is a primitive, rigid implementation that is being used only for expository purposes. The real linked list implementation comes later in this chapter. That is why the constructor still takes a maximum size, as with sequential lists — we're still (temporarily) dealing with a fixed-size array, though of nodes not elements.

Initialize/Finalize

The constructor for linked_list creates an array of nodes. Those nodes get initialized by the list_node constructor. A link from one node to another is simply the index in the array of the other node. Therefore, an impossible index value of –1 (the value of list::endmark) is used to indicate that there is no next node. For safety, each new node starts out with endmark as its link value. Each node's element pointer is initialized to 0, since it doesn't yet contain an element.

As in the sequential list implementation, a clear function is used to start the list off empty. It is also called by the list's **Copy** operations and may be called by application code to empty a list for reuse.

```
template <class elt> struct linked_list
{
    // . . .
    // Initialize/Finalize
  public:
    void clear();
    linked_list(int = 100);
    ~linked_list();
};
```

```
/* Initialize/Finalize */

template <class elt> void linked_list<elt>::clear()
{
    nextfree = 0;
    firstnode = endmark;
    cur = endmark;
    indx = no_index;
}

template <class elt> linked_list<elt>::linked_list(int maxlen) :
        allocation(maxlen), nodes(new list_node<elt>[maxlen])
{
    clear();
}
```

```
template <class elt> linked_list<elt>::~linked_list()
{
    delete [] nodes;
}
```

Access

Conceptually, the elements of a linked list are accessed like those of a sequential list — by position. However, because linked lists do not support direct access, the implementations of the functions are entirely different. In addition to the public positional **Access** operations, private functions are needed for locating specific elements within the list structure by position or by search. These functions return links to be used in the definitions of many of the other functions in the module. Note that public linked_list functions never return links — the locations of nodes within the structure is internal information that should not be made available to client code.

```
template <class elt> struct linked_list
{
    // . . .
    // Access
  private:
    link link_to(int);           // index of nth elt
    link link_to(elt);           // find an elt
    link link_to_prev(elt);      // support for insert_before
    link link_to_last();         // for convenience

  public:
    elt& nth(int);
    elt& operator[](int);
    elt& first();
    elt& last();
};
```

The definitions of the private **Access** operations illuminate the essence of linked list organization. The access process is a direct consequence of that organization. To find an element by position, the list is traversed starting from the first node until the nth node is reached. Likewise, to find a particular element, the list is traversed until a node containing it is located. The extreme is demonstrated in link_to_last, where the entire list must be traversed to reach the last element. Because these operations are so basic to the rest of the implementation, they are coded without using traversal operations, both for efficiency and so as not to disrupt application traversals in process.

Each node holds the index in the nodes array of the node that follows it in the list. Traversal simply follows these "links" from one node to the other until the target is reached. Traversals also ends if endmark is encountered. It is common practice to use the variable cur for the current node of a list traversal, and prev and next for the nodes before and after cur. Most of the internal **Access** operations return the location of the node that contains the target element. We'll see shortly that deletion of a node and insertion before a node actually modify the previous node. To support such actions, link_to_prev returns the location of the node *before* the one containing the target element.

```
/* Access: internal */

template <class elt> link linked_list<elt>::link_to(int n)
{
    link cur = firstnode;

    while (cur!=endmark && --n)
        cur = nodes[cur].getNext();

    return cur;
}

template <class elt> link linked_list<elt>::link_to(elt e)
{
    link cur = firstnode;

    while ((cur != endmark) &&
            e != nodes[cur].getElt())
        cur = nodes[cur].getNext();

    return cur;
}

// Caller must verify that elt is not in first node or result will be
// 'not there' (unless there's a subsequent repetition of the elt)
template <class elt> link linked_list<elt>::link_to_prev(elt e)
{
    if (firstnode == endmark) return endmark;

    link prev = firstnode;
    link cur = nodes[firstnode].getNext();

    while ((cur != endmark) && e != nodes[cur].getElt())
        {
            prev = cur;
            cur = nodes[cur].getNext();
        };

    if (cur == endmark)
        return endmark;                        // e not found
    else
        return prev;
}

template <class elt> link linked_list<elt>::link_to_last()
{
    if (firstnode == endmark) return endmark;

    link prev = firstnode;
    link cur = nodes[firstnode].getNext();
```

```
    while (cur != endmark)
    {
        prev = cur;
        cur = nodes[cur].getNext();
    }

    return prev;
}
```

Next are the definitions of the public **Access** functions. The internal **Access** functions return endmark if the desired element isn't found — for instance, if 1st.link_ to(5) is called on a list with fewer than five elements. The public functions are responsible for validating arguments provided by the use, checking values returned by the private functions, and signaling appropriate error conditions. In fact, that's most of what the public functions do, since they rely on the private ones to do the real work of locating elements.

```
/* Access */

template <class elt> elt& linked_list<elt>::nth(int n)
{
    link l = link_to(n);
    if (l == endmark) error("[linked_list::nth} index out of range");
    return nodes[l].getElt();
}

template <class elt> elt& linked_list<elt>::operator[](int n)
{
    return nth(n);
}

template <class elt> elt& linked_list<elt>::first()
{
    if (empty()) error("[linked_list::first] empty list");
    return nodes[firstnode].getElt();
}

template <class elt> elt& linked_list<elt>::last()
{
    if (empty()) error("[linked_list::last] empty list");
    return nodes[link_to_last()].getElt();
}
```

Modify

Linked lists exhibit a wide range of **Modify** operations, including several versions each of **Add**, **Remove**, **Exchange**, and **Replace**. As with **Access**, some private member functions that deal with node addresses are defined to be used by the public functions. In several cases, there are public and private functions with the same names: the destination arguments of the public ones are elements or positions, while the destination arguments of the private functions are links. The public functions traverse the list to obtain a link to the node corresponding to the destination argument, then pass that link to the appropriate private function.

Allocation and deallocation of nodes and the modification of their links are confined to the private functions. In an echo of our general modularization principles, we in effect have a submodule of private functions that do all the real work for the rest of the functions. This reduces the complexity of the whole module and limits the number of changes that have to be made to make some change to the list's representation. Nodes are allocated for use from the nodes list. The data member nextfree, initialized to 0, indicates the location of the next unallocated node. The function newnode sets the element and link of the newly allocated node and increments nextfree.

```
template <class elt> struct linked_list
{
    // . . .
    // Modify
  private:
    link newnode(elt, link = endmark);   // allocate from the array
    void insert_before_first(elt);
    void insert_after_last(elt);
    void insert_after(elt, link);
    void remove_first();
    void remove_after(link);

  public:
    // Modify: Add
    void add(elt);                        // insert at back
    void insert(elt, int pos = 1);        // add at pos, moving subsequent
                                          // elts down; pos can be 1 past end
    linked_list& operator+=(elt);         // insert at front
    void insert_before(elt new_elt, elt old_elt);
    void insert_after(elt new_elt, elt old_elt);

    // Modify: Remove
    void remove(elt);
    void remove1(elt);
    void remove(int pos);                 // remove nth elt
    linked_list& operator-=(elt);

    // Modify: Exchange
    void exchange(elt, elt);              // exchange first occurrences
    void exchange(int, int);              // exchange nth & mth elements

    // Modify: Replace
    void replace(elt old_elt, elt new_elt);
    void replace1(elt old_elt, elt new_elt);
};
```

```
/* Modify: Add Support */

// private:
template <class elt> link linked_list<elt>::newnode(elt e, link next)
{
    nodes[nextfree].setElt(e);
    nodes[nextfree].setNext(next);
    return nextfree++;
 }

template <class elt> void linked_list<elt>::insert_before_first(elt e)
{
    firstnode = newnode(e, firstnode);
}

template <class elt> void linked_list<elt>::insert_after_last(elt e)
{
    nodes[link_to_last()].setNext(newnode(e));
}

template <class elt> void linked_list<elt>::insert_after(elt e, link a)
{
    nodes[a].setNext(newnode(e, nodes[a].getNext()));
}
```

```
/* Modify: Add */

template <class elt> void linked_list<elt>::insert(elt e, int n)
{
    if (full()) error("[linked_list::insert(elt, int)] list full");

    if (n == 1)
        insert_before_first(e);
    else
        {
            link prev = firstnode;
            --n;
            while (--n > 0)
                if ((prev = nodes[prev].getNext()) == endmark)
                    error("[linked_list::insert] not that many elements");
            insert_after(e, prev);
        }
}

template <class elt> void linked_list<elt>::add(elt e)
{
    if (full()) error("[linked_list::add] list full");

    if (firstnode == endmark)
        insert_before_first(e);
    else
```

```
        insert_after_last(e);
}

template <class elt> linked_list<elt>& linked_list<elt>::operator+=(elt e)
{
    if (full()) error("[linked_list::operator+=] list full");

    insert_before_first(e);
    return *this;
}

template <class elt>
void linked_list<elt>::insert_after(elt new_elt, elt old_elt)
{
    if (full()) error("[linked_list::insert_after] list full");

    link oldlink = link_to(old_elt);

    if (oldlink == endmark)
        error("insert_after: elt not found");

    insert_after(new_elt, oldlink);
}

template <class elt>
void linked_list<elt>::insert_before(elt new_elt,elt old_elt)
{
    if (full()) error("[linked_list::insert_before] list full");

    if (old_elt == nodes[firstnode].getElt())
        insert(new_elt);                        // insert before firstnode
    else
        {
            link prevlink = link_to_prev(old_elt);

            if (prevlink == endmark)
                error("insert_before: elt not found");

            insert_after(new_elt, prevlink);
        }
}
```

Inserting a new node after an existing one is a simple procedure. The definition of insert_after contains a one-line implementation of the procedure diagrammed in Figure 8.3 on page 222. A new node is

- allocated
- initialized to hold a pointer to the new element and a pointer to the node pointed to by the old node
- made the node that the old node points to

Inserting a new node *before* an existing node is trickier because the link that has to be changed is in the predecessor of that node, and in a singly linked list there's no way to go from a node directly to its predecessor. We have to think of inserting before a node as equivalent to inserting the new one *after* the *predecessor* of the existing one instead of *before* the existing one. The definition of insert_before has to use a variant of link_to, called link_to_prev, to get the address not of the node containing the old element but of the node *before* that one. If the old element happens to be in the first node, it has no predecessor. In that case, it's the list's firstnode that gets changed.

Next we consider **Remove** operations. The private function remove_after implements node excision, as illustrated in Figure 8.4 on page 223. The node is modified to point to the node *after* the node to which it currently points. The excised node just hangs around still pointing to the same node, while nothing points to it. It's still in the array of nodes, but it is no longer part of the list.

```
/* Modify: Remove Support */

// private:
template <class elt> void linked_list<elt>::remove_first()
{
    firstnode = nodes[firstnode].getNext();
}

// private:
template <class elt> void linked_list<elt>::remove_after(link a)
{
    nodes[a].setNext(nodes[nodes[a].getNext()].getNext());
}
```

The definition of remove(int) runs into the same problem that insert_before ran into. The first node has to be treated as a special case. If the element is not in the first node, then remove just calls remove_after. Generally, **Remove** of an element from a collection structure has two flavors: remove one (usually the first occurrence found) and remove all. The first node must be specially treated in both of these.

```
/* Modify: Remove */

// remove nth element
template <class elt> void linked_list<elt>::remove(int n)
{
    if (firstnode == endmark) error("list is empty");
    if (n <= 0) error("invalid position");

    if (n == 1)
        remove_first();
    else
        remove_after(link_to(n-1));
}

template <class elt> void linked_list<elt>::remove1(elt e)
{
    if (firstnode == endmark) error("list is empty");
```

```
    if (e == nodes[firstnode].getElt())
        remove_first();
    else
        {

            link prevlink = link_to_prev(e);

            if (prevlink == endmark) error("remove1: elt not found");

            remove_after(prevlink);
        }
}

template <class elt> void linked_list<elt>::remove(elt e)
{
    // If e happens to be at the front (perhaps many times)
    // remove it until the first element is not e.
    while (firstnode != endmark && (e == nodes[firstnode].getElt()))
            remove_first();
    if (firstnode == endmark) return;

    // We can start on the second node knowing e is not the first element.
    link prev = firstnode;
    link cur = nodes[firstnode].getNext();

    // Traverse the rest of the list removing any occurrences of e.
    while (cur != endmark)
        {
            while (cur != endmark  && e != nodes[cur].getElt())
                {
                    prev = cur;
                    cur = nodes[cur].getNext();
                }
            if (cur != endmark)
                {
                    cur = nodes[cur].getNext();
                    remove_after(prev);
                }
        }
}

template <class elt> linked_list<elt>& linked_list<elt>::operator-=(elt e)
{
    remove_first(e);
    return *this;
}
```

Finally, we look at the definitions of the **Exchange** and **Replace** operations. These are much simpler than **Add** and **Remove** because they can be accomplished without modifying any links. Instead, the elements the nodes contain are changed, and the node sequence, as embodied in the links, is left untouched. The two exchange functions invoke the global exchange defined in standard.H and described in Section 1.4.4, page 84.

```
/* Modify: Exchange, Replace */

template <class elt> void linked_list<elt>::exchange(elt elt1, elt elt2)
{
    ::exchange(nodes[link_to(elt1)].getElt(),
               nodes[link_to(elt2)].getElt());
}

template <class elt> void linked_list<elt>::exchange(int pos1, int pos2)
{
    ::exchange(nodes[link_to(pos1)].getElt(),
               nodes[link_to(pos2)].getElt());
}

template <class elt>
void linked_list<elt>::replace1(elt old_elt, elt new_elt)
{
    link l = link_to(old_elt);
    if (l == endmark) error("[linked_list::replace] no such element");

    nodes[l].setElt(new_elt);
}

template <class elt>
void linked_list<elt>::replace(elt old_elt, elt new_elt)
{
    link cur = firstnode;

    while (cur != endmark)
        {
            if (old_elt == nodes[cur].getElt())
                nodes[cur].setElt(new_elt);
            cur = nodes[cur].getNext();
        }
}
```

8.2.4 Traversal

We've already seen a lot of traversals in the **Access** and **Modify** operations. Those, however, were coded in terms of internal representation details. The module must also encapsulate the mechanics of traversal in a form suitable for client code to use. Applications also need to traverse lists for many reasons beyond **Access** and **Modify**.

```
template <class elt> struct linked_list
{
    // . . .
    // Traversal
  private:
    static const int no_index;           // special 'uninitialized' value
```

```
    link cur;                              // traversal position
    int  indx;                             // traversal index
  public:
    void reset();
    bool finished();
    bool next();
    elt& current();
    int index();
};
```

Except for next, most of the **Traversal** operations are straightforward. Since there's no relationship between the location of a node and its position in the list, we have to keep a count of the number of nodes already seen in order to support the standard traversal function index. The awkwardness in the definition of next is due to the approach taken to traversals in this book, which requires a reset to be followed by a next before the first element can be used. In structures where the elements are stored contiguously, the traversal state can be initialized to –1. In a linked structure, however, there's no link value that means 'before the first'. Link values are either the location of nodes or endmark; there are no other special values available.

The best we can do, then, is have reset set the traversal state to endmark, and have next check for endmark every time it's called. In that case, though, how can the functions distinguish a traversal that had just ended from one that had just been reset? The definition here takes advantage of the fact that a separate count of the number of elements encountered must be maintained to support index. An otherwise impossible negative value is used to indicate a traversal that has just been reset. A traversal that has proceeded to the end will have a nonnegative count of the number of elements, even if, in an empty list, it's zero.

```
/* Traversal */

template <class elt> void linked_list<elt>::reset()
{
    cur = endmark;
    indx = -1;
}

template <class elt> bool linked_list<elt>::finished()
{
    return cur == endmark;
}

// Tricky because convention is to start traversal off before
// first position and there is no such thing with linked lists
// (can't do arithmetic on addresses).
template <class elt> bool linked_list<elt>::next()
{
    if (indx == no_index)
        error("[linked_list<elt>::next] traversal not yet initialized");
```

```
    if (endmark == cur)
        if (indx < 0)                        // traversal has been reset
            {
                indx = 0;                    // adjust to natural value
                cur = firstnode;
            }
        else
            error("[linked_list<elt>::next] traversal already finished");
    else
        cur = nodes[cur].getNext();          // advance to next node

    indx++;                                  // index ends 1 more than size
    return !finished();
}

template <class elt> elt& linked_list<elt>::current()
{
    if (endmark == cur)
        error("[linked_list<elt>::current] traversal not yet initialized");
    if (endmark == cur)
        error("[linked_list<elt>::current] traversal initialized "
                "but not yet stepped");
    if (finished())
        error("[linked_list<elt>::current] traversal already finished");

    return nodes[cur].getElt();
}

template <class elt> int linked_list<elt>::index()
{
    return indx;
}
```

8.2.5 Content Operations

Linked lists have the same **Content** operations as sequential lists. The implementations in the sequential list module took advantage of the presence of a length field, but the linked list versions will have to rely entirely on traversals. The definition of length, for example, just traverses the list counting as it goes. (Actually, it doesn't even have to count — it could use the value of index at the end of the traversal. Since counting is a typical application of traversal operations, it's worth showing a simple example of it here.)

In this implementation, a linked list becomes "full" when it has exhausted all of its nodes, a situation indicated by nextfree reaching allocation. An empty list is one with endmark as the value of firstnode. The **Compare** and **Combine** definitions are similar to the ones in the sequential list module, except that they can't take any shortcuts involving the length of the list, since that's not represented directly.

```
template <class elt> struct linked_list
{
    // . . .
  public:
    // Attributes
    int size();
    bool empty();
    bool full();

    // Compare
    friend bool equal(linked_list&, linked_list&);
    friend order compare(linked_list&, linked_list&);

    // Combine
    friend linked_list<elt> append(linked_list<elt>&, linked_list<elt>&);
    friend linked_list<elt> operator+(linked_list<elt>&,linked_list<elt>&);
    friend linked_list<elt> merge(linked_list<elt>&, linked_list<elt>&);};
};
```

```
/* Attributes */

template <class elt> int linked_list<elt>::size()
{
    reset();
    int count = 0;

    while(next()) count++;

    return count;
}

template <class elt> bool linked_list<elt>::empty()
{
    return firstnode == endmark;
}

template <class elt> bool linked_list<elt>::full()
{
    return nextfree == allocation;
}
```

The definition of length provides an interesting demonstration of the utility of generators. Here's a generator that is used only to count how many times it can produce a component. In fact, nothing is done in the loop other than producing the next component. The component itself is never used! (We don't have to increment a count in the function because operator++ already does that in support of the index function.)

```
/* Compare */

template <class elt>
order compare(linked_list<elt>& lst1, linked_list<elt>& lst2)
{
    if (&lst1 == &lst2) return EQUAL;        // same!
    lst1.reset();
    lst2.reset();
    order ord;

    while (lst1.next() && lst2.next() &&
            (EQUAL == (ord = compare(*lst1.current(), *lst2.current()))))
        /* do nothing! */;

    if (lst1.finished() && !lst2.next())
        // if lst1 is finished then lst2 never got stepped the last
        // time through the traversal so step one more time and test
        return EQUAL;
    else if (lst1.finished())
        return BEFORE;
    else if (lst2.finished())
        return AFTER;
    return ord;        // The traversal ended due to unequal elements
}

template <class elt
bool equal(linked_list<elt>& lst1, linked_list<elt>& lst2)
{
    lst1.reset();
    lst2.reset();

    while (lst1.next() && lst2.next())
        if (EQUAL != compare(*lst1.current(), *lst2.current()))
            return FALSE;

    if (lst1.finished())
        return !lst2.next();
    // if lst1 finished lst2 won't have been stepped in the while test
    // so step one more time and test

    return FALSE;            // here only if lst1 not finished and lst2 is
}
```

After checking whether the two arguments are actually the same list, compare traverses both lists in parallel comparing corresponding components. The traversal continues until two components are found that are not equal. The result in that case is the result of the unequal comparison, either BEFORE or AFTER. If one list runs out before the other, the shorter one is a prefix of the longer one and therefore BEFORE it according to the usual notion of (lexical) ordering. If both run out at the same time, they are equal.

```
/* Combine */

template <class elt>
linked_list<elt> append(linked_list<elt>& lst1, linked_list<elt>& lst2)
{
    linked_list<elt> lst(lst1.allocation + lst2.allocation);
    // not clear how many nodes to allocate: might as well add the maximums

    lst.firstnode = lst.copy_elements(lst1);
    lst.nodes[lst.link_to_last()].setNext(lst.copy_elements(lst2));

    return lst;
}

template <class elt>
linked_list<elt> operator+(linked_list<elt>& lst1, linked_list<elt>& lst2)
{
    return append(lst1, lst2);
}
```

The definition of append uses a private function called copy_elements that has been formulated to support append as well as the copy constructor and copy assignment operator. Its definition appears later, with the **Copy** operations. It constructs in one list (the list through which it is invoked) a copy of another list (its argument) and returns a pointer to the first node. Although a slight inefficiency is introduced, append is easily coded in terms of copy; the inefficiency is that after a copy is made of the first list, the partial copy must be traversed to find its last node.

8.2.6 Support Operations

Linked lists have a complete set of Support operations. **Search** appears as contains and contains_equal, which return Booleans, and position_of which returns the (offset-1) position of the target element in the list. As in the sequential list module, a **Sort** operation is declared but not defined, with discussion left for later in this chapter (Section 8.3, starting on page 251).

```
template <class elt> struct linked_list
{
    // . . .
    // Copy
  private:
    link copy_elements(linked_list<elt>&);
  public:
    linked_list(linked_list<elt>&);
    linked_list& operator=(linked_list<elt>&);

    // Process
    linked_list<elt> reverse();
```

```
    bool contains(elt);
    bool contains_equal(elt);
    int position_of(elt);
    void sort();

    // Output
    friend ostream& operator<<(ostream&, linked_list<elt>&);
};
```

The private function that implements the heart of **Copy** constructs a copy of its argument list's elements and returns the location of the firstnode, but it does not set firstnode. This allows it to also be used in append. The straightforward **Add** operation inserts elements at the front of a list. If we were to use that to construct the copy, we'd get a reversed list. Code to construct the copy with the same order as the original is somewhat more ntricate than if we could just insert elements at the front of the copy being built.

```
/* Copy */

// private:
template <class elt>
link linked_list<elt>::copy_elements(linked_list<elt>& lst)
{
    if (lst.empty()) return endmark;             // empty list
    if (full()) error("[linked_list::copy_elements] list full");

    link start = newnode(lst.current()); // handle firstnode node specially
    link prev = start;
    link newcur;

    lst.reset();
    lst.next();

    while (lst.next())
        {
            if (full()) error("[linked_list::copy_elements] list full");

            newcur = newnode(lst.current());
            nodes[prev].setNext(newcur);
            prev = newcur;
        }

    return start;
}

template <class elt> linked_list<elt>::linked_list(linked_list<elt>& lst)
    : allocation(lst.allocation), nodes(new list_node<elt>[lst.allocation])
{
    clear();
    firstnode = copy_elements(lst);
}

template <class elt>
```

```
linked_list<elt>& linked_list<elt>::operator=(linked_list<elt>& lst)
{
    if (this == &lst) return *this;              // assignment to self!

    if (allocation < lst.size())
        {
            delete nodes;
            allocation = lst.size();
            nodes = new list_node<elt>[allocation];
        }

    clear();
    firstnode = copy_elements(lst);
    return *this;
}
```

The **Process** operations are expressed quite tersely using traversal operations. Note how simple reverse is compared to copy. Adding to the front of a linked list, as in reverse, is much easier than adding to the end — just the opposite of how it is with sequential lists.

```
/* Process */

template <class elt> linked_list<elt> linked_list<elt>::reverse()
{
    linked_list lst(allocation);
    reset();
    while (next()) lst.insert(current());

    return lst;
}

template <class elt> bool linked_list<elt>::contains(elt e)
{
    reset();
    while (next()) if (e == current())) return TRUE;

    return FALSE;
}

template <class elt> bool linked_list<elt>::contains_equal(elt e)
{
    reset();
    while (next()) if (EQUAL == compare(*e, *current())) return TRUE;

    return FALSE;
}

template <class elt> int linked_list<elt>::position_of(elt e)
{
```

```
    reset();
    while (next()) if (e == current())) return index();

    return FALSE;
}
```

The definition of the **Output** operator is identical to the one for the sequential list module.

```
/* Output */

template <class elt>
ostream& operator<<(ostream& strm, linked_list<elt>& lst)
{
    lst.reset();
    strm << '(';

    if (lst.next()) strm << *lst.current();

    while (lst.next()) strm << ' ' << *lst.current();

    strm << ')';

    return strm;
}
```

8.2.7 Free Lists

Deleted nodes still occupy space, and the initial implementation of linked lists we've been examining provides no way to reuse them. The standard technique for reusing nodes is to maintain a *free list* — a list of all the nodes available for insertions. The implementation is changed so that every node in a list's nodes array belongs to one of two chains: one consisting of nodes pointing to elements of the list and one consisting of nodes available for reuse. The latter — the free list — will of course not be visible to clients of the list module.

Figure 8.6 illustrates the coexistence of the free list with the actual list. Note that there are two endmark values present in the array: one for the list and another for the free list. It doesn't matter what the nodes on the free list point to, since the node's elem will be set to a new value when the node gets reused.

The value of nextfree will now be the location of the first node on the free list. **Add** operations will remove a node from the free list and add it to the actual list. **Remove** operations will remove the node from the actual list and add it to the front of the free list. **Initialize** will now link all the nodes of the array together and set nextfree to the index of the first node.

Only two changes are needed in the header file. We add a new private member function to construct the free list for new lists — setup_freelist — and another —

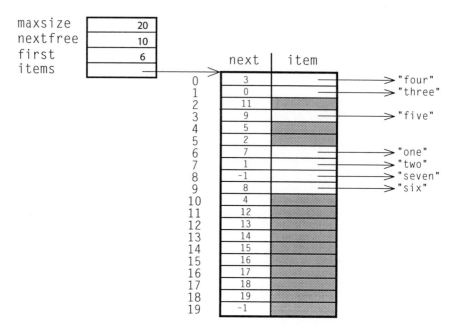

Figure 8.6   Coexistence of List and Its Free List in the Same Node Pool

recycle — to return nodes to the free list. The definition of newnode will be changed to take nodes off the free list, but we don't need a new member for that. *The rest of the header file is unaffected.* An application that included the original linked list module could now use this new, improved version without any code being changed.

```
template <class elt> struct linked_list
{
    // . . .
    // Free list operations
  private:
    link setup_freelist();    // initialize free list
    void recycle(link);       // return node at link to free list
};
```

```
/* Free list operations */

// private
template <class elt> link linked_list<elt>::setup_freelist()
{
    for (int i = 0; i < allocation-1; i++)
        nodes[i].setNext(i+1);
    nodes[allocation-1].setNext(endmark);
```

```
    return 0;                                    // index of first free node
}

// private:
template <class elt> void linked_list<elt>::recycle(link a)
{
    nodes[a].setNext(freelist);
    freelist = a;
}
```

In addition to adding definitions for the two new private member functions, the use of a free list requires modifying the definitions of some of the original functions. The definition of newnode changes entirely. Its job now is to remove the first node of the free list and return it as the new node. This completes the recycling of the previously deleted node. The two private functions that support **Remove** return nodes to the free list by calling recycle.

The function clear, called by the constructors and assignment operator and available to users for emptying lists, now invokes setup_freelist to link all the nodes in the nodes array together into a free list instead of just setting nextfree to 0. The definition of full used to test whether nextfree had reached the end of the nodes array; now, it tests whether there are any nodes left on the free list. All in all, the changes are not very substantial considering how much power they add to the module. The list can now grow and shrink indefinitely, as long as its size never exceeds the number of nodes allocated for it.

```
// member functions affected by the use of a free list

template <class elt> link linked_list<elt>::newnode(elt e, link next)
{
    if (full()) error("list full");

    link newnod = freelist;
    freelist = nodes[freelist].getNext();
    nodes[newnod].setElt(e);
    nodes[newnod].setNext(next);
    return newnod;
}

template <class elt> void linked_list<elt>::remove_first()
{
    link remnode = firstnode;
    firstnode = nodes[firstnode].getNext();
    recycle(remnode);
}

template <class elt> void linked_list<elt>::remove_after(link a)
{
    link remnode = nodes[a].getNext();
    nodes[a].setNext(nodes[nodes[a].getNext()].getNext());
    recycle(remnode);
```

```
}
template <class elt> void linked_list<elt>::clear()
{
    freelist = setup_freelist();
    firstnode = endmark;
    cur = endmark;
    indx = no_index;
}
template <class elt> bool linked_list<elt>::full()
{
    return freelist == endmark;
}
```

8.2.8 A Common Node Pool

In the new implementation, each list has its own free list. Each list's length is limited to a size established when it is created. Because of their flexibility, linked lists are generally used when there are a lot of insertions and deletions to be made. Thus, linked lists tend to grow and shrink a lot. It doesn't make much sense to have such flexible structures stored in fixed-size arrays. Most of the space in these arrays will be wasted most of the time, and it may not be possible to estimate the length a list might attain.

Better would be to have just one pool of nodes shared by *all* linked lists the program uses. There really is no reason to have a separate node pool for each linked list. We can start off with one very large free list and allocate the next node from it regardless of which list needs it. The array would contain nodes from the various lists, including the free list, but the link of any node will point only to another node of the same list.

Few changes are required to achieve this crucial modification. Because there is only one free list shared by all instances of the linked_list struct, nodes, nextfree, and allocation become static (i.e., global to the class), as do the functions setup_freelist and recycle.

Constructors and other functions will no longer allocate an array of nodes or initialize the free list, and the destructor doesn't have to deallocate the nodes. Since there's just one node pool and one free list shared by all linked lists, these just get initialized once and for all when the program begins execution. The basic constructor now takes no arguments, since it no longer needs a size. Any size arguments provided to a constructor in another function (e.g., append) would now be omitted, though these changes aren't shown here.

```
template <class elt> struct linked_list
{
    // members made static:
  private:
    static list_node<elt>* nodes;
    static link nextfree;
    static void recycle(link);
    static link setup_freelist();
```

```
    static int allocation;

    // changed constructor declaration:
  public:
    linked_list();
};
```

   With this implementation, lists are never full! However, the entire module can still run out of nodes if the free list becomes empty. The tests in various member functions that guard against trying to allocate new nodes when the free list is empty are still valid. Their meaning changes, though: instead of the individual list having run out of nodes, the entire module has run out of nodes to allocate. The corresponding error messages could be reworded to reflect this change, but the definition of full is unaffected.

   To initialize the free list, setup_freelist has to be executed at program start-up. Static data members, like ordinary global variables, are initialized by evaluating the initializer found in their definition. Adding the following statement to the implementation file causes setup_freelist to be called when the program starts:

```
        link list::nextfree = list::setup_freelist();
```

C++ allows static data members to be accessed at file scope even if they are private (otherwise, how would they ever get initialized?). Similarly, initializers of private data members are allowed access to private member functions. The use of an initializer for freelist is something of a trick: we are using it to invoke setup_freelist for its side effects, not really to get an initial value for freelist. We know that the initial value should be 0; however, there's no other way to force a global function to be automatically executed when the program starts up and we don't want users to have to explicitly invoke any module initialization routines.

   Since nodes and allocation are static, they too have to be initialized at file scope in the implementation file. Note that the list structure is left with only one nonstatic data member — the address of the first node. The amount of memory each instance will now occupy, therefore, is just the space for a single pointer! Here, the power of data abstraction comes at no cost in space: the list objects behave as structure instances at the software level while taking up only the space an ordinary pointer would occupy at the hardware level. The implementation file now includes the following definitions of static data members. (A file's static variables are initialized in the order their definitions appear, so by the time setup_freelist is called the nodes array has already been allocated.)

```
template <class elt> int linked_list<elt>::allocation = 100;
template <class elt> list_node<elt> * linked_list<elt>::nodes =
              new list_node<elt>[linked_list<elt>::allocation];
template <class elt> link linked_list<elt>::freelist =
              linked_list<elt>::setup_freelist();
```

   Initialization of nodes and allocation are removed from the constructors and the assignment operator, but the rest of the constructor definitions are unchanged. The only significantly affected functions are the linked list destructor and clear! Before, the destructor deleted the nodes array, and `clear` reinitialized the free list, linking all the nodes in the `nodes` array together. Now things are more complicated — the free list serves *all* the program's linked lists, so destroying one list should not cause any nodes to be deallocated, and clearing one list should not reinitialize the free list. Instead, the destructor should just clear the list, and `clear` should return all of the list's nodes to the free list. It is not necessary to return the nodes individually: they are already linked together, so they can be spliced onto the free list by simply changing the list's last node to point to the current free list.

```
template <class elt> void linked_list<elt>::~linked_list()
{
    clear();
}

template <class elt> void linked_list<elt>::clear()
{
    // splice list on to front of free list to recycle all its nodes
    nodes[link_to_last()].setNext(nextfree);
    nextfree = firstnode;

    // now reset list, as before
    firstnode = endmark;
    cur = endmark;
    indx = no_index;
}
```

8.2.9 Dynamic Linked Lists

The above discussion of array-based linked lists was designed to introduce the concept of nodes and links in a very concrete form. In practice, there's rarely any reason to preallocate a separate array of nodes. The `nodes` array may be removed from this implementation of the linked list representation. Instead, nodes can simply be allocated as needed from the heap, using `new`.

One approach would be to start with an empty free list, then allocate a new node any time one is needed but the free list is empty. Another approach is to allocate a chunk of nodes each time the free list is empty, linking them together after they are allocated. This reduces the overhead involved in calling `new` (since `new` would be called many fewer times) and the space involved in heap maintenance (since each call to `new` results in information being stored on the heap about how much space the newly allocated chunk occupies). Also, when nodes are allocated in chunks they end up clustered near each other in memory, which may, depending on the program, reduce paging activity as pointers are followed from one node to another.

Whether nodes are allocated one at a time or in groups, dynamic allocation introduces an important shift in the module's implementation. With dynamically allocated nodes, there's no array of nodes from which nodes are accessed — they just live independently on the heap. Therefore, instead of referring to nodes by array index, the code will point directly to nodes. In the previous implementations the type link was a synonym for int and was used for indices to an array of list_nodes. Now, link will be a synonym for a pointer to a node — i.e., list_node*.

To modify the code for this new approach, every occurrence of nodes[a]. in the module gets replaced by a->. (We actually could have used the pointer formulation in the array-based implementation — you can *always* use pointers instead of arrays — but there wouldn't have been any real reason to do so.) The value for linked_list::endmark changes also, from -1 to 0, representing the special null pointer. As with the typedef for link this change is much easier to make when it affects only the value of a constant data member rather than all the function definitions that refer to it.

The static member allocation gets reinterpreted not as the total size of the node pool, but the number to allocate whenever the free list is empty and a new node is needed. Therefore, it can be initialized to a much smaller number. Following is an example of a definition changed to use pointers instead of array indexing.

```
template <class elt> link linked_list::link_to(elt e)
{
    link cur = firstnode;

    while ((cur != endmark) && e != cur->getElt())
        cur = cur->getNext();

    return cur;
}
```

By going to the heap for more nodes whenever the free list runs out, this implementation guarantees that lists will never be full (unless the heap is exhausted). Other than that, only two functions are substantially affected by the change to dynamically allocated nodes and the use of pointers instead of array indices, and they are both private: setup_freelist and newnode. Any application that works with any one of the various linked list implementation's will work with any of the others. The public functional interface is unaffected by the implementation differences, so no modifications would be necessary.

```
template <class elt> link linked_list<elt>::newnode(elt e, link next)
{
    if (endmark == freelist)
        {
            freelist = new list_node<elt>[allocation];
            if (0 == freelist) error("[linked_list] heap exhausted");
            setup_freelist();
        }

    link newnod = freelist;
    freelist = freelist->getNext();
    newnod->setElt(e);
    newnod->setNext(next);
    return newnod;
}
```

```
template <class elt> link linked_list<elt>::setup_freelist()
{
    // Called whenever a new chunk of nodes is allocated from the heap.
    // Assumes that freelist points to an array of allocation
    // newly allocated nodes.
    for (int i = 0; i < allocation-1; i++)
        freelist[i].setNext(freelist+i+1);
    freelist[allocation-1].setNext(endmark);

    return freelist;
    // still have to return it because this gets
    // invoked by global initializer for linked_list::freelist
}
```

We've been exploring various ways to implement free lists. What kind of fundamental operations are the functions that manipulate the free list — `setup_freelist`, `newnode`, and `recycle`? Since it creates nodes that weren't there before, `setup_freelist` is clearly a **Create** operation. We haven't seen any **Create** operations since they were introduced in Chapter 1 (cf. Section 1.2.1, page 56 and Section 1.3.1, page 61). Normally, application programs create instances of structs through variable declarations and calls to `new`. Internally, the modules we've seen up to this point use `new` only to allocate dynamic arrays of pointers. The dynamic implementation of linked list is the first time we've seen the need for a module to create instances of structs. Dynamic allocation of structs inside the module is a special property of linked structures resulting from their use of private node types.

When do the nodes allocated with `setup_freelist` get deallocated? They get returned to the free list by `recycle` and taken from the free list by `newnode`, but they aren't destroyed until the program exits, when the heap itself goes away. What fundamental operations do these implement? From the list's viewpoint, they **Create** and **Destroy** nodes. However, the nodes don't really get created and destroyed — they get recycled instead. Perhaps we should call these **Allocate** and **Deallocate**. Those terms could also have been used instead of **Create** and **Destroy** throughout the book, as well as for these. Alternatively, we could use **Allocate** and **Deallocate** instead of **Create** and **Destroy** and use **Reallocate** for functions like `newnode` (but what would we then call functions like `recycle`?). Another choice — the one actually adopted here — is to view all this from the perspective of the code using the operations. The list struct asks the node struct for a node, but it doesn't care whether the one it gets is new or a recycled. We therefore consider recycling operations to be variants of **Create** and **Destroy**.

8.2.10 Variations

There are two important variations on the theme of linked lists that are often useful: lists that keep track of their end and lists whose nodes point to their predecessors in addition to their successors. The representational changes are straightforward and are described next. Code for these is left for exercises (cf. Exercises 22 and 23).

Keeping track of the last node is effective where additions are made frequently at the end of the list. Otherwise, each time an element is added to the end of a list, the list must be completely traversed. Other operations that access the last node of the list would also benefit from this modification. To avoid having to traverse the list until the end is reached each time access to the last node is needed, we can add a `lastnode` member to the `linked_list` structure and alter various **Modify** operations to maintain and take advantage of that pointer. At the small cost of one extra pointer per list, traversal to reach the last node is greatly speeded up.

Sometimes it is important to be able to traverse the list backward as well as forward. To support two-way traversal, we need a way to get from a node to its predecessor. In fact, the absence of a link to the predecessor made for some awkward code in some of the **Modify** functions seen earlier. In an ordinary linked list, the predecessor isn't represented, so to find it, code must traverse the list, starting at the beginning, looking for the node that points to the node whose predecessor is needed. That is obviously an inefficient way to proceed. An improvement would be to add a predecessor pointer to each node and change the various **Modify** operations to maintain both links. That would significantly simplify some of the module's own definitions, but most importantly it gives users new functionality: the ability to traverse the list in either direction. Lists whose nodes contain pointers to their predecessors as well as their successors are called *doubly linked lists*.

8.3 List Sorting

Sorting is a major part of many list-based applications. Naive algorithms for sorting are much slower than more sophisticated ones. These two facts combine to make sorting one of the most studied topics in computer science. Sorting algorithms also provide good examples for introducing the theoretical study of algorithm efficiency.

Sort is a **Process** operation like **Search**. Most data structures have meaningful Search operations, and this text are discusses them along with the other operations that implement the structures studied. Sort, however, is more closely associated with lists than with other kinds of structures, in part because of the correspondence between the linear nature of lists and the linear ordering sorting imposes. Other kinds of structures are either never rearranged, such as stacks and queues, or are always sorted, as we'll see in the section on association structures. Therefore, although **Search** is considered throughout the text, **Sort** appears only here.

8.3.1 Efficiency

A sorting algorithm rearranges the components of a list so that they are ordered according to some comparison function. This primarily involves comparing and moving components. The efficiency of a sorting algorithm can therefore be evaluated in terms of the number of comparisons and movements it performs. (The efficiency of a search algorithm depends on the number of comparisons alone, since it doesn't rearrange the structure.)

Consider a simple sequential search through a list containing N elements, such as the `contains` and `contains_equal` operations in the list implementations shown above. Each of the list's components is examined in turn until either a match is found or the list is exhausted. How many comparisons are performed? In the best case, the target happens to be the first component in the list, and only one comparison is needed. The worst case would be when the list did not contain a matching element or the target happened to appear last. In that case, the algorithm would perform N matches — one for each element in the list. In general, it would take K comparisons to find a target that happened to be the Kth element in the list. If no one element was any more likely to match than any other, the number of matches required on average would be approximately $N/2$:

$$\frac{(1 + 2 + \ldots + N)}{N} = \frac{N/2 \bullet (1 + N)}{N} = \frac{N(1 + N)}{2N} = \frac{1 + N}{2}$$

The efficiency of any search algorithm can be characterized this way — in terms of the number of comparisons it performs in the best, worst, and average cases. The exact execution time of an algorithm is rarely of interest. The important thing is how much longer a search takes as the number of elements in the collection increases.

This approach to evaluating efficiency gave rise to a notation used to characterize different kinds of algorithms, known as "Big O notation." The efficiency of a search algorithm requiring as many as N comparisons to locate a match among N elements is described as $O(N)$. The 'O' stands for 'order', and $O(N)$ is read as "order of N." An $O(N)$ algorithm is also called *linear*, since the time it takes to execute increases linearly with the size of the collection.

The goal of efficiency analysis is to relate the performance of an algorithm to the size of the collection it processes. Constant costs involved in setting up and controlling the algorithm are ignored, since as N increases, the fixed overhead is a less significant part of the total cost. With large enough N the fixed overhead becomes irrelevant. Also, with large enough N it doesn't really matter whether the actual cost is N (as in the worst case for sequential search through a list), $N+1$ (there may be one final comparison to distinguish between matching the last element or not finding a match at all), or even $(N+1)/2$ (as in the average case for sequential search). What matters is the *nature* of the increase in processing as N increases, not an exact formula for determining precise execution time. All of these values would be considered $O(N)$.

8.3.2 Simple List Sorting

We're going to look next at three simple methods for sorting lists. These algorithms are commonly used for sorting relatively small lists in simple programs. They are easy to understand and code. Analysis will show, however, that they are too inefficient to use for large lists.

Selection Sort

One straightforward way to sort a list is to find the element that is the "least" according to the specified ordering and swap it with the element that's at the beginning of the list. Then swap the element that belongs second with the element that's at the second position in the list. Next, the third-least element is swapped with the third element in the list, the fourth-least element with the fourth, and so on until the last position in the list is reached. This method is called *selection sort*, since it steps through the positions in the list selecting for each one the element that belongs there.

Here's how a simple sequence of numbers would get sorted. In each pass, the two numbers just exchanged (or the one that happened to be in the right place already) are underlined.

```
original:         5 8 3 6 7 2 4 1
after pass 1:     1 8 3 6 7 2 4 5
after pass 2:     1 2 3 6 7 8 4 5
after pass 3:     1 2 3 6 7 8 4 5
after pass 4:     1 2 3 4 7 8 6 5
after pass 5:     1 2 3 4 5 8 6 7
after pass 6:     1 2 3 4 5 6 8 7
after pass 7:     1 2 3 4 5 6 7 8
```

Any of the list implementations shown above could have included `selection_sort`. In fact, the algorithm doesn't depend at all on the list's representation, so the code would be the same in each module. The sorting function would compare pairs of elements using their type's `compare` function. Some types can be ordered in more than one way — for instance, names by first or last name. To allow for that possibility, sorting functions should take optional arguments that are functions of two elements returning an `order`. The default value for that optional argument would be `compare`.

The first pass of a selection sort of N elements must make $N-1$ comparisons to find the least element. The second pass makes one less comparison, since it skips the least element that was just moved to the first position. The third pass makes $N-3$ comparisons, and so on. The final pass just compares the last two elements in the list. The total number of comparisons is

$$(N-1) + (N-2) + (N-3) + \ldots + 3 + 2 + 1$$

Rearranging the terms so the first and last are paired, the second and second to last are paired, etc., gives

$$((N-1) + 1) + ((N-2) + 2) + ((N-3) + 3) + \ldots$$
$$= N + N + N + N + \ldots$$
$$= N/2 * N$$
$$= N^2/2$$

This shows that selection sort performs $O(N^2)$ comparisons. $O(N^2)$ denotes a *quadratic* algorithm.

What about the number of exchanges performed by selection sort? At most one exchange is performed on each pass, so at most the number of exchanges is $N-1$. (If the Kth least element happens to be in the Kth position, no exchange will take place on the Kth

pass.) The number of moves is therefore at most $3(N-1)$. This shows that selection sort is linear with respect to moves.

Insertion Sort

A similar approach turns things around: instead of selecting for each position the element that belongs there, each element is considered in turn and moved directly to the position where it belongs among the already sorted elements. As the sorted part of the list grows, the unsorted part shrinks. The first pass considers the first element already sorted and starts with the second element. Each pass starts at one element past where the previous pass started. This approach is called *insertion sort*.

Here's the result of the passes made for the sequence shown earlier. For each pass, the number that got moved into position is underlined. Note that subsequence numbers are moved down one position. A vertical bar separates the sorted part from the unsorted part and therefore indicates the number that will be repositioned on the next pass.

```
original:       5 | 8 3 6 7 2 4 1
after pass 1:   5 8 | 3 6 7 2 4 1
after pass 2:   3 5 8 | 6 7 2 4 1
after pass 3:   3 5 6 8 | 7 2 4 1
after pass 4:   3 5 6 7 8 | 2 4 1
after pass 5:   2 3 5 6 7 8 | 4 1
after pass 6:   2 3 4 5 6 7 8 | 1
after pass 7:   1 2 3 4 5 6 7 8 |
```

The first pass compares the second element only to the first. The second pass compares the third element with at most the first two — "at most" because the comparisons end once an element is found that does not belong before the one being inserted. The Kth pass compares the element at position $K+1$ to at most K others. Each pass performs at least one comparison. Since it is equally likely that the element being inserted will end up in one position as any other, and the Kth pass could make as few as 1 and as many as K comparisons, the average number of comparisons performed on the Kth pass is $K/2$. Since there are $K-1$ passes, the worst case number of comparisons is

$$1 + 2 + \ldots + N-2 + N-1$$
$$= N/2 * N$$
$$= N^2/2$$

Oddly, the worst case for insertion sort occurs when the list starts out in sorted order! (There are other ways to formulate the algorithm such that the already sorted list is the best case, but then a reverse-ordered list would be the worst case.) The average case would add the series of $K/2$ values instead of K's, so it's just half the worst case. Either way, the number of comparisons is again $O(N^2)$.

The number of moves on the first pass is either N or $N-1$, depending on whether the second element belongs before or after the first. The second pass will move as many as N and as few as $N-2$. Therefore, in the worst case, the number of moves performed on pass K is always N, corresponding to the situation in which the list starts exactly backward. Since there are N passes, the worst case is N^2. The average is also $O(N^2)$, though the algebra is a little more difficult to work out. Of course, if a linked list is used, then movements are dramatically reduced because the element to be moved can simply be removed from its current place in the list and inserted in its new place — subsequent elements do not have to be moved.

Bubble Sort

Another simple approach, called *bubble sort*, works by comparing and possibly exchanging pairs of adjacent elements. A pass is made through the list comparing successive pair of elements: the first two elements, then the second and third, then the third and fourth, and so on. Each pair of elements that are out of order relative to each other is exchanged. On the first pass, the element that belongs last in the ordering will "bubble" up to the end of the list because it will be swapped with each element and then compared to the next. On the second pass, the second-largest element will bubble up to the next-to-last position, and so on. Each pass can therefore make one fewer comparison, ignoring the elements that have already bubbled up to their proper place. The Kth pass makes $K{-}1$ comparisons and as many as $K{-}1$ exchanges. Note also that exchanges take three moves to perform.

An improvement is to notice whether any exchanges were made at all, and if not, terminate the algorithm without finishing the remaining passes. Once a pass makes no exchanges, subsequent passes will have no exchanges to make either. The list will already be sorted once no exchanges occur.

Here's an illustration of bubble sorting the example sequence. The pairs compared at each step of each pass are underlined.

```
original:        5 8 3 6 7 2 4 1

pass 1:          5 8 3 6 7 2 4 1
                 5 3 8 6 7 2 4 1
                 5 3 6 8 7 2 4 1
                 5 3 6 7 8 2 4 1
                 5 3 6 7 2 8 4 1
                 5 3 6 7 2 4 8 1
                 5 3 6 7 2 4 1 8

pass 2:          3 5 6 7 2 4 1 8
                 3 5 6 7 2 4 1 8
                 3 5 6 7 2 4 1 8
                 3 5 6 2 7 4 1 8
                 3 5 6 2 4 7 1 8
                 3 5 6 2 4 1 7 8

pass 3:          3 5 6 2 4 1 7 8
                 3 5 6 2 4 1 7 8
                 3 5 2 6 4 1 7 8
                 3 5 2 4 6 1 7 8
                 3 5 2 4 1 6 7 8

pass 4:          3 5 2 4 1 6 7 8
                 3 2 5 4 1 6 7 8
                 3 2 4 5 1 6 7 8
                 3 2 4 1 5 6 7 8

pass 5:          2 3 4 1 5 6 7 8
```

```
                                                    2 3 4 1 5 6 7 8
                                                    2 3 1 d 5 6 7 8

pass 6:                                             2 3 1 4 5 6 7 8
                                                    2 1 3 4 5 6 7 8

pass 7:                                             2 1 3 4 5 6 7 8
```

Ignoring the improvement that stops as soon as the list happens to be sorted, the $\mathcal{K}^{\text{th}}$ pass makes $\mathcal{N}-\mathcal{K}$ comparisons. The sum over all the passes is

$$\mathcal{N}-1 + \mathcal{N}-2 + \ldots + 2 + 1$$
$$= \mathcal{N}/2 * \mathcal{N}$$
$$= \mathcal{N}^2/2$$

The original order of the list does not affect the number of comparisons at all — it's the same in the best, average, and worst cases! Although the worst case isn't any worse than insertion or selection, bubble sort's best and average cases are as bad as its worst case, which is decidedly not true for the other two approaches.

Stopping when the list is already sorted reduces the number of comparisons made in the best case to $O(\mathcal{N})$. The best case would be when the list is already sorted, and only one pass of $\mathcal{N}-1$ comparisons would be needed to determine that the list is already sorted.

The number of actual exchanges, and therefore moves, does depend on the initial order. In the best case, when the list is already sorted, no exchanges occur. In the worst case, an exchange will occur on every comparison, which is $O(\mathcal{N}^2)$. All in all, this is not a useful sorting technique.

Implementation for Linked Lists

Here is code implementing these three simple sorting methods for linked lists. The **Sort** member functions will take an argument that indicates how the elements will be compared. The argument must therefore be a pointer to a function that takes two elements and returns an order (AFTER, EQUAL, or BEFORE). A null pointer will indicate that the normal compare function for the element type should be used. (Actually, since the structures shown in this book are constrained to contain pointers to elements, and compare is defined to compare objects rather than pointers, for a null comparison function the **Sort** functions will also dereference the pointers stored in the list before calling compare.) For convenience, we'll include a typedef for this pointer-to-function argument.

Two other member functions are added here. The code for the sorting functions will be somewhat simplified by pulling out the awkward expression that compares the elements to a separate (private) member function elts_in_order. We also add a public member function that is more convenient to introduce here but is actually an **Attribute**: sorted. Like the **Sort** functions, it takes a pointer to a comparison function as an argument; it returns a Boolean indicating whether or not the list is sorted according to that comparison function.

```
template <class elt> struct linked_list
{
    // . . .
    typedef order (*compfn)(elt, elt);
  private:
    static bool elts_in_order(link, link, compfn);
  public:
    bool sorted(compfn = 0);                      // Attribute!
    void selection_sort(compfn = 0);
    void insertion_sort(compfn = 0);
    void bubble_sort(compfn = 0);
    void merge_sort(compfn = 0);
};
```

The selection sort routine divides the list into sorted and unsorted parts. The variable end points to the end of the sorted part. The function loops repeatedly, removing the element following end, inserting it in its proper place in the sorted part of the list, and incrementing end. In essence, this is a nested traversal. Bubble sort is a similar nested traversal, but it always restarts at the beginning of the list and stops at one position earlier each time.

```
template <class elt>
bool linked_list<elt>::elts_in_order(link l1, link l2,
                                     order (*fn)(elt, elt))
{
    return AFTER != ((0 == fn)
                    ? compare(*l1->getElt(), *l2->getElt())
                    : fn(l1->getElt(), l2->getElt()));
}

template <class elt> bool linked_list<elt>::sorted(order (*fn)(elt, elt))
{
    reset();
    if (!next()) return TRUE;          // empty lists are inherently sorted!
    link prev;                         // internal traversal can grab pointer
    while (prev = cur, next())
        if (!elts_in_order(prev, cur, fn))
            return FALSE;
    return TRUE;
}

template <class elt>
void linked_list<elt>::selection_sort(order (*fn)(elt, elt))
{
    // a two-level traversal: for each outer, find the least element inner
    // remaining from outer to the list end and switch it with outer.
    link outer = firstnode;
    while (endmark != outer)
        {
            link inner = outer;
            link least = inner;
```

```
            while (endmark != (inner = inner->getNext()))
                if (elts_in_order(inner, least, fn))
                                        least = inner;
            ::exchange(least->getElt(), outer->getElt());
            // Note that this leaves the nodes in place and just
            // exchanges their elements.
            outer = outer->getNext();
        }
}

template <class elt>
void linked_list<elt>::insertion_sort(order (*fn)(elt, elt))
{
    if (endmark == firstnode || endmark == firstnode->getNext())
        return;                  // empty and 1-elt lists are inherently sorted

    link end = firstnode->getNext();
    link x;                                // the node being inserted

    // To facilitate coding, we'll start with the third node,
    // after exchanging the first two if they are out of order.
    if (!elts_in_order(firstnode, end, fn))
        ::exchange(firstnode->getElt(), end->getElt());

    while (endmark != (x = end->getNext()))
        {
            end->setNext(x->getNext()); // remove x

            if (elts_in_order(x, firstnode, fn))
                {
                    x->setNext(firstnode);
                    firstnode = x;
                }
            else
                // l is a link to the node just before the one we will
                // compare x with: to insert x before the node it belongs
                // before, we'll need the predecessor of that node.
                {
                    link l = firstnode;
                    while (l != end &&
                           !elts_in_order(x, l->getNext(), fn))
                        l = l->getNext();
                    // x goes after l, either because it belongs
                    // before l's successor or because l is the end
                    // of the sorted part of the list.
                    x->setNext(l->getNext());
                    l->setNext(x);
                    if (l == end) end = x;    // x is the new end
                }
        }
}

template <class elt>
void linked_list<elt>::bubble_sort(order (*fn)(elt, elt))
{
```

```
if (endmark == firstnode) return;    // empty lists are sorted

// We don't trail a pointer because we just exchange pairs of elements,
// leaving the nodes in place. This simplifies the coding.

link end = endmark;

while (firstnode != end)
    {
        link l = firstnode;
        while (end != l->getNext())
            {
                if (!elts_in_order(l, l->getNext(), fn))
                    ::exchange(l->getElt(), l->getNext()->getElt());
                l = l->getNext();
            }
        end = l;
    }
}
```

8.3.3 Better List Sorting

The three of the previous algorithms are fundamentally quite similar. All work by making a series of passes over the list. With each pass, one more component is placed in its proper place. A list of N components therefore requires N passes to sort. With selection and bubble sort, each pass considers one fewer component than the previous one, while in an insertion sort, each pass considers one more component than the previous one. Either way the number of comparisons averages out to about $N/2$. The algorithms are quadratic because they require N passes of $N/2$ comparisons — a total of about N^2.

A more efficient approach is to rearrange and divide the list into sublists that are sorted separately then brought back together. Here are two classic algorithms based on that idea.

Quicksort

The Quicksort algorithm was discussed in Section 5.4.3 on page 163 as an example of recursion. Recall that it works by splitting an array into two parts around a pivot value, in the process swapping elements so that all the elements in the first part are less than or equal to the pivot and all the elements in the second part greater than the pivot. Then the process is repeated recursively on each of the two subarrays — from the beginning through the pivot and from the element after the pivot through the end. Because sequential lists are implemented using arrays of elements, Quicksort can be used to sort them. However, the algorithm as described would not be applicable to linked lists, since it depends on indexed access of the list's components.

Since the pivot is not included in either sublist, both sublists are guaranteed to be smaller than the original list, even if one of them is empty. A sublist with just one element doesn't need sorting. A sublist with two elements can be sorted directly by conditionally exchanging its two elements. Only lists with more than two elements are sorted recursively.

Here's the process for the short sequence of integers used to illustrate the other sorting methods. The pivot is underlined, and the location of the upper and lower indices are shown as they move through the list until they cross.

```
to sort original:                    [ 5 8 3 6 7 2 4 1]

prepare split:                       [ 5 8 3 6 7 2 4 1 ]
                                         L           U

traverse:                            [ 5 8 3 6 7 2 4 1 ]
                                         L           U

                                     [ 5 1 3 6 7 2 4 8 ]
                                           L       U

                                     [ 5 1 3 6 7 2 4 8 ]
                                             L     U

                                     [ 5 1 3 4 7 2 6 8 ]
                                             L U

                                     [ 5 1 3 4 2 7 6 8 ]
                                             U L

swap pivot with U:                   [ 2 1 3 4 5 7 6 8 ]
                                               U L
return 4 (0-offset), leaving tasks 1A and 1B

(1A) to sort 0 thru 3:               [ 2 1 3 4 ] 5 7 6 8

prepare split:                       [ 2 1 3 4 ] 5 7 6 8
                                         L   U

traverse:                            [ 2 1 3 4 ] 5 7 6 8
                                         U L

swap pivot with U:                   [ 1 2 3 4 ] 5 7 6 8
                                         U L
return 1, leaving tasks 2A and 2B

(2A) to sort 0 thru 0:               [ 1 ] 2 3 4 5 7 6 8

(2B) to sort 2 thru 3:               1 2 [ 3 4 ] 5 7 6 8

(1B) to sort 5 thru 7:               1 2 3 4 5 [ 7 6 8 ]

prepare split:                       1 2 3 4 5 [ 7 6 8 ]
                                                 L U

traverse:                            1 2 3 4 5 [ 7 6 8 ]
                                                 U L
```

```
swap pivot with U:                      1 2 3 4 5 [ 6 7 8 ]
                                                    U L
return 6, leaving tasks 3A and 3B

(3A) to sort 5 thru 5:                  1 2 3 4 5 [ 6 ] 7 8

(3B) to sort 7 thru 7:                  1 2 3 4 5 6 7 [ 8 ]
```

The exact analysis of Quicksort can become fairly sophisticated. There are various ways to choose the pivot, with different consequences for best-, average-, and worst-case performance. We can take a simple look at Quicksort's basic characteristics, though, without getting into such details. The analysis is simplified by assuming that the size of the file is a power of two, because the split process can be thought of as dividing the file in half.

In each split, the traversals end up comparing each element with the pivot, as can be seen by examining the initial split in the above example, so splitting an subarray of $\mathcal{K}$ elements takes $\mathcal{K}{-}1$ comparisons. Then the list is split into two subparts whose combined size is just one less than the original list. (The pivot is not in either part.) The split of each of those parts will make one fewer comparison than the size of the part. Since the size of the two parts together is $\mathcal{N}{-}1$, the total number of comparisons for splitting the two sublists is $(\mathcal{N}{-}1){-}(1{+}1)$, or $\mathcal{N}{-}3$. Each of those two sublists will then be split into two, giving four altogether, but their sum too will be approximately $\mathcal{N}$, and nearly $\mathcal{N}$ comparisons will be made while splitting those four.

We can consider a "pass" to be the splitting of each of the sublists produced from a previous pass. Initially there are $\mathcal{N}$ elements and one sublist. The first pass produces two sublists, the second pass four sublists, etc. Each split removes a pivot element from further consideration, and some of the sublists may have zero, one, or two elements, but ignoring such complications doesn't disturb this analysis. In fact, since sublists of two elements still require a comparison to be sorted, they too perform one fewer comparison than the number of elements they contain. The splitting can continue pass by pass until no sublist has more than one element.

Suppose that every pivot happens to split its sublist exactly in half. Then with $\mathcal{N}$ the size of the initial list, the size of the pass 1 sublists will be (approximately, since the pivot is in neither sublist) $\mathcal{N}/2$, the size of the pass 2 sublists $\mathcal{N}/4$, etc. Each pass performs approximately $\mathcal{N}$ comparisons in splitting its sublists.

How many passes are needed to get down to lists of only one element? Since the $\mathcal{K}^{\text{th}}$ pass produces sublists of size $\mathcal{N}/2^{\mathcal{K}}$, the question can be rephrased as "for what value of $\mathcal{K}$ is $2^{\mathcal{K}} = \mathcal{N}$?" The answer is the base 2 logarithm of $\mathcal{N}$, since the definition of a logarithm of a number is the power to which a base must be raised to equal that number.

Thus, when all the splits happen to produce sublists of essentially equal size, approximately $\mathcal{N}$ comparisons will be made on each of $log_2\mathcal{N}$ passes. Therefore, the algorithm performs $O(\mathcal{N} log_2\mathcal{N})$ comparisons — more than $\mathcal{N}$ but less than $\mathcal{N}^2$. What about the number of exchanges? There is at most one exchange for every two comparisons, so there certainly won't be more moves than comparisons.

What happens if the split is less balanced? Consider an already sorted list:

```
prepare split:                          [ 1 2 3 4 5 6 7 8 ]
                                          L             U

traverse:                               [ 1 2 3 4 5 6 7 8 ]
                                          L             U

                                        [ 1 2 3 4 5 6 7 8 ]
                                          L           U
```

and so on, with L staying at 2 and U decreasing until:

```
                                        [ 1 2 3 4 5 6 7 8 ]
                                          U L
```

In other words, after $N–1$ comparisons, the pivot ends up being exchanged with itself (which of course could be skipped by a special test in the code). The resulting subarrays are an empty lower one and an upper one that's just the original without the pivot. This would continue, with each pass making one fewer comparison and generating an empty lower subarray and an upper subarray with one fewer element. This would take $N–2$ passes to produce an empty subarray and a subarray with just two elements, which could then be sorted with one comparison. The total number of comparisons will be

$$N–1 + N–2 + \ldots + 1$$
$$= N/2 * N$$
$$= N^2/2$$

An already sorted file leads to the worst-case result of $O(N^2)$ comparisons!

Different methods for choosing the pivot lead to different patterns of best and worst cases. The analysis for a list whose size is not 2^K for some integer K is more complicated, but produces the same results. More sophisticated analysis dispels the spectre of the worst case: it turns out that on average, Quicksort performs very close to $O(N \log_2 N)$ comparisons.

Note that the other three sorting methods shown above don't use any extra space, but that Quicksort requires either an explicit stack or the use of the program stack via recursive calls. This introduces further overhead. However, the stack can never grow deeper than N, since each split removes the pivot from further consideration. Consequently, this extra space, though a factor, grows only linearly with the size of the list to be sorted. All in all, Quicksort is generally about as good at sorting sequential lists as any algorithm could be, though it is not suitable for linked lists.

Merge Sort

Quicksort splits a list in half by rearranging it so that elements are placed into the sublist where they will ultimately belong. Then it recursively sorts each half. The comparisons are performed during the split process. Another approach, used by *merge sort*, splits the list in half without rearranging it, recursively sorts each half, then collates the two sorted halves. Merge sort does its comparisons during the collation steps. (There's no collation in Quicksort, because the exchanges make the two sublists independent of each other.)

Like Quicksort, therefore, merge sort is $O(N \log_2 N)$ for average cases. Unlike Quicksort, merge sort turns out to be $O(N \log_2 N)$ even in the worst case. For linked lists, merge sort is just about optimal. Merge sort would not be so useful with array-based lists because the split and merge process would have to copy elements into arrays allocated for the purpose, thus taking up significant amounts of extra storage and time allocating and deallocating it. Merge sort does not need extra storage for linked lists due to the pointer manipulations their nodes make possible.

The basic idea of merge sort is simple. A list is split in half by the manipulation of pointers to its nodes, which requires a traversal but no comparisons and thus is fast enough to ignore in the analysis. Each half is separately sorted; then the two halves are collated. Since the two halves were each in order before the collation, the collation results in a sorted list. Note the recursion: to sort the list, each of two halves is sorted; to sort a half, each of two of its halves are sorted, and so on. This continues until lists with only one element are reached, much as in Quicksort, which are inherently sorted.

Collation, or merging, is performed as follows: the first elements of the two halves are compared, and the smaller is added to an initially empty temporary list. The pointer to the beginning of the half that had the lesser element is stepped to point to the next node in its list. That node's element is compared with the element that remained at the front of the other list. The lesser of the two is added to the end of the temporary list, and so on, until one of the lists is exhausted. Then the remainder of the other list is added to the end of the temporary list. The temporary list can then be returned as the result of that sort step.

A brief illustration of the process follows. Implementation is left to Exercise 34.

```
original:                        5 8 3 6 7 2 4 1

sort:    (1A)                    5 8 3 6
(split) (1B)                     7 2 4 1

   sort 1A:(2A)                  5 8
      (split)(2B)                3 6

      sort 2A:                   5 8
      sort 2B:                   3 6
      merge 2A, 2B:              3 5 6 8

   sort 1B:(3A)                  7 2
      (split)(3B) 4 1

      sort 3A:                   2 7
      sort 3B:                   1 4
      merge 3A, 3B:              1 2 4 7

   merge 1A, 1B:                 1 2 3 4 5 6 7 8
```

8.3.4 Summary of Sorting Efficiency

We found that the three simple algorithms for sorting a sequential list are $O(N^2)$ for their worst and average cases, either in the number of comparisons or the number of elements moved. Each is $O(N)$ in the best case. Unfortunately, an algorithm's best case for comparison might not be its best case for movement. Variations on these algorithms improve their performance somewhat or affect what initial order actually is best or worst. (If the likely initial order is known, in particular that the list is almost sorted or that it is almost in reverse order, a variation for which that order is the best case could be selected for a particular program.) We also saw that Quicksort and merge sort are $O(N \log_2 N)$, though in pathological cases Quicksort can be as inefficient as the other methods.

The full mathematical analysis of an algorithm's sorting efficiency can get quite involved. The order of the algorithm — linear, quadratic, or whatever — is far more important a formula for computing the exact number of comparisons or moves. For small collections, it hardly matters how efficient an algorithm is. For large collections, the highest-power term of a formula expressing its efficiency so far outweighs the other terms, as well as its own coefficient, that it ends up being the only thing that matters. For large collections, an $O(N)$ algorithm will always be far faster than an $O(N^2)$ one. $O(N \log_2 N)$ is always faster than $O(N^2)$ and slower than $O(N)$.

Table 6 shows some representative values of these orders, to give a more concrete sense of how they increase.

N	N $\log_2$ N	N^2
10	33	100
100	664	10,000
1,000	9,966	1,000,000
10,000	132,877	100,000,000

Table 6   Representative Values for Common Efficiency Orders

A logarithmic graph of these sample numbers, such as the one shown in Figure 8.7, shows the relationship of the three different orders quite clearly.

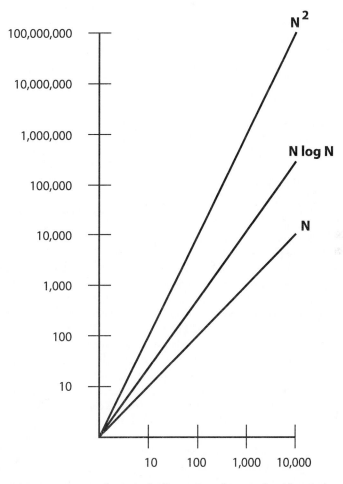

Figure 8.7   Logarithmic Scale Illustration of Some Algorithm Orders

8.4 EXERCISES

1. What term do you think best describes the various kinds of list structures? Discuss the applicability of each of the following terms to the list implementations discussed in this chapter. Point out where strictly speaking a term doesn't quite apply even though it may communicate an appropriate conceptual property. Also mention any other kinds of structures you know about that could be described by each of these terms, making it less useful for categorizing lists.
   (a) 'linked structures'
   (b) 'recursive structures'
   (c) 'dynamic structures'
   (d) 'linear structures'
   (e) 'sequential structures'

2. A common operation on linear structures is to extract a subpart of the structure, for instance the first (or last) n characters of a string or elements j through k of a list. Reasonable names for these functions are `prefix`, `suffix`, and `subX`, where X is the name of the structure (e.g., `substring`).
   (a) What kinds of operations are these in the framework of fundamental operations used in this book?
   (b) Should they be added to this chapter's list modules, or can you just program them with the facilities the list modules already provide?

Sequential Lists

3. Write a program that makes a list of all the words found in a file, using the sequential list module. The words can be listed in any order. Aim to make the program as simple as possible.

4. Write a program that uses sequential lists to write a very simple text editor, as follows:
   (a) A file is represented as a list of lines.
   (b) A line is represented as a list of words, defined as a sequence of printing characters, including punctuation.
   (c) "Current line" and "current word" positions are maintained; initially, they are both 1 (first word of first line).
   (d) Commands should include, for both lines and words, forward (changes current position), backward (changes current position), insert before, insert after, delete, replace, move forward, move backward, and move to. The only way to edit characters in this very simple editor is to replace the word in which they are contained.
   (e) A special insert mode should be available that allows the user to type lines of words at the keyboard and have them inserted at the current position.
   (f) Include a print function that prints a range of lines.

5. Modify the sequential list implementation from the first section of this chapter to dynamically grow and shrink the array holding the list elements. The old array should be replaced by a new one allocated from the heap, the old one's elements copied to the new one, and the old one freed.
   (a) What schemes can you think of for determining how much to grow or shrink the array?
   (b) This approach removes the most serious limitation of sequential lists, that they store elements in fixed size arrays; what new drawbacks does this approach introduce?

6. Write `seq_list::merge`, declared but not implemented in the code shown for the sequential list module. This should produce a new list by alternately adding elements from each of its two arguments until one runs out, then adding the rest of the other's elements.

7. Write `operator>>` for the sequential list module.

8. An alternative way to implement sequential lists uses a different strategy for delimiting the list within the array. No `length` field is maintained. Instead, the entire array is always considered, with a null pointer indicating an array element that does not contain a list element. Newly added elements may be stored anywhere there's a null pointer, though to preserve order it will still often be necessary to shift some elements down in the list.
   (a) Modify the sequential list implementation from the first section of this chapter to use this approach.
   (b) What are the advantages and disadvantages of this approach over using an explicit `length` field and shifting elements around for insertions and deletions?

9. Reimplement either the stack module of Chapter 5 or the queue module of Chapter 6 using a sequential list.
   (a) What are the advantages of using sequential lists as a foundation for stacks and queues?
   (b) What are the disadvantages?

10. Some of the sequential list member functions use sequential list traversal functions as opposed to more direct, lower-level code.
   (a) What advantages does this approach have?
   (b) What are its disadvantages?
   (c) Recode some of these member functions so that they don't use traversal functions.
   (d) Comment on the rewritten code.

11. In `sequential_list::operator=`, if the destination list's array is at least as large as the source list's, it is left alone rather than deleted and a new one allocated. The discussion of that function suggested that another approach would be to always delete the source list's elements array and allocate a new one. Compare the two approaches.
   (a) In what ways is the alternative better?
   (b) In what ways is the alternative worse?

12. The `allocation` of the new list in `seq_list::append` is set to the sum of the `allocations` of the lists being appended.
   (a) Is this a reasonable design choice?
   (b) What are some other approaches you can imagine?
   (c) What are the advantages and disadvantages of the other approaches?

13. Rewrite `seq_list::compare`, `seq_list::equal`, and `seq_list::append` to use traversal operators and compare the two versions.

14. Write a function `sublist` that takes two lists and returns a Boolean indicating whether the first list is a sublist of the second in the sense that the second list contains the same elements in the same order as the first list but may also have other elements following those.
   (a) What kind of fundamental operation is this?
   (b) Can you think of an application where it would be useful to have such a function?

15. The definition of `seq_list::append` begins by allocating an empty local list. It then traverses the two lists, adding each of their elements to the new list. Another approach would be to start with a copy of the first list, then traverse only the second.
   (a) Write, test, and debug a definition of `seq_list::append` that takes that approach.
   (b) Which do you prefer? Why?

16. The definition of `seq_list::reverse` is clever — perhaps so clever as to be highly artificial.
   (a) Rewrite the function taking a more natural approach.
   (b) Compare the two versions. Which do you like better? Why?

17. Augment the sequential list module to give the user control over how the output operator delimits lists (instead of always enclosing them in parentheses) and how it separates list elements. Use static members so that each list doesn't get its own output control state.

Linked Lists

18. Change the program in Exercise 4 so that it uses linked lists instead of sequential lists. How much did you have to change in the application program?

19. Add `remove_equals(elt)`, `remove1_equals(elt)`, `replace_equals(elt)`, and `replace1_equals(elt)` to the linked list module. What other functions might have different versions for equality, as opposed to identity, tests?

20. Other variations of operations that search for matches — in particular **Remove** and **Search** — are sometimes useful. In particular, several functions that take an element as their argument could also take a function of one element that returns a Boolean.

   (a) Add a function `contains_if` that tests whether the list contains an element for which the function argument returns `TRUE`.

   (b) Add a `remove_if` function to the linked list module that removes from the list any element for which the function argument returns `TRUE`.

   (c) Can you think of any other functions from the linked list module for which a similar variation would be useful?

21. Consider changing the linked list representation so that length is explicitly stored and maintained.

   (a) How does this affect the implementation?

   (b) Does this seem like a good idea?

22. Modify the linked list module to keep track of the last node, for efficiency.

   (a) How much of your code did you have to change?

   (b) Run some tests to compare the efficiency of adding elements to the end of the list in the two implementations.

   (c) What price is paid to keep track of the last node?

23. Modify your linked list module to be doubly linked, extend the traversal operations to handle generating predecessors (`prev`) in addition to successors (`next`), and try out reverse traversal.

24. Some of the linked list member functions use sequential list traversal functions as opposed to more direct, lower-level code.

   (a) What advantages does this approach have?

   (b) What are its disadvantages?

   (c) Recode some of these member functions so that they don't use traversal functions.

   (d) Comment on the rewritten code.

   (e) What criteria could you suggest for deciding whether to use traversal functions in coding a module's own functions?

25. The way computers store integers limits their magnitude. Applications may require integers of arbitrary (unlimited) size. One approach to implementing unlimited integers is to use a list to hold the pieces of an integer. At the extreme, each node could hold just one digit, but it is more practical to put a full-size regular integer in each node. For example, if 16-bit integers are stored in each node, a list of two nodes would represent one node's integer plus 2^{16} times the other's. Implement and demonstrate the use of an unlimited-size integers using a list module.

   (a) What kind of list makes sense?

   (b) What operations should be provided? Include them in your implementation.

   (c) Are these unlimited integers data structures?

   (d) If so, what are their components?

   (e) Write a program that allows a user to perform very simple operations on unlimited integers by typing expressions such as `1455523997360 + 559012424555` at the terminal.

26. Redo the card shuffle exercise from the chapter on streams (Exercise 4, page 141) using lists to represent decks.

   (a) How much of the program did you have to change?

   (b) The linked list module doesn't support splitting lists.

27. Implement a `set` module based on linked lists.

28. Reimplement either the stack module of Chapter 5 or the queue module of Chapter 6 using a linked list.

   (a) What are the advantages of using linked lists as a foundation for stacks and queues?

(b) What are the disadvantages?

(c) How does an implementation based on linked lists compare to one based on sequential lists? (Cf. Exercise 9.)

29. Consider the final version of the linked list module, where there is no node array.

(a) Should `freelist`, `newnode`, and `free(link)` be part of `list` or part of `list_node`?

(b) In the first versions, there are good reasons for putting these in `list`. What are they?

(c) How would the code be affected if you moved these from `list` to `node`?

(d) Recode the module making this change.

(e) Compare the two versions.

30. A *sparse matrix* is a large matrix (we'll assume two-dimensional here) most of the values of which are the same (normally zero). It may not make sense to allocate a huge amount of memory to hold a relatively small number of nondefault values. (Consider, e.g., the identity matrix of a thousand rows and a thousand columns.) Design, implement, and test a sparse matrix module based on the following approach. Make sure you allow the user to specify the default initial value for all elements of the sparse matrix.

(a) Have a sequential list of linked lists, one for each row. The entries in the lists are *cells* consisting of a column number and value. **Access** of the element in row r and column c is performed by searching the linked list for a cell whose column number is c. Adding an element to the matrix involves creating a cell for it and inserting it into the linked list corresponding to its row. How much space is taken for a sparse matrix with one nondefault value? What are the performance characteristics of **Access/Modify** operations?

(b) How would it help or hurt to store the lists so that the cells were ordered according to column?

(c) Once your module is working, considering changing it to work with sparse matrices of indefinite size. (That is, the size is never specified — if a larger row or column than has been seen before is specified, the matrix in effect grows.) Have lists only for rows with nondefault elements; this leads to using a linked list of rows instead of a sequential list, and now the cells have to include row numbers. What change had to be made in your test program or application to accommodate this change to the module? How have the performance characteristics of **Access/Modify** operations changed? How much space is required to store a sparse matrix with one nondefault value?

Sorting Lists

31. Show the sequence of passes involved in alphabetically sorting the names of the days of the week according to the insertion, selection, and bubble sort methods shown in Section 8.3.2, starting on page 252.

32. What is the best-case ordering for the insertion sort algorithm as described in Section 8.3.2 (page 254)?

33. The text in Section 8.3 explicitly shows base two for the logarithms in the efficiency analyses. Actually, the base is normally not specified in such discussions. What property of logarithms allows the base to be omitted in efficiency characterizations such as $O(N \log N)$?

34. Implement `merge_sort`, declared but not implemented in the linked list module.

35. Add simple **Sort** operations to the sequential list module, similar to the ones shown for linked lists:

(a) selection sort

(b) insertion sort

(c) bubble sort

36. Code for Quicksort was presented in Section 5.4.3 (page 163), but that was for sorting arrays.

(a) Add `quick_sort` to the sequential list module. (Use a recursive formulation instead of explicit stacks.)

(b) Was the code very different from the code for arrays? Why?

(c) Describe how you would implement Quicksort for linked lists (the final, pointer-based version) and comment on what that reveals about the nature of linked versus sequential lists.

37. The book's string struct contains a static data member `string::compares` that is initialized to 0 and initialized every time `compare(string&, string)` is called. It's public, so you can use and set its value directly. Gather statistics about the number of comparisons performed in sorting several different size lists of strings — say, 10, 50, 100, 500, and 1000 elements — as follows:

(a) Show results for sorted lists, reverse sorted lists, almost sorted lists, and random lists for insertion, selection, and bubble sort.

(b) If merge sort is available (provided by the instructor or implemented for Exercise 34), include that too.

(c) Similarly, if quick sort is available (provided by the instructor or implemented for Exercise 36), include that too.

(d) Use either the sequential or linked list implementations as convenient; you can even use different kinds of lists for different sorting methods.

38. An interesting question for a sorting method is whether it leaves equal elements in the same relative order. A sorting method is called *stable* if for every pair of elements in the original list, the first of the pair appears before the second in the sorted list.

(a) Which of the algorithms shown in the text are stable and which aren't?

(b) Construct an example that demonstrates instability for each of the algorithms you decide are unstable. (If you try to test your example with one of the sorting routines provided online, it will help to use as elements a type that distinguishes instances that test equal, perhaps by using an "id" field that is printed but not considered by `equal`.)

39. Bubble sort can be speeded up by reversing direction on each pass. In the formulation in the text, elements that belong near the end of the list quickly reach their final position, but elements that belong near the front move only one step closer to the front on each pass. By following each front to back pass with a back to front pass, elements that belong near the front reach their final positions quickly too.

(a) Implement this version.

(b) Gather statistics for the performance of both versions. (See Exercise 37 for information about `string::compares`.) Include sorted lists, reverse-sorted lists, almost-sorted lists, and random lists.

A Major Project

40. Linked lists are an excellent foundation for the representation of polynomials. Implement a complete polynomial module then write a program to perform interactive polynomial arithmetic. Details follow.

(a) For this exercise, define a polynomial as a sequence of terms, each consisting of a coefficient, one single-letter variable name, and an exponent. Each coefficient consists of a sign and an integer. Exponents consist of an optional sign and an integer. Terms do not have to be in any particular order, but assume that there's only one term with a particular exponent in any polynomial. White space is allowed between any two pieces of a term, including between a sign and an integer.

(b) Commands are to be read from `cin` and echoed along with appropriate responses to `cout`, though during development you'll probably want these to be files. Each command will occupy a single line. If there is any kind of input error, it should be reported and the entire line skipped.

(c) Single-letter names will be used to refer to polynomials. Use the array module from Chapter 2 to create an array of (pointers to) polynomials, indexed by character. You may allow either or both of upper- and lower-case letters, as convenient.

(d) The commands your program should handle include the following. In the description of these commands, *poly* refers to a polynomial, *name* refers to a single letter, *int* to an integer, and *op* to an operation (such as +). The command descriptions include C++-style comments.

```
let name be poly        // read poly and store in table[name]
eval name with int      // evaluate table[name] for int
show name               // output table[name]
copy name1 to name2     // copy table[name1] to table[name2]
do name1 op name2       // create & print the polynomial that
            // is the result of table[name1] op table[name2]
save name               // store result of last do in table[name]
free name               // destroy table[name]
end                     // exit program, printing all polynomials
                        // still in table, along with their names
```

(e) Polynomials should be represented as linked lists of terms. Store the terms in order of their exponents. Algebraic operations should be performed by creating a new (empty) polynomial for the result, generating the terms without worrying about zero coefficients, then eliminating terms with zero coefficient. (Be warned that the traversal operations of the linked list module do not support removing elements in the midst of a traversal. You should use the remove_if function described in Exercise 20. If that is not available, repeatedly traverse the list looking for an element with a zero coefficient, invoke remove on it, then restart the traversal, searching again until the traversal completes with no zero-coefficient term found.

(f) *Do not let yourself get bogged down in processing input.* Reading command lines and checking for errors can be a highly demoralizing coding challenge. One problem with a traditional approach to input is that there may be many nested levels of syntactic structures and each input operation has to report success or failure to its caller; then each caller has to check the result to make sure it's OK to proceed. Code is quickly swamped under all this testing and returning error conditions.

The way this assignment is constructed, a line is either correct or not. Your program does have to check for error conditions, but when one is found your program can just abort input and go on to the next line (freeing a partially constructed polynomial if applicable). The overall structure of the input process for a command is:

```
ReadCommandLine
    ReadCommand
    ReadName
    ReadKeyword
    ReadPolynomial
        ReadTerms
            ReadTerm
                ReadCoefficient
                    ReadSign
                    ReadValue
                ReadVariable
                ReadExponent
                    ReadSign
                    ReadValue
```

(The sign and value must be read separately for coefficients and exponents because white space may occur between them.) Suppose the program encounters an error while reading a coefficient. Should it go back through ReadTerm, then ReadTerms, then Read-Polynomial, and finally ReadCommand, each one checking whether the next succeeded or failed? No! The program should just abandon the whole mess, clean things up, and start fresh with the next line.

What's needed is a mechanism for aborting from within a series of function calls and returning to a designated place. True exception handling is ideal for this, but C's longjmp facility can work if used carefully. The main thing to watch out for is that the space used by the partially constructed polynomial is appropriately recycled.

(g) The polynomial module should be organized according to its fundamental operations. You should think first about what operations a polynomial module needs before worrying about what operations are needed for this particular program. You should at least include declarations for all appropriate functions, even if you only implement the ones you actually use.

(h) Comment on the advantages and disadvantages of the modularization approach advocated in this book based on your experience with this project.

9

Trees

Trees are important data structures with a wide variety of applications. In a tree, each item has one *or more* successors, called its *children*. Figure 9.1 shows a tree illustrating the organization of the data structure chapters of this book. Note that trees are drawn upside down relative to their real-world analogues.

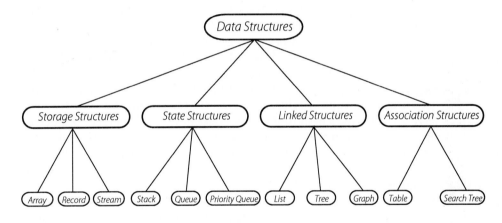

Figure 9.1 A Tree

An element's predecessor is its parent. Indirect predecessors are called *ancestors* and indirect successors *descendants*. *Binary trees*, in which each element may have at most two successors, are an important special case.

The first element of the tree is called its *root*. Every element has a predecessor except for the root. Elements with no successors are called *leaves* or *terminals*. Elements that do have successors are called *internal* nodes.

The *depth* of an element is its distance from the root. The depth of the root is defined to be 0, the depth of each of its children is 1, and so on. The nth *level* of a tree is the set of all its elements at depth n. The *height* of a tree is the maximum depth of its nodes.

A *subtree* is an element plus all its descendants. A *forest* is a collection of disjoint trees. The trees of a forest can be connected to form a single tree by joining them to a new common root.

Like linked lists, trees are composed of nodes connected by pointers. Whereas a linked list node has a pointer to one successor, a tree node may have pointers to more than one. This simple difference introduces some interesting complexity that profoundly affects the public interface of tree structures.

Because lists are linear, they combine the properties of simple sequential structures like arrays with the flexibility of other linked structures. As in an array, a list element may be accessed individually by specifying its position. Unlike arrays, streams, stacks, and queues, lists support insertion and deletion of elements at arbitrary positions. Because each node has at most one successor, traversals and traversal-like operations (such as finding the position of an element) can be coded as simple loops.

Trees are more complex than lists. Since each node can have more than one successor, trees are not linear structures. This affects their representation, the coding of their operations, and even the role their nodes play. There's no such thing as the nth element of a tree — access is always by navigation from one node to the next.

The representation and fundamental operations of trees are similar to those for linked lists, though complicated by the possibility of multiple successors. The tree representation will keep track of a current node for navigation operations. These will support moving around in the tree and accessing and modifying the current node. Corresponding to the back pointer of doubly linked lists is the option of having back pointers from a tree node to its predecessor (parent). Many operations on trees are necessarily recursive: they do something to a node's element and then to each of its subtrees. Recursive operations need to manipulate subtrees, not just traverse the structure one link at a time. We therefore sometimes need to interpret nodes not just as internal components of a tree structure, but as roots of their own subtrees. Although list operations may be expressed recursively, it isn't necessary to do so: because lists are linear, they can always be traversed iteratively. Consequently, the list implementations of the previous chapter did not need to support a sublist concept.

Code using a tree sometimes needs to construct or process the tree recursively. The usual navigation and traversal operations are fundamentally sequential in nature and so don't adequately support recursive operations. It therefore becomes necessary to make tree nodes available outside the module, along with appropriate operations for manipulating them. This contrasts with our list implementation, which was able to completely hide its private node structure. In effect we need two interfaces to trees: a tree-oriented one for most operations and a node- or subtree-oriented one for recursive operations. Of course, we could get by with just the node operations, but they are too low level for most purposes.

9.1 Binary Trees

A *binary tree* is either empty or consists of a root and two binary subtrees, designated *left* and *right*. (Note that this is a recursive definition.) Either or both of a tree's two subtrees may be empty. Figure 9.2 shows a binary tree.

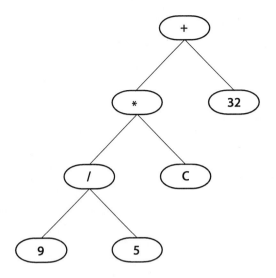

Figure 9.2   A Binary Tree

A tree's two subtrees are distinguished. The two binary trees of Figure 9.3 are *not* equivalent., even though they seem to contain the same information.

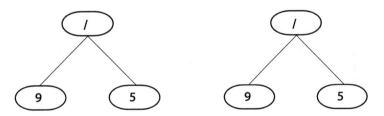

Figure 9.3   Two Similar but Different Binary Trees

The maximum number of items at the nth level of a binary tree (with the root at level 0) is 2^n. (Since each item can have a left and a right successor, the maximum number of items at one level is twice the number at the previous one.) A *full binary tree* is one in which each item has either 0 or 2 children, but not 1. A *complete binary tree* (of depth n) is a full one in which all leaves appear at the same level (level n). The number of nodes in a complete binary tree of depth n is $2^{n+1}-1$.

9.1.1 Representation

Binary tree nodes are a straightforward extension of linked list nodes. Each node has a pointer to an element and two pointers to nodes, as illustrated in Figure 9.4. The two pointers are normally designated `left` and `right`. The nodes will be allocated from a free

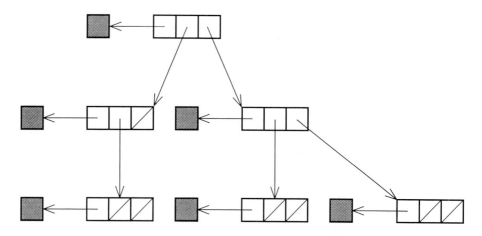

The shaded blocks represent the node contents.

Figure 9.4   Binary Tree Nodes

list, as in the linked list implementation of the previous chapter. For convenience we'll continue to use `link` as the name for a pointer to a node — it sure beats typing `binary_tree_node<elt>*` throughout the module!

When linked list nodes were introduced (cf. Section 8.2.2, page 221 ff.), definitions of all their operations were shown along with their declaration. The rest of the discussion dealt primarily with the lists themselves. Tree nodes must support richer functionality than list nodes due to the recursive nature of trees. Therefore, we'll discuss the various aspects of tree nodes in parallel with the discussion of trees, rather than preceding it.

```
#define link binary_tree_node<elt>*

template <class elt> struct binary_tree_node
{
  private:
    // Representation
    elt elem;
    link left;
    link right;
    // . . .
};
```

A tree is a root node and some subtrees. Internally, nodes will point to other nodes — 'subtree' will be a concept but not a separate type. We will need a tree type, though. All it will contain is a root node and the traversal state. Many operations on the tree will simply invoke similar operations on the root node. The tree and the root node are really two perspectives on the same structure.

```
template <class elt> struct binary_tree
{
  private:
    // Representation
    binary_tree_node<elt> root;
    // . . .
};
```

9.1.2 Lifetime Operations

Node Create/Destroy

Nodes will be allocated from their free list by the static function `binary_tree_node::newnode`. The only time nodes need to be created is when the free list is empty. Then a block of nodes will be allocated and linked together to form the free list. The static data member `allocation` will determine the number of nodes to be created when the free list runs out. We'll leave this public so user code can set it according to the needs of each application. Its value can even be changed repeatedly, to meet the varying needs of different parts of the program or phases of its execution. To allow applications to construct trees node by node — necessary to support recursive processes — we also make `newnode` public.

```
template <class elt> struct binary_tree_node
{
    // . . .
    // Create/Destroy
  private:
    static link freelist;
    static void make_freelist();
    void recycle();                       // return to freelist
  public:
    static int allocation;
    static link newnode(elt);             // allocate from freelist
};
```

For convenience, and since this is only an implementation detail, we'll link the nodes on the free list through their `left` member, rather than using a real list type. The free list is initially empty — there's no need to allocate nodes until they are required. Besides, this gives the application a chance to change the value of `allocation` before the first nodes are allocated. The default constructor (shown further below) links the nodes together, but the last node's `left` must be explicitly set to the null pointer to terminate the list.

The static function `newnode` removes a node from the free list, initializes its fields, and returns it to the caller. If the free list is empty, `newnode` invokes `make_freelist` to restock it. Note that nodes are always given a particular element, not left empty, and null `left` and `right` members.

Nodes are returned to the free list by `recycle` and don't get deallocated until the program exits. When a node is returned to the free list, its descendants must be returned too, so `recycle` must be recursive: it recycles its argument's left child, recycles its argument's right child, and finally puts its argument on the free list. This is the sort of code that normally appears in destructors. However, since the node isn't actually getting deallocated, the normal automatic invocation of the destructor doesn't occur, and we have to include it explicitly in `recycle`.

```
/* Free List Management */

template <class elt>
    binary_tree_node<elt>* binary_tree_node<elt>::freelist = 0;
template <class elt> int binary_tree_node<elt>::allocation = 100;

template <class elt> void binary_tree_node<elt>::make_freelist()
{
    freelist = new binary_tree_node<elt>[allocation];
    freelist[allocation-1].setLeft(0);
}

template <class elt>
binary_tree_node<elt>* binary_tree_node<elt>::newnode(elt e)
{
    if (!freelist) make_freelist();
    link nd = freelist;
    freelist = freelist->getLeft();
    nd->setLeft(0);
    nd->setRight(0);
    nd->setElt(e);
    return nd;
}

template <class elt> void binary_tree_node<elt>::recycle()
{
    if (left != 0) left->recycle();          // recursive call
    if (right != 0) right->recycle();        // recursive call
    left = freelist;
    right = 0;
    freelist = this;
}
```

Node Initialize/Finalize

Because the module manages its own nodes, client code never directly allocates a node, so the constructors are kept private. To allow the tree code to initialize its root node the tree constructor is made a friend of `binary_tree_node`. This is an interesting half-way kind of access: client code can *use* nodes through their operations (including the recycling versions of **Create** or **Destroy**), but it can't directly create new ones. The destructor is likewise kept private, and, since the tree destructor will cause the node destructor to be invoked, the tree destructor must be a friend.

```
template <class elt> struct binary_tree_node
{
    // . . .
    // Initialize/Finalize
  private:
    binary_tree_node();                         // free list constructor
    binary_tree_node(elt);                      // root constructor
    ~binary_tree_node();
    friend binary_tree<elt>::binary_tree();
    friend binary_tree<elt>::~binary_tree();
};
```

The code for the node constructor and destructors is trivial. The only noteworthy point is a little trick used to link nodes together when they are first added to the free list. In the linked list free list code, for clarity, there was an explicit loop that linked each node to the next. Here, we make use of two facts to streamline the process. One is that the nodes are all allocated in an array then all initialized. The other is that we can use C pointer arithmetic to get the next element of the array — the node we want the one being initialized to point to. Since the one being initialized is pointed to by this, the following node is pointed to by this+1.

```
/* Node Initialize/Finalize */

// private constructor: called only when free list is allocated
template <class elt> binary_tree_node<elt>::binary_tree_node()
        : elem(0), left(this+1), right(0)
{
}

template <class elt> binary_tree_node<elt>::binary_tree_node(elt e)
        : elem(e), left(0), right(0)
{
}

template <class elt> binary_tree_node<elt>::~binary_tree_node()
{
}
```

Tree Initialize/Finalize

The constructor and destructor for the tree itself are trivial. The constructor takes an element, which will be stored in the root. Strictly speaking, this implementation does not provide a way to make an empty tree — the tree always has at least a root node. However, if the root has not left or right subtree and its element is the null pointer, we'll consider the tree empty. A program can therefore create an empty tree by providing a null pointer, which it can later replace. The destructor is more substantial than the constructor: it recursively recycles the root's two subtrees.

```
template <class elt> struct binary_tree
{
    // . . .
    // Initialize/Finalize
    binary_tree(elt = 0);
    ~binary_tree();
};
```

```
/* Tree Initialize/Finalize */

template <class elt> binary_tree<elt>::binary_tree(elt e)
        : root(e), cur(0), count(-1)
{
}

template <class elt> binary_tree<elt>::~binary_tree()
{
    clear();
}
```

Node Access/Modify

Tree nodes have the same sort of simple **Access** and **Modify** operations that linked list nodes did. Here, of course, this a pair of operations for everything dealing with a successor — one for the left child and one for the right.

```
template <class elt> struct binary_tree_node
{
    // . . .
    // Access/Modify
    elt& getElt();                    // return node's contents
    void setElt(elt);                 // replace node's contents

    link getLeft();                   // return node's left subtree
    link getRight();                  // return node's right subtree

    void setLeft(link);               // replace left subtree
    void setRight(link);              // replace right subtree

    void addLeft(elt);                // add a new left child for elt
    void addRight(elt);               // add a new right child for elt
    void add(elt);                    // add a new child for elt --
```

```
                                              // left if available, else right

      void removeLeft();                      // remove left subtree
      void removeRight();                     // remove right subtree
};
```

There are some subtle decisions to make about what conditions these functions assume. For instance, if client code calls setLeft or addLeft, what happens if the node already has a left subtree? The choice was made to recycle the old subtree for setLeft, but to report an error for addLeft. Of course, setRight and addRight are treated similarly. The remove functions are coded to work whether or not the corresponding subtree is empty.

```
/* Node Access/Modify */

template <class elt> elt& binary_tree_node<elt>::getElt()
{
    return elem;
}

template <class elt> void binary_tree_node<elt>::setElt(elt e)
{
    elem = e;
}


template <class elt> link binary_tree_node<elt>::getLeft()
{
    return left;
}

template <class elt> link binary_tree_node<elt>::getRight()
{
    return right;
}


template <class elt> void binary_tree_node<elt>::setLeft(link tree_node)
{
    if (left) left->recycle();
    left = tree_node;
}

template <class elt> void binary_tree_node<elt>::setRight(link tree_node)
{
    if (right) right->recycle();
    right = tree_node;
}

template <class elt> void binary_tree_node<elt>::addLeft(elt e)
{
    if (left != 0)
```

```
        error("[binary_tree_node::addLeft] node already has left child");
    left = newnode(e);
}

template <class elt> void binary_tree_node<elt>::addRight(elt e)
{
    if (right != 0)
        error("[binary_tree_node::addRight] node already has right child");
    right = newnode(e);
}

template <class elt> void binary_tree_node<elt>::add(elt e)
{
    if (0 != left)
        left = newnode(e);
    else
        {
            if (0 != right)
                error("[binary_tree_node::add] node full");
            right = newnode(e);
        }
}

template <class elt> void binary_tree_node<elt>::removeLeft()
{
    if (left) left->recycle();
    left = 0;
}

template <class elt> void binary_tree_node<elt>::removeRight()
{
    if (right) right->recycle();
    right = 0;
}
```

Tree Access/Modify

Tree navigation always starts at the root node, and that's really the only **Access** function
the tree itself provides. Subsequently, other nodes are accessed and modified using node
Access and **Modify** operations. Similarly, the only **Modify** operation the tree needs is
clear, to empty the entire tree. That function starts at the root and recursively deletes
children using node operations.

```
template <class elt> struct binary_tree
{
    // . . .
    // Access/Modify
    link getRootNode();                  // for recursive processing
    void clear();                        // remove all the nodes
};
```

```
/* Tree Access/Modify */

template <class elt> link binary_tree<elt>::getRootNode()
{
    return &root;
}

template <class elt> void binary_tree<elt>::clear()
{
    if (root.hasLeft()) root.getLeft()->recycle();
    if (root.hasRight()) root.getRight()->recycle();
    root.setElt(0);
}
```

9.1.3 Traversal and Recursion

Trees are the first *nonlinear* structures we've encountered. They are inherently two-dimensional. We can even see the difference in the diagrams used to illustrate the various structures. For the other structures we've seen so far, the diagrams show organization in only one direction, left to right or top to bottom. In contrast, tree diagrams use both horizontal and vertical dimensions to show the structure's organization: vertical for parent-child relationships and horizontal to distinguish a node's descendants from each other. This two-dimensionality is the direct consequence of allowing an element to have more than one successor.

Consider the tree from Figure 9.2 on page 275, repeated here for convenience as Figure 9.5. Suppose we just wanted to print the items in the tree. We would start at the root,

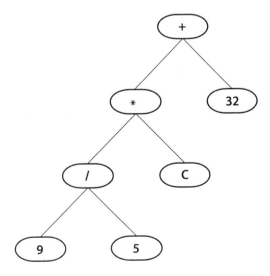

Figure 9.5   A Binary Tree

print +, then print the rest of the tree. If we go down the left branch, we would print *, then we could print the rest of that subtree, and so on. Eventually, we have to come back to the 32 that we ignored when we when followed the left branch from the root.

In traversing a linear structure there's only one next item, so nothing has to be remembered while that item is processed. In a nonlinear structure, items may have more than one successor. Only one next item can be processed at a time— the rest have to be recorded to be processed later. The state structures we studied in Part 3 of this book are exactly what is needed for recording these postponed tasks. But which one?

Traversal Orders

Actually, we can use any of them! The choice of state structure determines the order in which the items are visited by the traversal. Suppose we use a queue, so that after printing an item we add its successors to the queue:

```
                           add the root +      [ + ]
remove and print   +       add * and 32        [ * 32 ]
remove and print   *       add / and C         [ 32 / C ]
remove and print   32      nothing to add      [ / C ]
remove and print   /       add 9 and 5         [ C 9 5 ]
remove and print   C       nothing to add      [ 9 5 ]
remove and print   9       nothing to add      [ 5 ]
remove and print   5       nothing to add      [ ]

Resulting order of printing:  + * 32 / C 9 5
```

This order is called *breadth-first* because all the elements at one level of the tree are processed before going on to the elements at lower depths. Using a stack gives us a different order, called *depth-first*. Let's try the example with a stack (stacking the right successor before the left so that the left gets processed before the right):

```
                           push the root +     [ + ]
pop and print      +       push 32 then *      [ * 32 ]
pop and print      *       push C then /       [ / C 32 ]
pop and print      /       push 5 then 9       [ 9 5 C 32 ]
pop and print      9       nothing to push     [ 5 C 32 ]
pop and print      5       nothing to push     [ C 32 ]
pop and print      C       nothing to push     [ 32 ]
pop and print      32      nothing to push     [ ]

Resulting order of printing:  + * / 9 5 C 32
```

We could even use a priority queue to select the most promising or most important item of those remaining in the list of tasks. Game-playing programs based on artificial intelligence programming techniques do that, for example. Priority queues wouldn't make much sense in this example, however.

We saw in the chapter on stacks that stack-based processes can be expressed recursively. In effect, these implicitly use the subprogram call and return stack in place of an explicit stack. (See Section 5.4.1, page 160 and Section 5.4.3, page 163.) A depth-first traversal of a tree can therefore be expressed in code like the following.

```
template <class elt> void print(link nd, ostream& strm)
{
    strm << *nd->getElt() << ' ';
    if (nd->hasLeft()) print(nd->getLeft(), strm);
    if (nd->hasRight()) print(nd->getRight(), strm);
}
```

This is a typical recursive function on a binary tree. One step processes the current node, and the other steps add its children to the stack (whichever, if any, it has). We can even move the statement that processes the current node so that it comes between or after the recursive calls. This yields three variations on the depth-first approach, named according to when the node's element is processed relative to its successors. These are summarized in Table 7.

	order	sequence
first	preorder	node, left subtree, right subtree
between	inorder	left subtree, node, right subtree
after	postorder	left subtree, right subtree, node

Table 7   Depth-First Traversal Orders

Traversals of the tree above in the different depth-first orders produce the following outputs:

```
preorder:    + * / 9 5 C 32
inorder:     9 / 5 * C + 32
postorder:   9 5 / C * 32 +
```

These correspond to prefix, infix, and postfix algebraic expressions. (You may have encountered preorder or postorder algebraic expressions before, perhaps in using a scientific calculator.) Inorder corresponds to the usual way we write algebraic expressions. Note that preorder and postorder unambiguously indicate the intended computation, whereas inorder notation is ambiguous. The ambiguity of inorder expressions must be resolved with parentheses or precedence rules, a fact with which programmers are quite familiar.

Traversal Operations

Preorder traversal fits nicely into the framework we've been using for all the data structures. The state of the traversal can be maintained in a stack-valued data member of the tree. Reset clears the stack and pushes a pointer to the root node onto it. Next pops a (pointer to a) node from the stack and pushes its children. The traversal ends when the stack is empty. One extra capability is needed: since we allow applications to manipulate nodes in addition to the tree, **Traversal** must include a function to get the current node in addition to the usual function to get the current element.

Inorder and postorder traversals can also be coded using a stack, but not in any obvious way. The implementation of postorder traversal is left for Exercise 11, but inorder is shown here. An enum is used to identify which order a particular traversal should follow. The value for a traversal is provided as an argument to reset, which stores the value in the data member travord for the other **Traversal** functions to consult.

If we use a queue instead of a stack, we get breadth-first traversal. The implementation shown here uses a simple double-ended queue (a *deque*), a structure that allows addition and removal at each end. That way, the same structure can be used either as a stack or a queue.

```
enum traversal_order { preorder, inorder, postorder, breadth_first };

template <class elt> struct binary_tree
{
    // . . .
    // Traversal
  private:
    deque<link> tdeq;
    link cur;
    traversal_order travord;
    int  count;
    void push_children();
    void stack_lefts(link);                    // for inorder
  public:
    void reset(bool depth_first = TRUE);
    bool finished();
    bool next();
    elt& current();
    link current_node();
    int index();
};
```

A lot of power is packaged in these **Traversal** operations A user can traverse an entire tree one node at a time, in any of the depth-first orders or breadth-first, without bothering with the details of navigation. **Traversal** operations convert a fundamentally nonlinear structure into a linearly accessed sequence of indeterminate length — a stream!

The bulk of the work is handled by reset and two private auxiliary functions used to stack nodes according to the prevailing traversal order. The easy cases are inorder and breadth_first. The root node is stacked by reset, and whenever a node is popped its children are added to the deque at the front (for inorder) or back (for breadth_first). Children are handled by push_children, called by next.

The implementation of inorder is tricky and unintuitive but easy enough to understand. Reset begins by stacking the root, its left child, that node's left child, and so on, until a node is stacked that has no left child. Traversal then proceeds normally, except that every time a node is taken from the stack, push_children stacks all the left successors of its right child, just as reset began by stacking all the left successors of the root node.

```
/* Tree Traversal: Stacking */

template <class elt> void binary_tree<elt>::reset(bool depth_first)
{
    count = 0;
    cur = 0;
    travord = ord;

    switch (ord)
    {
      case preorder:
      case breadth_first:
        tdeq.push(&root);
        break;

      case inorder:
        stack_lefts(&root);
        break;

      case postorder:
        notimp("postorder binary tree traversal");
        break;
    }
}

template <class elt> void binary_tree<elt>::push_children()
{
    switch (travord)
    {
      case preorder:
        if (cur->hasRight())
            tdeq.push(cur->getRight());
        // right is pushed first so left is popped first
        if (cur->hasLeft())
            tdeq.push(cur->getLeft());
        break;

      case breadth_first:
        if (cur->hasLeft())
            tdeq.pushend(cur->getLeft());
        if (cur->hasRight())
            tdeq.pushend(cur->getRight());
        break;

      case inorder:
        if (cur->getRight())
            stack_lefts(cur->getRight());
        break;

      case postorder:
        notimp("postorder binary tree traversal");
    }
}
```

```
// Support function for push_children
template <class elt> void binary_tree<elt>::stack_lefts(link nd)
{
    while (nd)
        {
            tdeq.push(nd);
            nd = nd->getLeft();
        }
}
```

None of the rest of the functions are affected by the different traversal orders. Next calls push_children, but otherwise these all stand on their own. Traversal is finished when the deque is empty, regardless of the order.

```
/* Traversal: Other */

template <class elt> bool binary_tree<elt>::finished()
{
    return tdeq.empty();
}

template <class elt> bool binary_tree<elt>::next()
{
    if (count < 0)
        error("[binary_tree<elt>::next] traversal not yet initialized");
    if (finished()) return FALSE;
    cur = tdeq.pop();
    push_children();
    count++;
    return TRUE;
}

template <class elt> elt& binary_tree<elt>::current()
{
    assert(cur != 0);
    return cur->getElt();
}

template <class elt> link binary_tree<elt>::current_node()
{
    return cur;
}

template <class elt> int binary_tree<elt>::index()
{
    return count;
}
```

Processing a Tree Recursively

Using a stack to traverse a tree in preorder is straightforward. "Process a node; then process its children" corresponds directly to "pop a node; then push its children." What about inorder and postorder, though? These orders don't correspond to any straightforward use of a stack. It is possible to program them with a stack, but the code is awkward. We saw above that depth-first traversals can be quite concisely expressed by recursive code and that the only difference in the three orders is the position of the statement that processes a node relative to the statements that process its children. Therefore, we'll have the module's users program inorder and postorder traversals recursively, rather than through the sequential traversal mechanism our standard **Traversal** operations provides.

There's a more important reason to use recursion when processing a tree than for programming convenience. Sometimes information is derived from a node's contents together with information derived from its children. Consider function calls in programming languages: first a function's arguments must be evaluated; then the function itself must be evaluated *using the results of evaluating the arguments*. A process like this must imitate the recursive structure of the tree and can't use a sequential traversal. It isn't just that the tree must be processed in postorder: when a node is processed it needs not just the node's contents but the result of processing each of its children. (See Exercise 9 for an example involving trees that represent algebraic expressions.)

Recursive processing requires access to the nodes, as suggested in the introduction to this chapter. If we define a subtree as a node and its children, then clearly subtrees are inherently recursive since they are defined recursively. Moreover, each node *is* a subtree — nodes and subtrees are just two ways of looking at the same thing. The print function on page 285 is a good example of a recursive function that uses node **Access** functions to process a tree recursively.

Here's an interesting example of a tree that must be recursively processed.[1] Define a *binary mobile* as a tree of numbers in which each subtree represents a branch. The number in a terminal node represents a weight hanging from the branch represented by the node's parent. Note that a weight node will not have a sibling; that is, if a node's left subtree is a weight it will have no right subtree. The number in a nonterminal node represents the length of the branch. The number in the root is irrelevant. (Figure 9.6 shows an example.) The challenge is to determine if a given binary tree represents a *torque-balanced* mobile, defined as one in which the length of the left branch times the total weight hanging from it is equal to the length of the right branch times the total weight hanging from it.

This problem can be solved quite concisely with three functions, as follows. The expression balanced(t.getRootNode()) tests whether the binary tree t is balanced. This is a good demonstration of the conceptual power of recursion and a clever representation.

---

[1]Based on Exercise 2.27, Harold Abelson and Gerald Jay Sussman, *Structure and Interpretation of Computer Programs*, Cambridge: The MIT Press, 1985, pp. 99–100.

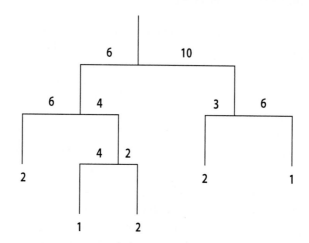

Figure 9.6   A Tree Representing a Binary Mobile

```
#define node binary_tree_node<int*>

int weight(node* nd)
{
    if (!nd->hasLeft())
        return *nd->getElt();          // a weight
    if (!nd->hasRight())               // left is a weight
        return weight(nd->getLeft());
    return weight(nd->getLeft()) + weight(nd->getRight());
}

int torque(node* nd)
{
    if (!nd->hasLeft())
        return(*nd->getElt());         // just a weight
    return *nd->getElt() * weight(nd)
}

bool balanced(node* nd)
{
    if (!nd->hasRight())
        return TRUE;
    return balanced(nd->getLeft()) &&
           balanced(nd->getRight()) &&
           (torque(nd->getLeft()) == torque(nd->getRight()));
}
```

Creating a Tree Recursively

One other kind of tree manipulation requires recursion. Sometimes new nodes are added to a tree by navigating from the root to the node that should become its parent. Search trees, discussed in Section 12.1 (page 403), use binary trees in this way. In other processes, nodes are added in a way that requires recursion because they construct a node along with its children. We could add a node, then one of its children, then a child of that child, and so on, but there is no convenient way to use navigation to return to ancestors to add their other child.

Consider the binary mobile example. How might a mobile be entered so that the program could construct a tree for it? Suppose we read an integer representing a new branch's length. We need to next read its left and right sub-branches. This forms a natural recursion. What terminates the recursion? Somehow we have to indicate that a number indicates just a weight so that its node doesn't get any children. Furthermore, a node with no children has no sibling, so its parent can tell not to attempt to read a right branch. The whole thing works very nicely if we follow a weight with a 0 representing its null right sibling. The input for the tree above would be

    6 6 2 0 4 4 1 0 2 2 0 10 3 2 0 6 11 0

All we need to create a tree is to declare one, then read its left and right subtrees with the following recursive function.

```
node* read()
{
    int n;
    in >> n >> ws;                    // skip white space to prepare for peek
    if (0 == n) return 0;
            // previous node was a weight; this is its null right sibling

    node* nd = node::newnode(new int(n));
    if (in.peek() != '0')
            // if next is 0, this is a weight, so don't read children
        {
            nd->setLeft(read());
            nd->setRight(read());
        }

    return nd;
}
```

9.1.4 Content Operations

Trees have a variety of **Attributes**. We'll show an equal **Compare** operation, but no compare: although orderings can be defined on trees, it's not common to do so. No **Combine** operations are appropriate for trees.

Attributes

Since we can view a binary tree node as either a node or a subtree, they will have two kinds of **Attribute** operations. The node-oriented **Attributes** tell whether the node has left or right children or any children at all. The subtree-oriented **Attributes** tell how many nodes are in the subtree and how deep the subtree is. We also include an nchildren function to tell how many children the node has, anticipating the attributes needed for trees that allow more than two children per node. Finally, it will sometimes be useful to determine the length of the free list, so a static function is included for that too.

```
template <class elt> struct binary_tree_node
{
    // . . .
    // Attributes
    bool full();
    bool hasLeft();
    bool hasRight();
    bool isTerminal();

    int nchildren();                    // number of immediate children
    int subtreeSize();          // size of subtree of which this is the root
    int maxdepth();    // maximum depth of subtree of which this is the root
    static int freelist_length();       // for monitoring behavior
};
```

Some of these functions are recursive (number_of_children and maxdepth), but most are simple. To find the number of nodes in the free list we actually have to count them.

```
/* Node Attributes */

template <class elt> bool binary_tree_node<elt>::full()
{
    return hasLeft() && hasRight();
}

template <class elt> bool binary_tree_node<elt>::hasLeft()
{
    return 0 != left;
}

template <class elt> bool binary_tree_node<elt>::hasRight()
{
    return 0 != right;
}

template <class elt> bool binary_tree_node<elt>::isTerminal()
{
    return !hasLeft() && !hasRight();
}
```

```
// includes the node itself to support the recursion
template <class elt> int binary_tree_node<elt>::subtreeSize()
{
    return 1 + (left==0 ? 0 : left->subtreeSize()) +
               (right==0 ? 0 : right->subtreeSize());
}

template <class elt> int binary_tree_node<elt>::nchildren()
{
    return left!=0 + right!=0;
}

// root is at depth=0
template <class elt> int binary_tree_node<elt>::maxdepth()
{
    return max((left==0 ? 0 : 1+left->maxdepth()),
               (right==0 ? 0 : 1+right->maxdepth()));
}

template <class elt> int binary_tree_node<elt>::freelist_length()
{
    link l = freelist;
    int n = (l != 0);
    while (0 != (l = l->left)) n++;
    return n;
}
```

Tree **Attributes** are those that apply to the tree as a whole rather than to a specific node. Some are shown here. Others are explored in Exercise 8.

```
template <class elt> struct binary_tree
{
    // . . .
    // Tree Attributes:
    int empty();
    int size();
    int maxdepth();
};
```

Definitions of the tree attribute functions just call similar functions on the root node.

```
/* Tree Attributes */

template <class elt> int binary_tree<elt>::empty()
{
    return (0 == root.getElt()) && !root.hasLeft() && !root.hasRight();
}
```

```
template <class elt> int binary_tree<elt>::size()
{
    if (empty())
        return 0;
    else
        return root.subtreeSize();
}

template <class elt> int binary_tree<elt>::maxdepth()
{
    return root.maxdepth();
}
```

Compare

We'll define simple `equal` operations for both trees and nodes, but since trees are rarely compared for order we won't show a `compare`. Essentially, two trees are compared like any collection structure: by traversing them in parallel, comparing each pair of elements encountered. In this case, the traversal has to preserve the tree structure, so it must be recursive. (Exercise 6 asks you to provide an example for which a sequential traversal generates the same elements from two trees that nevertheless are not equal because they have different shape.)

```
template <class elt> struct binary_tree_node
{
    // . . .
    // Compare
    friend bool equal(binary_tree<elt>&, binary_tree<elt>&);
};
```

```
/* Node Compare */

template <class elt> bool equal(binary_tree_node<elt>& node1,
                                binary_tree_node<elt>& node2)
{
    // first check that the two nodes have the same kinds of children
    if ((node1.left && !node2.left) || (!node1.left && node2.left) ||
        (node1.right && !node2.right) || (!node1.right && node2.right))
        return FALSE;

    // now check that their elements are equal and that their
    // subtrees are recursively equal
    return equal(*node1.elem, *node2.elem) &&
           (!node1.left || equal(*node1.left, *node2.left)) &&
           (!node1.right || equal(*node1.right, *node2.right));
}
```

Tree's compare just calls compare on the root node.

```
template <class elt> struct binary_tree
{
    // . . .
    // Compare
    friend bool equal(binary_tree<elt>&, binary_tree<elt>&);
};
```

```
/* Tree Compare */

template <class elt> bool equal(binary_tree<elt>& tree1,
                                binary_tree<elt>& tree2)
{
    return equal(tree1.root, tree2.root);
}
```

9.1.5 Support Operations

Copy

The usual copy constructor and assignment copy for nodes are programmed to generate errors because we don't want programs copying individual nodes, just whole trees. We can't just leave the functions undefined, because the compiler would generate default definitions if they were needed, and those would do the wrong thing. The only node **Copy** operation needed is duplicate, to support tree copying. That function returns (a pointer to) a node with the same element as and copies of the children of node for which it is called.

```
template <class elt> struct binary_tree_node
{
    // . . .
    // Copy
    binary_tree_node<elt>* duplicate();     // produce copy of self

    // individual node copying and assignment are disabled
    binary_tree_node(binary_tree_node<elt>&);
    binary_tree_node<elt>& operator=(binary_tree_node<elt>&);
};
```

```
/* Node Copy */

// return copy of self
template <class elt> link binary_tree_node<elt>::duplicate()
{
    link nd = newnode(elem);
```

```
    nd->left = (left ? left->duplicate() : 0);
    nd->right =( right ? right->duplicate() : 0);

    return nd;
}

template <class elt>
binary_tree_node<elt>::binary_tree_node(binary_tree_node<elt>&)
{
    notimp("binary_tree_node copy constructor");
}

template <class elt> binary_tree_node<elt>&
      binary_tree_node<elt>::operator=(binary_tree_node<elt>&)
{
    notimp("binary_tree_node copy assignment");
    return *this;
}
```

The tree **Copy** operations are as expected. As usual, we define a private copy function to capture the common actions needed by the copy constructor and the copy assignment operator.

```
template <class elt> struct binary_tree
{
    // . . .
    // Copy
  private:
    void copy(binary_tree<elt>&);
  public:
    binary_tree(binary_tree<elt>&);
    binary_tree<elt>& operator=(binary_tree<elt>&);
};
```

The **Copy** definitions use the node `duplicate` function. The assignment operator recycles the nodes of the old subtrees, but the constructor has no old nodes to worry about.

```
/* Tree Copy */

// private:
template <class elt> void binary_tree<elt>::copy(binary_tree<elt>& tree)
{
    root.setElt(tree.root.getElt());
    if (root.hasLeft())
        root.setLeft(tree.root.getLeft()->duplicate());
    if (root.hasRight())
        root.setRight(tree.root.getRight()->duplicate());
}
```

```
template <class elt> binary_tree<elt>::binary_tree(binary_tree<elt>& tree)
    : cur(0), count(-1), root(0)          // real work done in copy fn
{
    copy(tree);
}

template <class elt>
binary_tree<elt>& binary_tree<elt>::operator=(binary_tree<elt>& tree)
{
    if (this == &tree) return *this;       // assign to self!

    root.getLeft()->recycle();
    root.getRight()->recycle();
    cur = 0;
    count = -1;

    copy(tree);

    return *this;
}
```

Process

We need to be able to **Search** a tree for an element as with the other structures we've considered. For flexibility we'll provide subtree-oriented functions in the node module as well as whole-tree functions in the tree module. As always, two versions are included, one that tests identity of elements and one that tests equality.

```
template <class elt> struct binary_tree_node
{
    // . . .
    // Process
    bool contains(elt);
    bool contains_equal(elt);
};
```

```
/* Node Process */

template <class elt> bool binary_tree_node<elt>::contains(elt e)
{
    return (elem == e) ||
           (left && left->contains(e)) ||
           (right && right->contains(e));
}

template <class elt> bool binary_tree_node<elt>::contains_equal(elt e)
```

```
{
    return equal(*elem, *e) ||
           (left && left->contains_equal(e)) ||
           (right && right->contains_equal(e));
}
```

```
template <class elt> struct binary_tree
{
    // . . .
    // Process
    bool contains(elt);
    bool contains_equal(elt);
};
```

```
/* Tree Process */

template <class elt> bool binary_tree<elt>::contains(elt e)
{
    return root.contains(e);
}

template <class elt> bool binary_tree<elt>::contains_equal(elt e)
{
    return root.contains_equal(e);
}
```

Output

Output can mean one of two things: output the elements of the tree sequentially, or print a textual representation of the tree. We provide the latter, called show, in both modules, but a sequential output operator only in the tree module. For the most part, output will be used only by programmers debugging their code.

```
template <class elt> struct binary_tree_node
{
    // . . .
    // Output
    void show(ostream&, char* prefix, int tabsize, int level);
};
```

The formatted output will use indentation to show the shape of the tree. Each node will go on its own line, indented an amount proportional to its depth in the tree. Its children follow it, indented an extra level. For flexibility, we include arguments to specify a prefix to be printed on each line (possibly just extra indentation) and the number of spaces to indent for each level. If a node has one child, three dashes will be printed in place of its other child.

Although at first show might seem like a difficult function to write, a recursive approach makes it quite straightforward. This function includes an extra wrinkle on the usual recursive coding: the prefix and tabsize arguments have to be passed along to the next level of recursive call, but for level, level+1 is passed. As the recursive calls are stacked on and popped from the subroutine stack each retains its own value of level.

```
/* Node Output */

static void show_none(ostream& strm, char* prefix, int tabsize, int level)
{
    if (prefix) strm << prefix;
    spaces(level*tabsize);
    strm << "---" << '\n';
}

template <class elt>
void binary_tree_node<elt>::show(ostream& strm, char* prefix,
                                 int tabsize, int level)
{
    if (prefix) strm << prefix;
    spaces(level*tabsize, strm);
    strm << *elem << '\n';                  // print the element

    if (left)
        left->show(strm, prefix, tabsize, level+1);       // recursion
    else
        if (right)
            show_none(strm, prefix, tabsize, level+1);
        // if neither, don't do anything!

    if (right)
        right->show(strm, prefix, tabsize, level+1);
    else
        if (left)
            show_none(strm, prefix, tabsize, level+1);    // recursion
        // if neither, don't do anything!
}
```

The tree output operator just traverses the tree in depth-first preorder, printing each element followed by a space. (Exercise 10 asks you to write a recursive output function that indicates the structure of the tree without using indentation.) The tree show initiates a recursion by passing zero as the level argument of node's show.

```
template <class elt> struct binary_tree
{
    // . . .
    // Output
    friend ostream& operator<<(ostream&, binary_tree<elt>&);
    void show(ostream&, char* prefix = 0, int tabsize = 4);
};
```

```
/* Tree Output */

template <class elt>
ostream& operator<<(ostream& strm, binary_tree<elt>& tree)
{
    tree.reset();
    while (tree.next())
        strm << *tree.current() << ' ';
    return strm;
}

template <class elt>
void binary_tree<elt>::show(ostream& strm, char* prefix, int tabsize)
{
    root.show(strm, prefix, tabsize, 0);
}
```

9.2 N-ary Trees

The idea of a binary tree can be extended to allow more successors for each node. A tree in which each node has at most a fixed number of successors is called an *n-ary tree*. The *degree of a node* is how many subtrees (direct successors) it actually has. The *degree of a tree* is the maximum degree of its nodes; the term *order* is also used. (Figure 9.7 shows a small tree of degree 4.) An n-ary tree is *regular* if all its nonterminal nodes have their full complement of successors.

9.2.1 Representation

To implement an n-ary tree we can start with a copy of our binary tree module— after all, a binary tree is essentially just an n-ary tree of degree two. Symbolic names such as the 'left' and 'right' of the binary tree module are reasonable when there are just two things to distinguish. It might work to add 'middle' to distinguish among three successors, but it would be difficult to use symbolic names to distinguish among more than three. Instead, we would use ordinals like 'first', 'second', etc. We therefore need a collection structure that supports ordinal access. That structure must also be able to grow and shrink as children are added to a node.

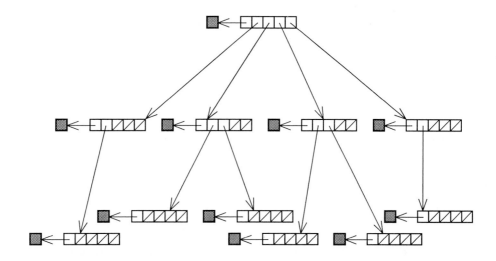

As in Figure 9.4 on page 276, the shaded blocks represent the node contents. That diagram can be interpreted as either a conceptual picture of a binary tree or as an illustration of the representational structure of binary tree nodes. Here, the diagram is only conceptual — the actual implementation has a layered internal structure.

Figure 9.7   An N-ary Tree of Degree 4

We've already seen a kind of structure that meets these requirements: an n-ary tree node can store its successors in a list. In particular, we can use a sequential list — since the number of successors is limited, we don't need the flexibility of linked lists. While we're considering this implementation, we'll also add a back pointer for the node's parent.

The main change in the representation is that there will be a `children` data member in `nary_tree_node` replacing the `left` and `right` of `binary_tree_node`. We'll also need a constant to specify the branching factor. We'll declare that as a static member of `nary_tree`, but leave it to the client program to actually define according to its own needs. Normally static data members are initialized in an implementation file with values appropriate to their role in the implementation as understood by the code in that file. Here, however, branching is really a parameter of the module that *client* code should set. (Cf. Exercise 14 for a discussion of this design decision.)

In the code below, changes from the binary tree implementation are underlined. Functions that are entirely unchanged (beyond the change to the types `nary_tree` and `nary_tree_node`) are not shown. The sparseness and simplicity of the changes demonstrates the great value of coding in terms of fundamental operations rather than directly accessing a structure's underlying representation. Although data abstraction is primarily aimed at supporting users of a structure, module writers and maintainers can benefit from it too, by writing more elaborate fundamental operations in terms of simpler ones rather than accessing data members directly.

```
#define link nary_tree_node<elt>*

template <class elt> struct nary_tree_node
{
  private:

    static link freelist;
    static int allocation;

    elt elem;
    seq_list<link> children;               // replaces left and right
    link parent;
    // . . .
};
```

The branching factor is a feature of the tree and determines the size of the seq_list used to hold pointers to a node children. In this implementation, different trees may have different branching factors, but within one tree every node will have the same branching factor. That list will be initialized by nary_tree_node constructors, so they have to be made friends of nary_tree.

```
template <class elt> struct nary_tree
{
  private:

    nary_tree_node<elt> root;

    static const int branching;
    friend nary_tree_node<elt>::nary_tree_node();
    friend nary_tree_node<elt>::nary_tree_node(elt);
    // . . .
};
```

9.2.2 Lifetime Operations

The free list functions don't change much from their binary tree implementation. In this implementation, the nodes get linked through their first child rather than through their left member as in the binary tree implementation. Because children is a data structure, whereas binary_tree_node's left and right were just pointers, nary_tree_node functions rely on seq_list functions rather than manipulating successor pointers directly. One minor difference is caused not by the change from binary to n-ary but rather by the addition of a parent pointer: newnode takes a second argument indicating the node that will be the parent of the newly created one.

```
/* Free List Management */

template <class elt> void nary_tree_node<elt>::make_freelist()
{
    freelist =  new nary_tree_node<elt>[allocation];
    freelist[allocation-1].children[1] = 0;
}


template <class elt>
link nary_tree_node<elt>::newnode(elt e, link par)
{
    if (!freelist) make_freelist();
    link nd = freelist;
    freelist = freelist->nthChild(1);   // link nodes by their first child
    nd->children.clear();
    nd->parent = par;
    nd->setElt(e);
    return nd;
}

// postorder recursion
template <class elt> void nary_tree_node<elt>::recycle()
{
    children.reset();
    while(children.next())
        children.current()->recycle();
    children.clear();
    children += freelist;
    freelist = this;
}
```

Initialize/Finalize

The nary_tree_node constructors change similarly. Here is where the maximum size of the successor list is established, based on the current value of nary_tree::branching. The destructors for nary_tree_node and nary_tree and the nary_tree constructors are unaffected by the change to a list of children.

```
/* Node Initialize/Finalize */

// private constructor: called only when freelist is allocated
template <class elt> nary_tree_node<elt>::nary_tree_node()
        : elem(0), parent(0), children(nary tree<elt>::branching)
{
    children.add(this+1);
}
```

```
template <class elt> nary_tree_node<elt>::nary_tree_node(elt e)
        : elem(e), parent(0), children(nary tree<elt>::branching)
{
}
```

Access/Modify

The only tree **Access** or **Modify** operation that needs to be changed in going from a binary tree to an n-ary one is `clear`. In the original version, `recycle` was explicitly invoked on the `left` and `right` children. Here, there are an unknown number of children stored in a sequential list, so `clear` must traverse the list invoking `recycle` on each of the nodes found there. Then, `recycle` recursively does the same thing on each node's list of children.

```
/* Tree Access/Modify */

template <class elt> void nary_tree<elt>::clear()
{
    root->getChildren().reset();
    while(root->getChildren().next())
        root->getChildren().current()->recycle();
    root.setElt(0);                              // why not
}
```

The node-level **Access** and **Modify** operations require extensive changes. Since we added a `parent` to each node, we need a new function to access it. The various pairs of binary tree or node functions with 'left' or 'right' in their name are replaced by single functions. Adding a child to a node puts it at the end of the successor list, so `add` doesn't specify where. In other functions, a specific child is designated by its position within the successor list. Changes in **Access** and **Modify** functions are not underlined, since these are essentially complete replacements for the binary versions.

```
template <class elt> struct nary_tree_node
{
    // . . .
    // Access/Modify
    link getParent();

    seq_list<link>& getChildren();        // for iteration, not modification
    link nthChild(int);

    link add(elt);
    void add(link);
    void remove(int);
};
```

```
/* Node Access/Modify */

template <class elt> link nary_tree_node<elt>::getParent()
{
    return parent;
}

template <class elt> seq_list<link>& nary_tree_node<elt>::getChildren()
{
    return children;
}

template <class elt> link nary_tree_node<elt>::nthChild(int n)
{
    return children[n];
}

template <class elt> link nary_tree_node<elt>::add(elt e)
{
    if (children.full())
        error("[nary_tree_node::add] children full");
    link child = newnode(e, this);
    children.add(child);
    return child;
}

template <class elt> void nary_tree_node<elt>::add(link l)
{
    if (children.full())
        error("[nary_tree_node::add] children full");
    children.add(l);
    l->parent = this;
}

template <class elt> void nary_tree_node<elt>::remove(int n)
{
    if (children.size() < n)
        error("[nary_tree_node::remove] no such child");
    children[n]->recycle();
    children.remove(n);
}
```

9.2.3 Traversal and Recursion

Recursion is significantly affected by the change to a list of successors. Binary tree nodes can have member functions that traverse the tree recursively in the following general form. Good examples include duplicate (page 295) and contains (page 297).

```
template <class elt> binary_tree_node<elt>::something(binary_tree* tree)
{
    do_something(itm);
    left->something();
    right->something();
}
```

We could have a ternary tree module with functions of the following form.

```
template <class elt> binary_tree_node<elt>::something(binary_tree* tree)
{
    do_something(itm);
    left->something();
    middle->something();
    right->something();
}
```

but there's no way to generalize this beyond three children using explicit function calls. Instead, n-ary tree traversal is accomplished by traversing the list of children.

```
template <class elt> nary_tree_node<elt>::something(nary_tree* tree)
{
    do_something(itm);
    children.reset();
    while(children.next()) something(children.current());
}
```

This is still recursive, since something calls itself on each child.

Another difference between binary tree and n-ary tree recursion is that inorder no longer makes sense. With only two successors the node's contents can be processed between the two successors, but there's no one "between" place when there are more than two successors. Preorder, postorder, and breadth-first traversals are still meaningful, however.

The implementation of **Traversal** operations, which support both preorder depth-first and breadth-first traversals, is unchanged, except for the definition of push_ children. That function incorporates all the knowledge of how to push a node's children onto the deque that maintains the state of the traversal. The other **Traversal** functions deal only with the current node and the deque and know nothing about how a node's children are obtained. This demonstrates the value of a subfunction like push_children, written solely to abstract out a separate detail of a more complicated operation. Next, responsible only for the high-level logic of moving to the next node in the traversal, is unaffected by the change from binary to n-ary nodes.

The implementation of push_children for binary_tree was simple, but nary_ tree::push_children performs its own traversal over the list of the current node's children! Actually, to ensure that the children get popped in the order in which they appear in the node's successor list, the traversal is performed on a reversed copy of the list. Since the number of children will in practice be quite small, reverse will be fast enough that this slight inefficiency won't be noticed.

```
/* Traversal */

template <class elt> void nary_tree<elt>::push_children()
{
    if (depthfirst)
        {
            seq_list<link> tmp(cur->children.reverse());
            // push in reverse order so popped in normal order
            tmp.reset();
            while(tmp.next())
                tdeq.push(tmp.current());
        }
    else     // breadthfirst
        {
            cur->children.reset();
            while (cur->children.next())
                tdeq.pushend(cur->children.current());
        }
}
```

9.2.4 Content Operations

Attributes

Changes to **Attribute** functions defined for binary trees and nodes are along the lines we've already seen, having to do with the way children are handled. Also, the addition of the parent back pointer supports an additional operation: depth of a node. Note how many of these functions delegate their responsibility to or traverse the children list.

```
/* Node Attributes */

template <class elt> bool nary_tree_node<elt>::hasNth(int n)
{
    return children.size() >= n;
}

template <class elt> bool nary_tree_node<elt>::full()
{
    return children.full();
}

template <class elt> bool nary_tree_node<elt>::isTerminal()
{
    return children.empty();
}
```

```
// includes the node itself to support the recursion
template <class elt> int nary_tree_node<elt>::subtreeSize()
{
    children.reset();
    int total = 1;
    while(children.next())
        total += children.current()->subtreeSize();
    return total;
}

template <class elt> int nary_tree_node<elt>::nchildren()
{
    return children.size();
}

// root is at depth=0
template <class elt> int nary_tree_node<elt>::maxdepth()
{
    int deepest = 0;
    children.reset();
    while (children.next())
        deepest = max(deepest, (1+children.current()->maxdepth()));
    return deepest;
}

template <class elt> int nary_tree_node<elt>::depth()
{
    int n = 0;
    for (link l = this; l->parent; l = l->parent) n++;
    return n;
}

template <class elt> int nary_tree_node<elt>::freelist_length()
{
    if (0 == freelist) return 0;

    link l = freelist;
    int n = 1;
    while (0 != (l = l->children[1])) n++;
    return n;
}
```

_____

_____

```
/* Tree Attributes */

template <class elt> bool nary_tree<elt>::hasNth(int n)
{
    assert(curnode != 0);
    return (curnode->hasNth(n));
}
```

```
template <class elt> int nary_tree<elt>::nchildren()
{
    assert(curnode != 0);
    return (curnode->nchildren());
}
```

Compare

As the conceptual level of the operation increases, the effects of changes to a structure's representation should decrease. The remaining functions in the binary tree node module are essentially the same, except that they replace the explicit use of left and right with traversals of the children list. If the change was just from one kind of collection structure to another, there would be no changes at all in these functions. The changes are because binary_tree_node was implemented with separate left and right members instead of some kind of collection of children.

The changes are too extensive at the code level to bother underlining them, but conceptually the changes are minimal. Since equal of two trees is implemented by just testing whether their root nodes are equal, that function doesn't change. None of our tree or node modules implements an order comparison (compare), so there's nothing to change there either.

```
/* Compare */

template <class elt> bool equal(nary_tree_node<elt>& node1,
                                nary_tree_node<elt>& node2)
{
    if (!equal(*node1.getElt(), *node2.getElt()))
        return FALSE;

    if (node1.nchildren() != node2.nchildren())
        return FALSE;

    node1->getChildren().reset();
    node2->getChildren().reset();

    while (node1->getChildren().next() && node2->getChildren().next())
        // both traversals will end at the same time
        if (!equal(*node1->getChildren().current(),
                   *node2->getChildren().current()))
            return FALSE;

    return TRUE;
}
```

9.2.5 Support Operations

Like the **Content** operations, the definition of some of the node **Support** operations
traverse successor lists rather than explicitly referring to left and right children. Otherwise, they are essentially the same as for binary tree nodes. The tree **Support** operations
are entirely unaffected.

Copy

Again taking advantage of a private subfunction that implements a complicated piece of
the main operation, the public **Copy** operations of nary_tree are unchanged from the binary tree versions. That function — copy — as well as nary_tree_node::duplicate
replace the explicit copies of the left and right subtrees with a traversal that adds a copy of
each child to a new node (or to an old node that was just cleared by nary_tree::opera-
tor=).

```
/* Node Copy */

// return copy of self
template <class elt> link nary_tree_node<elt>::duplicate()
{
    link nd = newnode(elem);

    children.reset();
    while (children.next())
        nd->add(children.current()->duplicate());

    return nd;
}
```

```
/* Tree Copy */

// private:
template <class elt> void nary_tree<elt>::copy(nary_tree<elt>& tree)
{
    root.setElt(tree.root.getElt());
    tree.root->getChildren().reset();
    while (tree.root->getChildren().next())
        root.add(tree.root->getChildren().current()->duplicate());
}
```

Process

```
/* Node Process */

template <class elt> bool nary_tree_node<elt>::contains(elt e)
{
    if (elem == e)
        return TRUE;

    children.reset();
    while (children.next())
        if (children.current()->contains(e))
            return TRUE;

    return FALSE;
}

template <class elt> bool nary_tree_node<elt>::contains_equal(elt e)
{
    if (equal(*elem, *e))
        return TRUE;

    children.reset();
    while (children.next())
        if (children.current()->contains_equal(e))
            return TRUE;

    return FALSE;
}
```

Output

```
/* Node Output */

template <class elt>
void nary_tree_node<elt>::show(ostream& strm, char* prefix,
                               int tabsize, int level)
{
    if (prefix) strm << prefix;
    spaces(level*tabsize, strm);
    strm << *elem << '\n';

    children.reset();
    while (children.next())
        children.current()->show(strm, prefix, tabsize, level+1);
}
```

9.3 General Trees

N-ary trees are an interesting generalization of binary trees, but as shown in the previous section, they turn out not to be all that useful. The problem is not the idea of having more than two children — it's the use of a fixed-size list to contain them. Often it isn't possible to determine a reasonable upper bound on the number of successors a node might have. Worse, n-ary trees are wasteful of space: every node has space for *n* successors regardless of how many the node actually has. As the degree is increased to accommodate larger numbers of possible successors the problem gets worse. In fact, you can prove that for any n-ary tree of any degree and shape, more than half the successor pointers in the tree are null! (The proof is left for Exercise 20.)

The final form of tree structure we'll consider is a further generalization of n-ary tree that will use successor lists that are not limited to a predetermined size. We'll call a tree with no fixed limit on the number of successors a node can have a *general tree* or just *tree*. General trees provide an attractive alternative to n-ary trees. They use space more efficiently, provide greater flexibility, and have straightforward implementations. Consequently, n-ary trees would be useful only in the simplest applications — typically only for degree 3, in which case, we might as well just implement "ternary trees," adding an explicit reference to a middle every place left and right are used. N-ary trees were used here only for pedagogical purposes, much as the array-based linked lists were used in the previous chapter.

General trees are just like n-ary trees but with a linked list used for a node's children instead of a sequential list. Figure 9.8 illustrates the resulting structure. The tree structure can be better appreciated by looking at a conceptual view rather than an implementation-level view: Figure 9.9 shows the same tree with lines going directly from a node to its children with no intervening linked list. A node's linked list of children uses only as many successor pointers as there happen to be children, so no space is taken up by null successor pointers in fixed-size arrays. Moreover, there's no need to specify a maximum degree in advance: each node's list of children just grows as necessary. Of course, linked lists have their own overhead, but surprisingly, the overhead will *always* be less than the space wasted for null successors! (The proof is left for Exercise 21.)

The module doesn't change much at all when sequential lists are replaced by linked lists. All the code is already generalized to use a list of successors. Selecting a different *implementation* of the successor list shouldn't affect the tree code that uses it. Of course, the seq_list in nary_tree_node's representation and in the couple of places it appears in function definitions changes to a linked_list. There's no branching, and children no longer needs a constructor argument. Otherwise, the only difference is that tree_node::add doesn't have to check whether the list is full!

These changes are so simple that they can be implemented by using language tricks rather than a separate copy of the module. A typedef changes seq_list to linked_list. Preprocessor directives determine which list module file to include and to control whether places branching is used are ignored. The provided code files are set up this way, and the n-ary tree module is changed to a general tree module simply by adding a #define GTREE. The typedef and preprocessor directives are controlled by other preprocessor directives that test whether or not GTREE is defined.

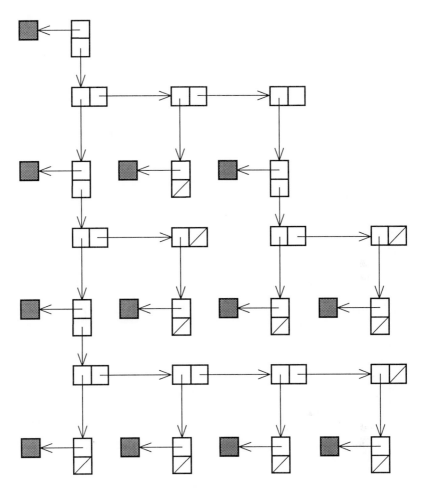

This view shows the representational relationships among the nodes of a general tree. The heavily outlined nodes tree nodes; the lightly outlined nodes are linked list nodes. Each tree node contains a linked list, which, as defined in Section 8.2.9 on page 248, consists solely of a pointer to its first node.

Figure 9.8   A General Tree — Representation View

9.4 EXERCISES

Binary Trees

1. In Table 5 on page 201 why is there no entry for a structure that has *n* predecessors and only one successor?

2. Answer the following questions:
   (a) What is the smallest number of levels a binary tree with 47 nodes can have?
   (b) What is the largest number of levels a binary tree with 47 nodes can have?
   (c) What is the smallest number of levels a ternary tree with 47 nodes can have?

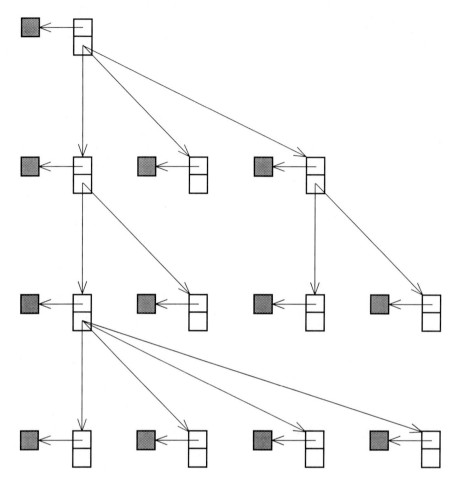

*This conceptual view shows nodes as directly connected to their parents
without the intervening linked lists that the implementation requires.*

Figure 9.9   A General Tree — Conceptual View

3. For the binary tree in Figure 9.5 on page 283 show the sequence of node visits that would result from each of the four possible traversal orders described in the text.

4. A lot of interesting results can be obtained from the analysis of trees. Here are a few more.

   (a) Prove that the maximum number of nodes at the nth level of a binary tree is 2^n.

   (b) Using that result, prove that the number of nodes in a complete binary tree of depth n is $2^{n+1}-1$.

5. What is the relationship between the number of leaves and the number of internal nodes in a full binary tree? Prove it.

6. Give an example of two binary trees that produce the same elements when traversed using the binary tree **Traversal** operations but are not equal because they have different shape.

7. Write a function that counts the number of terminal nodes of a binary tree.

8. 'Full' and 'complete' were defined for binary trees on page 275.
   (a) Write nonmember functions that implement them.
   (b) Rewrite them as member functions, adding them to a copy of the binary tree module.
   (c) Compare the two versions.
   (d) Should these have been included in the binary tree module?
   (e) What kind of (fundamental) operation are these?

9. Algebraic expressions are quite naturally represented as binary trees. In fact, we can write binary expressions in prefix, infix, or postfix notation, much as we can traverse trees depth-first in preorder, inorder, or postfix order. The easiest form of input for a program to process is preorder: since operators appear before their operands in prefix notation, it is straightforward to construct a node for an operator then nodes for each of its two operands.
   (a) Write a program that reads a prefix expression consisting only of integers and the operators + - * / and constructs the corresponding binary tree. The tree must be constructed recursively, so you'll use operations from the binary tree node module to operate on the tree being constructed. Use the binary tree module's **Traversal** operations to print the expression to verify that the program has constructed the proper tree.
   (b) Modify the program so that it prints the expression out in postfix notation. A program to convert an expression in prefix form to one in postfix form only needs to create a tree representing the expression read then output the tree's contents in a different order.
   (c) Extend the program so that it evaluates the tree for given input values and prints each input value along with the result of the corresponding evaluation.

10. Write a recursive function that prints a binary tree by printing each node in the form

    ```
    (element left-subtree right-subtree)
    ```

    For a null subtree, print dashes. As an example of what output should look like, the tree on page 283 should print out as (+ (* (/ 9 5) (C -- --)) (32 -- --)). The dashes are needed to distinguish nodes with just a left child from nodes with just a right child; however, you might want to try not printing the dashes for terminal nodes.

11. Code is shown in Section 9.1.3 for preorder, inorder, and breadth-first traversal (page 285 ff.).
    (a) Characterize the size of the stack needed for inorder traversal of a given tree.
    (b) Explain which nodes are stacked in an inorder reset and which during the traversal.
    (c) Implement postorder **Traversal** for the binary tree module.
    (d) Characterize the size of the stack needed for postorder traversal of a given tree, given the way your implementation works.
    (e) Explain which nodes are stacked in a postorder reset and which during the traversal, given the way your implementation works.

N-ary Trees

12. Determine and prove the answer to the following:
    (a) What is the maximum number of nodes at the nth level of an n-ary tree with degree n?
    (b) How many nodes are in a complete binary tree of depth n?

13. Predecessor links for lists and trees take up extra space. For lists, the number of links doubles, since each node must now have a pointer to its predecessor as well as its successors.
    (a) What happens to the total number of links in a binary tree when predecessor links are added?
    (b) How does the increase in the number of predecessor links in a complete n-ary tree change as n grows larger?

14. In the n-ary tree implementation, `branching` was made a private constant of `nary_tree`, and users are required to define it. Discuss each of the following proposals, presenting arguments for and against, and considering the ramifications of, their adoption. Ramifications may include changes to representation, addition of member functions, moving members from `nary_tree` to `nary_tree_node` or vice versa, differences in how users interact with the module, and so on. Don't forget effects on free list management. You might want to try actually making these changes in copies of the code files.
    (a) There should be a default value so that users don't have to define it.
    (b) Code in `nary_tree_node` shouldn't have to know about `nary_tree` at all, so there shouldn't be a reference to an `nary_tree` static member in the `nary_tree_node` constructor member initialization lists. Branching affects the nodes more than the tree anyway (in fact, it is never used at all in the `nary_tree` code), so we should move `branching` from `nary_tree` to `nary_tree_node`.
    (c) Programs should be able to set the value individually for each tree.
    (d) It should be possible to change a tree's branching at any point — perhaps nodes near the top of the tree have relatively few children but nodes near the bottom of the tree have relatively many, or the other way around.

15. The functions `nary_tree_node::duplicate` and `nary_tree::copy` are quite similar.
    (a) What led to this apparent redundancy?
    (b) Is there an efficient way to avoid it?
    (c) Can you suggest a way to avoid the redundancy that perhaps results in a lot of additional work but is conceptually very simple?

16. Add a member function `int* pathto(elt)` that returns a 0-terminated array of integers indicating the path from the root to the node containing that element: if the element is in the third subtree of the root, the path would begin with a 3, etc.

17. Define `bool regular(nary_tree<elt>&)` to test whether all nonterminal nodes of its argument have the maximum number of children allowed.

18. Exercise 10 asked for a recursive output function for a binary tree that used prentheses to show the tree's shape.
    (a) Try writing a similar function for n-ary trees.
    (b) No dashes are needed for n-ary trees. Why?

19. Write a function that produces a copy of an n-ary tree with every node's children reversed.

General Trees

20. Prove that for a tree of any degree > 1 and any shape, more than half the successor pointers in the tree are null. Hints:
    (a) How many successor pointers are there in a tree with k nodes?
    (b) How many nonnull successor pointers are there in a tree with k nodes?

21. Prove that no matter what the size or shape of a tree, using a linked list for a node's successors never takes more space than using an array of successor pointers. (Hint: pay special attention to terminal nodes.)

22. The `gtree` directory has a file depicting the descendants of Noah, as stated in Genesis X, and a file that reads them into a tree of strings. Add to a copy of that program the following operations and test code that demonstrates that they work. For the purpose of this exercise, assume that terminal nodes represent childless people.
    (a) `list<string*> children(string* p)`   `// children of p`
    (b) `list<string*> grandchildren(string* p)`   `// grandchildren of p`
    (c) `list<string*> descendants(string* p)`   `// descendants of p`

```
(d)  list<string*> ancestors(string* p)                    // ancestors of p
(e)  list<string*> parents()           // names of all people with children
(f)  list<string*> non_parents()        // names of people with no children
(g)  list<string*> prolific()// names of people with more than 3 children
(h)  bool isDescendantOf(string* p1, string* p2)
                                        // is p1 a descendant of p2?
```

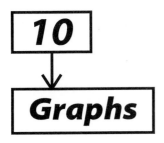

Graphs

Graphs are linked structures in which nodes may have any number of successors and predecessors (including none). The links of a graph are called *arcs*. (In more mathematical contexts arcs are called *edges* and nodes *vertices*.) Each arc represents some kind of connection between the elements of the nodes it connects.

In an *undirected graph*, the arcs don't have a direction. In a *directed graph* the arcs do have a direction: an arc is said to go *from* one node *to* another, and an arc from A to B is distinct from an arc from B to A. (The term *directed graph* is sometimes abbreviated *digraph*.) In an undirected graph, there's no distinction between 'successor' and 'predecessor'. In a directed graph, the successors of an element contained in node A are the elements contained in nodes *to* which there is an arc *from* node A; the predecessors are the elements contained in nodes *from* which there is an arc *to* node A.

A *directed acyclic graph* (DAG) is a directed graph with no cycles — that is, a graph that contains no node with a path from itself to itself. In practice, many situations that can be represented as a graph but not as a tree can be represented as a DAG. Although DAGs are conceptually and practically important, whether a graph has cycles or not has little bearing on its representation or the implementation of its operations.

Abstractly, an arc can be specified as a pair of nodes. If the graph is directed, the pair is ordered. In diagrams arcs are represented by lines, often curved. If the graph is directed, the arc includes an arrowhead to indicate its direction. Figure 10.1 shows an undirected graph and Figure 10.2 a directed graph.

If there is an arc between two nodes, those nodes are said to be *adjacent*, and the arc is said to be *incident on* the nodes. In a directed graph with an arc from node A to B, A is said to be *adjacent to* B and B to be *adjacent from* A. A is the *tail* of the arc, and B is the *head*.

The *degree of a node* is the number of arcs incident on it. In a directed graph, the *in-degree* of a node is the number of arcs having that node as their head, and the *out-degree* of a node is the number of arcs having that node as their tail. The degree of a graph is the maximum of the degrees of its nodes.

A *complete graph* is one with an arc between every pair of nodes. A *complete directed graph* is one with arcs in both directions between every pair of nodes.

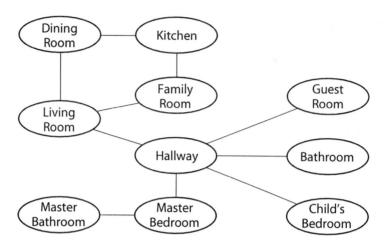

Figure 10.1   A Graph

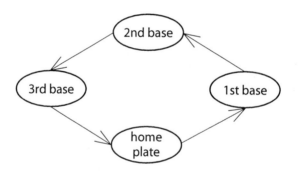

Figure 10.2   A Directed Graph

A *path* from node A to node B is a sequence of arcs that leads from A to B. The *length* of a path is the number of arcs it contains. A *cycle* is a path from a node back to itself. A graph is called *connected* if there is a path between any pair of nodes. Figure 10.3 shows an unconnected graph.

In most applications of linked lists and trees information is associated only with the nodes, not with the links. With graphs, however, information is often associated with arcs as well as with nodes (weights or distances, for example). Figure 10.4 shows an example of cities connected by lines showing the distance between them. Such graphs are called *labeled* or, if the extra information is quantitative, *weighted graphs*. The label can be any kind of value, even a complex struct. For example, Exercise 10 considers *state-transition graphs*, in which labels describe events and actions and the nodes represent states.

The representation of graphs is fairly complex. We'll look at two approaches in this chapter. The components of a linked list or tree are specified by its links and nodes. Graphs, however, must list their elements explicitly, rather than just linking them together. A node can be part of a graph without having any links at all, and there can be

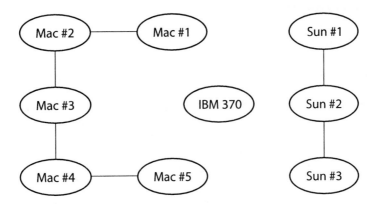

Figure 10.3   An Unconnected Graph

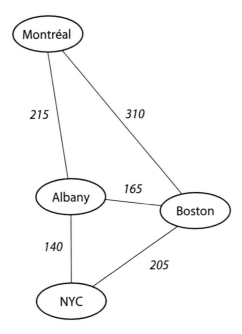

Figure 10.4   A Graph with Labeled Arcs

many paths from one node to another. Therefore, constituency must be separated from structure (shape, ordering, etc.), whereas in lists and trees — in most structures, actually — the two are expressed with the same linking mechanism.

10.1 Adjacency Matrices

One way to represent a graph structure is with an *adjacency matrix*. This is simply a square table with rows and columns headed by the nodes of the graph. An entry in the table indicates whether or not there is an arc between the node corresponding to the row and that corresponding to the column. The nodes themselves are stored in a separate list. If the arcs are labeled, the matrix entries would specify the arc labels; if unlabeled, a Boolean value would just indicate whether or not the arc was in the graph. (This representation takes the same space whether or not the graph is directed.)

The graph in Figure 10.4 would be represented as shown in Figure 10.5. The indices into the adjacency matrix are the positions of the corresponding city in the city list.

1	Albany, NY
2	Augusta ME
3	Boston, MA
4	Concord, NH
5	Hartford, CT
6	Montpelier, VT
7	Montréal, PQ
8	New York, NY
9	Providence, RI

Cities

	1	2	3	4	5	6	7	8	9
1	0	290	165	150	100	160	215	140	160
2	290	0	160	140	250	175	250	355	205
3	165	160	0	70	95	180	310	205	45
4	150	140	70	0	140	110	240	250	110
5	100	250	95	140	0	195	320	105	70
6	160	175	180	110	195	0	135	295	210
7	215	250	310	240	320	135	0	355	335
8	140	355	205	250	105	295	355	0	175
9	160	205	45	110	70	210	335	175	0

Approximate Mileages

Figure 10.5   Representing a Weighted Graph

10.1.1 Representation

The elements corresponding to the graph nodes will be stored in a sequential list whose maximum size is specified by the graph constructor and stored in the graph as maxelts. Arc labels are stored in a matrix of integers having dimensions maxelts by maxelts. We could use the multarray from Chapter 2, but we won't bother, since the only thing we need to do to this array is put and get values. Instead, we'll just allocate a C array and treat it as two-dimensional.

To simplify the rest of the code in the module and to reduce errors, all **Access** and **Modify** of the array elements will be performed through the private function arc(row, col). The nth row and column of the adjacency matrix correspond to the nth node, which contains the nth element of the list of elements. A nonzero value at arc(i,j) represents the label of an arc *from* the ith node *to* the jth node.

Note that there is no separate representation of the nodes themselves. The list stores the graph elements, and the adjacency matrix represents the arcs. The nodes are not data structures here, just conceptual entities whose data are stored in the other structures.

```
template <class elt> struct graph
{
  private:
    // Representation
    int maxelts;
    seq_list<elt> elts;          // node list, max size = maxelts
    int *arcs;                   // adjacency matrix, maxsize x maxsize

    int& arc(int, int);          // adjacency matrix lookup
    // . . .
};
```

```
/* Internal Access to arc label */

// Return reference to label of arc from i to j
// Positions are 1-offset
template <class elt> int& graph<elt>::arc(int row, int col)
{
    return arcs[((row-1)*maxelts) + col-1];
}
```

10.1.2 Lifetime Operations

Initialize/Finalize

The list of elements is part of the graph, so it is allocated automatically when the graph is created. The size of the array representing the adjacency matrix will depend on the maximum number of nodes that can be in the graph, which will be specified as a constructor argument. Therefore, the array must be allocated dynamically by the constructor rather than given a fixed size in the struct declaration. The constructor argument is also passed along to the sequential list via the constructor's member initialization list as well as stored in the graph.

```
template <class elt> struct graph
{
    // . . .
    // Initialize/Finalize
    graph(int maxsiz = 20);
    ~graph();
};
```

```
/* Initialize/Finalize */

template <class elt> graph<elt>::graph(int maxsize) :
    maxelts(maxsize), elts(maxsize), arcs(new int[maxsize*maxsize]),
    cur(0), arcrow(0), arccol(0), count(-1), arccount(-1)
{
    for (int i = 0; i < maxelts*maxelts; i++)
        arcs[i] = 0;
}

template <class elt> graph<elt>::~graph()
{
    delete arcs;
}
```

Access/Modify

There are two sets of **Access** and **Modify** operations, one for nodes and one for arcs. We want to be able to get the nth node, add a node for a new element to the graph (it doesn't matter where in the element list it goes), and remove an existing node. The node to be removed will be specified either by the element it contains or the position of its element in the sequential list. Another important kind of operation on graphs is getting the successors or predecessors of a particular element. This is almost an **Attribute** operation, but is central enough to the purpose of graphs to warrant treating it as a basic **Access** operation.

```
template <class elt> struct graph
{
    // . . .
    // Node Access/Modify
  private:
    void remove_at(int);                    // does the actual removal
  public:
    elt nth(int n);
    elt operator[](int n);                  // synonym for nth

    void add(elt);
    void remove(elt);
    void remove(int);

    seq_list<elt> successors(elt e);
    seq_list<elt> predecessors(elt e);
};
```

```
/* Node Access/Modify */

template <class elt> elt graph<elt>::nth(int n)
{
    return elts[n];
}

template <class elt> elt graph<elt>::operator[](int n)
{
    return nth(n);
}

template <class elt> void graph<elt>::add(elt e)
{
    elts.add(e);
}

template <class elt> void graph<elt>::remove_at(int pos)
{
    // remove node and therefore all adjacent arcs
    elts.remove(e);

    int siz = elts.size();
    int col, row;

    // shift rows of adjacency matrix
    for (row = pos; row < siz; row++)
        for (col = 1; col <= siz; col++)
            arc(row, col) = arc(row+1, col);

    // shift columns of adjacency matrix
    for (col = pos; col < siz; col++)
        for (row = 1; row < siz; row++)
            arc(row, col) = arc(row, col+1);
}

template <class elt> void graph<elt>::remove(int n)
{
    if (0 <= n || n > elts.size())
        error("[graph::remove(int)] no such element");

    remove(n);
}

template <class elt> void graph<elt>::remove(elt e)
{
    int pos = elts.position_of(e);
    if (0==pos)
        error("[graph::remove(elt)] no such element");

    remove(pos);
}
```

```
/* Node Access: successors and predecessors */

template <class elt> seq_list<elt> graph<elt>::successors(elt e)
{
    int row = elts.position_of(e);
    if (row <= 0) error("[graph::successors] elt not in graph");

    int siz = elts.size();

    seq_list<elt> lst(siz);                 // temp, will be copied on return

    for (int col = 1; col <= siz; col++)
        if (arc(row,col)) lst += elts[col];

    return lst;
}

template <class elt> seq_list<elt> graph<elt>::predecessors(elt e)
{
    int col = elts.position_of(e);
    if (col <= 0) error("[graph::predecessors] elt not in graph");

    int siz = elts.size();

    seq_list<elt> lst(siz);                 // temp, will be copied on return

    for (int row = 1; row <= siz; row++)
        if (arc(row,col)) lst += elts[row];

    return lst;
}
```

We also need to be able to **Access** and **Modify** arcs. The basic arc **Access** operation is to obtain the label of the arc going from one element's node to another's. A zero label will indicate that the graph does not contain such an arc. **Modify** involves adding or removing arcs between a pair of nodes. We'll call these join and unjoin. The same interface serves for both labeled and unlabeled graphs. For an unlabeled graph, the label argument will be omitted from calls to join, leaving the values 1 and 0 to indicate the presence or absence of an arc.

```
template <class elt> struct graph
{
    // . . .
    // Arc Access/Modify
    int label(elt, elt);
    void join(elt, elt, int val = 1);
    void unjoin(elt, elt);
};
```

```
/* Arc Access/Modify */

template <class elt> int graph<elt>::label(elt e1, elt e2)
{
    int pos1 = elts.position_of(e1);
    if (0 == pos1) abort0("[graph::label] first elt not in graph");

    int pos2 = elts.position_of(e2);
    if (0 == pos2) abort0("[graph::label] second elt not in graph");

    return arc(pos1, pos2);
}

template <class elt> void graph<elt>::join(elt e1, elt e2, int val)
{
    int pos1 = elts.position_of(e1);
    if (pos1<=0) abortv("[graph::join] first elt not in graph");

    int pos2 = elts.position_of(e2);
    if (pos2<=0) abortv("[graph::join] second elt not in graph");

    if (val == 0)
        error("[graph::join] arc label cannot be 0");
    else
        arc(pos1, pos2) = val;
}

template <class elt> void graph<elt>::unjoin(elt e1, elt e2)
{
    int pos1 = elts.position_of(e1);
    if (pos1<=0) abortv("[graph::unjoin] first elt not in graph");
    int pos2 = elts.position_of(e2);
    if (pos2<=0) abortv("[graph::unjoin] second elt not in graph");

    if (0 == arc(pos1, pos2))
        warning("[graph::unjoin] nodes are not joined");
    else
        arc(pos1, pos2) = 0;
}
```

10.1.3 Traversal

Two sets of **Traversal** operations are needed too — one for nodes and one for arcs. Node **Traversal** operations just invoke the same operation on the list of nodes. Arc **Traversal** is a more significant programming challenge. Also, traversing arcs calls for a more elaborate interface, since for each arc there are three pieces of information to be had: the node *from* which the arc goes, the node *to* which the arc goes, and, in labeled graphs, the label of the arc.

```
template <class elt> struct graph
{
    //. . .
    // Node Traversal
  private:
    int cur;
    int count;
  public:
    void reset();
    bool finished();
    bool next();
    elt &current();
    int index();

    // Arc Traversal
  private:
    int arcrow, arccol;
    int arccount;
  public:
    void reset_arc();
    bool finished_arc();
    bool next_arc();
    elt &current_arc_from();
    elt &current_arc_to();
    int current_arc_label();
    int index_arc();
};
```

```
/* Node Traversal */

template <class elt> void graph<elt>::reset()
{
    elts.reset();
}

template <class elt> bool graph<elt>::finished()
{
    return elts.finished();
}

template <class elt> bool graph<elt>::next()
{
    if (0 > count)
        error("[graph::next] traversal not yet initialized");
    if (finished())
        error("[graph::next] traversal already finished");

    return elts.next();
}

template <class elt> elt& graph<elt>::current()
```

```
{
    return elts.current();
}

template <class elt> int graph<elt>::index()
{
    return elts.index();
}
```

The arc traversal operations must traverse the adjacency matrix, looking for nonzero entries in the rows and columns up to the size of the `elts` list. The state of the arc traversal is captured by the number of the row and column of the most recently encountered nonzero label in the matrix. The definition of `next_arc` is complicated by the fact that after the last column of a row is reached, the column number gets reset and the row incremented. At least the details of accessing the label from the matrix are hidden by the private **Access** function `arc`.

```
/* Arc Traversal */

template <class elt> void graph<elt>::reset_arc()
{
    arccount = 0;
    arcrow = 0;
    arccol = elts.size();                    // to prepare for stepping
}

template <class elt> bool graph<elt>::finished_arc()
{
    return arccol >= elts.size() && arcrow >= elts.size();
}

template <class elt> bool graph<elt>::next_arc()
{
    if (0 > arccount)
        error("[graph::next_arc] traversal not yet initialized");
    if (finished_arc())
        error("[graph::next_arc] traversal already finished");
    do
        if (arccol >= elts.size())
            if (arcrow >= elts.size())
                return FALSE;
            else
                {
                    arcrow++;
                    arccol = 1;
                }
        else
            arccol++;
    while (!arc(arcrow, arccol));

    return TRUE;
}
```

```
template <class elt> elt& graph<elt>::current_arc_from()
{
    return elts[arcrow];
}

template <class elt> elt& graph<elt>::current_arc_to()
{
    return elts[arccol];
}

template <class elt> int graph<elt>::current_arc_label()
{
    return arc(arcrow, acorccol);
}

template <class elt> int graph<elt>::index_arc()
{
    return arccount;
}
```

10.1.4 Content Operations

Compare is hardly ever relevant to graphs. Combine has an obvious meaning and is worth providing. Many **Attribute** operations are possible. Some have to do with the elements in the graph, some with the connections in the graph, and some are more like **Combine** operations in that they produce new graphs.

Attributes

Graphs and their nodes have a variety of attributes, many implemented by interesting algorithms. (This is a favorite area of algorithm-oriented textbooks.) We'll show just a few here. Degree-related **Attributes** of nodes are straightforward to compute, but algorithms for computing some of the arc **Attributes** are quite elaborate.

```
template <class elt> struct graph
{
    // . . .
    // Node Degree Attributes
    int in_degree(elt);
    int out_degree(elt);
    int degree(elt e);
};
```

```
/* Node Degree Attributes */

template <class elt> int graph<elt>::in_degree(elt e)
{
    int col = elts.position_of(e);
    if (col <= 0) abort0("[graph::in_degree] elt not in graph");
    int siz = elts.size();

    int count = 0;
    for (int row = 1; row <= elts.size(); row++)
        if (arc(row,col)) count++;

    return count;
}

template <class elt> int graph<elt>::out_degree(elt e)
{
    int row = elts.position_of(e);
    if (row <= 0) abort0("[graph::in_degree] elt not in graph")

    int count = 0;
    for (int col = 1; col <= elts.size(); col++)
        if (arc(row, col)) count++;

    return count;
}

template <class elt> int graph<elt>::degree(elt e)
{
    return in_degree(e) + out_degree(e);
}
```

The size function will return the number of nodes in the graph. Although the graph includes other information, it does constitute a collection of elements, and some of its operations treat it that way. Size is one example; node **Traversal** operations are another. More complex **Attribute** operations produce new graphs based on the original. These can be used as the basis for determining other important **Attributes**, such as testing whether or not the graph is connected and whether there is a path from one node to another. (Cf. Exercise 2.)

```
template <class elt> struct graph
{
    // . . .
    // Graph Attributes
    int size();
    graph<elt> closure();                    // transitive closure
    graph<elt> shortest_paths();             // variation on closure
};
```

The *transitive closure* of a graph is a graph in which there's an arc between every pair of nodes between which there is a path (of perhaps many arcs) in the original. In other words, if there's no direct connection from one node to another, but there is an indirect path, a direct connection is added. A more formal statement is that the transitive closure is a copy of the original graph with an arc from node$_i$ to node$_k$ added wherever the original did not contain such an arc but did contain arcs from node$_i$ to node$_j$ and from node$_j$ to node$_k$ for some node$_j$.

The algorithm shown is a form of one known as Warshall's algorithm. It has been modified to work for labeled graphs by assigning newly added arcs the sum of the labels of the two arcs that led to its being added. (If the original graph is not labeled, all of its arcs will have label 1, and each arc in the closure will show how many arcs in the original it took to construct that path.)

The algorithm is subtle and difficult to grasp. It consists of nested loops over all possible values of i, j, and k. Once an arc is added, that arc can be used to construct further combinations. The algorithm orders the process in a way that guarantees that all possible combinations will be found. Note that the outer loop is over the intermediate node, not the starting or ending node. Thus, all two-arc paths that go through the first node are found, and corresponding arcs are added to the graph, before two-arc paths that go through the second node are considered; then all two-arc paths going through the second are considered before all two-arc paths going through the third.

```
/* Graph Attributes (Algorithms) */

template <class elt> graph<elt> graph<elt>::closure()
{
    graph<elt> g(*this);            // start with a copy of the graph
    int siz = elts.size();          // save size for convenience

    /*  for every node j,
            for every node i for which arc(i,j) exists,
                for every node k for which arc(j,k) exists
                    add arc(i,k) unless it already exists
    */
    for (int j = 1; j <= siz; j++)
        for (int i = 1; i <= siz; i++)
            if (g.arc(i,j))
                for (int k = 1; k <= siz; k++)
                    if (g.arc(j,k) && !g.arc(i,k))
                        g.arc(i,k) = g.arc(i,j) + g.arc(j,k);

    return g;
}
```

A simple modification of Warshall's algorithm due to Floyd produces a graph showing the shortest path from each node to each other node reachable from the first. In Warshall's algorithm, an arc from node$_i$ to node$_k$ is added (when it isn't one in the original graph) the first time a j is reached such that the graph contains an arc from node$_i$ to node$_j$ and one from node$_j$ to node$_k$. There's no guarantee that this new arc represents the shortest path. A larger j may later be encountered such that the path through it from node$_i$ to node$_k$ is shorter than the arc added. Floyd's modification checks for this possibility, and if the new path encountered is shorter than the current path, the current label for the node is replaced.

```
graph& graph::shortest_paths()
{
    graph<elt> g(*this);            // start with a copy of the graph
    int siz = elts.size();          // save size for convenience
    int val;                        // to save repeating additions

    for (int j = 1; j <= siz; j++)
        for (int i = 1; i <= siz; i++)
            if (g.arc(i,j))
                for (int k = 1; k <= siz; k++)
                    if (g.arc(j,k) &&
                        (!g.arc(i,k) ||
                         g.arc(i,k) > (val = g.arc(i,j) + g.arc(j,k)))
                        )
                        g.arc(i,k) = val;

    return g;
}
```

Combine

The simplest interpretation of Combine is that it makes a new graph whose node list is the combination of the original two. (Elements contained in both graphs appear only once in the new graph.) The new graph contains an arc between every pair of elements for which there was an arc in either graph. (If a pair of elements with an arc from one to the other is in both graphs, the implementation shown here will put the label of the second graph into the new graph — an adjacency matrix representation can store only one arc between a pair of elements.)

The implementation shown here is the obvious one. It starts by copying the first graph. Then it adds to the copy every element in the second graph that is not in the first. Finally, it traverses the arcs of the second graph adding a corresponding arc to the copy. The arc traversal is somewhat inefficient in that it repeatedly locates elements in the copy. Since several arcs may emanate from one node, the function could be improved by caching the node in the copy that corresponds to the node the arc is from in the second graph.

```
/* Combine */

template <class elt> graph<elt> operator+(graph<elt>& g1, graph<elt>& g2)
{
    graph<elt> g(g1.maxelts + g2.maxelts);  // make big enough for both
    g = g1;                                  // start with copy of g1

    int siz2 = g2.elts.size();
    for (int i = 1; i <= siz2; i++)
```

```
        if (!g1.elts.contains(g2.elts[i]))
            g.elts.add(g2.elts[i]);        // add any elements of g2 not in g1

    for (int row = 1; row <= siz2; row++)
        for (int col = 1; col <= siz2; col++)
            if (0 != g2.arc(row, col))
                g.arc(g.elts.position_of(g2.elts[row]),
                        g.elts.position_of(g2.elts[col])) = g2.arc(row, col);

    return g;
}
```

10.1.5 Support Operations

Copy

Using an adjacency matrix representation, copying a graph is simple: copy its list of elements and copy its adjacency matrix.

```
template <class elt> struct graph
{
    // . . .
    // Copy
  private:
    void copy(graph<elt>&);
  public:
    graph(graph<elt>&);
    graph<elt>& operator=(graph<elt>&);
};
```

```
/* Copy */

template <class elt> void graph<elt>::copy(graph<elt>& g)
{
    for (int i = 0; i < maxelts*maxelts; i++)
        arcs[i] = g.arcs[i];
}

template <class elt> graph<elt>::graph(graph<elt>& g) :
    elts(g.elts), maxelts(g.maxelts), arcs(new int[g.maxelts * g.maxelts]))

{
    copy(g);
}

template <class elt> graph<elt>& graph<elt>::operator=(graph<elt>& g)
{
```

```
    if (this == &g) return *this;        // assignment to self

    if (maxelts < g.size())
        {
            delete [] arcs;
            maxelts = g.maxelts;
            arcs = new int[maxelts * maxelts];
        }

    elts = g.elts;
    copy(g);

    return *this;
}
```

Process

As usual, we can ask whether or not a graph contains some element. Like size, this is another operation that treats the graph as primarily a collection, ignoring the arcs. **Other Search** operations involve finding paths between nodes. This is another rich area of algorithm study, but no implementations are shown here. As with trees, graphs can be searched in either a depth-first or breadth-first order. The same concepts apply, but in a graph, there isn't necessarily any node from which all the others are reachable, so searching a graph may involve searching many separate parts of the graph. Exercise 9 gives you the chance to write the code to search a graph for a path from one node to another. Note that searching for a path is different from just determining whether or not there is one — in this case we need to know the sequence of nodes that constitute the path, not just the path's label.

```
template <class elt> struct graph
{
    // . . .
    // Process
    bool contains(elt e);
    bool contains_equal(elt e);
};
```

```
/* Process */

template <class elt> bool graph<elt>::contains(elt e)
{
    return elts.contains(e);
}
```

```
template <class elt> bool graph<elt>::contains_equal(elt e)
{
    return elts.contains_equal(e);
}
```

Output

Given how complex graphs are, there is no simple, standard way to print out a textual representation. Here are some useful text-only **Output** operations. Modern graphical computing environments make it possible to display graph structures in various ways that show the arcs going from one node to another, but such display-oriented programming is not only beyond the scope of this book but requires information about the particular software being used. Different applications may have different requirements for graph output, whether textual or graphical. In the end, **Output** operations may be more the responsibility of the application than the graph module.

```
template <class elt> struct graph
{
    // . . .
    // Output
    void show_nodes(ostream& strm);
    void show_arcs(ostream& strm);
    friend ostream& operator<<(ostream& strm, graph<elt>& g);
};
```

```
/* Output */

template <class elt> ostream& operator<<(ostream& strm, graph<elt>& g)
{
    g.show_nodes(strm);
    g.show_arcs(strm);
    return strm;
}

template <class elt> void graph<elt>::show_nodes(ostream& strm)
{
    reset();
    while (next())
        strm << index() << '\t' << *current() << '\n';
    strm << "\n\n";
}

template <class elt> void graph<elt>::show_arcs(ostream& strm)
{
    // headers for adjacency matrix:
    for (int j = 1; j <= elts.size(); j++)
        strm << '\t' << j;
    strm << "\n\n";
```

```
// for each row, header and arcs
for (int i = 1; i <= elts.size(); i++)
    {
        strm << i;
        for (j = 1; j <= elts.size(); j++)
            strm << '\t' << arc(i, j);
        strm << '\n';
    }

strm << "\n\n";
}
```

10.2 Linked Representation

Because it uses a sequential list to store its nodes, the adjacency matrix implementation for graphs suffers from the same drawbacks as sequential lists: awkward removal, awkward insertion within the list (in fact this isn't supported at all in the version shown above), the need to estimate the maximum size to which it might grow, wasting space when smaller than the maximum size, etc. All this is compounded by similar problems with the rigid adjacency matrix.

As with lists and trees, flexibility is achieved by using a fully linked representation. There's a natural fit between the node and arc imagery used in talking about (and drawing) graphs and the node and link imagery used in talking about (and drawing) linked lists. Arcs can be represented as links (pointers), and nodes, in addition to their element, contain lists of links to their successors and predecessors. An interesting feature of this implementation that contrasts with the adjacency matrix implementation is that it is possible to have more than one arc from one node to another, which some applications require (e.g., finite state machine representation — cf. Exercise 10). Also, in a weighted graph (a graph with numerical labels), an arc can exist with weight 0, whereas the adjacency matrix representation used a matrix entry of 0 to indicate the absence of an arc.

10.2.1 Representation

Each node of the linked graph will be represented by an instance of graph_node, containing an elt plus lists of successors and predecessors. Since there are an indeterminate number of each, linked lists will be used. Graph nodes are similar to the nodes of a doubly-linked list except that the successors and predecessors are lists rather than single nodes. There is no separate adjacency matrix: all connectivity information is stored in the nodes themselves.

To support labels, the connections will be instances of an arc struct rather than just a pointer to another node. That struct will include a label and a pointer to the predecessor or successor node. (If the graph is unlabeled, it wouldn't need a separate arc structure — arcs would just be pointers to nodes — but for flexibility, this implementation will support both labeled and unlabeled graphs: we'll just put a 1 in every arc of an unlabeled graph.) Thus, the lists in a `graph_node` are linked_lists of `arc`s. Figure 10.6 shows how this fairly complex structure would be arranged for the graph of Figure 10.4 on page 321.

In a tree, there's a single marked starting place — the root — from which all the nodes can be reached, but that is not generally true of graphs. Graphs can include discontinuous pieces, and even if a directed graph is connected, there still may not be a node from which all the others can be reached. The graph structure will therefore contain a linked list of all the nodes rather than just a single root. In fact, that's all it contains — a graph is just a bunch of nodes.

```
// to make the code more readable:
#define glink graph_node<elt>*
#define arclink arc<elt>*

template <class elt> struct arc
{
  private:
    // Representation
    glink to_node;
    int label;
    // . . .
};
```

```
template <class elt> struct graph_node
{
  private:
    elt elem;
    linked_list<arclink> successors;
    linked_list<arclink> predecessors;
    // . . .
};
```

```
template <class elt> struct graph
{
  private:
    linked_list<glink> nodes;
    // . . .
};
```

10.2.2 Lifetime Operations

Create/Destroy

Nodes and arcs are managed by the graph structure, not created directly by application code. We'll provide the same sorts of **Create** and **Destroy** operations that we used to support recycling in the linked list implementation of Section 8.2.9, page 248. We won't

Key:

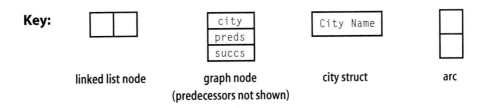

linked list node

graph node
(predecessors not shown)

city struct

arc

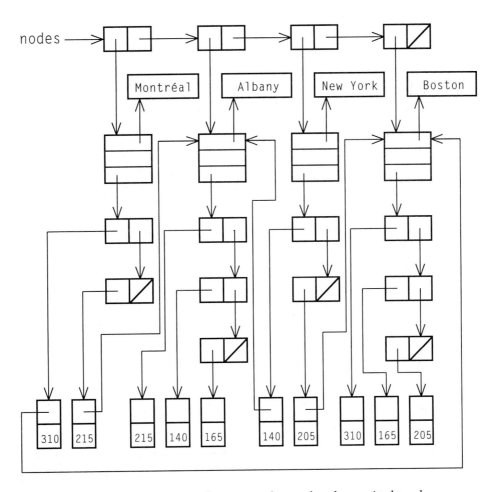

The arcs from the city *structs for* Albany *and* Boston *have been omitted to reduce the diagram's clutter. Links from graph nodes to their predecessors have also been omitted.*

Figure 10.6   Linked Graph Representation

bother to implement arc and node free lists, however. We'll just organize things to support adding that feature later without changing anything other than these **Create** and **Destroy** functions.

```
template <class elt> struct arc
{
    // . . .
    // Create/Destroy
    static arclink newarc(glink, int lbl = 1);
    void free();
};
```

```
/* Arc Create/Destroy */

template <class elt> arclink arc<elt>::newarc(glink nd, int lbl)
{
    return new arc<elt>(nd, lbl);
}

template <class elt> arclink arc<elt>::free()
{
    delete this;
}
```

```
template <class elt> struct graph_node
{
    // . . .
    // Create/Destroy
    static glink newnode(elt);
    void free();
};
```

```
/* Node Create/Destroy */

template <class elt> glink  graph_node<elt>::newnode(elt e)
{
    return new graph_node<elt>(e);
}

template <class elt> void graph_node<elt>::free()
{
    successors.reset();
    while (successors.next())
        successors.current()->free();              // free arcs

    predecessors.reset();
```

```
    while (predecessors.next())
        predecessors.current()->free();            // free arcs

    delete this;            // list nodes get freed by the list's destructor
}
```

Initialize/Finalize

The constructors and destructors for all three structs are trivial. Although graph contains one linked list and graph_node two, their constructors and destructors don't have to do anything about them. When a constructor or destructor is invoked, constructors and destructors of any struct-valued members are also invoked. Arguments can be passed to member constructors through the member initialization list, but the linked list constructor doesn't have any arguments.

```
template <class elt> struct arc
{
    // . . .
    // Initialize/Finalize
    arc(glink nd, int lbl = 1);
    ~arc();
};
```

```
/* Arc Initialize/Finalize */

template <class elt> arc<elt>::arc(glink nd, int lbl) :
        to_node(nd), label(lbl)
{
}

template <class elt> arc<elt>::~arc()
{
}
```

```
template <class elt> struct graph_node
{
    // . . .
    // Initialize/Finalize
    graph_node(elt);
    ~graph_node();
};
```

```
/* Node Initialize/Finalize */

template <class elt> graph_node<elt>::graph_node(elt e) : elem(e)
{
}

template <class elt> graph_node<elt>::graph_node(graph_node<elt>& nd) :
        elem(nd.elem)
{
}
```

```
template <class elt> struct graph
{
    // . . .
    // Initialize/Finalize
  private:
    void free_nodes();
  public:
    graph();
    ~graph();
};
```

```
/* Graph Initialize/Finalize */

template <class elt> void graph<elt>::graph() : arccount(-1)
{
}

template <class elt> void graph<elt>::~graph()
{
    clear();
}
```

Access/Modify

```
template <class elt> struct arc
{
    // . . .
    // Access/Modify
    glink getNodeTo();
    int getLabel();
    void setLabel(int);
};
```

```
/* Arc Access/Modify */

template <class elt> glink arc<elt>::getNodeTo()
{
    return to_node;
}

template <class elt> int arc<elt>::getLabel()
{
    return label;
}

template <class elt> void arc<elt>::setLabel(int lbl)
{
    label = lbl;
}
```

```
template <class elt> struct graph_node
{
    // . . .
    // Access/Modify
    elt& getElt();
    void setElt(elt);
    linked_list<arclink>& getSuccessors();
    linked_list<arclink>& getPredecessors();

    arclink arc_to(glink);
    arclink arc_from(glink);
    arclink arc_to(glink, int);
    arclink arc_from(glink, int);
};
```

```
/* Graph Node Access/Modify */

template <class elt> elt& graph_node<elt>::getElt()
{
    return elem;
}

template <class elt> void graph_node<elt>::setElt(elt e)
{
    elem = e;
}

template <class elt>
linked_list<arclink>& graph_node<elt>::getSuccessors()
{
    return successors;
}
```

```
template <class elt>
linked_list<arclink>& graph_node<elt>::getPredecessors()
{
    return predecessors;
}

template <class elt> arclink graph_node<elt>::arc_to(glink nd)
{
    successors.reset();
    while (successors.next())
        if (nd == successors.current()->getNodeTo())
            return successors.current();

    return NULL;
}

template <class elt> arclink graph_node<elt>::arc_from(glink nd)
{
    return nd->arc_to(this);
}

template <class elt> arclink graph_node<elt>::arc_to(glink nd, int lbl)
{
    successors.reset();
    while (successors.next())
        if (nd == successors.current()->getNodeTo() &&
            lbl == successors.current()->getLabel())
            return successors.current();

    return NULL;
}

template <class elt> arclink graph_node<elt>::arc_from(glink nd, int lbl)
{
    return nd->arc_to(this, lbl);
}
```

```
template <class elt> struct graph
{
    // . . .
    // Access/Modify
  private:
    glink node_for(elt);
    void remove_at(glink);

  public:
    elt nth(int n);
    elt operator[](int n);

    void add(elt);
    void remove(elt);
    void remove(glink);
```

```
    seq_list<elt> successors(elt);
    seq_list<elt> predecessors(elt);

    // Arc Access/Modify

    int label(elt, elt);

    void join(elt, elt);
    void join(elt, elt, int val);
    void unjoin(elt, elt);
    void join(glink, glink);
    void join(glink, glink, int val);
    void unjoin(glink, glink);
};
```

Lists of successors and predecessors are returned as newly created linked lists. Applications may traverse, search, and access specific elements of these in support of navigation and other such activities. They should not modify the graph through these lists, however.

```
/* Graph: Access to Nodes */

template <class elt> elt graph<elt>::nth(int n)
{
    return nodes[n]->getElt();
}

template <class elt> elt graph<elt>::operator[](int n)
{
    return nth(n);
}

template <class elt> glink graph<elt>::node_for(elt e)
{
    nodes.reset();
    while (nodes.next())
        if (e == nodes.current()->getElt()) return nodes.current();
    return NULL;
}


template <class elt> linked_list<elt> graph<elt>::successors(elt e)
{
    glink nd = node_for(e);
    if (!nd) error("[successors] elt not in graph");

    linked_list<elt> lst;                       // temp, will be copied on return
    nd->successors.reset();

    while (nd->successors.next())
        lst.add(nd->getSuccessors.current()->getNodeTo()->getElt());
```

```
    return lst;
}

template <class elt> linked_list<elt> graph<elt>::predecessors(elt e)
{
    glink nd = node_for(e);
    if (!nd) error("[predecessors] elt not in graph");

    linked_list<elt> lst;               // temporary - will be copied on return
    nd->getPredecessors().reset();

    while (nd->getPredecessors().next())
        lst.add(nd->getPredecessors().current()->getNodeTo()->getElt());

    return lst;
}
```

```
/* Graph: Modify of Nodes */

template <class elt> void graph<elt>::add(elt e)
{
    nodes.add(graph_node<elt>::newnode(e));
}

template <class elt> void graph<elt>::remove(elt e)
{
    glink nd = node_for(e);
    if (!nd) warning("elt not in graph");

    remove(nd);
}

template <class elt> void graph<elt>::remove(glink nd)
{
    nodes.remove(nd);
    nd->free();
}

template <class elt> void graph<elt>::clear()
{
    nodes.reset();
    while (nodes.next()) nodes.current()->free();
}
```

We'll need a variety of arc manipulation functions. Both join and unjoin need versions that take elements and, to support navigation-based applications, versions that take pointers to nodes. In addition, two flavors of unjoin are needed — one that takes a label and removes the arc with that label, another that just removes whatever arc it finds between the two elements or nodes. The element-based versions are coded to find the corresponding node and call the node-based versions.

```
/* Graph: Access/Modify of Arcs */

template <class elt> int graph<elt>::label(elt e1, elt e2)
{
    glink nd1 = node_for(e1);
    if (!nd1) abort0("first elt not in graph");

    glink nd2 = node_for(e2);
    if (!nd2) abort0("second elt not in graph");

    arclink a = nd1->getNodeTo((nd2));
    return a ? a->label : 0;
}

template <class elt> void join_nodes(glink nd1, glink nd2 ,int val)
{
    nd1->getSuccessors().add(arc<elt>::newarc(nd2, val));
    nd2->getPredecessors().add(arc<elt>::newarc(nd1, val));
}

template <class elt> void graph<elt>::join(elt e1, elt e2, int val)
{
    glink nd1 = node_for(e1);
    if (!nd1) abortv("first elt not in graph");

    glink nd2 = node_for(e2);
    if (!nd2) abortv("second elt not in graph");

    join(nd1, nd2, val);
}

template <class elt> void graph<elt>::unjoin(elt e1, elt e2)
{
    glink nd1 = node_for(e1);
    if (!nd1) abortv("first elt not in graph");

    glink nd2 = node_for(e2);
    if (!nd2) abortv("second elt not in graph");

    unjoin(nd1, nd2);
}

template <class elt> void graph<elt>::unjoin(elt e1, elt e2, int lbl)
{
    glink nd1 = node_for(e1);
    if (!nd1) abortv("first elt not in graph");

    glink nd2 = node_for(e2);
    if (!nd2) abortv("second elt not in graph");

    unjoin(nd1, nd2, lbl);
}

template <class elt> void graph<elt>::join(glink nd1, glink nd2, int val)
```

```
{
    if (nd1->arc_to(nd2, val))
        error("[graph::join] Cannot have two arcs with the "
                "same label from one node to another");
    else
        join_nodes(nd1, nd2, val);
}

template <class elt> void graph<elt>::unjoin(glink nd1, glink nd2)
{
    arclink to = nd1->arc_to(nd2);
    arclink from = nd2->arc_from(nd1);
    if (!to)
        warning("nodes are not joined");
    else
        {
            nd1->getSuccessors().remove(to);
            nd2->getPredecessors().remove(from);
        }
}

template <class elt> void graph<elt>::unjoin(glink nd1, glink nd2, int lbl)
{
    arclink to = nd1->arc_to(nd2, lbl);
    arclink from = nd2->arc_from(nd1, lbl);
    if (!to)
        warning("nodes are not joined by an arc with that label");
    else
        {
            nd1->getSuccessors().remove(to);
            nd2->getPredecessors().remove(from);
        }
}
```

10.2.3 Traversal

Since graphs contain both nodes and arcs, we'll need two sets of **Traversal** operations. Traversing the nodes of a graph is accomplished by traversing the graph's list of nodes, so node **Traversal** operations simply turn around and call the same functions on nodes. Traversing the arcs of a graph, however, is considerably more complicated. First of all, given a current arc, there are three different values an application might need: the element the arc is from, the element the arc is to, and the label. Separate versions of current have to be provided for each.

Then, some nodes may have more than one arc, and some may have none. The implementation of next_arc must move to the next node when the current one's list of successors is exhausted. It must also skip any nodes that have no arcs. There's no need to worry about node predecessors, however — every arc can be reached from both the node its from and the node its to, and we only want to encounter each arc once. The code for the arc **Traversal** operations also uses **Traversal** operations on nodes. It is assumed that applications will not intermix node and arc traversal. A more sophisticated implementation would maintain its own state for the nodes list traversal to allow arc **Traversal** operations to be performed in the midst of a node **Traversal**.

Since it's easier to read and write functions coded in terms of **Traversal** functions instead of more primitive data and function members, many of the other functions in this graph implementation use these. That means they might interfere with traversals the application is performing over the same graph. To avoid that problem a more sophisticated implementation would code these other operations without using **Traversal** functions.

```
template <class elt> struct graph_node
{
    // . . .
    // Node Traversal
  private:
    int count;
  public:
    void reset();
    bool finished();
    bool next();
    elt &current();
    int index();

    // Arc Traversal
  private:
    int arccount;
  public:
    void reset_arc();
    bool finished_arc();
    bool next_arc();
    elt &current_arc_from();
    elt &current_arc_to();
    int current_arc_label();
    int index_arc();
};
```

```
/* Node Traversal */

template <class elt> void graph<elt>::reset()
{
    nodes.reset();
    count = 0;
}

template <class elt> bool graph<elt>::finished()
{
    return nodes.finished();
}

template <class elt> bool graph<elt>::next()
{
    return nodes.next();
```

```
}

template <class elt> elt& graph<elt>::current()
{
    return nodes.current()->getElt();
}

template <class elt> int graph<elt>::index()
{
    return nodes.index();
}
```

```
/* Arc Traversal */

template <class elt> void graph<elt>::reset_arc()
{
    nodes.reset();
    arccount = 0;
}

template <class elt> bool graph<elt>::finished_arc()
{
    return nodes.finished();
}

template <class elt> bool graph<elt>::next_arc()
{
    if (arccount < 0)
        error("[graph::next_arc] traversal not yet initialized");
    if ((0 == arccount ) || !nodes.current()->getSuccessors.next())
        {
            do
                nodes.next();
            while (!nodes.finished() &&
                    nodes.current()->getSuccessors.empty());
            if (nodes.finished())
                return FALSE;
            nodes.current()->getSuccessors.reset();
            nodes.current()->getSuccessors.next();
        }
    arccount++;

    return TRUE;
}

template <class elt> elt& graph<elt>::current_arc_from()
{
    return nodes.current()->getElt();
}

template <class elt> elt& graph<elt>::current_arc_to()
{
    return nodes.current()->getSuccessors.current()->getNodeTo()->getElt();
```

```
}

template <class elt> int graph<elt>::current_arc_label()
{
    return nodes.current()->getSuccessors.current()->getLabel();
}

template <class elt> int graph<elt>::index_arc()
{
    return arccount;
}
```

10.2.4 Content Operations

Attributes

```
template <class elt> struct graph
{
    // . . .
    // Node Degree Attributes
    int in_degree(elt);
    int out_degree(elt);
    int degree(elt);

    // Graph Attributes
    int size();
    graph<elt> closure();            // transitive closure
    graph<elt> shortest_paths();     // variation on closure
};
```

```
/* Graph: Node Attributes */

template <class elt> int graph<elt>::in_degree(elt e)
{
    glink nd = node_for(e);
    if (!nd) abort0("elt not in graph");

    return nd->getPredecessors().size();
}

template <class elt> int graph<elt>::out_degree(elt e)
{
    glink nd = node_for(e);
    if (!nd) abort0("elt not in graph");

    return nd->getSuccessors.size();
}
```

```
template <class elt> int graph<elt>::degree(elt e)
{
    return in_degree(e) + out_degree(e);
}
```

The implementation of closure and shortest_paths should look pretty much the same for the linked representation as it did for the adjacency matrix representation. However, looking for an arc from one node to another ends up being quite a bit more complex here than a simple matrix lookup. We have to call arc_to on the source node and provide the destination node as an argument. That function then searches all the arcs of the source node looking for one that goes to the destination. The code is easy enough to express, but it's interesting how much more computation is involved in finding a specific arc using a linked representation compared to the adjacency matrix version.

A further issue involves how to get from one source node to another at each level of the triple iteration. Using for loops as before means accessing elements of the linked list of nodes by position. This is inefficient, since operator[] must start at the beginning and go from one node to the other until the nth node has been reached. This inefficiency could be avoided by using list traversal operations instead of for loops. (Since the way traversal operations are coded in this book does not support nested traversals, and the function performs a triple traversal over the same list of nodes, the traversals would have to be over *copies* of the nodes list.) To keep this definition of closure as similar as possible to the adjacency matrix version, the less efficient for loops are used.

```
/* Graph Attributes */

template <class elt> int graph<elt>::size()
{
    return nodes.size();
}

template <class elt> graph<elt> graph<elt>::closure()
{
    graph<elt> g(*this);
    int siz = nodes.size();
    glink ndi;
    glink ndj;
    glink ndk;
    arclink arc_ij;
    arclink arc_jk;

    for (int j = 1; j <= siz; j++)
    {
        ndj = g.nodes[j];
        for (int i = 1; i <= siz; i++)
        {
            ndi = g.nodes[i];
            if (0 != (arc_ij = ndi->arc_to(ndj)))
                for (int k = 1; k <= siz; k++)
```

```
                    {
                        ndk = g.nodes[k];
                        if (0 != (arc_jk = ndj->arc_to(ndk)) &&
                            0 == ndi->arc_to(ndk))
                          join_nodes(ndi, ndk,
                                        arc_ij->getLabel() + arc_jk->getLabel());
                    }
                }
            }

        return g;
}
```

Compare

Two graphs will be considered equal if they contain the same elements and arcs. The order of the elements and the order of the arcs are not relevant. Two arcs will be considered equal if they go from (nodes for) equal elements to (nodes for) equal elements. There's no meaningful definition of compare for graphs, so that's left unimplemented. Depending on the compiler, definitions may also need to be provided for equal and compare of two arcs and two graphs, since the linked list module expects to find those, but they won't be used and aren't shown here.

```
template <class elt> struct graph
{
    // . . .
    // Compare
    friend order compare(graph<elt>&, graph<elt>&);
    friend bool equal(graph<elt>&, graph<elt>&);
};
```

Coding equal is a little tricky because the graphs will contain entirely different nodes even though the nodes may contain the same elements and arcs. First, the number of elements the graphs contain are compared: if not equal, the graphs certainly are not. Then the nodes list of the first graph is traversed. For each node, the corresponding node of the second graph is located. (If there is none, the graphs are not equal. If there is a corresponding node for each of the first graph's nodes, the graphs are equal — we don't have to worry that the second graph may also contain some extra nodes because we've already compared their sizes.) Then the list of successor arcs for the first graph's current node is traversed. For each arc in the first graph, the node in the second graph is located that corresponds to the arc's destination node. (If there is no such node, the graphs are not equal.) Finally, we check whether there's an arc with the same label going between the two nodes of the second graph. (If not, the graphs aren't equal.)

```
/* Compare */

template <class elt> bool equal(graph<elt>& g1, graph<elt>& g2)
{
    if (g1.size() != g2.size()) return FALSE;

    g1.nodes.reset();
    while (g1.nodes.next())
        {
            glink nd1 = g1.nodes.current();
            glink nd2 = g2.node_for(g1.current());
            if (!nd2) return FALSE;

            if (nd1->getSuccessors().size() != nd2->getSuccessors().size())
                return FALSE;
            nd1->getSuccessors().reset();
            while (nd1->getSuccessors().next())
                {
                    arclink a1 = nd1->getSuccessors().getCurrent();
                    glink to2 = g2.node_for(a1->getNodeTo()->getElt());
                    if (0 == to2 ||
                        0 == nd2->arc_to(to2, a1->getLabel()))
                        return FALSE;
                }
        }

    return TRUE;
}
```

Combine

The implementation of operator+ here is similar to the one for adjacency matrices, except that it uses traversal operations to avoid the complexity they hide. The repeated search for the node in the copy that corresponds to the node the arc is from is potentially a worse source of inefficiency here than for the previous implementation. Not only may many arcs emerge from the same node, but many arcs may go from that node to the same other node, something not possible in an adjacency matrix implementation. More efficient implementations of operator+ would use some kind of caching scheme or code the arc traversal directly rather than using traversal operations.

```
template <class elt> struct graph
{
    // . . .
    // Combine
    friend graph<elt> operator+(graph<elt>&, graph<elt>&);
};
```

```
/* Combine */

template <class elt> graph<elt> operator+(graph<elt>& g1, graph<elt>& g2)
{
    graph<elt> g(g1);                        // start with a copy of g1
    glink nd;

    // add a node to g for each element of g2 that isn't in g1
    g2.reset();
    while (g2.next())
        if (!g1.contains(g2.current()))
            g.add(g2.current());

    g2.reset_arc();
    while (g2.next_arc())
        if (!g1.contains_arc(g2.current_arc_from(),
                             g2.current_arc_to(),
                             g2.current_arc_label())
           )
            g.join(g.node_for(g2.current_arc_from()),
                   g.node_for(g2.current_arc_to()),
                   g2.current_arc_label());

    return g;
}
```

10.2.5 Support Operations

Copy

The definition of **Copy** traverses the node list of the original graph adding a new node to
the copy for each element found in the original. The arc list of the original is also traversed, with a new arc added to the copy corresponding to each arc of the original. Since
the arc traversal operations return elements, not nodes, for the head and tail of the arc, we
can't just call `current_arc_from` and `current_arc_to`. Instead, we have to use code
similarly to theirs but without their `getElt()`.

```
template <class elt> struct graph
{
    // . . .
    // Copy
  private:
    void copy(graph&);
  public:
    graph(graph<elt>&);
    graph<elt>& operator=(graph<elt>&);
};
```

```
/* Copy */

template <class elt> void graph<elt>::copy(graph<elt>& orig)
{
    // called only on empty graphs
    arcount = -1;

    // add a node for each node of the original
    orig.reset();
    while (orig.next())
        nodes.add(graph_node<elt>::newnode(orig.current()));

    // add an arc for each arc of the original
    orig.reset_arc();
    while (orig.next_arc())
        join_nodes(orig.nodes.current(),
                   nodes.current()->getSuccessors.current()
                                    ->getNodeTo()->getElt(),
                   orig.current_arc_label());
}

template <class elt> graph<elt>::graph(graph<elt>& orig)
{
    copy(orig);
}

template <class elt> graph<elt>& graph<elt>::operator=(graph<elt>& orig)
{
    if (this == &orig) return *this;            // assignment to self

    clear();
    copy(orig);

    return *this;
}
```

Process

To **Search** for an element in a graph, the nodes list is traversed looking for a node that contains the element. As usual, two versions are provided: one that uses identity and one that uses equality.

```
template <class elt> struct graph
{
    // . . .
    // Process
    bool contains(elt);
    bool contains_equal(elt);
};
```

```
/* Process */

template <class elt> bool graph<elt>::contains(elt e)
{
    nodes.reset();
    while (nodes.next())
        if (e == nodes.current()->getElt())
            return TRUE;
    return FALSE;
}

template <class elt> bool graph<elt>::contains_equal(elt e)
{
    nodes.reset();
    while (nodes.next())
        if (equal(*e, *nodes.current()->getElt()))
            return TRUE;
    return FALSE;
}
```

Output

Output of a graph can mean either or both of two things: show the elements or show the arcs. We'll provide functions for each separately and have the output operator do both. To show the arcs, we'll just print them one to a line. We can't show them in a tabular format, as we did in the adjacency matrix implementation, because there may be many arcs between the same two nodes. Also, linked graphs tend to be sparse: if there are many nodes and relatively arcs, a tabular format wouldn't be of much use. For debugging purposes, simple **Output** operations would also be provided for arc and graph_node, but they aren't shown here.

```
template <class elt> struct graph
{
    // . . .
    // Output
    void show_nodes(ostream& strm);
    void show_arcs(ostream& strm);
    friend ostream& operator<<(ostream& strm, graph<elt>& g);
};
```

```
/* Output */

template <class elt> ostream& operator<<(ostream& strm, graph<elt>& g)
{
    g.show_nodes(strm);
    strm << '\n';
    g.show_arcs(strm);
    strm << '\n';
```

```
        return strm;
}

template <class elt> void graph<elt>::show_nodes(ostream& strm)
{
    reset();
    while (next())
        strm << index() << '\t' << *current() << '\n';
}

template <class elt> void graph<elt>::show_arcs(ostream& strm)
{
    reset_arc();
    while (next_arc())
        strm << index_arc() << ": "
             << *current_arc_from() << "--" << current_arc_label() << "-->"
             << *current_arc_to() << '\n';
}
```

10.3 EXERCISES

1. Now that you have been introduced to trees and graphs, in several different forms, what do you think of the term 'linked structures' to describe all the kinds of structures and implementations discussed in the three chapters of this part of the book? Discuss the applicability of each of the following terms to the tree and graph implementations discussed, in particular pointing out where strictly speaking they don't quite apply even though they may communicate an appropriate conceptual property. What do you think would be the best general term to categorize all forms of lists, trees, and graphs without also suggesting other less related kinds of structures?
   (a) linked structures
   (b) recursive structures
   (c) dynamic structures
   (d) linear structures
   (e) sequential structures

2. Add the following **Attribute** operations to the adjacency matrix implementation of graph. (*Hint:* these are meant to require very little programming given the facilities already provided by the graph module as shown in the chapter.)
   (a) `bool contains(elt)`
   (b) `bool contains_path(elt, elt)`
   (c) `bool connected()`

3. The adjacency matrix graph implementation limits each graph to a maximum number of nodes.
   (a) Why?
   (b) Why is it necessary to store the maximum number of elements the graph may contain?
   (c) Modify the implementation to allow the graph to grow beyond the initially specified maximum number of nodes.
   (d) What function definitions are affected by this modification?
   (e) Are the declarations of any public member functions of graph affected?

4. Implement `shortest_paths` for the linked implementation of the graph module. (Keep in mind that there may be more than one arc from one node to another.)

5. Suppose you have an application in which you often need to determine the length of the shortest path from one node to another. Floyd's algorithm, used in the implementation of `shortest_paths`, produces a graph with that information already computed. However, that algorithm could take up a lot of time each time it is called for a large graph.

   (a) Modify a graph implementation so that it "caches" the result of `shortest_paths`, invalidating it every time a node or arc is added or removed and recomputing it the next time the shortest path between two nodes is needed.

   (b) Is it really necessary to go through the whole algorithm again each time an arc is added or removed? If you can find one, describe an algorithm that would directly modify the existing shortest path graph instead of entirely recomputing it. If you don't think that's possible, explain why.

6. Use a debugger and/or add output statements to explore how Warshall's algorithm (page 332) works. Try to write a clear explanation of it for someone who has never seen it before.

7. Write a program that navigates a city graph like the one shown in Figure 10.4 on page 321 and Figure 10.5 on page 322.

   (a) You can use the program `demo.C` in the `graph` code directory as a starting point, perhaps substituting your own data.

   (b) Start the navigation at one of the cities.

   (c) Then repeatedly present the user with a choice of cities to go to from the current city, showing the miles to each one and navigating to the one the user selects.

   (d) One of the user's choices should always be "exit." When the user exits, print the final location and the total number of miles traveled.

8. Not all graphs have integer-valued labels. Labels may be other sorts of numbers (`double`, e.g.), strings, pointers, or struct instances. The graph implementations shown in this chapter support only integer-valued labels. Really, the type of the label should be a second template parameter.

   (a) Change one of the implementations to support whatever kind of label the user specifies. (Although this is conceptually sophisticated, the actual amount of editing required is fairly small.) You'll find that there's no reason to limit the label type to a pointer, as opposed to the elements of the structures we are studying.

   (b) Demonstrate the use of this module in a simple program.

A Project

9. (Optionally uses the results of Exercise 8.) *Adventure* was a computer program that introduced a whole new kind of game to the world in the late 1970s. The player navigates a complex cave, picking up tools and treasures while avoiding various obstacles and warding off various evil beings. From any room, there might be passages to another room in any of the directions East, West, North, South, up, and down. A passage from one room to another doesn't guarantee a passage in the opposite direction, and even if there is a passage in the opposite direction, it doesn't necessarily open in the opposite direction — a passage that leaves East from one room may hook around and enter at the North side of another room. Associated with each room is a text description that describes the special features of the room. A cave of rooms is easily represented as a directed graph. Use the linked graph module to write a program that constructs a moderate-size Adventure cave and allows a user to navigate around it.

   (a) Define a `Room` struct.

   (b) A passage from one room to another is represented as an arc between graph nodes containing the rooms. The label of the arc indicates the direction in which the player leaves the room to traverse the path represented by the arc. Unfortunately, the graph implementation provided assumes that arcs are weighted with integers. You can use the existing module by coding directions as integers. A more sophisticated approach would be to improve the module by parameterizing it by the type of value by which its arcs are labeled, as described in Exercise 8, so that you could then use an enumeration `direction` and a `graph<Room*, direction>`.

(c) After the program adds nodes and arcs to the graph, it should print the graph using one of the **Output** operations provided.

(d) Write a loop that allows a user to interactively explore the cave by entering one-letter directions.

(e) Write a function that finds a path from a designated entrance node to a designated exit node. This will be a recursive operation much like searching a tree. If there's a path from node A to some node B and a path from B to the exit, then of course there's a path, through B, from A to the exit. Use the `successors` operation to obtain all the nodes you can reach in the next step of the search. You'll have to keep track of the nodes you've already considered during the search to avoid infinite cycles — not an issue with trees, because nodes have only one predecessor.

(f) Have the program print the path it finds as a sequence of directions from the entrance.

(g) Have the program print out the descriptions of the rooms visited in following the path from the entrance to the exit.

(h) Why is a linked representation better than an adjacency matrix for this program?

(i) Why can't you just use node and arc **Traversal** operations to find a path from the entrance to the exit?

(j) Why couldn't you just use `closure` or `shortest_paths` to find a path from the entrance to the exit?

Another Project

10. (Optionally uses the results of Exercise 8.) A *state-transition graph* uses nodes to represent states a process may be in and arc labels to represent the events and actions that cause a transition from one state to another. In drawing the graph, the event may be shown as a label above the arc with the action a label below, or they may be shown as a single label in the form event/action. State-transition graphs are often used for parsing: the event is simply a character and the transition is the action to perform if that character is encountered while in the state represented by the node from which the arc comes.

(a) Draw a state-transition graph that represents some of the rules for parsing C++ symbols: numbers, identifiers, operators, etc. The nodes would contain strings naming the corresponding state. Show just the states and events, not the actions. For instance, when starting a new symbol, a digit would move the process to a state in which it is reading an integer. While reading the number, a digit returns to the same state, a space causes the completion of the symbol, and the first period encountered switches the process from reading an integer to reading a real.

(b) Represent your graph in a program, using a graph with string-valued labels. (The crude way would be to store pointers as integers and convert integers obtained from the graph to pointers. The proper way would be to use the modifications described in Exercise 8 and a `graph<string*, char>`.)

(c) Without actions, your graph represents legal sequences of characters, but doesn't say how they are used to construct identifiers. Add actions to your graph in the form of pointers to functions to call on the newly read character. For instance, while reading an integer, the response to a digit would be a function that multiplied the current value of the integer by ten and added the digit's numerical value.

(d) Represent this extended graph in your program as a `graph<string*, transition>`, where a `transition` is a struct containing a character and a pointer to a function that takes a character argument.

(e) Extend the program so that it actually uses the graph to parse input and generate symbols.

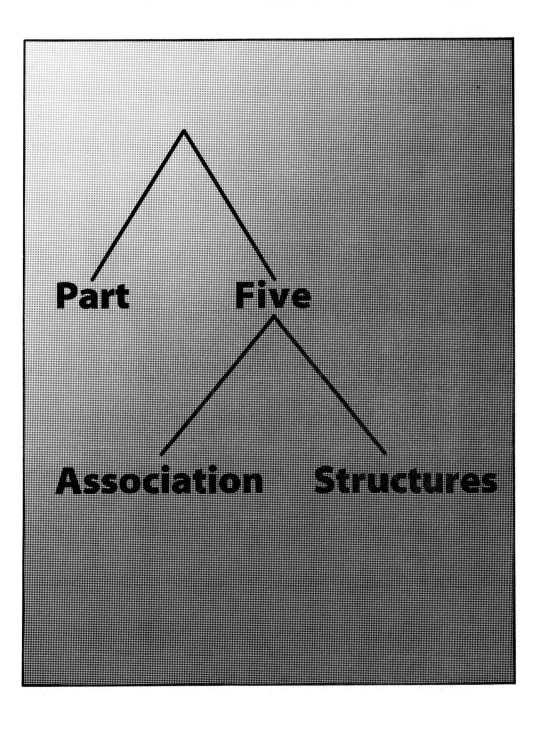

Part Five

Association Structures

Part Five:

Association Structures

An element of a linear structure (storage, state, or list) can be accessed by position (n^{th} element of an array or list, top of a stack, front of a queue, etc.). Linked structures (list, tree, or graph) support access by navigation. In either case the location of an element is determined entirely by the way elements are stored in the structure rather than by any properties of the elements themselves.

Association structures are different. Their elements are accessed according to some property of the elements themselves rather than by where they got stored. A library is a good real-world example: we look for a book on the basis of its title, author, subject matter, or number in some cataloguing system, but not on the basis of the shelf it happens to be stored on or where it is on that shelf.

The property by which an association structure accesses its elements is called a *key*. The key is a value obtained from elements. It may be something stored in the element or computed from the values stored in the element. For this reason, association structures are often called *content-addressable*. In essence, association structures are mechanisms for *mapping* a key to an element. Mathematically, they implement functions from a key domain to an element range. Access by key is often called *lookup*, and in C++ this is conveniently expressed with operator[], just as with positional access in linear structures like arrays and lists.

Association structures are built on top of other kinds of structures, reinterpreting the contents of the underlying structure for their own purposes. As Table 8 shows, the basic association structures are *tables* and *search trees*. Tables are implemented on top of lists or arrays, and search trees are implemented on top of trees or tree nodes. For the most part, we aren't going to see any new structuring techniques in this section — the emphasis shifts to algorithms for accessing what's stored in a kind of structure we've already examined. We will, however, see some variations on the concept of trees that don't quite fit into the forms described in Chapter 9 some very interesting ways of using trees to enforce various constraints on the organization of the structure's elements.

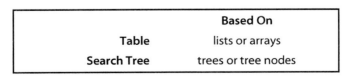

	Based On
Table	lists or arrays
Search Tree	trees or tree nodes

Table 8 Kinds of Association Structures

The implementations shown in this part of the book take advantage of some simplifying assumptions. One is that the key is unique for each element. That is, no association structure will ever contain two elements with equal keys. Another is that keys will be compared for equality, not identity. Also, like element types, key types are assumed to provide `equal`, `compare`, and `operator<<`. Finally, the element type must define a function `get_key` that takes an element and returns its key.

Keys can be any type for which `equal`, `compare`, and `operator<<` are defined. In contrast with their element type, the implementations here do not assume that keys are pointers, and in fact they generally won't be. Since tables involve two types — an element type and a key type — they have two type parameters in their template lists.

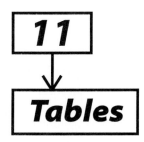

Tables

Tables, also known as *dictionaries*, are the most straightforward association structures. You are probably already familiar with simple kinds, as they are popular examples in introductory programming texts. They play major roles in a wide variety of system programs: compilers and linkers use symbol tables, operating systems use tables to manage resources, various kinds of database systems use tables to index their contents, and so on. Tables appear in many other kinds of applications, too.

This chapter begins with a review of *simple tables*. *Sorted tables* are considered next; although they share many characteristics with simple tables at the implementation level, the fact that they are sorted has significant implications. The last kind described are *hash tables*, important structures that support exceptionally efficient search.

The heart of a table mechanism is the associative lookup it supports. Arrays and lists can be accessed by position with expressions such as a[n]. Tables can be viewed as a generalization that allows access by *any* type instead of just integers — for instance, phonebook[name] where name is a string. The correspondence is particularly strong when the index of an element in an array or list is conceptually related to the element rather than just being the location at which the element happens to be stored. An example would be an array of month names in which the nth name corresponds to the nth month or an array storing counts of characters appearing in a file where a character's count is at the location in the array corresponding to the character's ASCII value. In fact, such uses of arrays and lists can really be viewed as degenerate forms of tables that organize their elements so that their integer-keys equal their position within the table.

Tables differ from arrays and lists in that the position of their elements is hidden from client code. Elements can be obtained by associative access or by traversal, but not by position. In a hash table, there might not even be an element at a specific position — elements are scattered around an array according to a scheme very different from the usual linear organization.

11.1 Simple Tables

A simple table is basically just a list plus an associative lookup operation. Elements are stored in a list (sequential or linked), but their order within the list is not significant. To find an element with a specified key, entries in the table are examined sequentially from the beginning until either one with that key is found or all the entries have been examined without success.

The cost of locating an element is a primary characteristic distinguishing different kinds of tables. A reasonable measure of that cost is the number of comparisons performed during the search, since other overhead (traversing the list, for instance) tends to increase more or less linearly with the number of comparisons. For a table with N elements, it could take anywhere from 1 to N comparisons to locate the one having a specified key. Because the target might be anywhere in the table, a successful search would take on the average $N/2$ comparisons. An unsuccessful search would of course take N comparisons. Consequently, the cost of searching a simple table increases *linearly* with the number of elements.

Other association structures support more efficient search at the cost of greater algorithmic and structural complexity. Simple tables are easy to implement, but their inefficiency normally outweighs the advantages of simplicity. Simple tables are rarely used for tables larger than tens of elements.

11.1.1 Representation

A simple table stores its elements in a sequential list. That's the only information it needs. An implementation of a simple table provides many of the same functions as the list on which it is based. In many cases, these functions would just turn around and call the same function on the list. However, there are many list functions that do not appear in a simple table module. The table has a more restricted interface than the list on which it is based. In particular, anything to do with the position of an element in a list is suppressed: **Access** is only by key. The list itself is not available to code using the table.

```
template <class elt, class key> struct table
{
  private:
    // Representation
    list<elt> elts;
    // . . .
};
```

11.1.2 Lifetime Operations

Lifetime operations for the table are essentially an interface to the lifetime operations of the underlying sequential list. The main difference between the two structures is capture here: access by key rather than by position.

Initialize/Finalize

The constructor initializes the list by forwarding it the allocation argument via the member initialization list. The constructor does nothing — the list's constructor will automatically be called when the table's is.

```
template <class elt, class key> struct table
{
    // . . .
    // Initialize/Finalize
    table(int alloc = 100);
    ~table();
};
```

```
/* Initialize/Finalize */

template <class elt, class key> table<elt, key>::table(int alloc)
        : elts(alloc)
{
}

template <class elt, class key> table<elt, key>::~table()
{
}
```

Access/Modify

The **Access** and **Modify** operations contain most of the differences between a simple table and the sequential list on which they are based. For convenience, overloadings of `remove` and `operator-=` are provided that take an element, but otherwise all of these functions are key oriented.

When a function searches for an element in the list with a specified key, it may or may not find one. It isn't clear *a priori* what to do when adding an element to a table that already has one for its key or removing the element with a key that isn't found. For greater flexibility, the definitions of functions dealing with key lookup will have an extra argument that allows the user to specify what is to be done. An enum `action` is added to `standard.H` to support this, with enumerators `IGNORE`, `WARN`, `ERROR`, and `REPLACE`. We'll see how those are used as we examine the various functions involved. These functions all include default values for their action arguments.

In most of the modules shown in this book, **Access** functions, as well as the `current` **Traversal** operation, return *references* to elements. This allows these operations to appear on the left side of an assignment, enabling code to easily replace the element returned. In fact, although **Replace** was described in the introductory materials as variant of **Access** (cf. Section 1.2.1, page 56), few of the implementations in this book show **Replace** operations. That is because in C++ putting a reference-returning function on the left side of an assignment is a sufficient implementation for **Replace**. Similar considerations apply to **Ex-**

change, another variant of **Access**. In this case, the template function exchange, provided in standard.H, serves as a universal implementation.

Association structures cannot allow the convenience of reference returns because they must be able to control where the new element goes within their structure. For simple tables this doesn't matter, but for most association structures it does. Consequently, these functions just return ordinary elements that cannot be replaced.

```
template <class elt, class key> struct table
{
    // . . .
    // Access/Modify
  private:
    int lookup_pos(key&);
  public:
    elt lookup(key&);
    elt operator[](key& k);

    void add(elt, action dup_action = IGNORE);
    table<elt, key>& operator+=(elt);
    elt remove(key&, action not_found_action = IGNORE);
    table<elt, key>& operator-=(key&);
    void remove(elt, action not_found_action = IGNORE);
    table<elt, key>& oper};
```

Access and **Modify** operations are based on a private function lookup_pos, that searches the list for an element with the specified key. If an element with the key is found, its position in the list is returned. If no element has the key, 0 is returned. Since sequential lists directly support positional access, this is a reasonable choice. Note the use of the get_key function the table module assumes is defined. Also, since lookup_pos uses the list's **Traversal** operations, it will interfere with any application-level traversal that might be in process, a problem we've seen in many other function definitions throughout the book.

```
/* Access */

// offset-1, like seq_list
template <class elt, class key> int table<elt, key>::lookup_pos(key& k)
{
    reset();
    while (next())
        if (equal(k, get_key(*current())))
            return index();

    return 0;
}

template <class elt, class key> elt& table<elt, key>::lookup(key& k)
{
    int pos = lookup_pos(k);
```

```
    if (pos <= 0)
        return 0;
    else
        return elts[pos];
}

template <class elt, class key> elt& table<elt, key>::operator[](key& k)
{
    return lookup(k);
}
```

Adding an element to a simple table ultimately just means adding it to the table's list. However, it must also take into account the possibility that the new element has a key equal to the key of an element already in the table. Curiously, that means searching the table as in an **Access** before going ahead and adding the element. This can make adding an element quite slow. To support applications coded in such a way as to foreclose this possibility, the action value IGNORE means to skip the search.

If action is not IGNORE, the search is performed. If no old element with they new one's key is found, the new one is added to the list. If a conflict occurs, an action value of REPLACE means to remove the old one and add the new one. So does WARN, but in that case a warning is also printed. ERROR means to print an error message and exit the program.

```
/* Modify: Add */

template <class elt, class key>
void table<elt, key>::add(elt e, action dup_action)
{
    int oldpos;

    if (IGNORE == dup_action) || (0 == (oldpos = lookup_pos(get_key(*e)))))
        elts.add(e);
    else
        if (ERROR == dup_action)
            error("[table::add] the table already contains an elt "
                "with the same key");
        else                                    // WARN or REPLACE
            {
                if (WARN == dup_action)
                    warning("[table::add] the table already contains an "
                            "elt with the same key");
                elts.remove(oldpos);
                elts.add(e);
            }
}

template <class elt, class key>
```

```
table<elt, key>& table<elt, key>::operator+=(elt e)
{
    add(e);
    return *this;
}
```

Remove operations are simpler. A key or, for convenience, an element is provided
and the list is searched. If the target if located, it is removed from the list. What happens
when the target is not found depends on the action argument provided. For the version
that takes an element, rather than a key, lookup is still based on the key, but then the element has to be compared with the one found to see if they are in fact equal, since the table
may contain a different one with the same key. The function is coded this way instead of
just calling the list module's position_of function so that it won't need to be modified
for different kinds of table implementations. Besides, equality tests are used here, and
they can get quite expensive — it might be a lot cheaper to get the keys out of two elements
and compare them than to compare the elements themselves.

```
/* Modify: Remove */

template <class elt, class key>
elt table<elt, key>::remove(key& k, action not_found_action)
{
    int pos = lookup_pos(k);

    if (0 != pos)
        return elts.remove(pos);
    else if (ERROR == not_found_action)
        error("[table::remove] the table does not contain an "
                "elt with the specified key");
    else if (WARN == not_found_action)
        warning("[table::remove] the table does not contain an "
                "elt with the specified key");

    return 0;
}

template <class elt, class key>
table<elt, key>& table<elt, key>::operator-=(key& k)
{
    remove(k);
    return *this;
}

template <class elt, class key>
void table<elt, key>::remove(elt e, action not_found_action)
{
    int pos = lookup_pos(get_key(*e));

    if ((0 != pos) && equal(*e, *elts[pos]))
        elts.remove(pos);
    else if (ERROR == not_found_action)
```

```
            error("[table::remove] element not in table");
    else if (WARN == not_found_action)
            warning("[table::remove] element not in table");
}

template <class elt, class key>
table<elt, key>& table<elt, key>::operator-=(elt e)
{
    remove(get_key(*e));
    return *this;
}
```

11.1.3 Traversal

Traversal operations are simply forwarded to the table's list.

```
template <class elt, class key> struct table
{
    // . . .
    // Traversal
  public:
    void reset();
    bool finished();
    bool next();
    elt& current();
    int index();
};
```

```
/* Traversal */

template <class elt, class key> void table<elt, key>::reset()
{
    elts.reset();
}

template <class elt, class key> bool table<elt, key>::finished()
{
    return elts.finished();
}

template <class elt, class key> bool table<elt, key>::next()
{
    return elts.next();
}

template <class elt, class key> elt& table<elt, key>::current()
{
    return elts.current();
}
```

```
template <class elt, class key> int table<elt, key>::index()
{
    return elts.index();
}
```

11.1.4 Content Operations

Tables have a typical set of **Content** operations. **Combine**, however, is omitted here and deferred to Exercise 2.

Attributes

The **Attributes** of a table are those of the underlying list.

```
template <class elt, class key> struct table
{
    // . . .
    // Attributes
    bool empty();
    bool full();
    int size();
};
```

```
/* Attributes */

template <class elt, class key> bool table<elt, key>::empty()
{
    return elts.empty();
}

template <class elt, class key> bool table<elt, key>::full()
{
    return elts.full();
}

template <class elt, class key> int table<elt, key>::size()
{
    return elts.size();
}
```

Compare

We'll provide an equal but no compare. The order in which elements are stored in a simple table is irrelevant, so there's no notion of ordering appropriate to them. It does make sense, however, to ask if one table is a subset of another, meaning that all of the first table's elements are also found in the second. Testing whether one structure is a "sub" of another is a fairly common operation with unordered structures.

```
template <class elt, class key> struct table
{
    // . . .
    // Compare
    friend bool equal(table<elt, key>&, table<elt, key>&);
    friend bool subtable(table<elt, key>&, table<elt, key>&);
};
```

The implementation of subtable is direct, though not necessarily efficient. It traverses the elements of the first looking to see if each is contained in the second. Wherever a "sub" test like subtable is implemented, an easy, though not necessarily efficient, way to code equal is to check if the two structures are "subs" of each other. As a simple improvement in efficiency, both functions compare the sizes of the two tables, which sequential lists can provide directly, before doing any real work.

```
/* Compare */

template <class elt, class key>
bool subtable(table<elt, key>& tbl1, table<elt, key>& tbl2)
{
    if (tbl1.size() > tbl2.size()) return FALSE;

    tbl1.reset();
    while (tbl1.next())
        if (!tbl2.contains_equal(tbl1.current())
            return FALSE;

    return TRUE;
}

template <class elt, class key>
bool equal(table<elt, key>& tbl1, table<elt, key>& tbl2)
{
    if (tbl1.size() != tbl2.size()) return FALSE;

    return subtable(tbl1, tbl2) && subtable(tbl2, tbl1);
}
```

11.1.5 Support Operations

Copy

Tables are copied by copying their underlying lists. They have no other information associated with them, so there's nothing to do beyond that.

```
template <class elt, class key> struct table
{
    // . . .
    // Copy
    table(table<elt, key>& tbl);
    table<elt, key>& operator=(table<elt, key>& tbl);
};
```

```
/* Copy */

template <class elt, class key>
table<elt, key>::table(table<elt, key>& tbl) : elts(tbl.elts)
{
}

template <class elt, class key>
table<elt, key>& table<elt, key>::operator=(table<elt, key>& tbl)
{
    if (this == &tbl) return *this;        // assignment to self!

    elts = tbl.elts;
    return *this;
}
```

Process

Most of the time tables are accessed by key to obtain the corresponding element. Occasionally, however, it may be useful to ask if a table contains a specific element. That's not the same thing as accessing the table with that element's key — the table might contain a different element stored with that key. Therefore, the usual contains and contains_ equal functions are provided. As with many other linear structures, it might make sense to provide a **Sort** operation for simple tables, but other types of tables either won't support that or automatically maintain elements in sorted order. Since it won't be in the other table implementations, it isn't included here.

```
template <class elt, class key> struct table
{
    // . . .
    // Process
    bool contains(elt);
    bool contains_equal(elt);
};
```

The definition of contains_equal first does a search of the table using the target element's key. Then, if a corresponding element is found, it is compared to the target element. The considerations for doing things this way, rather than traversing the list testing each element for equality with the target, are those described for the version of remove that takes an element (cf. page 372). The definition of contains, however, just asks the list whether it contains the element because identity comparisons will be faster than comparing keys or elements for equality.

```
/* Process */

template <class elt, class key> bool table<elt, key>::contains(elt e)
{
    return elts.contains(e);
}

template <class elt, class key> bool table<elt, key>::contains_equal(elt e)
{
    int pos = lookup_pos(get_key(*e));

    return (0 != pos) && equal(*e, *elts[pos]);
}
```

Output

Output of a table should be organized around the conceptual pairing of keys and elements. We'll print each element on a separate line preceded by its key. Even though the key might be printed by the element type's **Output** operation, it's still worth highlighting the correspondence between key and element, and in some situations the key will not be printed as part of printing the element.

```
template <class elt, class key> struct table
{
    // . . .
    // Output
    friend ostream& operator<<(ostream&, table<elt, key>&);
};
```

```
/* Output */

template <class elt, class key>
ostream& operator<<(ostream& strm, table<elt, key>& tbl)
{
    tbl.reset();
    while (tbl.next())
        strm << '\t' << get_key(*tbl.current()) << ":\t"
             << *tbl.current() << '\n';
    return strm;
}
```

11.2 Sorted Tables

One way to improve the efficiency of table search is to store elements in order according to their keys. Certain common search algorithms use element order to rapidly home in on the target element rather than searching blindly through the entire table. A sorted table is like a simple table, except that it adds elements to its list in such a way as to preserve ordering and takes advantage of that in its more efficient implementation of lookup.

11.2.1 Using an Ordered List

To keep the elements in order, **Add** operations have to determine where to insert a new element. It can do this at the same time it is checking whether the list contains an element with a key equal to the element being added. A straightforward implementation would perform a linear search with code something like the following.

```
template <class elt, class key> void sorted_table<elt, key>::add(elt e)
{
    for (int i = 1; i <= elts.size(); i++)
        if (AFTER != compare(get_key(*e), get_key(*elts[i])))
            break;
    if (equal(get_key(*e), get_key(*elts[i])))
        // ... handle complexities of different actions to take
        //     when an element with equal key is already in the table ...
    else              // e belongs before elts[i]
        elts.insert(e, i);              // i is allowed to be size+1
}
```

Adding an element at its proper position is more expensive due to the shifting of subsequent elements down in the list. A minor tradeoff is that add can stop as soon as it encounters an element whose key is after the key of the element being added instead of examining the entire list. A more significant tradeoff is that **Access** operations can similarly be made more efficient by taking advantage of ordering. Since applications using tables generally **Access** them much more frequently than they **Modify** them, the net improvement can be substantial.

Even though the elements are stored in order, a successful linear search takes the same number of comparisons — $N/2$ on average — as with a simple table, since the target element may still be anywhere in the list. However, an unsuccessful linear search would be faster, since, as in `add`, it can stop as soon as an element is encountered whose key is after the target. This is an interesting tidbit, but it doesn't fundamentally change the linear nature of the search. Costs still go up linearly with the number of elements in the table. What's needed is a search method that takes better advantage of the ordered elements.

11.2.2 Binary Search

That faster search method is *binary search*, a simple but powerful technique similar to what you do when you look up a word in a dictionary or a name in a phone book. A location in the middle of the table is selected and the target key compared to the key of the element at that location. If the keys are equal, the desired element has been found. If the target key is before the element's key, then search proceeds with the part of the table before the selected location. If the target key is after the element's key, search proceeds with the part of the table after the selected location.

The algorithm continues to cut the table into successively smaller portions, until either the target is located or the search has been narrowed to a single location in the table. In the latter case, the target is not in the table. If the search is for an `add`, the new element belongs either just before or just after the final location. Figure 11.1 illustrates this process for a table in which keys are names of fruits.

Each pass of the loop reduces the search's attention span by half. For a table of size N, the first pass reduces the attention span to $N/2$ elements, the second to $N/4$, and so on. After the kth pass, $N/2^k$ elements remain to be considered. It may happen that by chance the target is located in an early pass, but in any case the worse that can happen is for the search to continue until a range only one element large is reached. The number of passes this will take is the number of times N must be divided by 2 to reach 1. This is (by definition) the base two logarithm of N (i.e., $log_2 N$). The search time is therefore *logarithmic*, a great improvement over linear search. Since this algorithm depends on numerical calculations, it can be used only with structures that support positional index, such as sequential lists.

11.2.3 Implementation

A sorted table module is just like a simple table module in most respects. Nothing whatsoever changes in the header file. The only fundamental change is to `lookup_pos`, which implements binary search. (The preliminary version of `add` shown above was for expository purposes only: the improved search technique should really be implemented in `lookup_pos` rather than in `add`, so that **Access** functions can take advantage of it, too.)

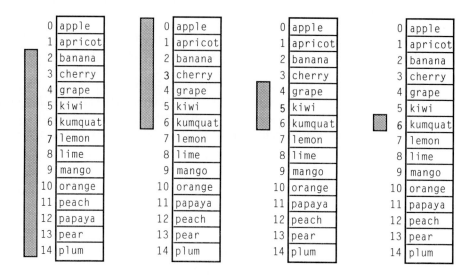

Searching for "kumquat": shading shows the region being considered; the highlighted index is the location of the next cut.

Figure 11.1   Binary Search

```
template <class elt, class key>
int sorted_table<elt, key>::lookup_pos(key& k)
{
    if (elts.empty()) return 0;

    int middle, lower = 1, upper = elts.size();
    order ord;

    while (lower < upper)
        {
            middle = (lower + upper) / 2;
            ord = compare(k, get_key(*elts[middle]));
            if (ord == EQUAL) return middle;
            if (ord == BEFORE)
                upper = middle - 1;
            else
                lower = middle + 1;
        }

    return lower;
}
```

This new version of lookup_pos returns the position of an element whose key may be after, equal to, or before the target key. Consequently, some incidental changes have to to be made to lookup and add to take that into account. Note that many other functions call lookup_pos, including remove and contains_equal, and they all benefit from the improved performance binary search provides.

```
template <class elt, class key> elt sorted_table<elt, key>::lookup(key& k)
{
    int pos = lookup_pos(k);

    if (0 == pos)
        return 0;

    if (equal(k, get_key(*elts[pos])))
        return elts[pos];

    return 0;
}

template <class elt, class key>
void sorted_table<elt, key>::add(elt e, action dup_action)
{
    if (elts.empty())
        {
            elts.add(e);
            return;
        }

    int pos = lookup_pos(get_key(*e));

    switch(compare(get_key(*e), get_key(*elts[pos])))
    {
      case BEFORE:
        {
            elts.insert(e, pos);
            break;
        }
      case AFTER:
        {
            elts.insert(e, pos+1);
            break;
        }
      case NO_ORDER:
        error("[sorsorted_table::add] compare returned NO_ORDER");
      case EQUAL:
        switch (dup_action)
          {
            case ERROR:
              error("[sorted_sorted_table::add] the sorted_table already "
                    "contains an elt with the same key");
              /* error exits, so no break */
            case WARN:
              warning("[sorted_sorted_table::add] the sorted_table already "
                      "contains an elt with the same key");
```

```
        /* no break */
      case REPLACE:
      case IGNORE:
        elts[pos] = e;
    }
  }
}
```

Finally, subtable can be made much more efficient than it was in the simple table module. Before, it had to search the entire second list for each element of the first list. It would be a great improvement to search the second list using the improved lookup_pos, via lookup, but we can do even better than that. Because the elements of each of the two tables are in order, we just have to traverse the two tables in parallel. When the key of the current element of the second table is less than the key of the current element of the first table, we can just do another next() on the second table. When the current element of the second table has a key that is *after* the key of the current element of the first table, we can stop and return FALSE, since we would know that the second table did not contain an element whose key is equal to the key of the first table's current element.

```
template <class elt, class key>
bool subtable(sorted_table<elt, key>& tbl1, sorted_table<elt, key>& tbl2)
{
    if (tbl1.size() > tbl2.size()) return FALSE;

    tbl1.reset();
    tbl2.reset();
    while (tbl1.next())
        {
            order ord;

            while (tbl2.next() &&
                  (AFTER ==
                      (ord = compare(*tbl1.current(), *tbl2.current()))))
                /* do nothing */;

            if (tbl2.finished() || (EQUAL != ord))
                return FALSE;
        }

    return TRUE;
}
```

11.3 Hash Tables

Suppose that every possible value of a table's element type had its own unique integer key and that those integers were all smaller than the size of the table. Under these highly restricted conditions, searching can be entirely eliminated by just storing each element at the location in the list corresponding to its key. These situations are not uncommon: examples include the number of days in a month indexed by the number of the month or a monthly calendar with a list of appointments for each day.

This situation is so straightforward that programmers typically just use arrays to represent this information rather than a more elaborate table structure: the array *is* the table, the indices are the keys, and the entries are the information associated with the keys! The keys are implicit in the structure of the array and aren't even necessarily part of the elements being stored.

It would be nice if the range of keys for a set of possible elements were often so well behaved, since direct lookup is so much more efficient than searching (no matter how good a search algorithm we use). Normally, of course, the keys aren't integer values, or they aren't unique, or they span such a wide range relative to how many items need to be stored that the array would be unacceptably large. Surprisingly, a clever technique called *hashing* approximates the efficiency of direct indexing with no restrictions on the keys other than that they be integers.

11.3.1 The Concept of Hashing

Suppose an application needed to store a few hundred strings in a table — names of people in an organization, for example. If we had a magic way of transforming a string to a unique integer between, say, 0 and 1000, we could use a direct-access table to store the strings and avoid expensive searching. Except for uniqueness, such a transformation would not be hard to implement: we just have to perform some integral computation on the characters of the string, perhaps not even using all of them. For instance, we could sum (or multiply) the ASCII value of the characters (or the first five, or the first, third, and last, or whatever) to obtain an integer.

The resulting integer n could not be used for an index directly, because there's no guarantee that it is less than the size of the array. That isn't hard to fix, though: $n\%size$ produces an integer between 0 and $size-1$ (inclusive). Thus, by first computing some integer value from an element, then taking the result modulo the table size, we can generate an index into the array. A function that generates indices like this is called a *hash function*, and its result can be used to directly access table elements.

The only problem with this scheme is that in general it isn't possible to find an integer-valued function that is quick to compute and produces a unique value for every possible key value. (If the hash function is too elaborate, it might end up taking more time than a binary search.) Moreover, unless the size of the table is bigger than the number of possible elements, which is generally out of the question, the remainder operation compresses a wide range of integers into a smaller one, precluding uniqueness. *Hash tables* are direct-access tables based on hash functions computed on keys along with mechanisms for *resolving collisions* — i.e., for distinguishing different keys that hash to the same index. They used to be called *scatter storage* because they distribute items around the table in what appears to be a haphazard manner, rather than sequentially as in simple or sorted tables.

11.3.2 Hash Functions

Before looking at collision resolution mechanisms, let's look at some of the characteristics of good hash functions. What makes hashing work is that the number of element values stored in the table is much smaller than the total number of possible element values. If we knew in advance which elements would be stored, we could perhaps find a function that *does* compute a unique hash index for each one. (In fact, algorithms for computing such *perfect hash functions* exist and are used for things like the keywords of a programming language in a compiler for that language.) In general, though, we don't have any idea what values will be stored and cannot even entertain the idea of devising a perfect hash function. This situation is characterized by the mathematical principle known as the *Pigeonhole Principle* which states that with N boxes and more than N objects to distribute among those boxes, at least one box must have more than one object in it.

Although collisions generally cannot be avoided, hash functions can be designed to minimize them. A good hash function spreads typical sets of elements relatively evenly over the index range of the table. Poor hash functions produce uneven distributions, in which the hash indices of most elements bunch up at relatively few index values. A good hash function must also be efficient to calculate, since it will be invoked frequently.

The first step in a hash function is to compute an integer value from a key. (Of course, if the key is already an integer, no further computation is necessary.) In C and C++, many kinds of keys can simply be cast to an integer! This strategy, not available in high-level languages, uses the machine-level representation of the key as if it were an integral value.

Keys are often strings. Typical hash functions on strings add some or all of the characters; they may also factor in the length of the string. It is surprisingly easy to design bad string hashing functions. For instance, adding all the characters produces the same value for anagrams (strings with the same characters in a different order). This problem is worse when only a few characters are used — say, the first two and the last — since in many applications many strings are closely related (similar names, addresses, titles, etc.). Addition of characters also fails to distinguish combinations of characters that sum the same, for example, "st" and "ru". For this reason, the bits representing the characters or the accumulated total are sometimes shifted before being added together, in an attempt to further scramble the result. Here's a simple-minded function to compute an index from a string.

```
long hash(string& s)
{
    int l = s.length();
    switch (l)
    {
        case 0:  return 0;
        case 1:  return s[0];
        case 2:  return s[0] * s[1];
        case 3:
        case 4:
        case 5:  return s[0] * s[1] + s[l-1];
        default: return s[0] * s[1] + s[l-4];
    }
}
```

Sometimes hashing is done on the memory address of a computational object instead of on its contents: the address of an object is an easily derived integer! This approach is useful for lookups based on object identity rather than equality of some key value.

The second step in computing a hash index is taking the remainder after dividing the integer produced in the first step by the size of the table. It turns out that due to some number theoretic considerations prime divisors produce much more even distributions than nonprime ones. Therefore, the size of an array used for a hash table should be a prime or at least a number with no small (less than about 20) prime divisors. Even numbers produce particularly bad distributions.

11.3.3 Resolving Collisions

As long as there are more possible key values than there are places in the table, collisions, where two different values produce the same hash index, can occur. The emptier the table, the less likely they are to happen, but we still need a mechanism for resolving collisions. There are many collision resolution techniques, but they are all based on a simple idea: the computed hash index is essentially a starting point for a search process. Given a target key and the corresponding hash index, an object located at that place in the table may be a different object whose key happens to hash to the same value as the target even though the two keys are not equal. The first step after computing a hash index is to *probe* the table by comparing the target key to the key of the object at the computed location: if they match, the target has been found; if not, search continues. Different resolution methods implement different search processes.

To illustrate, suppose we have elements to store whose keys are fruit names represented as strings. Figure 11.2 shows what a hash table might look like after several items have been added to the table using the hash function

```
hash(key) = (key[0] + key[3]) % 17
```

(This function only works with strings having at least 4 characters, and has the size of the table built into it; both are artificial limitations for the sake of constructing a simple example.) The next item to be added has key "kiwi", which happens to hash to 8, the same as "banana", which is already occupying location 8 of the table. This is a collision: the item whose key is "kiwi" cannot be stored there because the one whose key is "banana" already is.

Buckets

A simple collision resolution technique is to have the table contain *buckets* — small arrays of entries rather than individual entries. Each bucket contains objects whose keys all hash to the index of that location in the table, as shown in Figure 11.3. A hash value selects one of these buckets, which is then searched sequentially until the target object is located or an empty slot is encountered. If the selected bucket is empty, or none of its objects have keys that match the target key, the object is simply added to the end of the bucket.

In essence the bucket approach breaks the table down into lots of little ones. This simple scheme concedes the likelihood of a short search for most probes while making

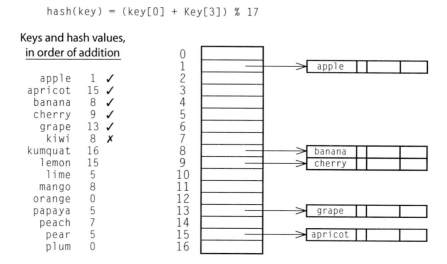

Figure 11.2 A Hash Table Collision

long searches very unlikely. The buckets must be fairly small, or far too much space will be wasted. One complication to this otherwise straightforward scheme is that buckets can overflow. One way to handle overflow is to have some other buckets off to the side somewhere, and include in each bucket a pointer to the next bucket to consider when that one is full.

As this amounts to a linked list of buckets, it may be better to acknowledge this from the beginning. The hash array can contain linked lists whose elements are pointers to hash buckets. (Remember, the implementation of linked lists ultimately developed in Chapter 8 includes just one data member — the pointer to the first node — so there is little overhead to a list.) Separate from the table would be an array of hash buckets, or they could even be allocated dynamically. That way, no bucket is used for hash indices that haven't yet been encountered.

Chaining

Another application of linked lists gives us another approach to collision resolution. Instead of buckets, the hash table simply contains linked lists of (pointers to) elements — in effect, hash buckets of size 1 (cf. Figure 11.4). The lists are referred to as *chains*, and the technique is called *chaining*. This is a pretty common technique where a straightforward implementation is desired and maximum efficiency isn't required. Each linked list contains all the elements whose keys hash to the same index. As with buckets, using chains minimizes search by dividing the set to be searched into lots of smaller pieces. There's nothing inherently wrong with linear search with small sequences; it's just that it gets slower and slower as the sequences to be searched get longer. In this approach to resolving collisions, each sequence of elements whose keys hash to the same value will stay relatively short, so linear search is adequate.

```
hash(key) = (key[0] + Key[3]) % 17
```

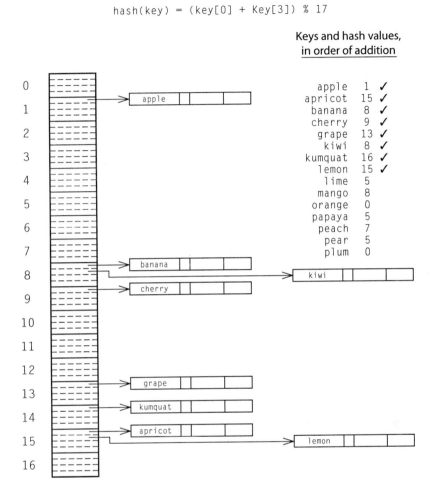

Keys and hash values,
in order of addition

apple	1	✓
apricot	15	✓
banana	8	✓
cherry	9	✓
grape	13	✓
kiwi	8	✓
kumquat	16	✓
lemon	15	✓
lime	5	
mango	8	
orange	0	
papaya	5	
peach	7	
pear	5	
plum	0	

Figure 11.3   Hash Buckets

Open Addressing

Using buckets or chains complicates the hash table structure. A structurally simpler approach is to store all the (pointers to) elements directly in the hash table. Collisions are resolved by looking somewhere else in the hash table. That "somewhere else" is a location generated by a deterministic mechanism so that subsequent hashes of the same key will reach that location. This approach is called *open addressing* or *rehashing*. In short, its strategy is as follows:

1. Compute the initial hash index for the key, and look in that location in the table.

2. If that location is empty, the target object is not in the table, and the search ends; if there is something stored there, compare its key to the target key.

```
hash(key) = (key[0] + Key[3]) % 17
```

Keys and hash values,
in order of addition

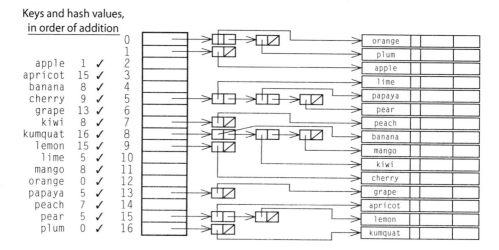

apple	1 ✓
apricot	15 ✓
banana	8 ✓
cherry	9 ✓
grape	13 ✓
kiwi	8 ✓
kumquat	16 ✓
lemon	15 ✓
lime	5 ✓
mango	8 ✓
orange	0 ✓
papaya	5 ✓
peach	7 ✓
pear	5 ✓
plum	0 ✓

Figure 11.4   Chaining

3. If the keys are equal, that object is the target, and the search ends; if not equal, that object is a different one whose key happens to hash to the same value (collision!).

4. *Compute a new index* into the table and go to step 3.

A variety of methods for determining the next location (step 4) are commonly used. The simplest form of open addressing is called *linear probing*: locations following the initial hash are examined in sequence. Eventually, one of three things happen:

1. An empty spot in the table will be found — the target element is not in the table.

2. The target element will be encountered.

3. The entire table gets searched (wrapping around from the end to the beginning), until the original hash location is reached again — the target element is not in the table, and the table is completely full.

The process is illustrated in Figure 11.5. In effect, the initial hash generates a location at which ordinary linear search begins. The initial hash is therefore just a *hint* giving a likely point to start the search, short-cutting a full sequential search but not guaranteeing how much searching will actually be necessary. People often find the concept of hash tables disconcerting when it is first introduced, since the idea of table lookup seems to require a specific known location for each element. However, what table lookup really requires is just that the process be deterministic — always producing the same result for any key. Hash tables are just a way of producing a deterministic result using a clever combination of indexing and search.

```
hash(key) = (key[0] + Key[3]) % 17
```

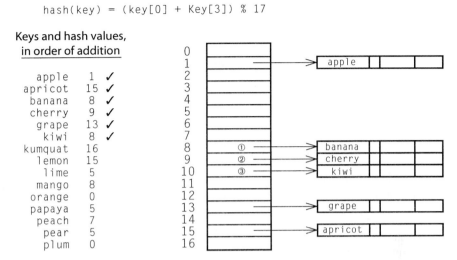

The item with key = "kiwi" ends up at location 10, though it hashes initially to 8: starting with the collision at 8, locations are examined sequentially (indicated by the numbers ①, ②, ③) until an empty one is found.

Figure 11.5   Linear Probing

Quadratic Probing

Linear probing is simple to implement, but it isn't all that effective. The problem is that as that table fills up, sequences of elements whose keys hash the same run into each other. In Figure 11.5, when the item with key = "kiwi" is added, there is a collision with the item having key = "banana"; sequential search immediately encounters another item (with key = "cherry") that happens to have a different initial hash value, so yet another probe is necessary.

To further illustrate this problem, suppose three elements hash to 7, occupying locations 7, 8, and 9, and that five other elements hash to 11, occupying locations 11 through 15. Now, if an element is added that hashes to 7, 8, or 9, it will be added in location 10. That's fine, but the next time that an element hashes to anything from 7 through 15, the rest of those locations have to be examined *even though their keys may well hash to different values*. Another element hashing to 7 will have to be compared to each of the other elements until an empty spot is found at location 16, though relatively few of those locations hold elements whose keys hash to 7. What has happened is that separate runs of same-hash elements have become entangled, causing much longer searches. This effect is called *clustering*, and it is in practice a very significant problem as hash tables fill up.

Other rehashing techniques are designed to reduce the clustering that occurs with linear probing. Instead of placing objects whose keys hash to the same index in close proximity, the index can be recomputed to spread the conflicting objects over more of the table. *Quadratic probing* increases the distance from one conflicting object to the next with each probe: for an object with hash value i, location i is checked first, then $i+1$, then

$i+4$, then $i+9$, etc. A formula for the nth index in a linear probe sequence (with n starting at 0, i the hash index, and m the table size) is

$$(i + n) \bmod m$$

A formula for the nth index in a quadratic probe sequence is

$$(i + n^2) \bmod m$$

The formulas are the same except for raising n to a different power. That power determines the "degree" of the probing, so to speak, thus the names 'linear' and 'quadratic'.

Multiplication is generally a slower hardware operation than addition. Note that a sequence of squares can be generated using only addition. Squares in a sequence manifest a simple pattern, which can be easily seen by lining up the squares in one row and the difference between successive squares in a row below them:

```
    0   1   4   9   16   25   36   49   64    . . .
        1   3   5   7    9    11   13   15    . . .
```

Each square is larger than the preceding square by two more than the preceding square is larger than the square before it. To generate the sequence, we can keep track of both the current square s (starting at 1) and the difference d that was added to the previous square to get the next one (also initially 1). Each step then involves computing a new difference by adding 2 to the previous one and a new square by adding the new difference to the previous square.

Quadratic probing wraps around after going past the end of the table, just like linear probing. For a given probe and given table size, the sequence of locations encountered in quadratic probing may eventual encounter some location a second time without hitting all the other locations in the table. It turns out, though, that if the size of the table, is a prime, at least half the locations in the table are encountered before returning to the initial location, which is good enough.

Since the distance between objects that hash the same increases as there are more of them, the clusters that appear in linear probing do not form with quadratic probing. Note that *any* function could be used to generate a new index, as long as it produces a reproducible sequence given an initial hash index. This is necessary because to find an object in the table the search must follow the same sequence of indices that led to an object's being placed at its (previously empty) location. A different sequence might encounter an empty location before the object, leading to the false determination that the object is not in the table.

11.3.4 Other Issues

Table Expansion

An element's location in a hash table is irrelevant to code using the table. No notion of linear ordering is supported. This has the advantage that the table can be reorganized during execution without client code even noticing. Client code provides a key, and the table mechanism finds the location that contains an element having that key or the location where the element should be added if not already there.

This property of hash tables makes it possible to dynamically expand tables as they get full. A larger array is allocated; then every element of the original array is hashed into the new array. Finally, the original array is deallocated. Note that the order of elements in the new array will have little, if any, relation to the order of elements in the old array, because the hash values are computed modulo a different size.

In practice it is desirable to rehash *before* the table is completely full. Regardless of the rehashing technique used to resolve them, the frequency of collisions increases dramatically as the table approaches saturation. Rehashing is worthwhile as soon as this effect becomes prominent. Different rehashing schemes have different performance characteristics, but typically performance starts to degrade significantly as the table reaches about 75–80% full. The definition of add can check how full the table is and trigger a rehash when a certain threshold has been reached. An alternative to coding a fixed fullness threshold is to have lookup_pos keep track of the average number of probes necessary to find a target and trigger expansion when that average exceeds a particular threshold.

Deletion

Hash tables are used primarily in applications where lookups are far more frequent than insertion. Furthermore, hash tables are normally used where objects are never deleted from a table once they are added to it. Deletion can be supported, but some collision resolution methods do so more easily than others.

With bucket or chaining methods, an object can be removed from the table simply by removing it from its list. Open addressing presents a more challenging problem: an object cannot simply be removed from the table, because it might be part of a cluster. When there is collision into a cluster, search must continue until either the target object is located or the cluster is passed. A search for an object might end prematurely if an earlier member of the cluster was deleted by just leaving a hole. Deleted entries must therefore be marked as such so they can be skipped during rehashing sequences. If an object is not found in the table, it can be stored in the first marked location encountered during the probe sequence *after* the sequence was followed to its end.

11.3.5 An Implementation

Here's the code for a hash table module, using quadratic probing and supporting expansion but not deletion. The implementation uses an array directly rather than a sequential list. The list contained in a simple or sorted table provides useful services, as evidenced by the large number of table functions that simply call the same function on the underlying list. In particular, the details of insertion, deletion, and size tracking are hidden from the table module, simplifying many of its function definitions. However, the way hash tables manage their elements is so different from how lists work that there is really nothing to be gained by using a list instead of a straight array.

The implementation assumes that the application supplies a function get_ hash(key&) that returns a long. That hash function only computes an integer from the element's key. The division by the table size is performed by the module, since it knows the size of the table.

We want to keep the size of the table prime, regardless of the size specified by the user. Also, the size of a newly expanded table should also be prime. We therefore include a function next_prime to compute the first prime equal to or greater than a given number. In general, tests for primeness form an interesting and challenging body of practical number theory, but real hash tables will be small enough for straightforward methods for finding primes. The algorithm shown here is based on a clever formulation by Knuth.

The public functions declared are essentially the same ones declared by the other table modules. **Remove** operations are omitted, and a few new attributes are included having to do with the fullness of the table. The representation and the definitions of the basic functions are entirely different, but many of the high-level functions — especially those using the **Traversal** operations — are just like their counterparts in the simple and sorted table modules.

```
template <class elt, class key> struct hash_table
{
    // Representation
  private:
    int allocation;
    int eltnum;                    // to track fullness and give user info
    elt *elts;                     // resizable array

    // Initialize/Finalize
    void init();
    void expand();
  public:
    hash_table(int = 103);
    ~hash_table();

    // Access/Modify
  private:
    int lookup_pos(key&);
  public:
    elt lookup(key&);
    elt operator[](key& k);
    void add(elt, action dup_action = IGNORE);
    hash_table<elt, key>& operator+=(elt);
    // no remove!

    // Traversal
  private:
    int curpos;
```

```
      int count;
  public:
    void reset();
    bool finished();
    bool next();
    elt current();
    int index();

    // Attributes
    bool empty();
    bool full();
    int size();
    int allocated_size();
    double fullness();

    // Compare
    friend order compare(hash_table<elt, key>&, hash_table<elt, key>&);
                                        // not implemented
    friend bool equal(hash_table<elt, key>&, hash_table<elt, key>&);
    friend bool subtable(hash_table<elt, key>&, hash_table<elt, key>&);

    // Combine
    // Left as an exercise

    // Copy
  private:
    void copy(hash_table<elt, key>& tbl);
  public:
    hash_table(hash_table<elt, key>& tbl);
    hash_table<elt, key>& operator=(hash_table<elt, key>& tbl);

    // Process
    bool contains(elt);
    bool contains_equal(elt);

    // Output
    static int keywidth;
            // min number of spaces to be used printing key; user can set
    friend ostream& operator<<(ostream&, hash_table<elt, key>&);
};
```

```
/* Miscellaneous Auxiliary Functions */

// based (loosely) on Algorithm A, Knuth, vol. 2, 1st. ed., p. 340
bool is_prime(int n)
{
    assert(n > 0);

    if (n%3 == 0) return 0;
    if (n%5 == 0) return 0;

    int lim = int(sqrt(n));
    for (int d = 5; d <= lim; d += 6)
```

```
        if ((n % (d+2)) == 0 || (n % (d+6)) == 0)
            return FALSE;

    return TRUE;
}

int next_prime(int n)
{
    if (n%2 == 0) n++;
    while (!is_prime(n)) n += 2;
    return n;
}
```

```
/* Initialize/Finalize */

template <class elt, class key> void hash_table<elt, key>::init()
{
    elts = new elt[allocation];
    for (int i = 0; i < allocation; i++) elts[i] = 0;
}

template <class elt, class key> hash_table<elt, key>::hash_table(int siz) :
    eltnum(0), allocation(next_prime(siz)), curpos(-2)
{
    init();
}

template <class elt, class key> hash_table<elt, key>::~hash_table()
{
    delete [] elts;
}
```

```
/* Access/Modify */

// private:
template <class elt, class key>
int hash_table<elt, key>::lookup_pos(key& k)
{
    extern long hash(key&);            // application must provide
    int i = hash(k) % allocation;
    int origi = i, diff = 1;           // to generate sequence of squares

    do  // look for empty slot or an element with equal key
        {
            if (!elts[i] || equal(k, get_key(*elts[i])))
                return i;

            i += diff;
            diff += 2;
            if (i >= allocation) i -= allocation;   // wrap around
```

```
        }
    while (i != origi);

    //  We've cycled back to the original index without finding a
    //  match for the key; time to expand the table!
    expand();
    return lookup_pos(k);        // looks recursive, but only happens once
}

template <class elt, class key> elt hash_table<elt, key>::lookup(key& k)
{
    return elts[lookup_pos(k)];
}

template <class elt, class key>
elt hash_table<elt, key>::operator[](key& k)
{
    return lookup(k);
}

//private:
template <class elt, class key> void hash_table<elt, key>::expand()
{
    int oldsize = allocation;
    elt *oldelts = elts;

    allocation = next_prime(2 * allocation);     // double the table size
    init();

    for (int i = 0; i < oldsize; i++)
        if (oldelts[i])
            elts[lookup_pos(get_key(*oldelts[i]))] = oldelts[i];

    delete [] oldelts;
};

template <class elt, class key>
void hash_table<elt, key>::add(elt e, action dup_action)
{
    int pos = lookup_pos(get_key(*e));

    if (0 == elts[pos])
        {
            elts[pos] = e;
            eltnum++;
            if (full()) expand();
        }
    else
        switch (dup_action)
        {
          case ERROR:
            error("[hash_table::add] the hash_table already contains "
                "an elt with the same key");
            /* error exits, so no break */
```

```
            case WARN:
                warning("[hash_table::add] the hash_table already contains "
                                            "an elt with the same key");

                /* no break */

            case IGNORE:
            case REPLACE:
                elts[pos] = e;
        }
}

template <class elt, class key>
hash_table<elt, key>& hash_table<elt, key>::operator+=(elt e)
{
    add(e);
    return *this;
}
```

```
/* Traversal */

template <class elt, class key> void hash_table<elt, key>::reset()
{
    curpos = -1;
    count = 0;
}

template <class elt, class key> bool hash_table<elt, key>::finished()
{
    return curpos >= allocation;
}

template <class elt, class key> bool hash_table<elt, key>::next()
{
    if (-2 == curpos)
        error("[hash_table::next] traversal not yet reset");

    while ((0 == elts[++curpos]) && !finished());

    return !finished();
}

template <class elt, class key> elt hash_table<elt, key>::current()
{
    if (-2 == curpos)
        error("[hash_table::current] traversal not yet reset");

    if (-1 == curpos)
        error("[hash_table::current] traversal reset but not yet stepped");

    if (finished())
        error("[hash_table::current] traversal already finished");

    return elts[curpos];
```

```
}

template <class elt, class key> int hash_table<elt, key>::index()
{
    return count;
}
```

```
/* Attributes */

template <class elt, class key> bool hash_table<elt, key>::empty()
{
    for (int i = 0; i < allocation; i++)
        if (0 != elts[i]) return FALSE;
    return TRUE;
}

template <class elt, class key> double hash_table<elt, key>::fullness()
{
    return double(eltnum)/allocation;
}

template <class elt, class key> bool hash_table<elt, key>::full()
{
    return 5*eltnum > 4*allocation;
    // semi-arbitrary choice of 80% cutoff
}

template <class elt, class key> int hash_table<elt, key>::size()
{
    return eltnum;
}

template <class elt, class key> int hash_table<elt, key>::allocated_size()
{
    return allocation;
}
```

```
/* Compare */

template <class elt, class key>
bool subtable(hash_table<elt, key>& tbl1, hash_table<elt, key>& tbl2)
{
    if (tbl1.size() > tbl2.size()) return FALSE;

    tbl1.reset();
    while (tbl1.next())
        if (!tbl2.contains_equal(tbl1.current()))
            return FALSE;

    return TRUE;
```

```
}

template <class elt, class key>
bool equal(hash_table<elt, key>& tbl1, hash_table<elt, key>& tbl2)
{
    if (tbl1.size() != tbl2.size()) return FALSE;

    return subtable(tbl1, tbl2);
}

template <class elt, class key>
order compare(hash_table<elt, key>&, hash_table<elt, key>&)
{
    notimp("compare(hash_table<elt, key>& tbl1, "
           "hash_table<elt, key>& tbl2)");
    return NO_ORDER;
}
```

```
/* Combine */
/* Left for Exercise 2 */


/* Copy */

template <class elt, class key>
void hash_table<elt, key>::copy(hash_table<elt, key>& tbl)
{
    eltnum = tbl.eltnum;
    for (int i = 0; i < allocation; i++) elts[i] = tbl.elts[i];
}

template <class elt, class key>
hash_table<elt, key>::hash_table(hash_table<elt, key>& tbl) :
    allocation(tbl.allocation), elts(new elt[tbl.allocation]), curpos(-2)
{
    copy(tbl);
}

template <class elt, class key>
hash_table<elt, key>&
hash_table<elt, key>::operator=(hash_table<elt, key>& tbl)
{
    if (this == &tbl) return *this;        // assignment to self!

    if (allocation != tbl.allocation)
        {
            delete [] elts;
            allocation = tbl.allocation;
            elts = new elt[allocation];
            // not init(), because don't need to zero since
            // about to copy to every location in the new array
        }
```

```
    copy(tbl);

    return *this;
}
```

```
/* Process */

template <class elt, class key> bool hash_table<elt, key>::contains(elt e)
{
    return e == elts[lookup_pos(get_key(*e))];
}

template <class elt, class key>
bool hash_table<elt, key>::contains_equal(elt e)
{
    return equal(*e, *elts[lookup_pos(get_key(*e))]);
}
```

```
/* Output */

template <class elt, class key> int hash_table<elt, key>::keywidth = 24;

template <class elt, class key>
ostream& operator<<(ostream& strm, hash_table<elt, key>& tbl)
{
    tbl.reset();
    while (tbl.next())
        {
            long curpos = strm.tellp();
            strm << '\t' << get_key(*tbl.current());
            long wdth = strm.tellp() - curpos;
            spaces(max(1, tbl.keywidth - wdth), strm);
            strm << *tbl.current() << '\n';
        }
    return strm;
}
```

11.4 EXERCISES

1. Complete the diagrams in Figure 11.2 (page 386), Figure 11.3 (page 387), and Figure 11.5 (page 389).

    (a) Show where the rest of the keys end up.

    (b) How many collisions occurred in each case? (Each element compared that isn't equal is a collision; for instance, if three different elements are in a bucket in 11.3, when a fourth different element is added to the same bucket, there will have been three collisions when that element was added.)

(c) Show a complete diagram like the one in Figure 11.5 based on quadratic probing instead of the linear probing used there. How many collisions occurred in adding all the keys?

2. Aiming for simplicity and clarity, rather than any special efficiency, write the obvious **Combine** operation(s) for the following.
    (a) simple tables
    (b) sorted tables
    (c) hash tables

3. Using public functions provided by the table modules, write a function `keys` that takes a table and returns a sequential list of its elements keys for the following.
    (a) simple tables
    (b) sorted tables
    (c) hash tables

4. Consider replacing the sequential list of the simple table module with a linked list.
    (a) Is there anything in the simple table module that depends on the list being sequential as opposed to linked?
    (b) If the answer to (a) is no, explain why. If yes, what changes would have to be made if using a linked list?
    (c) What would be the advantages of using a linked list?
    (d) What would be the disadvantages of using a linked list?

5. Modify the simple list module to automatically expand its list when full.
    (a) How many functions had to be changed?
    (b) Is the table's behavior significantly affected? If so, how? If not, why not?
    (c) Does this look like a worthwhile improvement?
    (d) Keeping in mind other uses of sequential lists, which seems more appropriate: that the table should expand its list or that the sequential list module should be extended to automatically expand when full?

6. The definition of `table::add` (page 371) checks to see if the table already contains an element with the same key. If its `action` argument is `REPLACE`, the old element is removed and the new one added. Since simple tables are based on sequential lists, and removing an element from a sequential list requires shifting all subsequent elements up to fill in the gap, this facet of `table::add` might be a source of significant inefficiency. A simple and more efficient alternative would be to store the new element in the old one's position, simply overwriting one pointer with another without disrupting the rest of the list.
    (a) Is this always more efficient? Consider where the new element is placed in the two approaches and see if you can imagine a situation in which the proposed change might actually make things worse.
    (b) Could a similar improvement be made to the definitions of `add` in the other kinds of tables shown in this chapter? If so, why; if not, why not?

7. Modify the implementation of one of the table modules to allow the user to specify what function is to be used to get the key (instead of assuming a global `get_key` function). There are three ways to do this. Choose one to implement, but discuss the advantages and disadvantages of each, along with the advantages in general in allowing users to specify the function. The three possibilities are as follows.
    (a) Add a pointer-to-function argument to every function that uses `get_key`, either directly or indirectly.
    (b) Give the constructor a pointer-to-function argument, store that in the table struct, and have functions use that instead of `get_key`.
    (c) Make the function a third parameter to the template.

8. An alternative form for a simple table is an *association list*. Typically based on linked lists, these store pairs of keys and elements. Lookup involves sequential search through the pairs for the specified key. Unlike the other tables discussed here, an association list would store arbitrary pairs of keys and elements: the element does not necessarily provide a function to get its key. More than one entry may contain the same key, in which case **Access** operations obtain the first one encountered in the list.
   (a) Implement and test an association list module.
   (b) Give examples of situations in which it would be useful to have a table in which keys were not part of the elements stored.

9. Compare simple tables and sets. (Hint: consider the abstract behavior of their fundamental operations.)
   (a) In what respects are they alike?
   (b) In what respects are they different?
   (c) Would a simple table be a reasonable foundation on which to build a set module?

10. The sorted list implementation shown in the chapter uses a sequential list, but insertion into a sequential list is inefficient (except at its end). An obvious possibility is to use a linked list instead.
    (a) Copy the sorted list module and modify your copy to use a linked list instead of a sequential list.
    (b) What functions did you have to change?
    (c) Were you able to implement binary search on a linked list? If not, why not? If you were able to, what compromises, if any, did you have to make to do so?
    (d) Compare the efficiency of this implementation to the one based on a sequential list. Can you think of situations in which the original would be faster?
    (e) Other than efficiency, what other reasons are there to choose one approach over the other?

11. Write a program that reads words from a file, representing them as instances of string, and counts how many times each appears. Have it report the number of words read, the number of different words found, and the number of comparisons performed. It should traverse the table and lookup the key of each element, and then report the number of comparisons performed in doing that. The string module in the include and lib directories provides a public static data member string::compares, which compare(string&,string&) increments; also, equal(string&,string&) calls compare. Your program can reset string::compares to zero whenever it wants.
    (a) Write versions of the program that use a simple table, a sorted table, and a hash table.
    (b) Compare the performance of the three methods on text files of several different sizes.
    (c) Comment on the differences between the numbers obtained while indexing the file and the numbers obtained while looking up each word.

12. In many applications of table lookup, the same relatively few keys get looked up repeatedly within a short time. A simple table implementation could take advantage of this by always moving the most recently located object to the front of the list, a technique sometimes called *self-organizing search*.
    (a) Make this change to the simple table module.
    (b) Repeat the experiment of Exercise 11 to get figures for the modified simple list and compare with the old figures.
    (c) What are the increased costs of this method?
    (d) When would the benefits outweigh the costs?
    (e) Ob viously, no such improvement is available for sorted tables, because they rely on the ordering of their list to implement binary search. It would seem that the improvement would be inapplicable to hash tables too; however, a similar modification can be made to hash ta-

bles by considering each chain of elements that have the same hash index as a list and reordering elements within that chain. Modify the hash table module to implement this change.

(f) Repeat the experiment of Exercise 11 to get figures for the modified hash table and compare with the old figures.

(g) If you don't see any significant difference between the new and old figures for hash tables, explain why not and under what conditions such a modification might pay off. If you do see a significant difference, can you characterize the tradeoff between the increased speed and the costs incurred to attain it?

13. Modify the hash table implementation to support deletion.

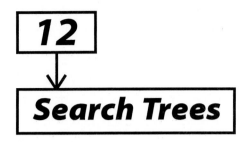

Search Trees

The list- and array-based tables examined in the last chapter are widely used structures. Simple tables and hash tables do not depend on or take advantage of the relative ordering of the keys of their elements, whereas sorted tables do. For key types that provide `equal` but not `compare`, simple tables or hash tables must be used. Sorted tables may be used with key types that do provide `compare`, but they are inefficient because of all the shifting of elements caused by insertions and deletions. Of course, a hash table can be used with elements whose keys happen to provide `compare`, but its **Traversal** operations process its elements in random order.

In sum, tables are useful when relatively small numbers of elements are involved or there is no need for ordered traversals. Applications that need ordered traversals over large numbers of associatively accessed elements must use a different kind of structure. *Search trees*, based on various kinds of tree structures, provide the needed power. This chapter looks at some of the many ways trees can be used to support searching.

12.1 Binary Search Trees

Binary trees may be used to implement search trees according to a very simple scheme:

- Each node contains a (pointer to) an element being stored.
- A node's left subtree contains only elements whose key is *before* the key of the node's element.
- A node's right subtree contains only elements whose key is *after* the key of the node's element.

Figure 12.1 shows a small search tree, with nodes represented only by their keys.

To find the element with a target key, the tree is searched by following a path starting at the root node. At each step the search key is compared to the key of the current node's element. If the keys are equal, the target has been located. If the target key is before the key of the current node's element, the node's left subtree is examined next; otherwise, the right subtree is examined. This continues until either the target is found or there's no sub-

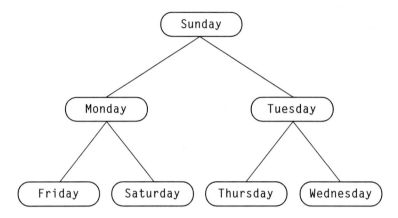

Figure 12.1   A Search Tree

tree in the appropriate direction of the current node. In the latter case, there is no element in the tree that matches the key. At that point, an **Access** operation would return 0, while an **Add** operation would add a node for the new element in the appropriate direction from the current node.

Here's an implementation. As with tables, the search tree modules shown in this chapter assume that get_key(elt, elt) is provided by the application.

12.1.1 Representation

A search tree can store its elements in a binary tree and use the binary tree to perform most of its operations. The binary tree is parameterized only in terms of the element type — it's only the search tree module that knows about keys.

```
template <class elt, class key> struct search_tree
{
  private:
    // Representation
    binary_tree<elt> elts;
    // . . .
};
```

Many of the modules shown in this and the previous chapter on tables are implemented on top of other structures we've already studied — in particular, lists and trees. Most of the operations on the higher-level structure are implemented by just calling the same operation on the lower-level structure. Only a few operations — typically **Access** and **Modify** — have to do something special in support of associative access.

This is a powerful use of data abstraction. We put aside the details of the lower-level structure's implementation in order to concentrate on the new way we are using it. A traditional implementation would code a search tree as a special kind of binary tree. A typical strategy would be to make a copy of the binary tree module and edit it where search tree behavior is different from a plain binary tree. The disadvantages of that approach include having to deal with two levels of complexity in the same module (the underlying binary tree and the specialized search procedures), having to duplicate any extensions or bug fixes later made to the original binary tree module in the copy, and leaving internal details in the public interface (access to tree nodes, navigation operations, etc.). A data abstraction approach avoids these problems at the cost of having to write a number of simple functions that call their lower-level equivalents.

12.1.2 Lifetime Operations

A search tree provides operations for lookup (**Access**), **Add**, and **Remove**. Action arguments control what happens when there are key conflicts in an **Add** or absent keys or elements in a **Remove** in just the same ways as the table modules of the previous chapter.

Initialize/Finalize

These are entirely trivial. There is nothing to code. If we let the compiler generate the do-nothing constructor and destructor instead of defining them, the results would be exactly the same.

```
template <class elt, class key> struct search_tree
{
    // . . .
  public:
    // Initialize/Finalize
    search_tree();
    ~search_tree();
};
```

```
/* Initialize/Finalize */

template <class elt, class key> search_tree<elt, key>::search_tree()
{
}

template <class elt, class key> search_tree<elt, key>::~search_tree()
{
}
```

Access

The real work of lookup is done by lookup_pos, which takes a key and locates the node in the tree having an element whose key is equal to the target key. Lookup will also be used by **Remove** operations to find the node in the tree to delete.

```
template <class elt, class key> struct search_tree
{
    // . . .
    // Access
  private:
    link lookup_pos(key&);
  public:
    elt lookup(key&);
    elt operator[](key&);
};
```

```
/* Access */

template <class elt, class key>
elt search_tree<elt, key>::lookup_pos(key& k)
{
    link cur = elts.getRootNode();
    if (0 == cur->getElt()) return 0;

    while (cur)
        switch (compare(k, get_key(*cur->getElt())))
        {
          case EQUAL:
            return cur;
          case BEFORE:
            cur = cur->getLeft();
            break;
          case AFTER:
            cur = cur->getRight();
            break;
          case NO_ORDER: error("[search_tree::lookup] "
                               "elts cannot be compared");
        }

    return 0;
}

template <class elt, class key> elt search_tree<elt, key>::lookup(key& k)
{
    link pos = lookup_pos(k);
    if (0 == pos)
        return 0;
    else
        return pos->getElt();
}
template <class elt, class key>
elt search_tree<elt, key>::operator[](key& k)
{
    return lookup(k);
}
```

Add

The only **Add** operations are add and its synonym operator+=. Add uses the key of the element it is given to locate the place in the tree where that element should be added. Complexity arises when there already is an element in the tree whose key is equal to the element being added, so code to handle that is split off to a private subfunction add_equal. Otherwise, adding is straightforward. It mimics the behavior of lookup, except that at the end, when there's no node in the direction it is trying to go, it adds a node for the new element at that point.

```
template <class elt, class key> struct search_tree
{
    // . . .
    // Add
  private:
    link add_equal(link, elt, action));
  public:
    elt add(elt, action);
    elt operator+=(elt);
};
```

```
/* Modify: Add */

// private:
template <class elt, class key>
void search_tree<elt, key>::add_equal(link cur, elt e, action dup_action)
{
    switch (dup_action)
    {
      case WARN:
        warning("[search_tree::add] the tree already "
                "contains an elt with the same key");
        /* no break */
      case IGNORE:
      case REPLACE:
        cur->getElt() = e;
        return;

      case ERROR:
        error("[search_tree::add] the tree already "
              "contains an elt with the same key");
    }
}

template <class elt, class key>
void search_tree<elt, key>::add(elt e, action dup_action)
{
    link cur = elts.getRootNode();

    if (0 == cur->getElt())
        {
```

```
                    cur->setElt(e);
                    return;
              }

      key k = get_key(*e);

      while (TRUE)
          switch (compare(k, get_key(*cur->getElt())))
          {
            case EQUAL:
              add_equal(cur, e, dup_action);
              return;

            case BEFORE:
              if (cur->hasLeft())
                  cur = cur->getLeft();
              else
                  {
                      cur->addLeft(e);
                      return;
                  }
              break;

            case AFTER:
              if (cur->hasRight())
                  cur = cur->getRight();
              else
                  {
                      cur->addRight(e);
                      return;
                  }
              break;

            case NO_ORDER:
              error("[search_tree::add] can't compare keys");
              break;
          }
}

template <class elt, class key>
search_tree<elt, key>& search_tree<elt, key>::operator+=(elt e)
{
    add(e);

    return *this;
}
```

Suppose we add the names of the months to a search tree, in calendar order. The structure of the tree after adding the names of each of the first seven months is shown in Figure 12.2. The structure of the tree after adding all of the months is shown a little later, in Figure 12.3 on page 412.

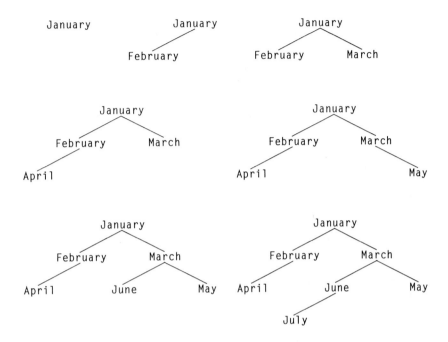

Figure 12.2   Adding Months to a Search Tree in Calendar Order

Remove

Remove is an intricate operation in a search tree. As with other ordered structures, removing an element should not disturb the conceptual ordering of the elements. With a
linear structure, elements have only one successor, so deleting an element leaves its successor in its place. Things are more complicated with a nonlinear structure like a search
tree, because the deleted element has more than one successor. The implementation here
has three levels: the public functions, a private function do_remove that implements the
actual removal (as lookup_pos implements search), and other private functions called by
do_remove.

```
template <class elt, class key> struct search_tree
{
    // . . .
    // Remove
  private:
    elt do_remove(link);
    void do_remove_terminal(link);
    void do_remove_left_only(link);
    void do_remove_right_only(link);
    void do_remove_both(link);
  public:
    void clear();
```

```
    elt remove(key&, action not_found_action = IGNORE);
    search_tree<elt, key>& operator-=(key&);
    void remove(elt e, action not_found_action = IGNORE);
    search_tree<elt, key>& operator-=(elt);
};
```

Two versions of remove and its synonym operator-= are provided: one that takes a key and one that takes an element. The two remove functions call do_remove to perform the actual work. For convenience, clear is also provided. There's nothing complicated about clear — it just clears the underlying tree. In all cases, recycling of nodes removed from the tree is handled by the binary tree and binary tree node modules.

```
template <class elt, class key> void search_tree<elt, key>::clear()
{
    elts.clear();
}

template <class elt, class key>
elt search_tree<elt, key>::remove(key& k, action not_found_action)
{
    link pos = lookup_pos(k);

    if (pos)
        return do_remove(pos);
    else
        switch (not_found_action)
        {
          REPLACE:  error("[search_tree::remove] REPLACE inapplicable");
          ERROR:    error("[search_tree::remove] no element with "
                          "specified key");
          WARNING:  warning("[search_tree::remove] no element with "
                            "specified key");
          default:
            return 0;
        }
}

template <class elt, class key>
search_tree<elt, key>& search_tree<elt, key>::operator-=(key& k)
{
    remove(k);

    return *this;
}

template <class elt, class key>
bool search_tree<elt, key>::remove(elt e, action not_found_action)
{
    link pos = lookup_pos(get_key(*e));

    if (pos)
        if (equal (*e, *pos->getElt()))
```

```
            do_remove(pos);
        else
            error("[search_tree::remove] the tree contains a element "
                    "with a key equal to the target's, but it is not "
                    "equal to the target]");
    else
        switch (not_found_action)
        {
          REPLACE:  error("[search_tree::remove] REPLACE inapplicable");
          ERROR:error("[search_tree::remove] no such element");
          WARNING:  warning("[search_tree::remove] no such element");
          default:
            return FALSE;
        }

    return TRUE;
}

template <class elt, class key>
search_tree<elt, key>& search_tree<elt, key>::operator-=(elt e)
{
    remove(get_key(*e));

    return *this;
}
```

There are four cases to consider for **Remove**, depending on what children the node being removed has. The main job of do_remove is simply to determine which case applies and call the applicable subfunction. It first saves the element to be removed so it can return it, because after the selected subfunction is finished that element won't be in the tree anymore. For convenience, it ends by returning the element removed.

```
/* Remove: dispatcher */

template <class elt, class key>
elt search_tree<elt, key>::do_remove(link pos)
{
    elt e = pos->getElt();

    if (!pos->hasLeft())
        if (!pos->hasRight())
            do_remove_terminal(pos);     // terminal node
        else
            do_remove_terminal(pos);     // right child only
    else
        if (!pos->hasRight())
            do_remove_right(pos);        // right child only
```

```
        else
            do_remove_both(pos);        // both children

    return e;
}
```

We can see what should happen in each case by looking at examples. Figure 12.3 shows the tree that results from completing the addition of (elements whose keys are) month names to the tree started above (cf. Figure 12.2 on page 409). The simplest case is

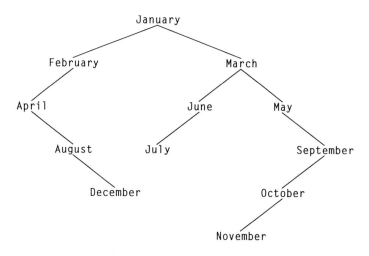

Figure 12.3   Search Tree of Months Added in Calendar Order

the deletion of a terminal node, for instance `July`: the node can just be removed from the tree without any further consequences, as shown in Figure 12.4.

Also straightforward is a node with just one subtree. There are two cases — one a node with just a left subtree and one a node with just a right subtree. The necessary modifications are in essence the same in either case: the node being removed can simply be replaced by its only subtree. Figure 12.5 shows the month tree after the removal of `February`, with just a left subtree, and `May`, with just a right subtree.

The difficult case is when the node being removed has both a left and a right subtree. The presence of two subtrees dictates the node that can replace the one being deleted. Whatever key ends up replacing the one being deleted must, by the rules by which search trees are constructed and maintained, belong after all the keys in the left subtree and before all the keys in the right subtree. Which key is that? A moment's thought should show that it must be *the inorder successor* to the key of the element being removed, since that key comes after all the left subtree keys (which come before the one being removed) and before all the right subtree keys (which come after the one being removed), other than the successor itself. Since the successor by definition comes *after* the key being removed, it must be somewhere in the right subtree.

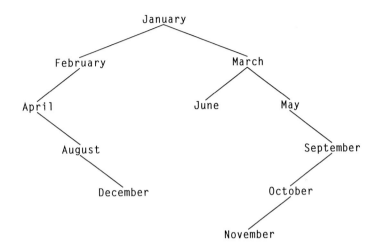

Figure 12.4   The Month Tree with July Removed

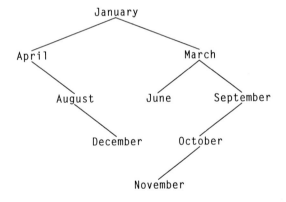

Figure 12.5   The Month Tree with February and May Removed

But where? It's not the root of the right subtree — the right child — because that comes after the node being removed. It must be somewhere in that node's left subtree, since its elements come before that node. Is it the left child of that right child? Not if that also has a left child, since that would come before it. In the end, the way to find the inorder successor of a node is to navigate first to its right child, then, as long as the node navigated to so far has a left subtree, go to its left child — in short, go right, then take lefts as far as you can. The node where the navigation stops is the inorder successor of the original node.

The inorder successor takes the place of the node being removed. But what about its subtrees? It can't have a left subtree, or the navigation process that found it would have continued on past it. If it doesn't have a right subtree — i.e., it's a terminal node — than there's nothing further to worry about: in effect, it's like removing a terminal node. If it does have a right subtree, it is replaced by its right subtree: in effect, it's like removing a node with just a right subtree. Figure 12.6 shows the remaining month name tree with March removed.

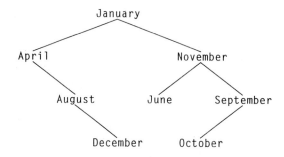

Figure 12.6   The Month Tree with March Removed

Implementations of the four cases follows. They use parent-oriented node functions not shown in the discussion of binary tree but provided by the on-disk module. All of this code will correctly delete the element that happens to lie at the root of the tree. (The only special case is when the root is the only node of the tree, in which case by the convention specified earlier, we show an empty tree by setting the root's element to 0.) The way this uniformity is accomplished is by using a trick often used for deleting a node in a linked list: move the information contained in the node's successor and then delete the successor instead. This avoids having to find the predecessor of the node in a singly linked list. The tactic is used here not to avoid having to find the predecessor, as that can be obtained simply by calling getParent, but because the resulting code ends up being more compact and easier to understand when the node containing the element being removed is left in place and the node with the element taking its place removed from the tree instead.

```
/* Remove */

template <class elt, class key>
void search_tree<elt, key>::do_remove_terminal(link pos)
{
    if (elts.getRootNode() == pos)
        elts.getRootNode()->setElt(0);
    else
        pos->getParent()->replace(pos, 0);
}

template <class elt, class key>
void search_tree<elt, key>::do_remove_right_only(link pos)
{
    link l = pos->getLeft();

    // Now, save the left node's information so it can be recycled
    link ll = r->getLeft();
    link lr = r->getRight();
```

```
    elt le = l->getElt();

    // prepare left node for recycling
    l->setLeft(0);
    l->setRight(0);

    // recycle left node and give pos its former information
    pos->replace(l, ll);              // recycles l
    pos->setRight(lr);
    pos->setElt(le);
}

template <class elt, class key>
void search_tree<elt, key>::do_remove_left_only(link pos)
{
    link r = pos->getRight();

    // Now, save the right node's information so it can be recycled
    link rr = r->getRight();
    link rl = r->getLeft();
    elt re = r->getElt();

    // prepare right node for recycling
    r->setRight(0);
    r->setLeft(0);

    // recycle right node and give pos its former information
    pos->replace(r, rr);              // recycles r
    pos->setLeft(rl);
    pos->setElt(re);
}

template <class elt, class key>
elt search_tree<elt, key>::do_remove_both(link pos)
{
    // locate pos's inorder successor:
    // the leftmost node of its right subtree
    for (link succ = pos->getRight();
        succ->hasLeft();
        succ = succ->getLeft());

    pos->setElt(succ->getElt());
    // elevate successor elt to take the place of pos's elt

    link r = succ->getRight();
    // succ guaranteed to have no left to worry about

    succ->setRight(0); // prepare for recycling
    succ->getParent()->replace(succ, r);
    // replace succ by it's right child and recycle succ. replace knows
    // whether succ was the right or left child of its parent.
}
```

Note that each of the above four functions ends with a call to `replace`. That function figures out which of the parent's child the node being replaced is, and replaces it with another node (or 0), setting that node's parent accordingly. It also recycles the node being replaced. Each of the functions ensures that before this happens the node being replaced has no successors — those successors already having gotten reattached to a different node — so that the recycling does not recursively delete any other nodes.

12.1.3 Traversal

The rest of the functions provided by the search tree module are trivial, or nearly so — nothing like the monster that **Remove** turned out to be! The **Traversal** operations just use the **Traversal** operations of the underlying binary tree. Recall that the binary tree module provides several different flavors of traversal: breadth-first, preorder, inorder, and, although left unimplemented, postorder. For a search tree, we always want an inorder traversal, as that is the one that presents the elements in order of their keys.

```
template <class elt, class key> struct search_tree
{
    // . . .
    // Traversal
    void reset();
    bool finished();
    bool next();
    elt& current();
    int index();
};
```

```
/* Traversal */

template <class elt, class key> void search_tree<elt, key>::reset()
{
    elts.reset(inorder);
}

template <class elt, class key> bool search_tree<elt, key>::finished()
{
    return elts.finished();
}

template <class elt, class key> bool search_tree<elt, key>::next()
{
    return elts.next();
}

template <class elt, class key> elt search_tree<elt, key>::current()
{
    return elts.current();
}
```

```
template <class elt, class key> int search_tree<elt, key>::index()
{
    return elts.index();
}
```

12.1.4 Content Operations

Attributes are those of the underlying binary tree. No **Combine** or **Compare** operations are shown here, although they could be coded directly using **Traversal** operations over the trees involved.

```
template <class elt, class key> struct search_tree
{
    // . . .
    // Attributes
    bool empty();
    bool full();
    int size();
    int maxdepth();
};
```

```
/* Attributes */

template <class elt, class key> bool search_tree<elt, key>::empty()
{
    return elts.empty();
}

template <class elt, class key> bool search_tree<elt, key>::full()
{
    return FALSE;
}

template <class elt, class key> int search_tree<elt, key>::size()
{
    return elts.size();
}

template <class elt, class key> int search_tree<elt, key>::maxdepth()
{
    return elts.maxdepth();
}
```

12.1.5 Support Operations

As with tables, there are no separate **Process** operations: **Search** and **Sort** have been absorbed into the **Access** and **Modify** operations, and others (like **Reverse**) don't apply here.

Copy

```
template <class elt, class key> struct search_tree
{
    // . . .
    // Copy
    search_tree(search_tree<elt, key>&);
    search_tree<elt, key>& operator=(search_tree<elt, key>&);
};
```

```
/* Copy */

template <class elt, class key>
search_tree<elt, key>::search_tree(search_tree<elt, key>& t) : elts(t.elts)
{
}

template <class elt, class key> search_tree<elt, key>&
search_tree<elt, key>::operator=(search_tree<elt, key>& t)
{
    if (this == &t) return *this;        // assignment to self!

    elts = t.elts;

    return *this;
}
```

Output

As usual, **Output** involves traversing the tree, printing out its elements. As with the table implementations of Chapter 12, each element will be printed on a separate line, preceded by its key.

```
template <class elt, class key> struct search_tree
{
    // . . .
    // Output
    static int keywidth;
    // min number of spaces to be used printing key; user can set
    friend ostream& operator<<(ostream&, search_tree<elt, key>&);
    void show(ostream&, char* prefix = 0, int tabsize = 4);
};
```

```
/* Output */

template <class elt, class key> int search_tree<elt, key>::keywidth = 24;
// This is just an initialization - user can reset

template <class elt, class key>
ostream& operator<<(ostream& strm, search_tree<elt, key>& t)
{
    t.reset();
    while (t.next())
        {
            long curpos = strm.tellp();
            strm << '\t' << get_key(*t.current());

            long wdth = strm.tellp() - curpos;
            spaces(max(1, t.keywidth - wdth), strm);
            strm << *t.current() << '\n';
        }

    return strm;
}

template <class elt, class key>
void search_tree<elt, key>::show(ostream& strm, char* prefix, int tabsize)
{
    elts.show(strm, prefix, tabsize);
}
```

12.2 Balanced Search Trees

Search trees are normally quite efficient. Lookup in a search tree is much like the binary search of a sorted table: at each decision point, half the remaining tree is eliminated. Thus, search time should be on the order of the base two logarithm of the number of elements in the tree. Ideally, search trees combine the flexibility of linked structures with the power of binary search, which normally requires an inflexible linear structure.

12.2.1 Unbalanced Searching

However, in a search tree, the decision to go left or right is a *structural* one, not an arithmetical one, made with no knowledge of what the rest of the tree looks like in the chosen direction. The sizes of the two subtrees depend on their previous pattern of growth, which depends in turn on the order in which elements have been added to the tree. Uneven growth makes worst-case searches take longer, since the tree ends up deeper than is theoretically necessary to store the given number of elements.

Consider the search tree of Figure 12.3 on page 412, repeated here for convenience as Figure 12.7. That tree was constructed by adding elements with month name keys in

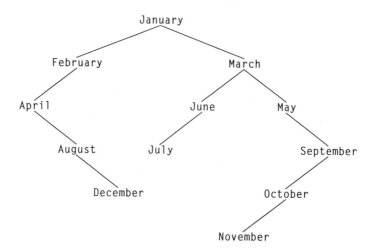

Figure 12.7   Search Tree of Months Added in Calendar Order

calendar order. Twelve elements can be stored in a binary tree whose maximum depth is three, so finding one should require no more than four comparisons. (The root is at depth 0.) Yet, in the tree of Figure 12.7, it would take 6 comparisons to locate November.

Figure 12.8 shows what happens if we add the elements in alphabetical order of their month names. Now it can take as many as 12 comparisons to find an entry! In the worst case, a search tree degenerates into a linked list, and a search can end up examining every node in the tree. Strangely enough, the worst case for a search tree arises when elements are added in the order defined by their keys, or the reverse of that order. The price of structural sophistication is often less natural behavior!

12.2.2 Maintaining Balance

The basic idea of the search tree can be improved by organizing things so the tree stays more balanced. 'Balanced' can mean several things:

Leaf balanced: All terminal nodes appear at either depth $\mathcal{D}$ or depth $\mathcal{D}-1$, for some positive integer $\mathcal{D}$.

Almost balanced or *height balanced*: For each node of the tree, the heights of its two subtrees differ by no more than one.

Strictly balanced: For every node in the tree, the number of nodes in its left and right subtrees differ by no more than one.

To maintain a balanced tree according to any of these definitions it is necessary to consider the way insertions and deletions affect balance. If an insertion or deletion throws the tree out of balance, nodes have to be moved around to restore balance. Leaf balance turns out to be too weak a notion to produce worthwhile improvements in overall efficiency. Strict balance is too strong a criterion, since it requires examining the entire

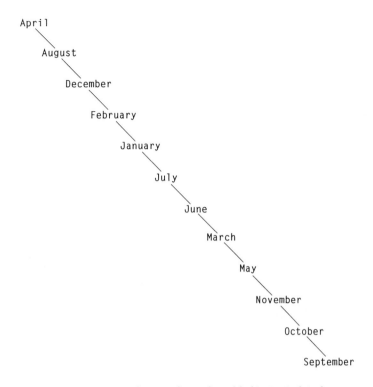

Figure 12.8 Search Tree of Months Added in Lexical Order

tree — far too much work for the search efficiency gained. Height balance turns out to be a reasonable compromise between the extra work required to maintain balance and the resulting increase in search efficiency.

The reason height balance proves feasible is that it can be maintained through only *local* changes in the neighborhood of the node that was just added or removed. Height balance allows terminal nodes to appear at varying depths in the tree, while nevertheless maintaining a reasonable overall balance. To implement *height-balanced search trees* (often called *AVL trees* after Russian mathematicians who invented them.), we define the *balance factor* of a node to be the height of its right subtree minus the height of its left subtree. The criterion for a height-balanced tree is that every node has a balance factor of −1, 0, or +1.

Suppose that at some point, every node of an existing tree has a balance factor of 0. The addition of a new node will change its parent's balance factor to either −1 or +1, according to whether it's added on the left or right, respectively. In fact, since its parent had a balance factor of 0, the parent must have either no children or two: if it had only one, it would not have had a balance factor of 0, and if it had two, it could not have accepted another. This changes the balance factor of all the parent's ancestors too, by the same amount.

Figure 12.9 shows the tree obtained by starting with an empty tree and adding the first five month names in calendar order. The resulting tree is balanced in any sense of the word. By the definition of height balance, the nodes for January, April, and May have

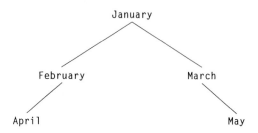

Figure 12.9   A Balanced Tree of Month Names

balance factors of 0, the balance factor of the node for February is –1, and the balance factor of the node for March is +1. Adding a new child to a node that has a balance factor of ±1 and just one child restores that parent node's balance factor to 0. (That parent's other child must have been a terminal node, otherwise there would have been more than one node in the parent's only subtree, and the absolute value of the parent's balance factor would be greater than 1.) The parent's ancestors aren't affected, because the height of the subtree of which the parent is the root is not changed by the addition of a second terminal child. Figure 12.10 shows an example: adding June has restored the balance factor for

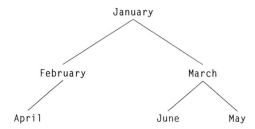

Figure 12.10   March's Balance Restored to 0 by Addition of June

March to 0 but left the balance factor for January unchanged.

More difficult cases to handle are those in which a node is added in a way that further unbalances a node with balance factor ±1. For instance, adding August to April in the tree of Figure 12.10 would make February's balance factor 2. The resulting tree is shown in Figure 12.11. Because February's balance factor is greater than 1, that tree is no longer balanced, and nodes will have to be rearranged to restore the tree's balance.

In this example, the unbalance is close to where the new node was added, so the situation is relatively easy to see. Sometimes, however, the unbalance occurs further up within the tree, a situation that's harder to visualize. We'll later look at an example (Figure 12.17 on page 426) where adding a node to a terminal node leaves the (formerly) terminal node, its parent, and its grandparent with balance factors of 1, but changes the balance factor of its terminal node's great-grandparent, which happens to be the root, from 1 to 2. Though internal unbalances are more difficult to visualize, the actions performed to restore balance in such situations turn out to be essentially the same as for unbalance near the bottom of the tree.

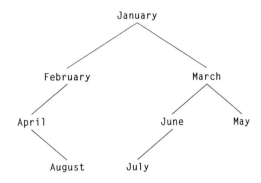

Figure 12.11   The Month Tree Unbalanced at February

Whenever some node's balance factor becomes ±2 as a result of an addition, nodes must be shifted around to restore balance. Fortunately, there are only four generic cases to consider, and they form symmetric pairs, so really there are only two different kinds of rebalancing maneuvers to understand. Rebalancing is accomplished by rearranging three nodes relative to each other: the new node, its parent, and its grandparent. The four cases and their remedies — often referred to as *LL, LR, RL,* and *RR* — are illustrated schematically in Figure 12.12.

The rebalancing actions are usually described as a *rotation*, corresponding to the way the nodes change position relative to each other in diagrams like those in Figure 12.12. The label for each kind of rebalancing indicates the directions taken (left or right) to arrive at the new node's location. *LR*, for instance, means that starting at the node that just became unbalanced, the new node was added to the *left* subtree as its *right* child. *LL* and *RR* are symmetric to each other, as are *LR* and *RL*.

Rebalancing is accomplished simply by changing a few pointers, so it is not expensive. For instance, LL rotation is performed as follows. Calling (a pointer to) the newly unbalanced node gpar (for 'grandparent'), (a pointer to) the new node nd, and (a pointer to) the new node's parent par, we have the following steps.

```
gpar->setLeft(NULL);
par->setRight(gpar);
```

LR rotation is more intricate. Using the same terminology for the nodes involved, its steps are as follows.

```
gpar->setLeft(NULL);
par->setRight(NULL);
nd->setLeft(par);
nd->setRight(gpar);
```

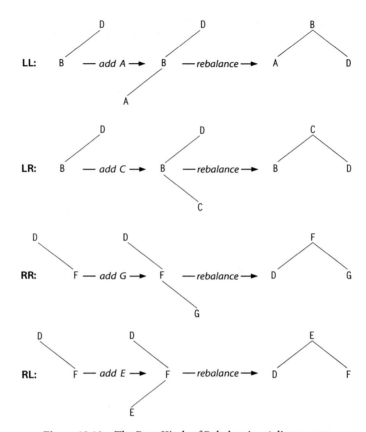

Figure 12.12   The Four Kinds of Rebalancing Adjustments

Let's continue adding month names to the tree and see what happens. The first step is to rebalance the tree of Figure 12.11 on page 423 by performing an LR rotation. (In the symbols of Figure 12.12, 'D' is February, 'B' is April, and 'C' is August.) Figure 12.13 shows the result.

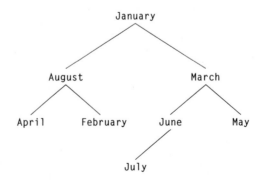

Figure 12.13   The Month Tree Rebalanced by an LR Rotation at February

Next, September may be added without unbalancing the tree. However, October unbalances May, as shown in Figure.12.14 Performing a RL rotation produces the tree in

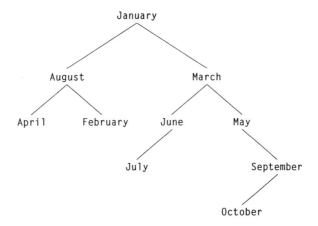

Figure 12.14   The Month Tree Unbalanced at May

Figure 12.15, in which balance has been restored to all nodes.

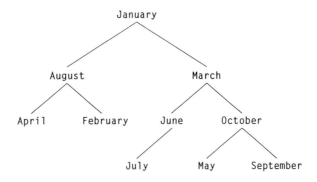

Figure 12.15   The Month Tree Rebalanced by an RL Rotation at May

12.2.3 Rebalancing Further Up in the Tree

Although the basic idea of rebalancing is straightforward, the details make it seem quite complicated. Unfortunately, rebalancing is even more intricate than the discussion to this point indicates. Rotations have been described as if they involved isolated nodes, but nodes further up the tree are affected too. Note that in all four kinds of rotation, gpar moves down one level in the tree, becoming a terminal node. This affects gpar's parent, which will have to replace gpar with the node that took its place.

This involves a further pointer change beyond those described for the rotations. The situation is slightly complicated by needing to know whether gpar was on the left or right side of its parent. If we let `left` be a Boolean indicating whether or not `gpar` was the left child of its parent, then we need to add the following step to LL rotation:

```
if (left)
    gpar->parent->setLeft(par);
else
    gpar->parent->setRight(par);
```

and similarly to LR rotation, with corresponding changes made to RR and RL rotations:

```
if (left)
    gpar->parent->setLeft(nd);
else
    gpar->parent->setRight(nd);
```

This is still not enough. Further complications arise when the unbalance develops further up the tree than at the grandparent of the new node. Also, sometimes `par` already had a child before the new one was added. Consider the tree at the top of Figure 12.16,

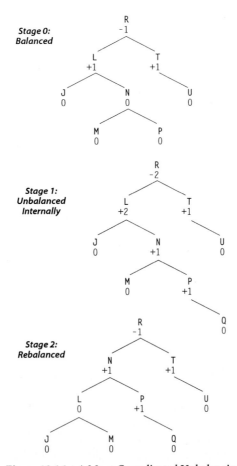

Figure 12.16   A More Complicated Unbalancing

which shows single-letter keys and balance factors for nodes. When node Q is added to this tree, the following balance factors change in sequence:

```
P:   0  →  +1
N:   0  →  +1
L:  +1 →  +2
R:  -1 →  -2
```

The result is shown in the diagram's middle tree. The tree has become unbalanced at L, and an RR rebalancing is needed. This will make N the left child of R, and L the left child of N. However, N already had a left child M — what happens to that node? As the diagram shows, M must become the right successor of L when L is moved. The bottom tree of the diagram is the final result. Note that once balance is restored at the lowest unbalanced node it is automatically restored at all higher-level unbalanced nodes.

Returning to the tree of month names, adding November produces the tree shown in Figure 12.17. Adding November to May does not unbalance May, nor does it unbalance

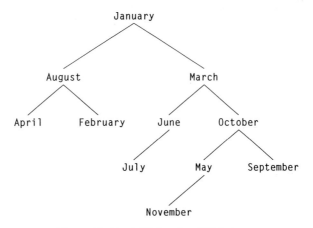

Figure 12.17   A Higher-Level Unbalance

October, or even March, but it does unbalance January! That node's left subtree has a depth of 2, but now its right subtree has a depth of 4, so its balance factor is now +2. An RR rotation is necessary to restore balance. Figure 12.18 shows the result of performing

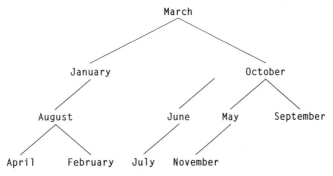

Figure 12.18   The Tree Partially Rebalanced by an RR Rotation

the RR rotation. There's a problem! An RR rotation makes the top node the middle node's left child and elevates the top node. But in this case, the top node — March — already had a left child! June and its child July have been orphaned!

Where can the orphaned subtree be attached? Notice that when the parent-child relationship between January and March was reversed, January lost its right subtree. It turns out that January right is just the place to attach the orphaned subtree. Figure 12.19 shows the result. The tree is once again balanced, and December can be added without

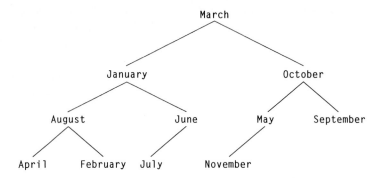

Figure 12.19 The Rebalance Completed by Attaching June to January

further incident. Figure 12.20 shows the final tree, with all 12 month names. It's not

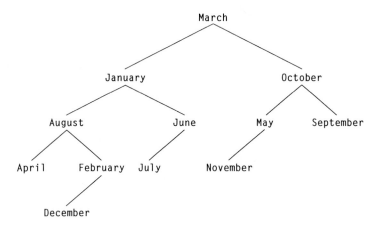

Figure 12.20 The Final Month Tree

strictly balanced, but it's a considerable improvement over the unbalanced search tree.

12.2.4 Implementation

The code for a balanced tree is just like the code for an ordinary search tree, with two differences. First, the representation must be changed slightly to accommodate balance factors. In a search tree, the underlying binary tree holds elements. Here, the underlying binary tree holds pointers to an auxiliary structure, called `balanced_element`, that holds an element and a balance factor. Therefore, all the calls to `getElt` have to also call another function to extract the element out of the `balanced_element` that `getElt` returns. That function is also named `getElt`, consistent with the conventions used for all the code in the book. The other difference is that **Modify** operations must be changed to maintain balance.

The Auxiliary Structure

The declaration of `balanced_element` and the definitions of its functions are quite simple, as the structure doesn't do anything except hold an element and manage a balance factor. All the decisions and manipulations involving balance factors are handled by the `balanced_tree` functions.

```
template <class elt> struct balanced_element
{
  private:

    elt elem;
    int balance;

  public:

    balanced_element(elt);
    ~balanced_element();

    elt& getElt();
    void setElt(elt);

    int getBalance();
    int operator++();
    int operator--();

    friend order compare(balanced_element<elt>&, balanced_element<elt>&);
    friend bool equal(balanced_element<elt>&, balanced_element<elt>&);
    friend oaastream& operator<<(ostream&, balanced_element<elt>&);
};
```

```
/* Balanced Tree Element -- packages an element with a balance factor */

template <class elt> balanced_element<elt>::balanced_element(elt e) :
        elem(e), balance(0)
{
}

template <class elt> balanced_element<elt>::~balanced_element()
{
}
```

```cpp
template <class elt> elt& balanced_element<elt>::getElt()
{
    return elem;
}

template <class elt> void balanced_element<elt>::setElt(elt e)
{
    elem = e;
}

template <class elt> balanced_element<elt>::getBalance()
{
    return balance;
}

template <class elt> int balanced_element<elt>::operator++()
{
    assert(-2 <= balance && balance <= 1);
    // may be called on a node being rebalanced with bal = -2
    return ++balance;
}

template <class elt> int balanced_element<elt>::operator--()
{
    assert(-1 <= balance && balance <= 2);
    // may be called on a node being rebalanced with bal = +2
    return --balance;
}

template <class elt>
bool equal(balanced_element<elt>& be1, balanced_element<elt>& be2)
{
    return equal(*be1.getElt(), *be2.getElt());
}

template <class elt>
order compare(balanced_element<elt>& be1, balanced_element<elt>& be2)
{
    return compare(*be1.getElt(), *be2.getElt());
}

template <class elt>
ostream& operator<<(ostream& strm, balanced_element<elt>& be)
{
    if (be.balance > 0)
        strm << "(+";
    else if (be.balance < 0)
        strm << "(";
    else strm << "( ";

    return strm << be.balance << ") " << get_key(*be.getElt());
}
```

Add

Only the operations implementing **Add** will be shown here. **Remove**, combining the complexities of search tree **Remove** with the complexities of balanced tree **Add**, is left to Exercise 6 lest it swamp this part of the chapter. There's little to be gained looking at definitions of the other functions, since they are so similar to the code of the ordinary search tree module. One thing worth noting, though, is that **Traversal** produces the elements in the same order as if the tree were not balanced: the rules of search trees determine the resulting traversal order, though the internal structure of the tree will vary depending on the order of the elements and whether balance is being maintained.

The usual `add` function is supported by three sets of private functions. One set implements the various rotations. Another set propagates balance changes. A third set manages the actual addition of the element according to whether it belongs at, to the left, or to the right of the node located by a call to `lookup_pos`.

```
#define blink binary_tree_node<balanced_element<elt>*>*   // for convenience

template <class elt, class key> struct balanced_tree
{
  private:
    binary_tree<balanced_element<elt>*> elts;
    // . . .
    // Add
    void addEqual(elt, blink, action dup_action);
    void addLeft(elt, blink);
    void addRight(elt, blink);
    void decrementBalance(blink);
    void incrementBalance(blink);
    void LLrotate(blink);
    void LRrotate(blink);
    void RRrotate(blink);
    void RLrotate(blink);

  public:
    void add(elt, action dup_action = IGNORE);
    balanced_tree<elt, key>& operator+=(elt);
};
```

The implementation of `add` is essentially the same as it was in the ordinary search tree module. It searches the tree to determine where the new element belongs; then it hands off the job of actually adding the element to `addLeft`, `addEqual`, or `addRight`.

```
/* Modify */

template <class elt, class key>
void balanced_tree<elt, key>::add(elt e, action dup_action)
{
    blink cur = elts.getRootNode();
    if (0 == cur->getElt())
```

```
                        {
                            cur->setElt(new balanced_element<elt>(e));
                            return;
                        }
            key& k = get_key(*e);

            while (TRUE)
                switch (compare(k, get_key(*cur->getElt()->getElt())))
                {
                  case EQUAL:
                    addEqual(e, cur, dup_action)
                    return;

                  case BEFORE:
                    if (cur->hasLeft())
                        {
                            cur = cur->getLeft();
                            break;
                        }
                    else
                        {
                            addLeft(e, cur);
                            return;
                        }

                  case AFTER:
                    if (cur->hasRight())
                        {
                            cur = cur->getRight();
                            break;
                        }
                    else
                        {
                            addRight(e, cur);
                            return;
                        }

                  case NO_ORDER:
                    error("[balanced_tree::add] can't compare keys");
                    break;
                }
}

template <class elt, class key>
balanced_tree<elt, key>& balanced_tree<elt, key>::operator+=(elt e)
{
    add(e);

    return *this;
}
```

The definition of addEqual is unchanged from the regular search tree module, except for having to call setElt to set the element of the balanced_element returned by the node's getElt. The definitions of addLeft and addRight call the corresponding functions for the binary node to which the new node will be added. In the regular search tree module, that's all that was required, so no separate functions were defined. Here, these functions also have to call decrementBalance or incrementBalance respectively.

```
/* Add: addLeft, addEqual, and addRight private functions */

template <class elt, class key>
void balanced_tree<elt, key>::addEqual(elt e, blink cur, action dup_action)
{
    switch (dup_action)
        {
          case WARN:
            warning("[balanced_tree::add] the search tree "
                    "already contains an elt with the same key");
            /* no break */
          case IGNORE:
          case REPLACE:
            cur->getElt()->setElt(e);
            return;

          case ERROR:
            error("[balanced_tree::add] the search tree "
                    "already contains an elt with the same key");
        }
}

template <class elt, class key>
void balanced_tree<elt, key>::addLeft(elt e, blink cur)
{
    cur->addLeft(new balanced_element<elt>(e));
    decrementBalance(cur);
}

template <class elt, class key>
void balanced_tree<elt, key>::addRight(elt e, blink cur)
{
    cur->addRight(new balanced_element<elt>(e));
    incrementBalance(cur);
}
```

The definitions of decrementBalance and incrementBalance change the balance factors, invoke a rebalancing function when necessary, and propagate changes up the tree. We'll show decrementBalance only — the definition of incrementBalance is identical with lefts and rights and pluses and minuses switched.

```
template <class elt, class key>
void balanced_tree<elt, key>::decrementBalance(blink cur)
{
    switch(--(*cur->getElt()))          // decrement balance factor
        {
```

```
      case 0:                              // do nothing
        break;

      case -1:                             // tell parent
        if (cur->getParent())              // stop at root
            if (cur == cur->getParent()->getLeft())
                decrementBalance(cur->getParent());
            else
                incrementBalance(cur->getParent());
        break;

      case -2:
        // rotate.  Happens only on propagation up --
        // never on the first increment due to a new leaf
        if (cur->getLeft()->getElt()->getBalance() < 0)
            LLrotate(cur);
        else
            LRrotate(cur);
        break;

      default:
        internal_error("[balanced_tree::decrementBalance] "
                       "illegal balance factor");
    }
}
```

Finally, rotations are performed by `LLrotate`, `LRrotate`, `RRrotate`, and `RLrotate`. Only the first two are shown here. As with `decrementBalance` and `incrementBalance` the other two are symmetrical with the ones shown. There's not much one can say about this intricate code other than that it directly implements the rotations shown in Figure 12.12 on page 424 by moving pointers around. No new nodes are created, and no old ones are destroyed: these are just rearrangements of existing nodes.

```
template <class elt, class key>
void balanced_tree<elt, key>::LLrotate(blink cur)
{
    blink par = cur->getParent();
    blink child = cur->getLeft();

    // in an immediate (not propagated) unbalance child->right will be 0
    ++(*cur->getElt());                    // -> -1
    ++(*cur->getElt());                    // -> 0
    ++(*child->getElt());                  // -> 0

    // replace cur with child in par
    if (par)
        {
            cur->setLeft(child->getRight());
            child->setRight(cur);
            if (cur == par->getLeft())
                par->setLeft(child);
            else
```

```
                        par->setRight(child);
        }
    else        // cur is the root;
        {       // handle specially since root is not pointer
            balanced_element<elt>* tempelt = cur->getElt();
            cur->setElt(child->getElt());
            child->setElt(tempelt);

            cur->setLeft(child->getLeft());
            child->setLeft(child->getRight());

            child->setRight(cur->getRight());
            cur->setRight(child);
        }
}

template <class elt, class key>
void balanced_tree<elt, key>::LRrotate(blink cur)
{
    blink par = cur->getParent();
    blink child = cur->getLeft();
    blink gchild = child->getRight();

    // in an immediate (not propagated) unbalance gchild->left and
    // ->right will be 0; in an internal unbalance, one will not be 0.
    ++(*cur->getElt());   // -> -1
    ++(*cur->getElt());   // -> 0
    --(*child->getElt()); // -> 0
    child->setRight(gchild->getLeft());

    // replace cur with grandchild in par
    if (par)
        {
            cur->setLeft(gchild->getRight());
            gchild->setLeft(child);
            gchild->setRight(cur);
            if (cur == par->getLeft())
                par->setLeft(gchild);
            else
                par->setRight(gchild);
        }
    else        // cur is the root;
        {       // handle specially since root is not pointer
            balanced_element<elt>* tempelt = cur->getElt();
            cur->setElt(gchild->getElt());
            gchild->setElt(tempelt);

            gchild->setLeft(gchild->getRight());
            assert(child == cur->getLeft());

            gchild->setRight(cur->getRight());
            cur->setRight(gchild);
        }
}
```

12.3 B-Trees

B-trees are a clever representation with important applications and a rich literature. There are many variations; we'll look at only the basic form. B-trees are particularly useful for storing large numbers of disk-based records, as in databases, but they are useful for in-memory storage as well.

Each node of a B-tree holds several elements as well as several pointers to other nodes. In file-based applications, nodes are sized so that they each occupy a single unit of disk memory (block, page, etc.) to make optimal use of each disk access, since getting information from disk is far slower than getting it from the computer's memory. The way B-trees grow keeps the tree relatively balanced and maintains *locality* — that is, records near each other as ordered by their keys end up near each other in the tree, ideally in the same node.

B-tree growth exhibits some unusual patterns. Leaf nodes are all at the same level of the tree, so the trees have an orderly shape. B-trees grow deeper at the root instead of at the leaves. Finally, the growth process ensures that every node is at least half full.

The maneuvers involved in manipulating B-trees are quite similar to those for balanced trees, but complicated by their being more than one element in each node. Although the code ends up being too complicated to be worth showing and explaining in the text, a full implementation is contained in the B-tree directory of the code files accompanying this book. We'll discuss here only representation and the operations that are significantly different from those of balanced trees: **Access**, **Add**, and **Remove**.

12.3.1 Representation

The implementation shown here assumes in-memory storage. Some details change when B-trees are represented on disk. In particular, disk block numbers replace pointers to nodes. For a disk-based B-tree, the size of its nodes is usually determined by how many child pointers and elements can fit into a disk block or page. Also, disk-based B-tree nodes would typically store actual elements, rather than pointers to elements. We won't consider disk-based B-trees any further, but they do play central roles in a variety of file-based systems, including databases.

Structurally, B-trees can be viewed as n-ary trees in which each node has a *list* of elements instead of just one. We therefore can use the tree node from the n-ary tree module. Each node will each hold a (pointer to) a sequential list of elements. The *order* of a B-tree is the number of successors each node can have, so that will be the tree node's branching factor (number of children). Each node's list will contain up to *order*–1 elements. That number will be provided as an argument to the sequential list constructor. The n-ary tree representation stored a root node directly, but here we must store a pointer for reasons that will soon become apparent.

```
template <class elt, class key> struct btree
{
  private:
    // Representation
    tree_node<seq_list<elt>*>* root;
    // . . .
};
```

B-trees are an extension of the basic idea underlying search trees. Within a node's list of elements, the elements are stored in order of their key field, as in a sorted table. All the elements of the first subtree are before the list's first element, according to the ordering defined by their key type. All the elements of the second subtree come between the first and second elements of the list, and so on. All the elements of the last subtree belong after the last element of the list. The list of elements stored at each node and the node's list of successors are structurally unrelated to each other, but conceptually they are parallel to each other — the B-tree functions manage things so that their elements correspond in the way just described.

Figure 12.21 illustrates a partially full B-tree node of order 8, showing just integer keys of its elements. All the nodes in the subtree labeled 1 will have keys less than 20, all

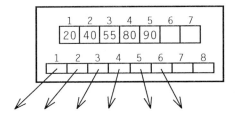

Figure 12.21   A Partially Full B-Tree Node

the nodes in subtree 2 will have keys between 20 and 40, and so on. Note that the number of subtrees is one greater than the number of elements. Corresponding to each element is a subtree of elements that come before it. In addition, there is also a subtree of elements that come after the last element.

12.3.2 Lookup

Search begins at the root node, as with all search trees. The current node's list is searched. If an object with the target key is discovered in the table, the search is over. When no match is found, the search stops at an element before or after which a new element with the specified target key would go if it were added to the list.

Because the pointers in the node's list of children correspond to the elements in the element list, the identified location in the element list also identifies one of two positions in the child list, depending on whether the key comes before or after the key of the element at the identified location. The appropriate child is made the current node and the search continues recursively. Search ends successfully when an element with the target key is found and fails when a terminal node is reached that does not contain such an element. Note that a successful search may terminate at any node in the tree, but failure can only be determined when a terminal node has been reached. Whether or not the search is successful, no backtracking occurs — a direct path is followed from the root to the node containing the target element, if there is one, or a terminal node if there isn't.

12.3.3 Add

Suppose it has been determined that the key of an element to be added to the tree follows the key of element k of the current node and precedes the key of element $k+1$, but the current node is a terminal. The new element can simply be inserted into the element list at location $k+1$. Subsequent elements in the list get shifted down to accommodate the new element. Since this node has no children, its list of children is empty and can be ignored. Figure 12.22 illustrates this situation.

insert component with key =32

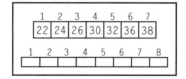

Figure 12.22   Insertion into a Terminal B-Tree

Of course, if the terminal node's element list is full, the new element can't be added to it. In this case a new node is allocated, and some reorganization occurs. To visualize this reorganization, assume the list had room for an extra element (i.e., had *size* = *order* instead of *size* = *order*–1). The following would occur to reorganize the tree:

  • Elements 1 through (*order*/2)–1 stay in the old node.
  • Elements (*order*/2)+1 through order are removed from the old node and stored in the new node.
  • The middle element, at (*order*)/2, gets moved up to (inserted into) the node's parent.

This is demonstrated in Figure 12.23. (Siblings of the old and new nodes are not shown there — just pointers to them.)

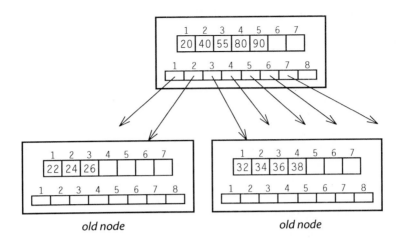

A component with key = 34 is inserted, causing the terminal node to be split; half its components are moved to a new node. Siblings of the two nodes are omitted — only the pointers to them are shown.

Figure 12.23   Insertion into a Full Terminal B-Tree Node

B-tree insertion always begins at a terminal node. If that node is full, its elements are split between it and a newly created sibling, except for the middle element, which is inserted into the terminal node's parent. If the parent is full, another split occurs, with one of its elements moving up the parent's parent. This process works its way up until a middle element is raised to a node that has room for it. The only way a node ever gets a new child is when one of its existing children is split. A surprising consequence of this is that terminal nodes always remain terminal, no matter how the tree continues to grow.

Insertion into a nonterminal (as a result of a child splitting) must also adjust the list of children, as shown in Figure 12.23. When the element moving up from an old child is inserted into the node's list of elements, a pointer to the newly created child must be inserted after the corresponding position of that list, causing subsequent elements list to move over. If the element list is full, the nonterminal must be split. The only difference between splitting a terminal and a nonterminal is that when an element of the nonterminal is moved to the newly created node, the corresponding child pointer must go with it. (In a full nonterminal node both the element list and the child list are full.)

Thus, items and children nodes are normally paired. The only time they separate is when an item is raised to a parent node in conjunction with a split. The child corresponding to the raised item becomes the first child of the newly created node. (The first child of a node has no item partner.) The new node becomes the partner of the raised item.

Eventually, the splitting process will back all the way up to the root. If the root node is full, it too must be split. However, there would be no parent to accept one of the root's items. A new root node must be created. The old root will no longer be the root, and the tree will be one level deeper — the tree grows in height at its root, not at its leaves! Unlike ordinary trees, B-trees actually replace their root nodes, demoting the old root. This is why their representation requires a *pointer* to a root node, as mentioned in Section 12.3.1 above.

The splitting procedure ensures that the root node is the only one that can ever be less than half full. More precisely, the minimum number of items in a nonroot node is (*order*–1)/2 if *order* is odd, and (*order*/2)–1 if *order* is even, as in the current example. When a new root node is created, it gets only one item, the one being raised from the old root. This relatively even distribution of objects among nodes is the central feature of B-trees and the source of their efficiency. The tree is always fairly balanced and fairly full, and therefore it stays relatively shallow. Yet, the procedure for ensuring this balance is quite minimal computationally, though somewhat complex conceptually.

Let's look at an example. We'll use month names again, adding them in calendar order to a B-tree of order 4. (To save space, we'll use just three-letter month names this time.) The root node starts out empty. Acting like a sorted table, the root can accept the first three month names without any splitting. Figure 12.24 shows the sequence of states resulting from adding the first three month names to an empty B-tree.

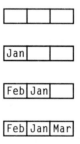

Figure 12.24   Insertion of Month Names into an Empty B-Tree

Adding Apr causes the first split. A new node is created, and the elements of the old node are redistributed. Half the elements stay in the original node, one gets elevated, and the rest go into the new node. Then, since it was the root node that got split, a new root is created to hold the elevated element. After that rearrangement, there's room in the original node for the next month — May — without any further rearrangement. Figure 12.25 shows the changes to the tree that result from adding Apr then May.

The element with key Jun would go in the right terminal node, but there's no room for it there. As a result, that node gets split, and the middle element (including the newly added one) gets elevated. In this case it happens that the new element is the one that gets elevated. Since there's room in the parent node, the elevated element is inserted there, along with a pointer to the new node. The pointer to the node that got split remains where it was, and the pointer to the new node gets inserted after it. In this case it happens that the node getting split was at the end of its parent's list of children, so the pointer to the new node gets added to the end of that list. With those changes, there is room for Jul, Aug, and Sep to be added without causing any further splitting. Figure 12.26 illustrates all this activity.

1. No room for Apr.

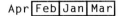

Apr Feb Jan Mar

2. Node splits; Feb moves up.

Feb

Apr   Jan Mar

3. New root node created for Feb; children linked.

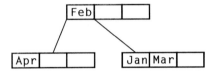

Feb

Apr   Jan Mar

4. May added.

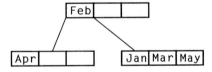

Feb

Apr   Jan Mar May

Figure 12.25   Insertion of Apr Causes the First Split

Adding Oct causes the next split, as shown in Figure 12.27. After that split Nov and Dec can be added, completing the tree. To increase the size of the tree and illustrate further details of B-tree **Add**, we'll add some more elements, this time with (three-letter) names of days as keys.

An element with key Sun causes an immediate split, since it would go in the rightmost terminal node, which is already full. That split, as Figure 12.28 shows, elevates the element with key Oct to the root. However, since the root is full, a second split is necessary, resulting in a new root node. Mon and Tue then fit in the tree, but Wed causes another split. At that point, there's room for the rest of the day names without any further splits. Figure 12.29 shows the final tree.

12.3.4 Remove

The logic of **Remove** operations resembles that of **Add**, but in reverse. Instead of splitting when they overflow, nodes are combined when one has too few elements. As stated earlier, the minimum number of elements in nonroot nodes is $(order-1)/2$ if $order$ is odd, $(order/2)-1$ if $order$ is even. Ignoring the required minimum, for a moment, removing an

1. No room for Jun.

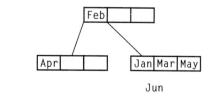

Jun

2. Node splits; Jun moves up.

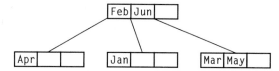

3. Jul, Aug, and Sep are added.

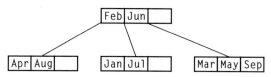

Figure 12.26   Insertion of Jun Causes Another Split

element that turns out to be in a leaf node is trivial: it is simply removed from that node's list, and there are no children to worry about. Removing an element from an internal node is similar to removing an element from a height-balanced tree.

Note that the immediate predecessor and successor of an element in a nonterminal node must be located in terminal nodes. (If the immediate predecessor was in another internal node, then that node would have a subtree containing elements that come after that predecessor, but then the predecessor would not be the immediate predecessor, since there would be other elements that come after it but before the element being removed. Likewise, if the immediate successor was in an internal node, then that node would have a subtree containing elements that come before that successor.)

Because the immediate predecessor and successor are in terminal nodes, either one of them can be moved from its terminal node to take the place of the element being removed, as in height-balance removal. Figure 12.30 shows the result of removing Sat and Sun from the finished tree of Figure 12.29. Thu, the immediate successor of Sun, is removed from its node to replace the element whose key was Sun.

Thus, even when the element being removed is in a nonterminal node, some element ends up being removed from a terminal node. If an element is removed from a terminal node that has only the minimum number of elements allowable, it is necessary to move an element from another terminal node to maintain the required minimum. Suppose the terminal node is the nth child of its parent, for $n > 1$. The removed element's im-

1. No room for Oct.

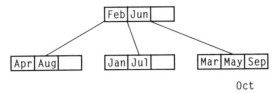

2. Node splits; May *moves up.*

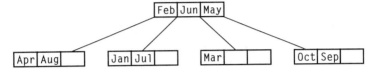

3. Nov *and* Dec *are added.*

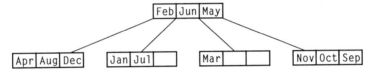

Figure 12.27   Insertion of Oct Causes the Next Split

mediate predecessor is at position $n-1$ in the parent node's successor list. The predecessor's immediate predecessor must be the last element of the terminal node's sibling immediately to its left.

If that sibling has more than the required minimum number of nodes, the predecessor can be moved from the parent down to the terminal node, and the predecessor's predecessor can be moved up from the left sibling to take the predecessor's place. Similarly, if the terminal node is n^{th} child of its parent, for $n > order$, and the sibling immediately to its right has more than the required minimum number of nodes, the nth element of the terminal's parent can be moved down to the terminal, with the first element of the terminal's right sibling taking its place.

Figure 12.31 illustrates this with the removal of Sep: Thu is moved down from the parent, and Tue moved up from the right sibling to take its place. It would also work to move Oct from the parent and move Nov from the left sibling to take its place, as shown by the removal of Thu in the last step in that figure.

If none of the terminal node's siblings has more than the required number of elements, one of the siblings can be combined with the terminal node. (The elements of the right-most of the two nodes get moved to the other node, and the right-most node of the pair gets deleted or recycled.) In that case, the element in the parent between the two terminal nodes gets moved down into the combined node and the child pointer that follows it gets removed from the children list.

1. No room for Sun.

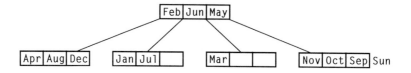

2. Node splits; Oct moves up, but there's no room in the parent.

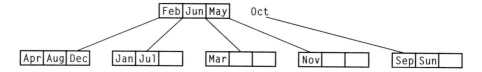

3. Root splits; Jun moves up.

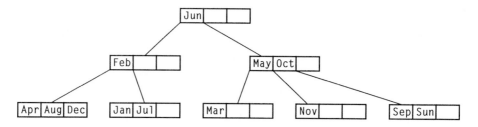

3. Mon and Tue are added.

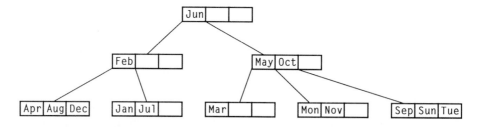

Figure 12.28   Insertion of Sun Causes Two Splits

There is always going to be enough room for the elements of both terminals plus the element from the parent, because the terminal from which the element was removed has less than the required minimum, and its sibling has exactly the required minimum. In fact, there will always be room for another element in the combined nodes even after the parent element has been moved down. (Twice the minimum is either *order*–1, if the order

1. No room for Wed.

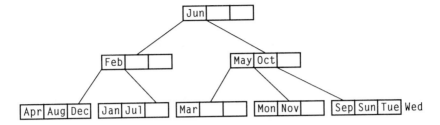

2. Node splits; Sun moves up.

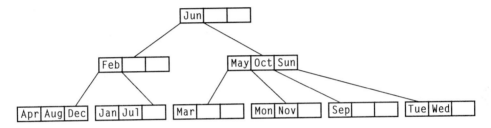

3. Thu, Fri, and Sat are added.

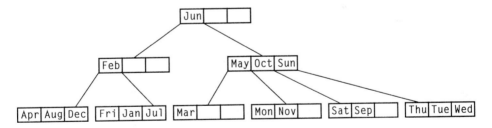

Figure 12.29   Insertion of Wed Causes the Final Split

is odd, or *order*–2 if the order is even. Therefore, there's always room for the parent, and since the node from which the element was removed has one *less* than the minimum, there's room for one or two more elements, depending on whether the order is odd or even.)

Figure 12.32 shows how this works when Mon is removed. When the order of the tree is 3 or 4, as in this case, the minimum number of elements a node may have is one, so the only nodes that get merged are empty ones without a sibling that has more than one element. In this example, the empty node is merged with the sibling to its right, but it also

0. Starting with the finished tree.

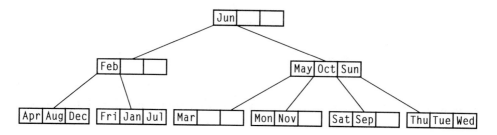

1. Sat is removed.

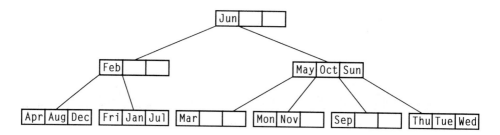

2. Sun is removed; Thu takes its place.

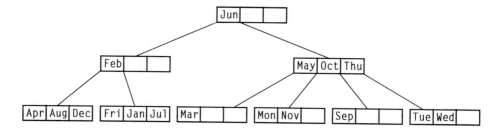

Figure 12.30   Simple Removal of Sat and Sun

could have been merged with its left sibling. (Obviously, the implementation of the algorithm would have to be coded to choose one or the other.)

Finally, if moving the parent down into the merged node leaves the parent node with too few nodes, the process repeats at the next level up. This continues until either a rearrangement leaves all nodes involved with a sufficient number of elements or the last element has been moved down from the root. The latter case can occur only when the root has exactly one element and both its children have the minimum number of elements.

1. Removing Sep leaves a terminal node with too few elements.

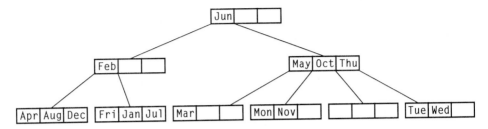

2. Thu is moved down from the parent node and Tue moved up to take its place.

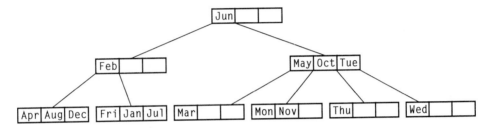

3. Removing Thu again leaves the terminal node with too few elements; this time, predecessors are 'rotated': Oct is moved down from the parent node and Nov moved up to take its place.

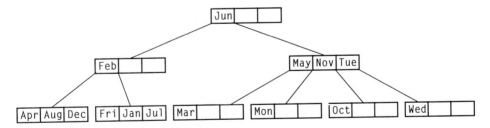

Figure 12.31   Fixing a Terminal Node with Too Few Elements

(An element may get moved from the root in other situations, but then another element would take its place. The only time an element is removed from a parent without another element being elevated to take its place is when two children are merged.) In that case, the root is left with no elements and one child. The child becomes the new root, and the root node is deleted or recycled.

1. Removing Mon leaves a terminal node with too few elements.

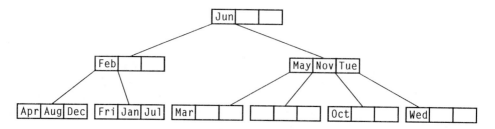

2. The terminal node is combined with a sibling, and Nov, the parent between them, moved down.

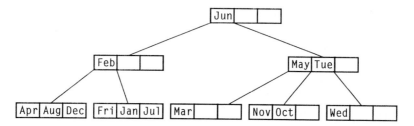

Figure 12.32   A Removal May Require Merging Two Nodes

12.4 EXERCISES

1. Show a best-case search tree for elements having as keys the names of the days of the week.
   (a) How many such trees are there?
   (b) Why?
   (c) Can you describe a procedure for ordering insertions into an initially empty search tree to achieve maximum balance?

2. Manually simulate the process of adding elements with the following keys to an initially empty B-tree:

   > 4 12 10 14 60 62 64 6 8 20 22 24 70 74 72 52 54 50 80 82 84
   > 92 94 90 30 32 34 42 44 40 36 38 46 48 75

3. The implementation of search tree **Remove** sometimes needs to find the node with the inorder successor of the node being deleted (cf. do_remove_both, page 415).
   (a) Do you think that bit of functionality should be pulled out as a separate, publicly available function?
   (b) Can you give an example or two of how it might be useful in a particular application you can imagine?
   (c) If it were a separate function, what kind of fundamental operation would it be?

4. Do Chapter 11's Exercise 11 on page 401 for search trees, balanced trees, and B-trees. Compare the numbers you obtained to each other and to those for the tables.

5. In the discussion of the functions implementing search tree **Remove** the claim was made that the code was simplified by removing the node of the element taking the removed element's place instead of removing the removed element's node. (That discussion is found on page 414.) The latter is certainly a more natural approach.

   (a) Recode the four functions so that they remove the node of the element being removed. This approach requires detaching and reattaching various subtrees that might be affected —the subtrees of the node being removed and the subtrees of the one taking its place — as well as the parent of the one being removed (if it has one — that node might be the root!). It might help to consult one or more other data structure textbooks to see the code they present for removing an element from a search tree. Your code may use any functions of the search tree module — private or public — but only the public functions provided by the binary tree and binary tree node module.

   (b) Test your code by using the `tst.C` program in the search tree directory where the book's code is found. It makes a tree out of the names of fruits used to illustrate tables in Chapter 11, then deletes them in an order that purports to test the various possible removal situations. This program goes beyond just the four cases based on the number of subtrees by considering various further combinations for the case where both subtrees are present based on whether or not the element being deleted is at the root, whether or not the element taking its place has a right subtree, and even whether or not the inorder successor of the element being deleted is its right child rather than something down the left side of its right child's left subtree.

   (c) If you do consult other textbooks, you might find it interesting to try to compare the code they show to the code shown here in terms of factors that affect readability.

6. Implement the **Remove** operations for the balanced tree, following the lead of the **Remove** operations of the ordinary search tree and the **Add** operations of the balanced tree.

7. The B-tree implementation discussed here and included with the on-disk code uses a sequential list to hold each node's elements. However, it uses it to maintain the elements in order. Since that's what a sorted table does, isn't this duplicating some of the work that went into implementing the sorted table module? Shouldn't the nodes contain sorted tables of elements, not lists?

   (a) Change the implementation to use sorted tables.

   (b) What advantages or disadvantages of one approach over the other did you discover?

   (c) Is a sorted table appropriate for this implementation, or should it be left using a sequential list? Explain.

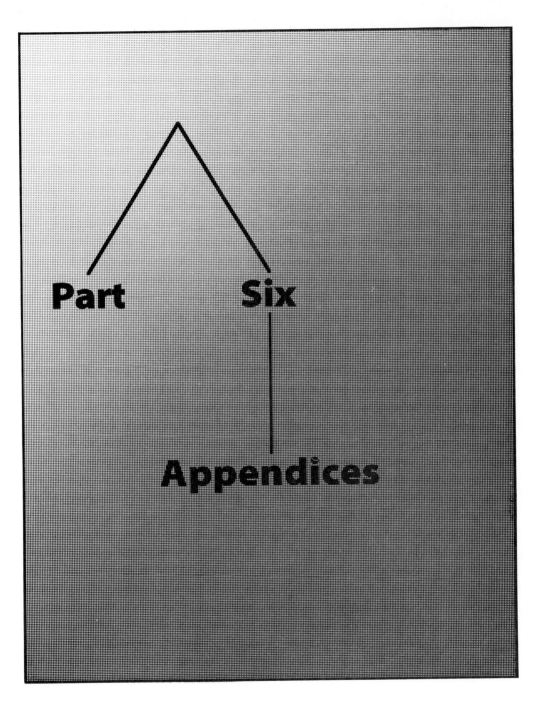

Part Six

Appendices

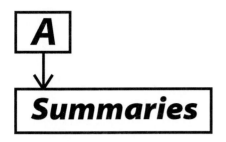

A

Summaries

A.1 Fundamental Operations

Lifetime	Traversal	Content	Support
Create/Destroy	Foreach	Attributes	Copy
Initialize/Finalize	Collect	Compare	Process
Access/Modify	Generate	Combine	Input/Output

Table 9   Summary of Fundamental Operation Categories

Common Variations

Modify	**Add** (+=), **Remove** (-=), **Exchange, Replace,** `clear`
Iterate	**Foreach, Collect, Merge, Sum; Traversal** operations
Attributes	`empty`, `full`, `size`
Compare	`equal` (==, !=), `compare` (==, !=, <, <=, >, >=)
Combine	+, -, ⋆
Copy	copy constructor, copy assignment, **Reverse, SubCollection**
Process	**Sort, Search**
Output	unformatted, formatted, graphical, external storage

A.2 Fundamental Structures

Storage	Homogeneous?	Access
Array	yes	direct
Record	no	direct
Stream	yes	sequential

Table 10 Kinds of Storage Structures

State	Next Task
Stack	newest
Queue	oldest
Priority Queue	best

Table 11 Kinds of State Structures

Linked	Predecessors	Successors
List	1	1
Tree	1	1 or more
Graph	1 or more	1 or more

Table 12 Kinds of Linked Structures

Association	Based On
Table	lists or arrays
Search Tree	trees or tree nodes

Table 13 Kinds of Association Structures

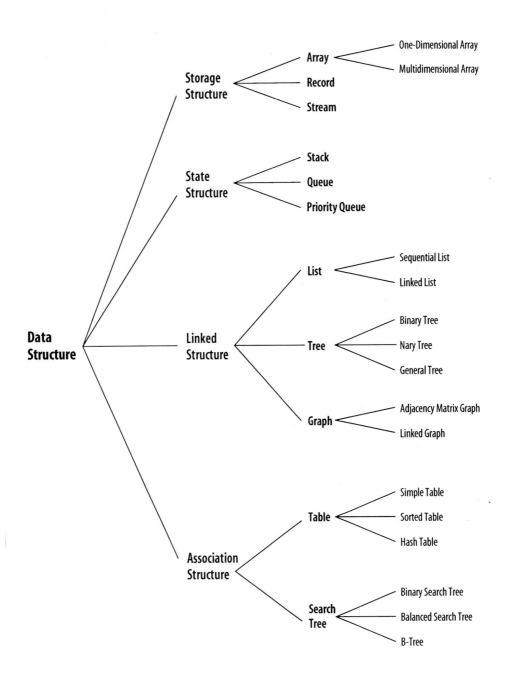

Figure A.1   A Taxonomy of the Data Structures Discussed in This Book

Review of C Data Types

This Appendix provides a quick review of some C basics that are particularly important for understanding C++. The emphasis is on scoping and types, especially pointers. This book assumes general knowledge of C, so procedural aspects such as expression, statements, and functions won't be reviewed here. However, even people with substantial experience writing C programs are often unclear about important aspects of C's type system. Many details that are relatively unimportant in ordinary C programming become quite important in C++, so programmers moving to C++ are often confronted with new ideas or information that turn out to have been in C all along, though generally ignored.

With very few exceptions, everything about C data types is also true in C++. The few exceptions are noted.

B.1 Basics

B.1.1 Primitive Types

All types in C are ultimately built from primitive types. The basic data types in C are as follows.

char	a single byte, usually used to hold a character
int	an integer
float	a "single-precision" floating-point number
double	a "double-precision" floating-point number

A *qualifier* is a reserved word that modifies types. To specify integers of different size, one of the qualifiers long or short are used. An example would be long int. It is not necessary to include the int — a long is the same as a long int. Although the type char is usually used to hold characters, it may be used as a shorter short.

Except for char, which is always 1 byte, the language does not specify any particular size for these fundamental types. The intention is that ints are the size that is natural for the host hardware, typically either 16 or 32 bits, and that if possible, short and long are different sizes. The only constraint imposed by the language is that

```
sizeof(char) ≤ sizeof(short) ≤ sizeof(int) ≤ sizeof(long)
```

An integral type may be modified by signed or unsigned to indicate whether or not it includes negative numbers.

B.1.2 Constants

Constants include numbers, characters, and strings (sequences of characters). An integer constant beginning with a 0 is an octal number, and an integer beginning with 0x is hexadecimal. A constant with a decimal point is a double, unless followed by an F (upper- or lowercase), in which case it is a float. Numeric constants may be followed by an L to indicate long. Following are some examples of constants.

```
12                          /* decimal */
012                         /* octal */
0x12                        /* hexadecimal */
12u                         /* unsigned decimal */
12L                         /* signed long decimal */
'a'                         /* character */
"string"                    /* string */
```

Nonprinting characters are indicated with special *escape* sequences. The most common are

```
'\n'                        /* new line */
'\t'                        /* tab */
'\0'                        /* null */
```

Other nonprinting characters may be specified by their octal or hexadecimal byte value, for example:

```
'\007'                      /* ASCII BEL */
'\xFF'                      /* ASCII DEL */
```

Finally, there are *enumeration constants*. These are lists of constant values specified in a program using the reserved word enum, as in the following example.

```
enum Boolean { true, false };
```

In C, enumeration constants are really just other names for equivalent constant integers. In fact, an enum declaration may specify the integer equivalents, as follows.

```
enum order { before = -1, equal = 0, after = 1 }
```

The default integer value for the first constant of an enumeration is zero. Each constant that does not specify an integer equivalent gets one that is one more than the previous constant's.

In C++, each enumeration is actually a separate type, and a name may not appear in multiple enumeration lists. Although in C++, an enumeration is not equivalent to an integer, the compiler may automatically cast an enumeration to its integer value. However, casts, whether implicit or explicit, from an integer to an enumeration are not allowed:

there is no guarantee that the enumeration contains a value corresponding to the integer, and more than one constant in the same enumeration may have the same integer value.

```
enum direction {left=1, right, up, down, dn=down, none=0};
```

B.1.3 Variables

Variable *declarations* specify a type and a name, as in the following.

```
int n;
```

A variable declaration may include an initializer, in which case it is also a *definition*.

```
int n = 0;
```

In C the initializer of a *static variable* (cf. Section 0.3.1, page 19 for a discussion of static variables) must be a constant expression (i.e., one whose value can be computed at compile-time). In C++ any valid expression is allowed, including function calls. In both languages, initializers of automatic variables may be any valid expression.

A variable may be declared more than once, as long as all the declarations agree. Different versions of C have had different rules for how many definitions of a variable a program is permitted to contain; in C++, only one definition is permitted.

Several variables may be specified in one declaration, as in the following.

```
char ch1, ch2, ch3;
```

Each variable appearing in a declaration may have its own initializer.

```
char ch1='A', ch2, ch3='\0';
```

In that declaration, ch2 is left uninitialized. Static variables that are declared but not defined (i.e., none of the declarations includes an initializer) are initialized to zero. Automatic variables without initializers start out with whatever bits they happen to contain.

B.2 Derived Types

Various mechanisms exist for building more complex types out of the primitives described above. Such nonprimitive types are called *derived types* in C. Derived types may be derived from combinations of primitives and other derived types. The three major derived data types are arrays, structs, and pointers.

B.2.1 Arrays

An array in C is a sequence of values of the same type. Arrays are declared using square brackets to show the number of elements they contain. Arrays are always one-dimensional; however, an array may be a sequence of other arrays, approximating the multidimensional arrays of other languages. Some examples follow.

```
int month_days[12];              /* 12 ints */
char buffer[256];                /* 256 chars */
int calendar[5][20];             /* 5 arrays of 20 ints */
```

There is no string type in C, but arrays of characters are conventionally interpreted as strings. The representation assumed by the library functions provided through string.h ends the string with a null character. There may, of course, be characters following the null byte — the size of the array the string occupies and the (conceptual) length of the string are two different things.

Arrays may be initialized with a list of values enclosed in curly braces. In such initializations, the size of the array may be omitted, in which case enough space is allocated to hold elements in the initializer. Character arrays may be initialized by string constants, which include a final null character. Following are two examples.

```
int month_days[12] = {31,28,31,30,31,30,31,31,30,31,30,31};
char title[] = "untitled";       /* an array of 9 chars */
```

Array elements are referenced with square-bracket notation: array[index]. The first element is always at index 0. Arrays of arrays are indexed with the same notation. Since an element of an array of arrays is itself an array it may be followed by another index expression. Some examples are

```
month_days[n]
buffer[0]
calendar[month-1][day-1]
```

B.2.2 Structures

Structs, called *records* in most languages, are another mechanism for building compound types. A struct consists of named *members* (*fields* in other languages). Each field has its own type. Here's a simple struct.

```
struct date
{
    short day, month, year;
};
```

Inside the struct are simply variable declarations, just as they would appear inside a function. However, these are strictly declarations — initializations are not allowed here.

In C, the name of the struct is not itself a type: it must be prefaced by the reserved work struct wherever it is used. In C++, once a struct is declared it can be used anywhere one of the built-in type names can be. The struct name may *not* be prefaced by struct, except in declarations of the struct itself. In C a variable is declared with a struct type as follows.

```
struct date TODAY;
```

In C++, the same declaration would read

```
date TODAY;
```

A value of struct type is called an *instance* of the struct; here, for example, TODAY's value is
an instance of the struct date.

Like arrays, structs may be initialized with a list of values enclosed in curly braces.
The values are assigned to the fields of the struct in the order that the fields appear in the
struct's declaration. Each one's type must correspond, or be coercible to, the type of the
corresponding field. An example of defining a date in this way would be

```
date BICENTENNIAL = {4, 7, 1976};
```

To access members of an instance of a struct, a period is used: TODAY.month would
be the value of the month field of TODAY. Structs can be passed as arguments to functions
and returned as values. (Of course, if C++ references aren't used, then structs are passed
and returned by value, which means that they get copied to and from instances local to the
function.) A function to test if a day of a month might be written in C as follows, using the
array of the number of days in each month shown earlier and ignoring leap years.

```
int is_last_day_of_month(struct date dt)
{
    return (dt.day == DAYS[dt.month];
}
```

B.2.3 Pointer Types

Pointers are another kind of derived type, though, unlike arrays and structs, they have no
internal structure. At bottom, a pointer is just the address in the computer's memory
where some data is located. For a variety of reasons, it is often more convenient, flexible,
or efficient to program in terms of pointers instead of the actual data. For example, passing a pointer to a struct as a function argument avoids the copying that passing the struct
itself would entail. Whenever a pointer is used, there are always two different values involved, as illustrated in Figure A.1: the value of the pointer itself (an address) and the value
of what the pointer points to.

Figure A.1   A Pointer is the Address of Another Data

A pointer type is declared using an asterisk to modify the type from which the pointer type is derived. Similarly, asterisks are used to *dereference* the pointer — i.e., to convert
the pointer from something that just *refers* to a computational object to the object itself.
Pointer values are obtained by the *address-of* operator (&); for example, &dt produces a
pointer to the value of dt. If the pointer points to a struct, then a hyphen followed by a
greater-than sign (->) — an arrow — is used as a shorthand equivalent to dereferencing

the pointer with an asterisk and accessing a field with a period. Thus, if `ptr` is a pointer to a `date` instance, `ptr->day` is equivalent to `(*ptr).day`. Without the parentheses, this would be read as "dereference the value of the `day` field of `ptr`, which would not be legitimate given that `ptr` is a pointer not a `date`, and would not be what was intended in any case.

Pointers are legitimate types in their own right and may be included in structs and arrays. Here are some representative declarations. (Unfortunately, C declaration syntax gets quite devious as various derived types are mixed.)

```
struct date dt;                 /* a date */
struct date *dtptr;             /* ptr to date */
struct date *dtptrs[5];         /* array of 5 ptrs to date */
struct date (*dtsptr)[5];       /* ptr to array of 5 dates */
struct date *(*dtptrs_ptr)[5];  /* ptr to array of 5 ptrs
                                   to date */
struct date (*dtfn)();          /* ptr to a function that
                                   returns a date */
struct entry
{                               /* a struct containing a   */
    date* dt;                   /* pointer to a date and   */
    char* what;                 /* a string (ptr to char) */
};
```

White space may appear before and/or after the asterisk. It may even be omitted altogether. Thus, the following are all equivalent.

```
struct date *dtptr1;
struct date* dtptr2;
struct date * dtptr3;
struct date*dtptr4;
```

However the declaration is written, the asterisk is parsed as modifying the variable name. Some people prefer the first usage because the declaration reads the way the compiler interprets it. Some prefer the second usage because conceptually the asterisk is part of the type, even if that isn't how the parser treats it. Because the asterisk is parsed with the variable name, the second usage is as misleading when there are more than one variables in the declaration as it is clear when there is only one. The following, for instance, declares a pointer to date and a date — not another pointer.

```
struct date* d1, d2;
```

As a result, some people prefer to put white space on *both* sides of the asterisk, to avoid the shortcomings of either of the first two usages. Hardly anyone ever omits white space entirely.

A special value called the *null pointer* may be assigned to any pointer value, regardless of type. Technically, there is no way to refer to the null pointer itself. In C++, a 0 is automatically converted to the null pointer where it is assigned to a pointer-valued variable. It is common practice in the C community to #define NULL to some kind of zero expression, often in a system header file. Certain arcane consequences in C++ make this unadvisable, and, because C++ code can simply use a 0 to mean the null pointer, it is unnecessary.

B.2.4 Aliases

The reserved word typedef is used to define an alias, or synonym, for a type. Following
the typedef is an ordinary variable declaration, except that instead of declaring a variable
the declaration declares a type alias. The variable name in the declaration is the alias for
the type in the rest of the declaration. Following are some examples.

```
typedef char* string;
typedef int boolean;
typedef struct entry calendar[12][31];
```

After a typedef, the name can be used as if it were the type for which it is an alias.

```
string str1;                     /* str1 is a char* */
bool equal(string, string);
            /* equal takes two char*'s and returns an int */
```

Note, however, that despite what its name sounds like, typedef does not define a new
type. It's just as if the type were substituted for its alias in the program text. There is little
difference between using a typedef and a #define to define a type alias, except for the
syntax. In the following, the compiler will not object to the assignment of an int to a bool
or a char to a byte.

```
typedef int boolean;         /* intent is boolean = 0 or 1 */
boolean flag = 100;          /* permitted! */

typedef char byte;
byte b;
b = 'a';                      /* no conversion: a byte is a char */
```

Iterators in C++

Traversal operations perform some action for each element of a collection. Traversals, often expressed as iterations, are one of the major sources of errors and complexity in programs. The power of traversal functions is that they encode in one place the mechanics of performing the traversal. Client code need only supply the action to be performed for each element of the collection. It doesn't have to know anything about the representation of the collection or any of the details involved in getting from one element to another, and the code doesn't have to be edited if the collection's implementation changes.

C.1 Kinds of Traversals

Traversals differ with respect to what they do with the result of the action performed on each element. Most traversals just perform an action that has no result, or whose result is simply ignored. Some traversals collect the results into a new structure. For instance, a list of full path names may be traversed to obtain a set of directories the path names include. In the style used in this book, this would be coded as follows.

```
struct pathname;
struct directory;
template <class elt> struct seq_list;
// . . .
seq_list<pathname*> filenames;
// . . .
set<directory*> dirs;
filenames.reset();
while (filenames.next())
    dirs += filenames.current();
```

Another traversal pattern that appears regularly is one that combines all the values encountered not into a new collection, but into a single value. Summing the elements of a list, or some value derived from the elements of the list, would be an example of that. Continuing the above example, we might have

```
int sum;
filenames.reset();
while (filenames.next())
    sum += filenames.current()->getSize();
```

C.2 Iterators

These patterns are common enough that it would be nice to have a single function to perform the action on each element of the collection rather than having to piece together the traversal with calls to reset, next, and current. The argument to such a function would specify the action to be performed, and the function would perform that action for every element in the collection before returning. (Such a function is often called an *iterator*, but C++ uses that term for the one-at-a-time traversal mechanisms such as those shown throughout this book. People who call these functions *iterators* call the traversal operations, especially next, *generators*.)

A function that just performed the action for each element is often called either do or foreach. One that collects the results is often called collect. There isn't a commonly used name for the kind that produces an element-type value instead of a collection. We might call it combine, but we've used that for a kind of fundamental operation throughout the book. The language APL had operations like this and called them *reduction operators*, in that they reduced the dimension of their argument by one: a three-dimensional array — an array of two-dimensional arrays — would produce a two-dimensional array, and so on. A list is a one-dimensional sequence, and an element is a zero-dimensional sequence, so reduce might be a reasonable name for this kind of iterator function.

C.2.1 Function Arguments

In traditional algorithmic languages the only way to supply an action is to pass a function or procedure to be invoked on each element.[1] Sometimes called parametric procedures, function arguments are a very powerful mechanism in the abstraction toolbox. Unfortunately, programmers are rarely taught much, if anything, about them, so function arguments end up seeming mysterious.

The basic idea is really quite simple. C's type system allows the declaration of a *pointer-to-function*. The syntax for a pointer-to-function variable or argument is similar to a function declaration, except that the function name is preceded by an asterisk and enclosed in parentheses. For instance, the type of a C string comparison function would be

```
int (*compfn)(char*, char*)
```

(The parentheses are necessary because otherwise the asterisk would be interpreted as modifying the return-type!)

---

[1] This tends to lead to the gratuitous definition of functions just for the sake of being able to pass them. Other languages, in particular Lisp and Smalltalk, have constructs that allow bits of code to be packaged and passed as arguments without having to define a named function.

In the body of a function with a pointer-to-function argument, the name of the argument is used just as if it were the name of the function to which it points.[2] A routine to sort an array of strings according to whatever comparison function is passed might be defined as follows.

```
void sort(char* strings[], int length,
          int (*cmpfn)(char*, char*))
{
    . . .
    if cmpfn(strings[i], strings[j]) . . .
    . . .
}
```

Pointers to functions are part of ordinary C and can be used the same way in C++. Sometimes what you want to do is pass a member function as an argument, not an ordinary global function. For this C++ has a *pointer-to-member-function* type, in which the asterisk is preceded by a struct name and the scope resolution operator. In the call, the member function is accessed through an object with the operator .* or the operator ->*, depending on whether it is being accessed through an object or a pointer to an object.

The above pointer-to-function examples could be rewritten for our string module. If the comparison were to be performed by a member function, the type could be

```
int (string::*)(string*)
```

and the sort function could look like the following.

```
void sort(string* strings[], int length,
          int (string::*cmpfn)(char*))
{
    . . .
    if (strings[i]->*cmpfn)(strings[j]) . . .
    . . .
}
```

C.2.2 Defining Iterator Functions

We can use function arguments to define true iterators — functions that take a collection and an action and perform the action on each element of the collection. In the simplest case, an iterator's function argument will have one argument that is they type of the collection's elements. Its return value will depend on the kind of traversal pattern captured: a void, a collection, or an element. We could define the following instead of or in addition to the Traversal functions of our modules. (The name collection is used here to stand for any of the structures we studied. Note also that argument names may always be omitted in function declarations; in this case, omitting the argument name of the function argument leaves a strange-looking parenthesized asterisk.)

---

[2]Strictly speaking, using the pointer-to-function requires dereferencing the pointer and enclosing it in parentheses, just as in the pointer's declaration, for example (*fn)(*current()). However, because the usage is unambiguous, C also allows omitting the asterisk and parentheses around the function variable: fn(*current()). Some people prefer the first style because it makes clear that fn is a variable; others prefer the second because it's less intricate.

```
template <class elt> struct collection
{
    // Traversal
    void foreach(void (*)(elt));
    collection<elt> collect(elt (*)(elt));
    elt reduce(elt (*)(elt));
};
```

Implementations in terms of our Traversal operations are straightforward. They look just like the kind of code shown above and throughout the book. The only difference is that instead of calling a specific function on the current element, it calls whatever function that was passed in as an argument.

```
template <class elt> void collection<elt>::foreach(void (*fn)(elt))
{
    reset();
    while (next()) (*fn)(*current());
}

template <class elt>
collection<elt> collection<elt>::collect(elt (*fn)(elt))
{
    collection<elt> coll;
    reset();
    while (next()) coll += (*fn)(*current());
    return coll;
}

template <class elt> elt collection<elt>::reduce(elt (*fn)(elt))
{
    elt result;
    reset();
    while (next()) result += (*fn)(*current());
    return result;
}
```

C.3 Problems with Implementing Iterators in C++

There is nothing wrong with the above. It is valid, and it does what we want. However, it isn't good enough. There are many details that were carefully avoided. For instance, reduce has to start with a zerolike value for result, but we don't have a general way of getting one. Another problem is that some collects collect a different type of element or produce a different type of collection than the elements and collections over which they traverse. The above example showing the extraction of a set of directories from a list of path names did both: it produced a `set<directory*>` from a `seq_list<pathname*>`. Similarly, a `reduce` may produce a different kind of value than the collection's element type, as in summing the `int` sizes of a list of `pathname*` above.

A major deficiency is that there is no provision in these functions for extra arguments. For instance, suppose we want to print every element of a collection. It's simple enough to write a function `print(elt e)` that just does `cout << *e` and pass `print` to a `foreach`. That's fine, but what if we want to provide the particular stream to output to as an argument? Not only do we need a `foreach` that takes an extra argument, but its functional argument also needs a second argument. Since different kinds of functions would require different kinds of arguments, we might make the argument type a `void*` and leave it to the function argument to explicitly convert it to what it expects. Templates provide a new solution to that old problem, though. For instance, we could define a generic `foreach` that took any kind of second argument by making its type a second template parameter.

```
template <class elt, class argtype>
void collection<elt>::foreach(void (*fn)(elt, argtype&), argtype& arg)
{
    reset();
    while (next()) (*fn)(*current(), arg);
}
```

Soon we'd realize we'd sometimes need versions of `foreach`, `collect`, and `reduce` that took *two* extra arguments. (For every point, move the point by `dx` and `dy`.) Occasionally, we might need iterators that took three or four extra arguments. We'd end up with a large number of very similar functions.

Another major deficiency in the above iterators is they don't support premature termination or filtering. The most common kind of premature termination is a search: "For each element, do nothing, but stop when an element matching this one is found!" Filtering occurs when the action should only be applied to some of the elements: "For each `filename*`, delete the corresponding file if it is older than ninety days." These are common variations on straight iteration, so we'd like to be able to pass in termination and filter tests. Either or both could be specified with pointer-to-function arguments with signature `bool (*)(elt)`. This leads to further proliferation of different versions of the basic three iteration functions. One can end up with a collection module that has more iterators than all its other functions combined!

Yet another important problem is even worse than a proliferation of iterator functions: C lacks a mechanism allowing a function to refer to another function's local variable. In Pascal, for instance, a function can contain not just local variables but also local functions. This has many uses. Among others, it would solve some of the zero-value and extra-argument problems described above. We would be able to write code like the following.

```
int sum_sizes(seq_list<pathname*> lst)
{
    int total = 0;
```

```
        void add1(pathname*) { total += pathname->getSize(); }
        lst.foreach(add1);
    }

    template <class elt>
    void print_all(ostream& strm, seq_list<elt> lst)
    {
        void print1(elt e) { strm << e; }
        lst.foreach(print1);
    }
```

This is quite elegant, when you get used to this way of thinking and programming. Inside add1, when it refers to total, there are only two possibilities in C: total is either local to the function or global (ignoring the difference between file-scope (static) and program-scope (extern) variables). Nested functions give us intermediate possibilities: if a variable is not local, maybe it's local to the function that contains this function, or the function that contains that one, etc. This allows passing one function (add1) to another (foreach) that invokes it, while allowing the function passed to refer to variables defined in the context where it was defined. (This style of programming is not common in the Pascal community, although Pascal's nested functions make it possible. It is really Lisp and its important dialect Scheme in which nested scopes are commonly used for this purpose.)

Some of the proliferation of iterator variations could be controlled by the careful use of optional arguments, but not all. In the end, the whole approach proves unwieldy, however interesting. The structure of the language simply does not support this kind of traversal packaging in an effective way. Under these conditions, it makes little sense to provide any iterator operations except perhaps the basic foreach. Instead, collection modules provide lower-level traversal functions such as those shown throughout the book, and users are left to build whatever kinds of iterations they want out of those building blocks. It isn't ideal, but it's workable.

Object-Oriented Programming

Since it encompasses C, C++ supports traditional programming. As this book shows, it also supports data abstraction. In fact, it goes beyond even that, and supports a kind of programming called *object oriented*. Although object-oriented programming has a long history, it has only recently achieved popularity in the mainstream academic and commercial communities.

Though it would have facilitated some of the maneuvers made in implementing the modules shown in this book, object-oriented programming is not necessary for the study of data structures. The book's discussion and examples were carefully restricted to data abstraction programming. Getting accustomed to all the C++ mechanisms used is enough of a challenge without the addition of the features supporting object-oriented programming. Similarly, it's enough to ask the reader to learn the more modern style of data abstraction programming without also demanding a further shift to object-oriented programming. Nevertheless, object-oriented programming is a natural extension of data abstraction programming, and it's worth taking a peek at what it has to offer.

The roots of object-oriented programming lie in the Simula language, introduced in the late 1960s. The language most responsible for the development and popularization of the approach is Smalltalk, a "pure" object-oriented language that evolved in the 1970s and started being distributed commercially in the early 1980s. The Lisp community also investigated object-oriented programming extensively during the 1970s and 19802. The first language to add object-oriented features to C was Objective-C, which was inspired by Smalltalk. C++ is another hybridization of object-oriented programming with the C language, inspired by Simula. For a variety of technical, sociological, and economic reasons, C++ rapidly became dominant in the professional software development community as it came to be distributed and supported commercially in the late 1980s and early 1990s.

We'll look briefly here at the concept of object-oriented programming, some of the benefits it provides, and the basic C++ mechanisms that support it. Everything about data abstraction as studied in this book is part of object-oriented programming. It really takes only a few new features to go from the base of facilities for data abstraction programming that C++ provides to full support for object-oriented programming.

The treatment here is quite brief. Its purpose is to point out the direction in which the programming mechanisms and style shown in this book lead, and therefore the next step in one's study of C++.[3] It also focuses exclusively on object-oriented *programming*. It does not begin to cover the rich topics of object-oriented analysis, design, databases, and user interfaces.

D.1 The Object Metaphor

The people who developed Smalltalk introduced a metaphorical way of talking about computation that became the standard way of discussing object-oriented programming. The basic concepts are simple.

1. Computation consists of *objects* that interact with each other.
2. An object interacts with another by sending it a *message* then waiting for its response.
3. A *class* describes a kind of object, in terms of its *state* and *behavior*.
4. Every object is an *instance* of a class.
5. Each object has its own independent state, represented by values stored in its *instance variables*.
6. The response an object makes to a message it receives is determined by its class.
7. Actions taken in response to a message are specified in *methods*.
8. A class may *inherit* state and behavior from another class; the class inherited from is called a *superclass*, and the inheriting class is called a *subclass*.

Data abstraction has much in common with object-oriented programming, though its concepts and mechanisms were largely developed in a different part of the computer science community. In retrospect, it is clear that data abstraction forms the foundation of object-oriented programming, even though things didn't actually evolve that way. We can say similar things about the structs and functions shown throughout the book.

1. Computation consists of *functions* that interact with each other.
2. A function interacts with another by *calling* it and waiting for its return.
3. A *struct* describes a kind of data structure as a sequence of *variables* and *functions*.
4. Every data structure is an *instance* of a struct.
5. Each data structure has its own independent state, represented by values stored in its *fields* (or *members*).
6. The code actually executed for a given function call depends on the types of its arguments, including, in the case of member functions, the type of the expression through which it is invoked.
7. Actions taken to execute a function are specified in *function definitions*.

---

[3]A good book to read for further information is *Programming in C++*, by Dewhurst and Stark. A more thorough introduction is *C++ Primer*, by Lippman. Both books are included in Appendix F.

These two lists are quite parallel. What are the differences? The primary conceptual difference is one of emphasis: computation as functions calling each other versus objects that send messages to each other. Traditional programming is organized around *functions* (or *procedures*), whereas object-oriented programming is organized around *objects*. This ends up having far more substantial effects than can easily be described here. The primary technical difference is that there is nothing corresponding to inheritance in traditional or data abstraction programming. In the above lists, the one for data abstraction programming does not contain a parallel to the eighth item of the one for object-oriented programming.

A third difference, though absolutely central, is less apparent from the above descriptions. In traditional programming, the actual function that will get invoked for a particular function call is determined during compilation, but in object-oriented programming the actual method that gets invoked is determined when a message is actually sent during program execution. In both cases, the decision is based on the types involved, but in data abstraction programming the decision is a *static* one (i.e., made at compile time) whereas in object-oriented programming the decision is a *dynamic* one (i.e., made at run time). (In traditional programming, there is really nothing to decide — without function overloading, each name refers to just one actual function.) The term *binding* is often used in computer science to refer to the connection between a name and what it refers to, and this third distinguishing feature of object-oriented programming is called *dynamic binding*.

D.2 Benefits of Object-Oriented Programming

In short, object-oriented programming goes beyond data abstraction by adding *inheritance* and *dynamic binding*. It also causes subtle yet profound shifts in the way programs are designed and developed. We won't address these mysterious shifts here, but we will briefly describe some of the advantages that inheritance and dynamic binding provide.

D.2.1 Benefits of Inheritance in Programming

The main advantage of inheritance in programming is that it allows *programming by differences*. (It has further, and perhaps more significant, consequences for analysis and design, but that goes far beyond the scope of the present discussion.) When one data structure is a lot like another, it is far more effective to describe it in terms of its differences from the other, rather than copying and editing the entire implementation of the other data structure to implement the differences. Moreover, changes made to the other structure's implementation — bug fixes, new features, more efficient functions, etc. — don't magically appear in modified copies of the module. In fact, when people copy and modify a module such as a linked list implementation, there is usually no way to even find out where all the copies are. Even if the copies could somehow be tracked down or an announcement of changes sent to all their owners, the same modifications would have to be made to each copy, a major source of tedium and error.

A class that inherits from another class typically adds further state and behavior. It may also *replace* inherited functions with its own versions. Dynamic binding involves looking in an object's class for the method for a message received. The superclass is examined only if no method is found in the subclass. Therefore, if a class includes a method that was already present in its superclass, the effect is to replace that method. Instances of the superclass will continue to use the superclass method to respond to the corresponding message, but instances of the subclass will use the method it provides.

Collection structures like the ones studied in this book are fertile ground for interesting uses of inheritance. In many cases, several implementations of a structure differed only in relatively few representation details and function implementations. These could be better expressed using inheritance so the individual structs would only contain the differences rather than all the repeated code. Examples include the following.

- sequential lists versus linked lists
- n-ary trees versus general trees
- simple tables versus ordered tables versus hash tables

In fact, several of the modules from the disk of code provided with the book incorporate several different implementations, with a preprocessor macro used to determine which code should actually be compiled for a given version. Inheritance is a much more powerful mechanism than preprocessor directives for this sort of thing. Moreover, it allows incorporating another module without modifying its text, a very important consideration for program maintenance and library distribution.

D.2.2 Benefits of Dynamic Binding in Programming

The ability to defer binding to run-time makes an enormous difference. It allows collections to contain a mixture of objects, rather than just objects of one type. As a collection is traversed during execution, one or more messages are sent to each object encountered. The method invoked for each object is the one defined (or inherited) by its class. The only way to accomplish this in traditional or data abstraction programming is with unions and switch statements that select appropriate actions according to the value of a type field associated with the union.

A minor problem with switch statements is that they are wordy and error-prone. Selecting behavior based on type is very repetitive in form, and like all repetitive things is best left to the computer rather than the programmer to manage. More importantly, the behavior of a type is not captured in any one place. Instead, it is distributed across all the switch statements that deal with it throughout the program. This dilutes the data-centered power of data abstraction, which ideally captures all the behavior of a type in a separate module that implements it. It means that when the behavior of the type is changed, those changes have to be made in all the relevant switch statements. In many cases, those changes will be redundant as the same tests and actions are performed in several different places in the program or data structure module.

A surprising advantage to using dynamic binding instead of switch statements is that new types can be added to the system *without changing any existing code*. If the system automatically determines the appropriate function to call at run time based on the type of the particular object encountered, then the programmer doesn't have to write type-based tests. That means that the names of types, or equivalent values of type fields, never appear in the program, which is why new ones can be added without changing anything. (This is a slight exaggeration: somewhere the program has to create instances of the new type, and there the type must be mentioned by name.) The only constraint on the new type is that it provide implementations for any function that might be called on it.

D.3 Object-Oriented Features of C++

We'll look at the mechanisms that C++ uses to implement inheritance and dynamic binding. Enormous subtlety and complexity confront the serious user of these facilities. Only the basics are shown here.

The C++ community's object-oriented terminology differs somewhat from the traditional vocabulary presented above. Instead of *inheritance*, the term *derivation* is used. Instead of *superclass* and *subclass*, the terms are *base class* and *derived class*. The term *function* is retained instead of switching to the term *method*. Functions that are dynamically bound are called *virtual functions*.

D.3.1 Classes and Instances

In C++ classes are just like structs. The reserved word `class` is used instead of `struct`. Actually, the two are essentially interchangeable. Classes are defined and instantiated just like structs. The only difference is that members of classes are *private* by default, whereas members of structs are *public* by default. (Once `private:` or `public:` is specified, the difference evaporates for the rest of the struct or class.) The keyword `class` was introduced to encourage the shift in perspective of an object-oriented point of view. The keyword `struct` was retained to allow existing C code to be used with C++.

D.3.2 Inheritance in C++

Inheritance is specified by following a class's name in its definition by a colon and the name of its superclass. For instance, the priority queue of Chapter 7 was implemented as a copy of the queue module shown in Chapter 6, with the constructors, assignment operator, and `add` replaced. Instead of copying the queue implementation, it would be preferable to use inheritance. Its declaration would be as follows. Its implementation file would contain only the functions specified in the declaration. Everything else is handled by the compiler.

```
template <class elt> struct pqueue : queue
{
    // Additional data members
  private:
    bool highfront;
    int (*evaluator)(elt);
```

```
    pqueue(bool highest_first = TRUE, int (*evfn)(elt) = 0, int siz = 100);
    // Different copy operations are needed to support extra data members.
    void copy_elts(pqueue<elt>& q);
    pqueue(pqueue<elt>& q);
    pqueue<elt>& operator=(pqueue<elt>& q);

    // A different add replaces the inherited one so it is declared here.
  public:
    void add(elt);

    // Additional, private Modify operations supporting add.
  private:
    bool before(elt itm, int pos);
    void insert(elt itm, int pos);

    // Nothing further appears here!
};
```

An important further detail must be explained. When a struct is instantiated, its constructor is called automatically. When a pqueue is instantiated, one of its constructors is invoked, of course. That constructor initializes pqueue data members. What about the data members inherited from queue? The queue module already contains code for handling those, so we don't want to have to repeat that here. Besides, the two modules might be maintained by two different programmers. Certainly we don't want the pqueue programmer to have to track changes in the internal implementation of queues. All in all, the way things should be organized is that each class is responsible for the initialization of the data members it declares.

To support that, C++ automatically causes base class constructors to be invoked. When a pqueue is instantiated, both the queue and the pqueue constructors are executed. That much happens automatically. What doesn't happen automatically is the passing of arguments to the base class constructor. If the derived class constructor doesn't pass arguments to the base class constructor that will be automatically invoked, the base class's default constructor will be the one executed. To pass arguments, the derived class constructor must include the base class and the arguments in the member initialization list, as if the base class were actually a member of the derived class (the way a seq_list is a member of the table module of Section 11.1).

The old definition of the pqueue constructor (page 187) was as follows.

```
/* Lifetime Operations */

template <class elt>
pqueue<elt>::pqueue(bool high, int (*fn)(elt), int siz)
    : highfront(high), evaluator(fn), maxelts(siz-1), elts(new elt[siz])
{
    assert(siz > 1);
    clear();
}
```

However, `maxelts` and `elts` were declared in `queue` and should be initialized there. The inheritance-based implementation of `pqueue` would omit those members from the member initialization list, replacing them with a mention of `queue` and the arguments to pass to its constructor. The effect of this is to pass along the `siz` argument to the `queue` module. In principle, any expression can be passed along to the base class constructor, but in practice it is almost always arguments to the derived class constructor that are simply forwarded to the base class for handling. Here's the new definition, with the change underlined.

```
/* Lifetime Operations */

template <class elt>
pqueue<elt>::pqueue(bool high, int (*fn)(elt), int siz)
    : highfront(high), evaluator(fn), queue(siz)
{
    assert(siz > 1);
    clear();
}
```

Classes may have more than one base class. This is known as *multiple inheritance*. Multiple bases just appear after the usual base class colon, separated by commas. Not all object-oriented languages support multiple inheritance. Originally C++ did not, but now it does. A class that inherits from more than one base inherits all the members of each base.

D.3.3 Dynamic Binding in C++

Pure object-oriented languages provide only dynamic binding for message execution. Traditional languages, of course, provide only static binding for function calls. C++, being a hybrid language, provides both. That means there has to be some way to distinguish which calls will be bound to specific functions statically (resolved at compile-time) and which will be bound dynamically (deferred until run-time).

The scheme used in C++ is that all calls of a particular member function are either static or dynamic. There is no way to indicate on a call-by-call basis which should be static and which dynamic. (It turns out, though, that only calls through pointers or references may be dynamically bound; calls through object values are always statically bound even if the function is normally dynamically bound.) Ordinary global functions and static member functions are always bound statically.

The default, of course, is static binding — what we've been using all along. To indicate that a function should be bound dynamically, the reserved work `virtual` precedes its declaration. Because both `queue` and `pqueue` provide an `add` function, that function should be declared `virtual`, as follows.

```
template <class elt> struct queue
{
    // . . .
    virtual void add(elt);
    // . . .
};
```

When a class declares a function `virtual`, the function is `virtual` in all the subclasses of that class. It is therefore not necessary to specify `virtual` for that function where it is redeclared in subclasses. However, it is good practice to specify `virtual` anyway, so that someone reading a class definition can tell immediately which functions are bound statically and which dynamically.

Declaring a function `virtual` is all that is necessary to cause it to be dynamically bound. The rest is taken care of automatically by the compiler. For each class that has at least one virtual function, a table of virtual functions is constructed. Each instance of such a class gets an extra hidden data member that is a pointer to the class's virtual function table. Instead of compiling in a call to a specific function, the compiler compiles in a call through a specific offset in the *virtual function table*. At run-time, the virtual function table of the current object is accessed and the function at the designated offset is called. In that way, different functions may be called for objects of different classes.

E

C++ *Justifications*

There are many ways in which the C++ style adopted for this book does not conform to standard professional practice. The differences are intentional, designed to reduce complexity and increase readability for people new to C++ and the study of data structures. To some extent, this is simply because this is a *computer science* book, not a book on professional software development. More importantly, the subject of this book is *data structures*, not C++. All discussions and uses of C++ are entirely subservient to the purposes they serve in supporting the main presentation. This Appendix is included for readers who want to know more about the choices made regarding the use (or more likely the nonuse) of various C++ features.

One general rule dominated all decisions about what C++ features to use and how to use them: although usage here may deviate from the professional norm, in no case should it introduce misconceptions, dangerous practices, or bad habits that will have to be fixed in later study or work. The deviations here are harmless simplifications the limitations of which students will easily transcend when it later becomes appropriate to do so. For instance, even though a major reason for defining certain binary functions as friends is to make sure both arguments get equal treatment under conversions to base classes, and that issue wouldn't arise here because inheritance is never used, it was still judged better to show such functions as binary friends rather than unary members in order to instill the correct habits and aesthetics for when students encounter inheritance later on. On the other hand, although `struct` is used instead of `class` in data structure definitions, this is just a style choice with no significant consequences and a usage that can easily be reversed later.

Classes, Inheritance, and Dynamic Binding

By far the most significant decision was to restrict the features used to those supporting data abstraction only, not object-oriented programming (cf. Appendix D). Avoiding inheritance and dynamic binding avoids a slew of subtle, complex, and difficult issues. (The features themselves are simple and powerful, but many difficulties arise when they combine with each other and the data abstraction features of C++. It is enough to ask the reader of this book to learn many new features that C++ adds to C and a new way of thinking about programming (data abstraction) in order to learn about data structures, the real subject of the book. It would simply be too much to pile on top of that the further shift to object-oriented features and programming.

Even without object-oriented programming, though, inheritance has important applications in the design and implementation of data structures. It would be nice to define structures that are essentially variations on similar other ones by defining only the differences they introduce. For instance, priority queues could be derived from queues. It was tempting to do this, but only a few of the book's structures would benefit from this treatment, and for the purposes of this book it seemed sufficient for the text to show only the changed functions and the on-line code to use preprocessor directives. Also, there is still a fair amount of turmoil in the field about the appropriate use of inheritance, and it isn't clear that teaching students at this level to use "implementation inheritance" is really in their best interests.

`struct` **versus** `class`

Given that no object-oriented features were used, and that `struct` and `class` are essentially equivalent in C++ (the only difference being the default accessibility of members and bases), it seemed appropriate to use `struct` instead of `class`. The book presumes acquaintance with C, so students should already be somewhat familiar with `struct`s. Nothing would be gained by introducing a new term. This is one of the most visible of the book's choices, and no doubt experienced C++ programmers will find the pervasive use of `struct` here odd, but really the issue is entirely trivial.

Unfortunately, the language does not allow using `struct` instead of `class` in specifying template parameters. It would have been better for this book if the reserved word used for that were `type`, which is what `class` means in that context. Even allowing `struct` in addition to `class` would have made it possible to avoid introducing the latter entirely. The way things are, the only choice was to use `class` and note that the word really means 'type'.

Ordering of Members

What should come first in the definition of a data structure — private or public members, data or function members, etc. — depends on who's going to read the definition. Since this book is about the design and implementation of data structures, as well as their use, the definitions start with representation, proceed to the core operations, and end with the less central functions. A different order would be appropriate in a class library of generally useful data structures. There, one would want to order things to present the public interface first and implementation details last. In fact, it would be better to put the implementation details in a separate header file that the main one `#includes`, so that *all* users see is the public interface. For this book, we definitely do not want to hide the implementation — that's what the book's about!

Friend Functions

Many functions were routinely declared as friends in their struct. It turns out that their are two quite different reasons to declare a friend function inside a struct. The obvious one is to give the function access to private members of the struct. More subtly, it allows defining an ordinary, nonmember function inside the struct. Stylistically, to support the encapsulation metaphor, it is better to declare all functions that are part of the module's interface inside the struct itself, rather than following it. To accomplish that, such functions may be made friends, regardless of whether or not they actually require access to private members. Note that such functions are still clearly part of the module's interface and are in no way secondary to member functions.

Most of these friend functions could, of course, be made members (with their first argument omitted). (A major exception is the output operator: if a member, it would have to be a member of `ostream`, not of the user's class, since its first argument is an `ostream`; however, that is not possible, `ostream` is already defined.) There are two reasons to make them global instead of members. First, you'll find that they are for the most part **Compare** and **Combine** operations, which are inherently binary. Stylewise, a binary function with one argument just looks odd: a natural response to seeing the declaration `bool equal(list<elt>&)` is "Equal to what?" Even Smalltalk, a very pure object-oriented language still provides binary operators like those of traditional languages because they are inescapably natural and preferred by programmers.

A more subtle reason to make binary operations global arises with the use of inheritance. Implicit conversions from derived to base classes may be performed on a function argument, but not on the expression through which it is called. It would be strange, and possibly dangerous, to have one argument of an operation that is conceptually binary treated differently from the other. Therefore, it is common practice to make such functions binary nonmember friends.

Inline Functions

In the early days of C++, inline functions drew a lot of attention. The traditional objection to data abstraction programming is: "All those function calls!" Inline functions answer that objection, since they allow simple functions to be replaced by their definitions instead of a slower function call. Instructional materials — books, articles, course overheads, etc. — are full of class definitions with inline member functions. In retrospect, that appears to be the effect of the pressure of space limitations inherent in such materials rather than a real commitment to programming that way. As the field has matured, people began to realize that inlining was exclusively an efficiency issue and should always be left for late stages of code development, when performance tuning becomes important. Before that, they complicate things by causing too much recompilation when changed (because they are in header files), evading the debugger, and obscuring other declarations in the class with their bulk. There is no reason at all to use them in an introductory context.

const

With the exception of a few constant values here and there, the use of `const` has been entirely avoided. This is perhaps the single biggest change that would have to be made to the code in this book to bring it up to professional standards. It is very important to make a function's reference arguments `const`, unless the function is meant to modify them. (This is so important that compilers routinely warn or even generate errors in the presence of nonconst reference arguments. Under the relentless pressure of such compilers, in fact, it proved infeasible to maintain this stance of innocence, and consts have been added to most reference arguments in the on-line code, though not in the book. However, the code just casts away the consts, so that nothing is really changed, except that the compiler is silenced.)

Although important in software distributed to others for real-world use, const declarations are obtrusive in too many ways to use them in this book. One problem is just that they make code wordier, and it's important in a book like this not to make things look too complicated. Often it is necessary to provide two definitions of many member functions — one const the other not, but otherwise identical. This is too tedious for a book like this.

Above all, there are many surprising consequences of const. The author's experience with his own programming, the programming his students have done, and the programming his consulting clients do has shown const to be the source of more difficulties than any other single C++ feature. For instance, it is a rule of the language that all members of a const object are const, but AT&T's cfront compiler got this wrong as recently as version 2.1! If one declares

```
struct point { int x, y; };
struct line { point start, end; }
const line l = { {0, 0}, {10, 10} };
```

then the following is illegal, but was accepted by cfront 2.1.

```
l.start.x = 5;
```

Most C++ programmers don't know this, and some don't even agree that const should be interpreted this way.

Traversal operations are a major difficulty here. To output a list, we might print a parenthesis, traverse the list printing each element followed by a comma, then print a final parenthesis (ignoring the problem of there being one fewer commas then elements). That process would be expressed in the list module's output operator, which would take a reference to an output stream and a reference to a list as arguments. The list argument should be const because it won't be modified. If it were const, then the calls to reset, next, and current used in traversing the list would have to invoke const member functions or the compiler wouldn't let them be called on a const list.

One difficulty is that although reset and next are const in one sense — they don't change the content or order of the list — they are not const in another, in that they modify a data member, and if we make them const, the compiler won't let them modify the traversal state of the list! Another difficulty is less obvious: since current returns a reference to an element, that reference is required to be const, because modifying it would be modifying the list, which is const. (This is closely related to the rule that all members of a const object are const.) That's all right for the output operator, but it means that traversals cannot obtain elements that are then modified. For instance, you couldn't replace one element with another, or change the value corresponding to a key in a table.

These problems can be eliminated by the simple expedient of casting the const list reference to a nonconst one at the start of the output operator, or perhaps doing that in the traversal operations. In that case, one might ask, what good is a feature that in reality provides no advantage and requires user intervention to circumvent? To handle such situations with more delicacy than just casting away the const is just too difficult for first-time users of C++ to have to confront. Endless compilation and link errors result, many with no apparent cause or solution.

Once you introduce `const` in a couple of places that look reasonable, you will find that it spreads like a virus until nearly everything in your system has to be `const` to get anything to compile. You are welcome to experiment with the on-line code, adding `const`s to reference parameters (without casting the `const`s away, as the on-line code does) and making member functions `const`. You will learn a lot about the language. You will also learn a lot about your tolerance for frustration. Just don't say you weren't warned!

Restricting Collection Elements to Pointer Types

The collection implementations of this book will work only for pointer-typed elements. Conceptually, we want to ignore the pointers and think of a `list<string*>` as containing strings, not pointers to strings. Three of each module's functions dereference the presumed pointer: `equal`, `compare`, and `operator<<`, in order to call the corresponding function on the objects to which the element pointers point. There are deep semantic issues and implementation requirements involved in any other approach. Storing objects instead of pointers may require copying an object when it is "added" to a collection, and raises difficult issues of ownership that complicate **Finalize** and **Destroy** operations. It is difficult to construct a collection structure that works well for both pointers and primitives such as `int`s; many widely distributed collection libraries, in fact, provide special `int` and `char*` versions of each collection in addition to a generic collection-of-pointers version.

What the data structure methodology in this book really required was a scheme that could be applied simply and consistently to every structure studied. Restricting elements to pointer types made that possible. It also made the implementations significantly simpler. It makes the collections more flexible too, by resolving subterranean ownership and identity issues. If you want to store an object, having to store a pointer to it is only an ampersand away. The converse is not true: if you want to use pointers — so that an object may be in several different lists or tables, for example — there is no way to accomplish that with collections that accept and provide objects. Again, you are welcome to experiment with modifying the on-line code to create collection templates that take objects instead of pointers. The experience will undoubtedly be educational.

Reference Returns

Many **Access** and related functions, in particular `current`, defined in the modules return references. There are important problems with this approach. Probably the most hideous one is that references are tied to the addresses of the data to which they refer, but a structure's implementation may relocate an object within its internal memory: elements may be shifted around or copied over to a newly allocated larger array, leaving the reference pointing to a wrong element or even deleted memory. Some functions of course should or must return references — in particular, assignment operators. However, most of the reference returns in this book's code are references to allow the function — especially `operator[]` — to appear on the left-hand side of an assignment statement. They may also be used as temporary aliases for convenience during the execution of a limited piece of code, but once the structure is modified they will no longer be valid. It is not intended that they be stored beyond such very limited contexts, and unpleasant surprises will occur if they are.

Separate Iterator Classes

Any real C++ collection module would implement traversal not through member functions of the collection structure but with a separate iterator struct. This approach has two important advantages. One is that no space is taken up by the representation of traversal state in a collection that is not currently being traversed, and constructors and assignment operators don't have to deal with the tricky details of initializing traversal state. The more important advantage is that if each traversal is embodied in a separate object, it is possible to have multiple traversals of the same structure going on at the same time. Certain patterns of computation require that. For example, in a selection sort that traverses a list exchanging the current element with the one that belongs in itself, finding the least remaining element is itself a traversal process over the same list.

The problem for this book is that these separate iterator classes introduce a fair amount of complexity. It is highly desirable that the student acquire an appreciation for the flexibility and elegance of traversal programming. The student is unlikely to encounter a situation in which it is truly important to save the little bit of space traversal state occupies or where multiple simultaneous traversals over the same collection are really necessary. The seemingly gratuitous complexity separate iterator classes entail would discourage many students and obscure the value of traversal operations.

Overloading `operator new`

The free list allocation and recycling of nodes found in linked structure modules should really be handled by overloaded `new` and `delete` operators. However, using those would not make the code any more readable, concise, efficient, or accurate. Client code rarely call these functions anyway, so the interfaces to the modules are not significantly affected by this choice.

Nested Types

In principle, C++ allows other types to be defined inside structs. The meaning of these nested types is the same as if they had been defined outside the struct. The difference is simply the scope of their names. In principle, enumerations like the traversal orders in the binary tree module and secondary structs like the various node structs encountered should be defined inside the structs that use them. That would appropriately restrict their names and avoid "polluting the global name space," as this concern is usually phrased. Unfortunately, the implementation of nested types in many current compilers is quite inadequate, and it became necessary to back off from the attempt to use this feature.

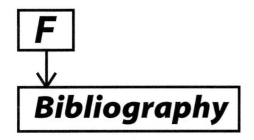

Bibliography

Listed here are some suggestions for other books that might prove useful for further explanations, examples, and exercises as well as topics not covered in this one. All use C or C++, unless indicated by their title or otherwise noted.

Abelson, Harold and Gerald Jay Sussman with Julie Sussman. *Structure and Interpretation of Computer Programs.* Cambridge, MA: MIT Press, 1985

Budd, Timothy. *An Introduction to Object-Oriented Programming* Reading, MA: Addison-Wesley, 1991.

Dewhurst, Stephen C., and Kathy T. Stark. *Programming in C++.* Englewood Cliffs, NJ: Prentice Hall, 1989.

Ellis, Margaret A. and Bjarne Stroustrup. *The Annotated C++ Reference Manual.* Reading, MA: Addison-Wesley, 1990.

Esakov, Jeffrey and Tom Weiss. *Data Structures: An Advanced Approach Using C.* Englewood Cliffs, NJ: Prentice Hall, 1989.

Gehani, Narain. *C: Food for the Educated Palate.* Rockville, MD: Computer Science Press, 1985

Harbison, Samuel P. and Guy L. Steele Jr. *C: A Reference Manual*, 3rd ed. Englewood Cliffs, NJ: Prentice Hall, 1991.

Helman, Paul, Robert Veroff, and Frank M. Carrano. *Intermediate Problem Solving and Data Structures: Walls and Mirrors*, 2nd ed. Redwood City, CA: Benjamin/Cummings, 1991. [Pascal used.]

Kernighan, Brian W. and Dennis M. Ritchie. *The C Programming Language*, 2nd ed. Englewood Cliffs, NJ: Prentice Hall, 1991

Kruse, Robert L., Bruce P. Leung, and Clovis L. Tondo. *Data Structures and Program Design in C.* Englewood Cliffs, NJ: Prentice Hall, 1988.

Lippman, Stanley B. *C++ Primer*, 2nd ed. Reading, MA: Addison-Wesley, 1991.

Liskov, Barbara and John Guttag. *Abstraction and Specification in Program Development.* Cambridge, MA: MIT Press, 1986.

McCracken, Daniel D. and William I. Salmon. *A Second Course in Computer Science with Modula-2.* New York: Wiley, 1987.

Meyers, Scott. *Effective C++: 50 Specific Ways to Improve Your Programs and Designs.* Reading, MA: Addison-Wesley, 1992.

Murray, Robert B. *C++ Strategies and Tactics.* Reading, MA: Addison-Wesley, 1993.

Plauger, P. J. *The Standard C Library.* Englewood Cliffs, NJ: Prentice Hall, 1992.

Sedgewick, Robert. *Algorithms in C++.* Reading, MA: Addison-Wesley, 1992.

Standish, Thomas A. *Data Structure Techniques.* Reading, MA: Addison-Wesley, 1980.

Stroustrup, Bjarne. *The C++ Programming Language*, 2nd ed. Reading, MA: Addison-Wesley, 1991.

Tenenbaum, Aaron M. and Moshe J. Augenstein. *Data Structures Using Pascal*, 2nd ed. Englewood Cliffs, NJ: Prentice Hall, 1986.

Tenenbaum, Aaron M., Yedidyah Langsam, and Moshe J. Augenstein. *Data Structures Using C.* Englewood Cliffs, NJ: Prentice Hall, 1990.

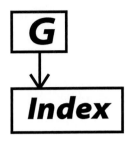

Index

Pages indicated here generally refer to conceptual discussions, not the code and discussion of its details that typically follow. After this index is an index of all function definitions shown in the book, arranged by struct.

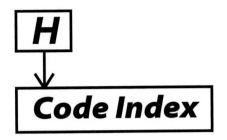

Code Index

This index lists function definitions by module, following the order in which the modules appear in the book. For convenience, nonmember functions are listed without their argument lists, which are uselessly repetitious. Their arguments should be obvious from their context. Most of them take references to two template structures of the type with which they are associated; these include equal and compare. The operator<< functions of course take an ostream& and a template structure.

Storage Structures

State Structures

Linked Structures

Association Structures

table
   ~table(), 369
   add(elt, action), 371
   contains(elt), 377
   contains_equal(elt), 377
   current(), 373
   empty(), 374
   equal, 375
   finished(), 373
   full(), 374
   index(), 374
   lookup(key&), 370
   lookup_pos(key&), 370
   next(), 373
   operator+=(elt), 372
   operator<<, 378
   operator-=(elt), 373
   operator-=(key&), 372
   operator=(table&), 376
   operator[](key&), 371
   remove(elt, action), 372
   remove(key&, action), 372
   reset(), 373
   size(), 374
   subtable, 375
   table(int), 369
   table(table&), 376

sorted_table
   add(elt), 378
   add(elt, action), 381
   lookup(key&), 381
   lookup_pos(key&), 380
   subtable, 382

hash_table
   ~hash_table(), 394
   add(elt, action), 395
   allocated_size(), 397
   compare, 398
   contains(elt), 399
   contains_equal(elt), 399
   copy(hash_table&), 398
   current(), 396
   empty(), 397
   equal, 398
   expand(), 395
   finished(), 396
   full(), 397
   fullness(), 397
   hash_table(hash_table&), 398
   hash_table(int), 394
   index(), 397
   init(), 394
   lookup(key&), 395
   lookup_pos(key&), 394
   next(), 396
   operator+=(elt), 396
   operator<<, 399
   operator=(hash_table&), 398
   operator[](key&), 395
   reset(), 396
   size(), 397
   subtable, 397

About the Book

This book was printed from camera-ready copy provided by the author. Early drafts were written on a Macintosh SE/30 using Microsoft Word and Claris MacDraw II. Late drafts and final copy were prepared on a Macintosh Quadra 700 using FrameMaker 3.0.1. Final diagrams were prepared from the author's drafts by Ron Cillizza using Adobe Illustrator, then imported into FrameMaker. The cover was produced using Quark Xpress by Jayne Conte at Prentice Hall based on a preliminary design by the author, who was assisted by Janet Shapiro Model (his wife) and Nancy Stoodt (of Stoodt Design).

The typefaces are from Adobe Systems. Code is in Letter Gothic Bold; everything else is set in some version of the multiple master faces Minion (body) and Myriad (headings, diagram labels, cover, etc.). The ability to tune the multiple master faces for each of their particular applications proved extremely valuable in the formatting of this book. Final copy was printed on a Hewlett-Packard LaserJet 4M (600 dpi with Resolution Enhancement Technology) on Hammermill LaserPrint paper.

About the Author

Mitchell L Model received his Ph.D. in Computer Science from Stanford University in 1979, specializing in artificial intelligence. His dissertation research was performed at Xerox Palo Alto Research Center, where he was involved in early work on knowledge representation languages and graphical user interfaces. He was an assistant professor at Brown and Brandeis universities before leaving academics to become a consultant, first in symbolic computation and expert systems then in object technology.

As an independent consultant Dr. Model provides courses, consulting, and mentoring to software engineers learning to use object technology. He is particularly active in the areas of object-oriented design, application prototyping, user interfaces, and object-oriented databases. He has extensive experience in traditional, symbolic, and object-oriented programming, including a wide variety of systems and languages. Though a compulsive hacker, his real commitments are to teaching and the quality of people's lives. Dr. Model may be reached via email at `mlm@acm.org`.